THIRD
EDITION

Groups: Process and Practice

THIRD
EDITION

Groups:
Process and Practice

Marianne Schneider Corey
Private Practice

Gerald Corey
California State University, Fullerton
Diplomate in Counseling Psychology,
American Board of Professional Psychology

Brooks/Cole Publishing Company
Pacific Grove, California

Brooks/Cole Publishing Company
A Division of Wadsworth, Inc.

Printed in the United States of America
10   9   8   7

Library of Congress Cataloging-in-Publication Data
Corey, Marianne Schneider, [date]
    Groups: process and practice.

    Rev. ed. of: Groups / Gerald Corey, Marianne
Schneider Corey.   2nd ed.   c1982.
    Includes bibliographies and index.
    1. Group psychotherapy.   I. Corey, Gerald.
II. Corey, Gerald.   Groups.   III. Title.
RC488.C5935   1986   616.89'152   86-2595
ISBN 0-534-06540-6

Sponsoring Editor: *Claire Verduin*
Editorial Assistant: *Linda Ruth Wright*
Production Editor: *Fiorella Ljunggren*
Manuscript Editor: *William Waller*
Permissions Editor: *Carline Haga*
Interior and Cover Design: *Katherine Minerva*
Cover Photo: *Lisa Thompson and Lee Hocker*
Authors' Photos: *Judy K. Blamer*
Typesetting: *TCSystems, Shippensburg, Pennsylvania*
Cover Printing: *The Lehigh Press Company, Pennsauken, New Jersey*
Printing and Binding: *The Maple-Vail Book Manufacturing Group, York, Pennsylvania*

To our families and friends

■■ *Marianne Schneider Corey*, a licensed marriage and family therapist in private practice in Idyllwild, California, is a National Certified Counselor and holds a master's degree in marriage, family, and child counseling from Chapman College. She is a clinical member of the American Association for Marriage and Family Therapy and holds membership in the American Association for Counseling and Development, the Association for Specialists in Group Work, and the California Association of Marriage and Family Therapists. Marianne and Jerry Corey were the co-chairs of the Professional Standards and Ethics Committee of the Association for Specialists in Group Work in 1981–1982.

For years Marianne has been actively involved in leading groups for various populations and in providing training and supervision workshops in group process. With her husband, Jerry, she has conducted workshops, continuing-education seminars, and personal-growth groups in Germany, Mexico, and China, as well as the United States. With her colleagues, Marianne co-leads weeklong residential workshops in Idyllwild each summer. She also counsels individuals and couples in her private practice.

The Coreys have been married since 1964. They have two teenage daughters, Heidi and Cindy.

Marianne has co-authored several articles on group work, as well as the following books (published by Brooks/Cole Publishing Company):

- *I Never Knew I Had a Choice*, Third Edition (1986, in collaboration with Gerald Corey)
- *Issues and Ethics in the Helping Professions*, Second Edition (1984, with Gerald Corey and Patrick Callanan)
- *Casebook of Ethical Guidelines for Group Leaders* (1982, with Gerald Corey and Patrick Callanan)

· *Group Techniques* (1982, with Gerald Corey, Patrick Callanan, and J. Michael Russell)

■■ *Gerald Corey,* Professor and Coordinator of the Human Services Program at California State University at Fullerton and a licensed psychologist, received his doctorate in counseling psychology from the University of Southern California. He is a Diplomate in Counseling Psychology of the American Board of Professional Psychology, is a National Certified Counselor, and is registered as a National Health Service Provider in Psychology. He is a Fellow of the American Psychological Association (Counseling Psychology) and holds membership in the American Association for Counseling and Development, the American Group Psychotherapy Association, the Association for Humanistic Psychology, the Association for Counselor Education and Supervision, the Association for Specialists in Group Work, the Western Association for Counselor Education and Supervision, and the Western Psychological Association.

Jerry serves on the editorial board of the *Journal of Counseling and Human Service Professions* and in the past has been on the editorial board of the *Journal for Specialists in Group Work* and the ASGW's Commission for Teaching of Group Counseling. With his colleagues, he regularly gives presentations at professional conventions, conducts in-service training workshops, offers weeklong residential growth groups, and conducts seminars and workshops in the United States and abroad.

Jerry was the recipient of the ASGW's 1984 Professional Career Award for Distinguished Service in the Field of Group Work. In that year he also received the Distinguished Faculty Member Award from the School of Human Development and Community Service of California State University at Fullerton.

Recent publications by Jerry—all with Brooks/Cole Publishing Company—include:

· *Case Approach to Counseling and Psychotherapy,* Second Edition (1986)
· *Theory and Practice of Counseling and Psychotherapy,* Third Edition (and *Manual*) (1986)
· *I Never Knew I Had a Choice,* Third Edition (1986, with Marianne Schneider Corey)
· *Theory and Practice of Group Counseling,* Second Edition (and *Manual*) (1985)
· *Issues and Ethics in the Helping Professions,* Second Edition (1984, with Marianne Schneider Corey and Patrick Callanan)
· *Casebook of Ethical Guidelines for Group Leaders* (1982, with Marianne Schneider Corey and Patrick Callanan)
· *Group Techniques* (1982, with Marianne Schneider Corey, Patrick Callanan, and J. Michael Russell)

PREFACE

This book outlines the basic issues and key concepts of group process and shows how group leaders can apply these concepts in working with a variety of groups.

In Part One we deal with the basic issues in group work. The introductory chapter presents our own perspective on theory applied to practice, a discussion of group-leadership issues, and an overview of types of group. In this new edition we give increased coverage in Chapter 2 to the ethical, legal, and professional aspects of group leadership.

In Part Two separate chapters deal with group-process issues at each phase in the evolution of a group. A few of these issues are: designing a group and getting it started; working effectively with a co-leader at each stage of a group; member roles and leader functions; problems that can occur at different times in a group; and techniques and procedures for facilitating group process. There is new material summarizing the practical applications of research literature at each of the stages of a group. We also encourage practitioners to include evaluative research in the design of their groups. Each chapter concludes with an exercise section.

Some other topics that receive expanded coverage in the third edition are: concrete examples of group process in action; illustrations of leader interventions; therapeutic factors in a group accounting for personal change; examples of effective and ineffective member behaviors; the role of cohesion, self-disclosure, and feedback; and ways of combining research and practice. Chapter 8 provides concise summaries of each stage of a group's development. This chapter puts all the topics covered in Parts One and Two in a nutshell for easy reference and review. The reading list at the end of Part Two, which has been updated and expanded considerably, is offered to help readers round out their knowledge of the topics discussed in the first two parts of the book and pursue a deeper understanding of areas of special interest.

In Part Three we show how the basic concepts examined in Part Two can be applied to specific types of therapeutic group. We offer guidelines for group leaders who want to design groups specifically for children, adolescents, adults, and the elderly. These guidelines are based on our experiences and those of our colleagues. New to this edition is an expanded coverage of a variety of groups appropriate to many settings. Although we describe a number of techniques, we discourage readers from using any of them without first developing a sound rationale for doing so in a particular situation. We focus on the unique needs of each age group and how to meet them, and we offer ethical, legal, practical, and professional guidelines, as well as an expanded and updated list of suggested readings for each type of group. In many ways this is a "how-to" book, but it is also a book about the "why" of group leadership.

For whom is this book intended? It is for graduate and undergraduate students majoring in psychology, sociology, counseling, social work, education, and human services who are taking courses in group counseling or group leadership. It is also a practical manual for practitioners who are involved in leading groups and for counselors who are training to lead various types of group. Others who may find this book useful in their work are social workers, rehabilitation counselors, teachers, pastoral counselors, correctional workers, and marriage and family therapists. Mental-health professionals and paraprofessionals are increasingly expected to possess the skills necessary for group counseling. We have found that students in counseling psychology and related programs must often complete an internship involving work with a variety of people—children or adolescents, the elderly, clients with substance-abuse problems, inpatient groups in a hospital, and outpatient groups in a community agency. On their jobs as mental-health workers, they may be asked to set up and lead one or more of these groups. This is our reason for writing about a range of therapeutic groups. We hope to get readers thinking in creative ways about how they might design groups to effectively meet the needs of diverse clients.

An *Instructor's Resource Manual* for this third edition of *Groups: Process and Practice* is now available. It contains multiple-choice test items, questions for reflection and discussion, additional exercises and activities, reading suggestions for instructors in preparing classes, a survey of current practices in the teaching of group-counseling courses, and examples of course outlines. We also describe our approach to workshops in training and supervising group leaders, which can be incorporated into many group courses.

■■ Acknowledgments

We want to express our appreciation to J. Michael Russell and Patrick Callanan, both of whom continue to be very influential in helping us refine our views of group process and practice. They have been co-leading weeklong residential personal-growth groups with us for 14 summers, as well as working with us in the residential training workshops we offer for group leaders. We wish to recognize Mary Moline and Helga Kennedy, who also co-lead groups and workshops with us. These valued friends and colleagues have an influence on our style of group leadership that is reflected in the pages of this book.

The reviewers of this third edition have been instrumental in our making important changes from the earlier editions. We extend our appreciation to the following people who reviewed the manuscript and made useful comments: Lupe and Randy Alle-Corliss, clinical social workers in agency work and private practice; Marguerite (Peg) Carroll of Fairfield University; Barbara Herlihy of the University of Houston at Clear Lake; Walt Lifton, a community consultant; Mary Moline of California State University at Fullerton; Beverly Palmer of California State University at Dominguez Hills; Rex Stockton of Indiana University; Craig Washington of Northern Virginia Community College; and Jim Wigtil of Ohio State University. The following student reviewers were most helpful: Diana Cowles, Joanna Doland, Carl Johnson, Jan MacFarlane, Andrea Mark, Donna Robbins, Jane Sipe, Helen Smith, and Veronika Tracy. We especially appreciate Joanna Doland's fine work in compiling the index for the book.

We thank the following people for granting us permission to describe their groups in Part Three: Lupe and Randy Alle-Corliss, Marilyn Chandler, Wayne Huey, Michael Nakkula, and Phil Piechowski. We hope that their innovative programs inspire those who read this book to think of their own special designs for a group.

The dedicated members of the Brooks/Cole team offered once again support as well as challenge. We wish to express our gratitude to Fiorella Ljunggren, senior production coordinator, and Claire Verduin, managing editor and psychology editor, for their continued keen interest in the revision process of our books and for their sense of humor and perspective, which don't seem to fail even under the most demanding circumstances. And we are especially indebted to William Waller, the manuscript editor, whose talent has contributed much to the readability and clarity of our book.

Marianne Schneider Corey
Gerald Corey

CONTENTS

■■ Chapter 11   Groups for Adults   307

■■ Chapter 12   Groups for the Elderly   345

Introduction: Basic Issues in Group Work

■■ Through the workshops we offer around the country, we have become aware of a growing interest in using group approaches with a wide variety of populations. In these visits to other states, however, we still hear comments like "What are those Californians up to now?" Those who are not familiar with groups are often suspicious about the purpose and value of them. Even though the reputation of groups has suffered from some poor practices in the past, we are convinced that groups have much to offer. The effort involved in setting up and leading groups is considerable, yet we think that this commitment is essential if the group movement is to be viewed with respect. In Part One we discuss the fundamentals of group work and provide guidelines for beginning your own work as a group leader.

1

A Perspective on Group Process and Practice

1. If you were applying for a job that entailed leading groups, how would you address these questions: "What theoretical orientation guides how you lead groups? How would you set up a group? How do you view your role as a leader?"
2. What are some advantages of practicing within a single theoretical perspective? some disadvantages? What value can you see in developing an eclectic stance by drawing on concepts and techniques from diverse theoretical perspectives? Are there any drawbacks?
3. Beginning group leaders face a number of concerns in setting up and leading groups. What worries do you have about leading your first group? If you have had some experience in group work, what problems did you face when you began?
4. What personal characteristics, skills, and specialized knowledge do you associate with effective group leaders? Which of these attributes do you see as being most crucial in competently leading groups?
5. What are some advantages and disadvantages of co-leadership of a group, both for the group members and for the co-leaders?

■■

Introduction

Our hope is that, from its very beginning, this book will get you excited about the prospect of leading groups and about the value of group work. This chapter discusses our theory of group work, which obviously influences the way we function in groups. It also deals with the personal characteristics desirable in group leaders, describes basic skills needed for effective leadership, and explains our preference for co-leadership. The chapter includes an overview of the various types of group, and it ends with a look at recent trends in group work.

The Theory behind the Practice

■■ Our Theoretical Orientation

We are sometimes asked to declare what theory we follow. Neither of us subscribes to any single theory in totality. Rather, we function within an eclectic framework that we continue to develop as we practice. We respect the contributions that many theorists have made to the field. We freely borrow concepts and techniques from most of the contemporary therapeutic models and adapt them to our own unique personalities. Thus, our theoretical orientations and leadership styles are primarily a function of the individuals we are.

Our conceptual framework takes into account the *feeling, thinking,* and *behaving* dimensions of human experience.

In working with group members, first of all we help them identify and express their *feelings*. We find the following theories of value in facilitating emotional expression in group sessions: Carl Rogers' person-centered approach emphasizes the value of listening with understanding and encouraging people to put into words what they are feeling in the moment. The experiential therapies, such as psychodrama and Gestalt, place value on expressing feelings in action-oriented ways; techniques are available to facilitate the opening up of sometimes buried feelings and to enable members to work through some emotional barriers.

Although we believe that it is important to deal with feelings in most of the groups we lead, we do not think that this focus alone will lead to personality change. We also value those therapies that emphasize the *thinking* dimension. Though many clients can benefit from an emotional catharsis (release of pent-up feelings), some kind of cognitive work is also essential. Therefore, we draw heavily on transactional analysis, behavior therapy, and rational-emotive therapy. From transactional analysis we focus on early parental messages that group members incorporated and the early decisions they made about themselves and others in response to these parental injunctions. We typically challenge group members to begin to think about decisions they made as children, some of which may have been necessary for their psychological survival at one time yet are clearly out of date. We hope that members will eventually be able to make necessary revisions that can lead them to live more freely. From cognitive-behavioral therapy and rational-emotive therapy, we stress paying attention to one's "self-talk." How are members' problems actually caused by the assumptions they make about themselves, about others, and about life? How do members create their problems by the thoughts and beliefs they cling to? How can they begin to free themselves by critically evaluating the sentences they feed themselves? In other words, many of our group techniques and procedures are designed to tap members' thinking processes, to help them think about events in their life and how they have interpreted these events, and to work on a cognitive level to change certain belief systems. We have even suggested that members experiment with saying aloud new sentences, even if they don't believe what they are saying, just to have the experience of telling others something different about themselves.

Feeling and thinking are vital components in the therapeutic process, yet we see another dimension as essential if the goal is behavior or personality change; this is the *behaving*, or *doing*, component. Members can spend countless hours in gaining insights and ventilating pent-up feelings, but at some point they need to get involved in an action-oriented program designed for change. Doing is a way of bringing feelings and thoughts together by applying them to real-life situations. In Chapter 7, on ending a group, we focus on techniques and strategies to assist members in consolidating what they've learned in their group experience and applying new behaviors to situations they encounter every day. We focus on contracts, "homework assignments," action programs, self-monitoring techniques, support systems, and self-directed change programs. These approaches all stress the role of commitment on the members' part—commitment to practice new behaviors, to follow through with a realistic plan for change, and to develop practical methods of carrying out this plan in everyday life.

Underlying our integrated focus on feeling, thinking, and behaving is our philosophical leaning toward the existential approach, which places primary emphasis on the role of choice and responsibility in the therapeutic process. We do not perceive or treat group members as helpless victims of forces determining their life. Although we can appreciate that people are strongly influenced by certain traumatic events, we do not subscribe to the view that people are *hopelessly* "scripted" during early childhood or that they can do nothing now to change any negative conditioning from the first five years of life. Basically, we challenge people to look at the choices they *do* have and to accept the responsibility for choosing for themselves. Most of what we do in our groups is based on the assumption that people can exercise their freedom to change situations. In those cases where it is not possible to change a difficult situation, we work with members on changing their attitudes toward it or the way they behave or react to it. The group context offers people opportunities to learn how to use the freedom they have.

Of necessity, this discussion of our theoretical orientation has been brief. Readers who want a more elaborate discussion of the various theoretical orientations, along with their implications for group work, are referred to *Theory and Practice of Group Counseling* (Gerald Corey, 1985).

■■ Developing Your Own Theory of Group Practice

Attempting to lead groups without having an explicit theoretical rationale is like flying a plane without a flight plan. Though you may eventually get there (and even find the detours exciting), you're equally likely to run out of patience and gas and do nothing but fly aimlessly in circles. Group leaders without any theory behind their interventions will probably find that their groups never reach a productive stage.

We don't see theory, however, as a rigid set of structures that prescribes, step by step, what the leader should do. Rather, we see theory as a general framework that helps leaders make sense of the many facets of group process, provides them with a map that gives direction to what they do and say in a group, and helps them think about the possible results of their interventions. We encourage you to look at all the contemporary theories to determine what concepts and techniques you can incorporate into your leadership style. The theoretical stance you develop is most meaningful if it is closely related to your values, beliefs, and personal characteristics.

In co-leading groups we do not consciously think about what theory we are using with what type of client. Yet sometimes we rely more on one type of intervention than another, depending on the needs of the clients. We are inclined to use more confrontive interventions with relatively well-functioning members, for example, and to draw on supportive approaches when we work with clients who are unable to benefit from confrontation. With members who are highly emotional, we challenge them to think about decisions they have made about themselves and how these beliefs and decisions affect the way they feel and what they do. With individuals who have a tendency to intellectualize or rehearse what they say, we employ emotive techniques as a way of helping them overcome some of their blocks to effective functioning. We have a rationale for using the techniques we employ, and our interventions generally flow from some particular theoretical framework. Our concern is to help clients identify and experience whatever they are feeling, identify ways in which their assumptions influence how they feel and behave, and experiment with alternative modes of behaving.

Unfortunately, too many leaders are practice oriented, which means that they use certain techniques but can't say why. By thinking about the different therapeutic group models, leaders may be stimulated to examine questions such as:

· What is the basic nature of human beings?
· How can I incorporate my philosophy of human nature into the way I lead groups?
· Can people be trusted to determine their own direction in a group, or do they need strong intervention from the leader to keep them moving productively?

· Who should determine the goals of the group, the members or the group leader?
· How specific should the goals be?
· What is the group leader's role? Facilitator? Director? Expert? Consultant? Resource person?
· How much responsibility for the group's work lies with the leader? with the members? To what degree should the group be structured by the leader?
· What are your views on selecting a co-leader and working with one? Ideally, how would you divide responsibility with a co-leader?
· Should the leader work with one person at a time or encourage maximum interaction among members?
· How much personality change is desirable? Should the focus be on attitude change or on behavior change?
· What are the functions of group members?
· What techniques are the best? Why?
· What are the criteria for measuring the success of a group?

A theory can help group leaders clarify such issues. Ultimately, the most meaningful perspective is one that is an extension of the values and personality of the group leader. A theory is not something divorced from the essence of the person; at best, it is an integral part of the person and an expression of the person's uniqueness. It is unrealistic to expect group leaders in training to have integrated a well-defined theoretical model with their practice. This may take years of extensive reading and practice in leading groups. Group leaders should devote considerable time to thinking about and discussing with others their ideas about group practice.

Developing a personalized group model that guides one's practice is obviously an ongoing process; the model continuously undergoes revision. With increased experience the leader develops new questions. Experiments are tried and clinical hunches put to the test. By talking to fellow group leaders, leaders can get ideas for modifying old practices to fit new knowledge. Good group leaders constantly question their mode of operation and make changes over time.

You can limit yourself by subscribing totally to the tenets of a single theoretical viewpoint. If you become a devotee of one approach, you may overlook critical aspects of human experience and unduly limit your effectiveness with different clients by attempting to force them to fit your theory. Although you need a theoretical perspective to guide you as a group practitioner, it is useful to keep in mind that each theory has something unique to offer and that effective group leaders are continually refining a personalized theory of group process that guides the interventions they make.

In fairness, we need to say that some writers are highly critical of encouraging students to formulate a personalized theory. Patterson

(1985) has long contended that students are not capable of formulating a theory because theories can be developed only by mature individuals on the basis of a thorough knowledge of existing theories and long experience. He also asserts that the idea of individual theories is based on the faulty assumption that there are an infinite number of theories and that all theories are equally valid.

Patterson's contentions merit some consideration, for we ourselves see some dangers in encouraging an eclectic approach. At its worst, eclecticism can be an excuse for sloppy practice, a practice that lacks a systematic rationale. It can be a disorganized process of merely picking bits and pieces from various theories without any integrating framework. At its best, however, eclecticism can be a creative synthesis of the unique contributions of diverse theories.

Throughout this book we refer to your ability to draw on your life experiences and your personal characteristics as one of your most powerful therapeutic tools. Particularly important is your willingness to examine how your personality and behavior either hinder or facilitate your work as a group leader. Although it is essential to become well grounded in the theories underlying group work, to acquire those needed skills in conducting groups, and to gain supervised experience as a group leader, we do not see this as enough to make you an effective leader. It is also essential that you be willing to take an honest look at your own life to determine if you are willing to do for yourself what you challenge group members to do.

An Overview of the Various Types of Group

Throughout the book *therapeutic group* is used as a general term to indicate any of various types of group. By *therapeutic* we don't mean having to do with treatment of emotional and behavioral disorders but rather having as a broad purpose increasing people's knowledge of themselves and others, assisting people to clarify the changes they most want to make in their life, and giving people some of the tools necessary to make these desired changes. By interacting with others in a trusting and accepting environment, participants are given the opportunity to experiment with novel behavior and to receive honest feedback from others concerning the effects of their behavior. As a result, the participants learn how they appear to others. We use the term *therapeutic group* to refer to group counseling, group therapy, T-groups, structured groups, awareness groups, consciousness-raising groups, self-help and leaderless groups, and personal-growth groups, among others. Different types of group differ with respect to goals, techniques used, the role of the leader, and the kind of people involved. The following brief descriptions will give you some idea of the diversity of these groups.

■■ Group Therapy

Group therapy originated in response to a shortage during World War II of personnel trained to provide individual therapy. At first, the group therapist assumed a traditional therapeutic role, frequently working with a small number of clients with a common problem. Gradually, leaders began to experiment with different roles. Many of them discovered that the group setting offered unique therapeutic possibilities. The dynamics of a group provided support, caring, confrontation, and other unique qualities not found in individual therapy. Within the group context members could practice new social skills and apply some of their new knowledge.

Many people participate in group therapy to try to alleviate specific symptoms or problems, such as depression, sexual difficulties, anxiety, and psychosomatic disorders. Some therapy groups are organized for the purpose of correcting a specific emotional or behavioral disorder that impedes people's functioning. In group therapy attention is given to unconscious factors and one's past as well as to personality change. Such groups are thus typically of longer duration than most other types.

■■ Group Counseling

The counseling group usually focuses on a particular type of problem, which may be personal, educational, social, or vocational. It is often carried out in institutional settings, such as schools, college counseling centers, and community mental-health clinics and agencies. This type of group differs from a therapy group in that it deals with conscious problems, is not aimed at major personality changes, is generally oriented toward the resolution of specific and short-term issues, and is not concerned with treatment of the more severe psychological and behavioral disorders.

Group counseling has both preventive and remedial aims. The group involves an interpersonal process that stresses conscious thoughts, feelings, and behavior. The focus of the group is often determined by the members, who are basically well-functioning individuals who do not require extensive personality reconstruction and whose problems relate to the developmental tasks of the life span or finding means to cope with stresses of a situational crisis. The group is characterized by a growth orientation, with an emphasis on discovering inner resources of personal strength and helping members to constructively deal with barriers preventing optimal development. The group provides the support and the challenge necessary for honest self-exploration.

The group counselor's job is to structure the activities of the group, to see that a climate favorable to productive work is maintained, to facilitate member interaction, and to encourage the members to translate their insights into concrete action plans. To a large extent group leaders carry out this role by teaching the members to focus on the here and now and to establish personal goals that will provide direction for the group.

Participants in group counseling often have problems of an interpersonal nature, which are ideally explored in a group context. Members are able to see a reenactment of their everyday problems unfold before them in the counseling group. The group is viewed as a microcosm of society, in that the membership is diverse. The group process provides a sample of reality, with the struggles people experience in the group situation resembling their conflicts in daily life. Members are encouraged to see themselves as others do through the process of receiving feedback. They have a chance to experience themselves as they did in their original family, reliving conflicts they had with significant people in their life. There is also the chance to practice new ways of behaving, for the empathy and support in a group help members identify what they want to change and how to change. Participants can learn to respect cultural and value differences and can discover that, on a deep level, they are more alike than different. Although their circumstances may differ, their pain and struggles are universal.

■■ Personal-Growth Groups

Personal-growth groups offer an intense experience intended to help relatively healthy people function better on an interpersonal level. Rather than being aimed at curing personality problems, such groups are developmental, being concerned with exploring personal issues that most people struggle with at the various transition periods in life. The rationale for these groups is that the support and challenge they provide help participants make an honest self-assessment and determine specific ways in which to change their patterns of thinking, feeling, and acting. Although participants can benefit from the feedback they receive from others, it is ultimately up to them to decide what changes they want to make. Participants can compare the perceptions they have of themselves with the perceptions others have of them, and then they can decide for themselves what they will do with this information.

Personal-growth groups range from those with an open structure, in which participants shape the direction of the group, to those characterized by a specific focus. But they share the following goals:

· helping people develop more positive attitudes and better interpersonal skills
· using group process as a way of facilitating personality change
· helping members transfer behavior and skills developed in the group to situations outside of the group (Zimpfer, 1981)

Although personal-growth groups are often led by social workers, psychologists, or counselors, they may also be led by paraprofessionals in some settings. Regardless of who leads these groups, we think that training and supervision in a group process is essential, even if it is on-the-job training. Although the clients in these groups are typically not highly disturbed, such groups can be counterproductive if they are led by people who lack the knowledge and skills to facilitate interaction.

▪▪ T-Groups, or Laboratory-Training Groups

T-groups, also referred to as training groups, laboratory-training groups, or sensitivity-training groups, tend to emphasize the human-relations skills required for successful functioning in a business organization. In such groups the stress is on education through experience in an environment in which experimentation can occur, data can be analyzed, new ideas are encouraged, and decisions can be made or problems solved. Frequently these groups are task oriented, and the focus is on specific organizational problems, such as: How can leadership become a more shared function? By what vehicle can employees creatively express themselves?

The focus of T-groups is on the group process rather than on personal growth. (*Group process* refers to the stages of development of a group and the interactions that characterize each stage.) Members are taught how to observe their own processes and also how to develop a leadership role so that they can continue the groups on their own.

▪▪ Structured Groups

Groups structured to focus on one theme are being increasingly used by agencies, schools, and college counseling centers. Although the specific topic varies according to the interests of the leader and the population of the group, such groups share the aim of providing members with increased awareness of some life problem and the tools to better cope with it. Generally, the sessions are about 2 hours each week, for 4 to 15 weeks. Depending on the population, some group sessions may be as short as 30 to 45 minutes, especially with children or clients with a short attention span.

At the beginning of these structured groups it is common to ask members to complete a questionnaire on how well they are coping with the area of concern. Such groups make use of structured exercises, readings, homework assignments, and contracts. When the group comes to an end, another questionnaire is often used to assess the members' progress.

This list will give you some idea of the scope of topics for structured groups:

- stress management
- assertion training
- eating disorders (bulemia and anorexia)
- women in transition
- dealing with an alcoholic parent
- learning coping skills
- managing relationships and ending relationships
- overcoming perfectionism
- support for incest victims

■■ Self-Help Groups

Self-help groups serve a critical need for certain populations that is not met by professional mental-health workers. Such groups, composed of people with a common interest, provide a support system that helps reduce psychological stress and gives the members the incentive to begin changing their life. Self-help groups stress a common identity based on a common life situation to a far greater extent than do most other groups. The members share their experiences, learn from one another, offer suggestions for new members, and provide encouragement for people who sometimes see no hope for their future.

Examples of self-help groups include Alcoholics Anonymous, Weight Watchers, Mended Hearts, and Recovery, Inc. These groups are led by people who are struggling with the same issues as the members of the group, and by intention they are not professionally led. At times professionals are used as consultants, however.

Group Leadership

■■ Problems and Issues Facing Beginning Group Leaders

Those who are just beginning to lead groups typically feel overwhelmed by the number of potential problems. New leaders ask themselves questions such as:

- Will I be able to get the group started? How?
- What techniques should I use?
- Should I wait for the group to initiate?
- Do I have what it takes to follow through once something has been initiated?
- What if I make mistakes? Can I cause someone serious psychological damage?
- Do I know enough theory? Can I apply whatever I do know in groups?
- Should I share my anxiety with my group?
- How much should I participate as a member?
- What do I do if there is a prolonged silence?

· What if the entire group attacks me?
· How do I know whether the group is helping people change?
· How can I work with so many people at one time?

Group leaders, whether inexperienced or seasoned, cannot be guaranteed effectiveness. Hence, courage is necessary, the courage to function under conditions of uncertainty. Group leaders will make mistakes, and, if they can admit them, they will learn from them. It is important that leaders not be harshly critical of themselves—that they not work under self-imposed standards of perfection.

One problem that will probably confront new group leaders is negative reactions from group members. On the one hand, if a leader structures a group by using specific techniques, he or she may be accused by members of constricting their freedom. The members may rebel by refusing to cooperate with the structure. On the other hand, members may criticize a nonstructuring leader for allowing them to flounder, and they may wait passively for the leader to initiate some exercise. Group leaders need to learn how to constructively confront those who have these reactions. If leaders become tight and defensive, the members may, in turn, become increasingly defensive. Such an undercurrent of unresolved hostility will sabotage any further work. How to deal with these situations will be discussed later in this section.

Beginning group leaders should realize that it will take time to develop leadership skills to the point that they feel effective. Many feel like quitting after leading only a few sessions; such people usually want to be accomplished leaders without experiencing the self-doubts and fears that may be necessary to the development of a leader. Some feel devastated if they don't receive an abundance of positive feedback. It probably cannot be mentioned too many times that some struggle and uncertainty are almost always a part of learning how to lead well. Nobody expects to perfect any skill (skiing, playing the guitar, making pottery) in a few introductory lessons. Those who finally experience success at these endeavors are the ones who have the endurance to progress in increments. The same can be said of group therapists, although their success depends not only on native skill and supervision but also on involvement in their own personal therapy. There is probably no better teacher than experience, but unguided experience may be less than helpful. Immediate feedback—from a supervisor, from co-leaders, or from other leader trainees in a training group—enables leaders to profit from their experience.

■■ Personal Characteristics of the Effective Group Leader

We believe that the personhood of the leader is the most important determinant of group outcomes. In discussing the personality characteristics of the effective group leader with some of our colleagues, we found that it was difficult to list all of the traits of effective leaders and even more difficult to agree on one particular personality type associated with effective group leadership. The following are some characteristics that we deem important elements of the group leader's personhood.

Courage.   One of the most important personal traits of effective group leaders is courage. Leaders show courage in their willingness (1) to be vulnerable at times, admitting mistakes and imperfections and taking the same risks that they expect group members to take; (2) to confront another, even though they might not be sure that they're right; (3) to act on their beliefs and hunches; (4) to be emotionally touched by another and to draw on their experiences in order to identify with the other; (5) to continually examine their inner self; (6) to be direct and honest with members; and (7) to express to the group their fears and expectations about the group process. Leaders should not use their special role to protect themselves from honest and direct interaction with the rest of the group.

Willingness to Model.   One of the best ways to teach desired behaviors is by modeling those behaviors in the group. Group leaders would do well to recognize the extent to which their behavior influences the group. Through their behavior, and the attitudes conveyed by it, leaders can create such group norms as openness, seriousness of purpose, acceptance of others, and the desirability of taking risks. Leaders exercise this influence on the group process by virtue of their position as leader.

   We believe that group leaders teach largely by example—by doing what they expect members to do. They must realize that their role differs from that of the group member, but they mustn't hide behind a professional facade. By engaging in honest, appropriate, and timely self-disclosure, group leaders can both participate as members in the group and fulfill the leadership function of modeling.

Presence.   The ability to be emotionally present with group members is extremely important. It involves being touched by others' pain, struggles, and joys. Some members may elicit anger in a group leader, and others may evoke pain, sadness, guilt, or happiness. Leaders can become more emotionally involved with others by paying close attention to their own reactions and by permitting these reactions to become intense. This does not mean that they must talk about the situation in their own life that caused them the pain or evoked the anger. It means that they allow themselves to experience their feelings, even for just a few moments. Fully experiencing emotions gives leaders the ability to be compassionate and empathic with their clients. At the same time as they're moved by others' experiences, leaders must remain separate persons with their own experiencing. This mode of relating is extremely important, for group members as well as for group leaders.

To increase the ability to be present, it is important for the leader to spend some time alone before leading a group and to shut out distractions as much as possible. The leader can then prepare for the group by thinking about the group members and preparing to become involved with them. If this reflection time is not allowed for, the group members will probably get far less from the leader, for he or she is likely to be psychologically detached from the members' experiencing.

Goodwill and Caring.   A sincere interest in the welfare of others is essential in a group leader. This means that group leaders must neither abuse their role by using the group mainly for their own purposes nor exploit members to enhance their ego.

Caring involves respecting, trusting, and valuing people. It may be exceedingly difficult for a leader to care for certain group members, but the leader should at least want to care. It is vital that group leaders become aware of what kinds of people they care for and what kinds they find it difficult to care for. Leaders can gain this awareness by openly exploring their reactions to members.

That the leader cares about the members must be demonstrated to the group; merely saying so is not enough. There are various ways for leaders to exhibit a caring attitude. One way is by inviting a person to participate but allowing that person to decide how far to go. Another way is for the leader, aware of discrepancies between a person's words and behavior, to confront that person but to do so in a way that doesn't scare the member off. Another way for the leader to express caring is by giving warmth, concern, and support when, and only when, he or she feels it toward a person. Still another way to show caring is not to tolerate dishonest behavior but rather to encourage people to be what they could be without their masks and shields.

Belief in Group Process.   Some therapists really don't believe that groups can effect significant change in clients, yet they continue to lead therapy groups. We think that a deep belief in the value of group process is positively related to constructive outcomes. We have found that our enthusiasm and convictions are powerful both in attracting a clientele and in providing an incentive to work. Our belief in group process gives a sense of hope to potential and current group members. We're not suggesting that leaders should uncritically embrace groups as the only means of achieving growth; it would be naive not to recognize the limitations of group process. We are suggesting that, to lead successfully, leaders must believe in the value of what they are doing and trust the therapeutic forces in a group. Group leaders who do not genuinely believe in the value of therapeutic group work, and who do it only for money or power, we consider unethical.

Openness.   To be effective, group leaders must be open with themselves, open to others in groups, open to new experiences, and open to lifestyles and values that differ from their own. Leaders must not only openly reveal their own experiences but also openly show their reactions to members in the group. Openness does not mean that leaders reveal every aspect of their personal life; it means that they reveal enough of themselves to give the participants a sense of the person.

Leader openness tends to foster a spirit of openness within the group; it permits members to become more open about their feelings and beliefs, and it lends a certain fluidity to the group process. Self-revelation cannot be manipulated as a technique, however; it is best done spontaneously, when it seems appropriate.

Nondefensiveness in Coping with Attacks.   Dealing frankly with criticism is related to openness. Group leaders who are easily threatened, who are insecure in their work of leading, who are overly sensitive to negative feedback, and who depend highly on group approval will encounter major problems in trying to carry out a leadership function. Members sometimes accuse leaders of not caring enough, of being selective in their caring, of structuring the sessions too much, of not providing enough direction, of being too harsh, and so forth. Some of the criticism may be fair—the leader may be inept—and some of it may be unfair—an expression of jealousy, testing of authority, power seeking, or projection onto the leader of feelings for other significant people. The crucial thing is for the leader to nondefensively explore with the group the feelings that are behind the criticism and to differentiate between feelings that are produced by the leader and feelings that mainly represent transference.

Personal Power.   Personal power does not entail domination of members or manipulation of them toward the leader's end; rather, it is the dynamic and vital quality of the leader. Leaders have it when they know who they are and what they want. Their life is an expression of what they espouse. Personal power also involves a sense of confidence in self; the group members realize that this person knows what he or she is doing. And it involves a certain charisma; the members like the personal qualities of the group leader and want to develop some of these same characteristics. Rather than talking about the importance of being alive, powerful leaders express and radiate an aliveness through their actions.

Power and honesty are closely related. In our view, powerful people are the ones who can show themselves. Although they may be frightened by certain qualities within themselves, the fear doesn't keep them from examining these qualities. In contrast, powerless people need very much to defend themselves against self-knowledge. Powerless people are very vulnerable and, what's more, can't face this fact. Powerful people recognize and accept their weaknesses and don't expend energy concealing them from themselves and others.

There is often a great need in clients to see leaders not only as powerful but also as having all of the qualities that the members are striving for. Clients may view leaders as perfect. Such members tend to undercut their own power by giving their leader all of the credit for the insights that they, the members, are in fact responsible for. Powerful group leaders can accept credit where it's due and at the same time encourage clients to accept their own share of credit for their growth. There is a danger that leaders will become infatuated with clients' perceptions of them as finished products. Group leaders who fall prey to this are likely to stifle their own ongoing growth.

Stamina.   Group leading can be taxing and draining as well as exciting and energizing. Therefore, a leader needs physical and psychological stamina and the ability to withstand pressure in order to remain vitalized throughout the course of a group. Some novice counselors begin a group feeling excited and anticipate each session—until the group becomes resistive, until members begin to drop out, or until members say that they feel the group is going nowhere. If a leader gives in to fatigue at this point, any possibility that the group will be productive may be lost. This means that group leaders need to be aware of their own energy level. Furthermore, they need to have outside sources of psychological and emotional nourishment; if they depend primarily on their group's progress for this, they run a high risk of being undernourished and thus of losing the stamina so vital to their success as leaders. Unrealistically high expectations can affect a leader's stamina. Those leaders who cling to such expectations of dramatic change are often disappointed in themselves and what they perceive as "poor performance" on the part of their group. Faced with the discrepancy between their visions of what the group *should* be and what actually occurs, these leaders often lose their enthusiasm and begin to needlessly blame both themselves and the group members for what they see as failure.

Willingness to Seek New Experiences.   A therapist's personhood is partly determined by his or her experiences with various facets of living. A narrow range of life experiences restricts the capacity of a leader to understand the psychological worlds of clients, who may have different values resulting from different life experiences. If a group leader has lived a fairly sheltered life and has known little pain and struggle, how can he or she empathize with clients who have suffered and have made dramatic life choices? Can those therapists who have never experienced loneliness, joy, anguish, or uncertainty understand these conditions in their clients? Although it is not possible for leaders to experience directly everything they may encounter in others, they should at least be willing to identify ways in which they can draw on their own emotions in working with group members. It is unrealistic to expect counselors to have experienced the same problems as their clients. But the emotions that all of us experience are much the same. We all experience psychological pain, even though what leads to this pain may be different. One basis for empathizing with clients is being open to the sources of pain in our own life, without becoming swept up by this pain.

Self-Awareness.   A central characteristic of any therapeutic person is awareness of self, including one's goals, identity, motivations, needs, limitations, strengths, values, feelings, and problems. The therapist who has a limited understanding of who he or she is will surely not be able to facilitate this kind of awareness in clients. As we've mentioned, being open to new life experiences and divergent lifestyles is one way leaders can expand their awareness. Involvement in their own personal therapy, both group and individual, is another way for leaders to become more aware of who they are and who they might become. Awareness of why they choose to lead groups is crucial. What needs are served by being a group leader? Group leaders with dim self-awareness or leaders who keep themselves blinded for fear of what they might discover are dangerous people in groups. How can they encourage others to risk self-discovery if they themselves refuse to do it? Group leaders should be committed to becoming increasingly aware of their own needs and motivations. Group leaders have a rich source of information about themselves; all they need to do is reflect on interactions they've had with members of their group.

Sense of Humor.   Although therapy is serious business, there are many truly humorous dimensions of the human condition. The ability to laugh at oneself and to see the humor in one's own human frailties can be extremely useful. At times, people take themselves so seriously that they miss an opportunity to put into perspective the importance of their problems. Groups occasionally exhibit a real need for laughter and joking—simply for release of the tension that has built up. This is particularly true of intensive groups after sustained periods of dealing seriously with weighty problems. This release should not be viewed as an escape, for genuine humor can heal. The leader who can enjoy humor and infuse it effectively into the group process has an invaluable asset.

Inventiveness.   The capacity to be spontaneously creative—to approach each group with fresh ideas—is a most important characteristic for group leaders. Freshness may not be easy to maintain, particularly if a therapist leads groups frequently. Leaders must somehow avoid becoming trapped in ritualized techniques or a programmed presentation of self that has lost all life. Leaders who are good at discovering new ways of approaching a group and who are willing to suspend the use of established techniques are unlikely to grow stale. Working with interesting co-leaders is one way for leaders to get fresh ideas. Getting some distance from groups—for example, by doing fewer of them, doing other things, or taking a vacation—also may help a leader gain a fresh perspective.

Inventiveness in leaders involves the ability both to detect clues that someone gives them and to create some way of exploring with the person the problem that is hinted at. In this regard it is important for group leaders to have a theoretical perspective, for this will guide their selection of techniques. For instance, we have been influenced by the psychoanalytic view of development, so when we lead groups, we invent techniques that aid people in tapping their memories of early childhood experiences. In this way, leaders can use the theory or combination of theories they endorse as a source of fresh techniques.

■■ Survey of Group-Leadership Skills

Although the personality characteristics of the group leader are among the most important determinants of group outcomes, we think it is a mistake to assume that being a person of goodwill and approaching your group enthusiastically are all you need to lead effectively. Some personality attributes seem positively related to effective leadership, but these characteristics by themselves are not sufficient. Basic counseling skills specific to group situations must be developed. Like most skills, counseling skills can be taught to some degree, but there is also an element of art involved in using these skills in a sensitive and timely way. Learning how and when to use these skills is a function of supervised experience, practice, feedback, and confidence in one's use of the skills.

We will now consider some of the skills that you will need to acquire as a competent group leader. As you read, keep in mind that these skills, like personal qualities, are essential but not sufficient for effective leadership. Unless you are also the kind of person who provides a positive model that your clients can benefit from, your success as a leader will be limited.

Active Listening.   It is most important to learn how to pay full attention to others as they communicate, and this process involves more than merely listening to the words. It involves absorbing the content, noting gestures and subtle changes in voice or expression, and sensing underlying messages. Group leaders can improve their listening skills by first recognizing the barriers that interfere with paying attention to others.

Some of these roadblocks are not really listening to the other, thinking about what to say next instead of giving full attention to the other, being overly concerned about one's role or about how one will look, and judging and evaluating without putting oneself in the other person's place. Like any other therapeutic skill, active listening exists in degrees. Some leaders are so intent on being in the spotlight that they can't focus on anything outside themselves; other leaders have developed a high degree of perceptivity in discerning others' messages. The skilled group leader is sensitive to the congruence (or lack of it) between what a member is saying in words and what he or she is communicating through body posture, gestures, mannerisms, and voice inflections. For instance, a man may be talking about his warm and loving feelings toward his wife, yet his body may be rigid and his fists clenched. A woman recalling a painful situation may both smile and hold back tears.

Reflecting.   Reflecting, a skill that is dependent on active listening, is the ability to convey the essence of what a person has communicated so the person can see it. Many neophyte group leaders find themselves confining most of their interaction to mere reflection. Somehow it seems safe. And, since members continue to talk, leaders continue to reflect. Carried to its extreme, however, reflection can become a hollow echo, empty of any substance:

> **Member:** I really didn't want to come to the group today. I'm bored, and I don't think we've gotten anyplace for weeks.
> **Group Leader:** You didn't want to come to the group because you're bored and the group isn't getting anywhere.

There was plenty of rich material here for the leader to respond to in a personal way, or with some confrontation, or by asking the person and the group to examine what was going on in the group. Beginning on a reflective level may have value, but staying on that level produces blandness. The leader might have done better to reply "You feel like quitting the group because you don't sense any involvement; you sound discouraged about the possibility of getting much from this experience." The leader would then have been challenging the member to look at the emotions that lay beneath his words and, in the process, would have been opening up opportunities for meaningful communication.

Clarifying.   Clarifying is a skill that can be valuably applied during the initial stages of a group. It involves focusing on key underlying issues and sorting out confusing and conflicting feelings. Thus, a girl might say: "I hate my father, and I wish I didn't have to see him anymore. He hurts me so often. I feel guilty when I feel this way, because I also love him and wish he would appreciate me." And the therapist might clarify:

"You have feelings of love and hate, and somehow having both of these feelings at once doesn't seem OK." Clarification can help the client sort out her feelings so that she can eventually experience both love and hate without experiencing guilt. However, stronger intervention methods than clarification may have to be used before she can accept this polarity.

Summarizing.   The group process can get bogged down or fragmented, and the skill of summarizing is useful. On the basis of a summary, decisions about where to go next can be made. For example, some members may be arguing that the leader is not providing enough structure and direction while other members are maintaining that the leader is handling the group correctly. If the interaction seems to be turning into a debate, the group leader might interrupt and have each person state briefly how he or she feels about the issue. The leader can then summarize and offer possible alternatives.

At the end of a session the leader might make some summary statements or ask each member to summarize. For instance, a leader might say "Before we close, I'd like each of us to make a statement about his or her experience in the group today and tell where he or she is left." It's a good idea for the leader to make the first summary statement, so that the members will have a model for this behavior. Sometimes, however, the leader may want to close the session with his or her own reactions.

Facilitating.   The group leader can facilitate the group process by (1) assisting members to openly express their fears and expectations, (2) actively working to create a climate of safety and acceptance in which people will trust one another and therefore engage in productive interchanges, (3) providing encouragement and support as members explore highly personal material or as they try new behavior, (4) involving as many members as possible in the group interaction by inviting and sometimes even challenging members to participate, (5) working toward lessening the dependency on the leader, (6) encouraging open expression of conflict and controversy, and (7) helping members overcome barriers to direct communication. The aim of most facilitation skills is to help the group members reach their own goals. Essentially, these skills involve opening up clear communication among the members and helping them increase their responsibility for the direction of their group.

Empathizing.   An empathetic group leader can sense the subjective world of the client. This skill requires the leader to have the characteristics of caring and openness already mentioned. The leader must also have a wide range of experiences to serve as a basis for identifying with others. Finally, the leader must be able to discern subtle nonverbal messages as well as messages transmitted more directly. It is impossible really to know what another person is experiencing, but a sensitive group leader can make a good guess. It is also important, however, for the group leader to avoid blurring his or her identity by overidentifying with the group members. The core of the skill of empathy lies in being able to openly grasp another's experiencing and at the same time maintain one's separateness.

Interpreting.   Group leaders who are highly directive are likely to make use of interpretation, which entails offering possible explanations for certain behaviors or symptoms. If interpretations are accurate and well-timed, they may result in a member's moving beyond an impasse. It is not necessary that the leader always make the interpretation for the client; in Gestalt therapy, clients are encouraged to make their own interpretation of their behavior. A group leader can also present an interpretation in the form of a hunch, the truth of which the client can then assess. For instance, an interpretation might be stated as follows: "Harry, I've noticed that, when a person in the group talks about something painful, you usually intervene and become reassuring and in some way try to take that person's pain away. Does this say that you fear painful experiences yourself?" It is important that the interpretation be presented as a hypothesis rather than as a fact. Also important is that the person have a chance to consider the validity of this hunch in the group.

Questioning.   Questioning is really not much of a skill, and it is overused by many group leaders. Interrogation seldom leads to productive outcomes, and more often than not it distracts the person working. If a member happens to be experiencing intense feelings, questioning is one way of reducing the intensity. Asking "Why do you feel that way?" is rarely helpful. However, appropriately timed "what" and "how" questions do serve to intensify experiencing. Examples are questions such as: "What is happening with your body now, as you speak about your isolation?" "In what ways do you experience the fear of rejection in this group?" "What are some of the bad things you imagine happening to you if you reveal your secrets to this group?" "How are you coping with your feeling that you can't trust some of the members here?" These questions direct the person to heighten feelings of the moment. Leaders should develop the skill of asking questions like these and avoiding questions that remove people from themselves. Questions that are not helpful include those that search for causes of behavior, probe for information, and the like—for example: "How long have you been seeking your father's approval?" "Why do you feel depressed?" "Why don't you leave home?"

Linking.   A group leader who has an interactional bias—that is, who stresses member-to-member rather than leader-to-member communication—makes frequent use of linking. This skill calls on the insightfulness of the leader in finding ways of relating what one person is doing or saying to the concerns of another person. For example, Katherine might be describing her feeling that she won't be loved unless she's perfect. If Pamela has been heard to express a similar feeling, the leader could ask Pamela and Katherine to talk with each other in the group about their fears. By being alert for cues that members have some common concern, the leader can promote member interaction and raise the level of group cohesion.

Confronting.   Beginning group leaders are often afraid to confront group members for fear of hurting them, of being wrong, or of inviting retaliation. It doesn't take much skill to attack another or to be merely critical. It does take both caring and skill, however, to confront group members when their behavior is disruptive of the group functioning or when there are discrepancies between their verbal messages and their nonverbal messages. In confronting a member, a leader should (1) challenge specifically the behavior to be examined, avoiding labeling the person, and (2) share how he or she feels about the person's behavior. For example, Danny has been interrupting the group, pelting people with "why" questions and offering interpretations. The leader might intervene: "Danny, I find it difficult to listen to all your questioning and telling people how they are. Most of the time when you enter the group interaction, you interpret others' behavior for them, and I still don't know much about you. I fear that, if you don't look at this, when the group ends you'll be a stranger. If that were to happen, I'd be disappointed."

Supporting.   The skill in supportive behavior is knowing when it will be therapeutic and when it will be counterproductive. A common mistake is offering support before a participant has had an opportunity to fully experience a conflict or some painful feelings. Although the intervention may be done with good intentions, it may abort certain feelings that a given member needs to experience. Another mistake is supporting game-playing behavior. For instance, if a woman is playing helpless and trying to convince everyone of how fragile she is, a leader who offers support will, in effect, foster her dependency. What the leader might do instead is confront the member with the fact that she can do for herself what she's pleading for others to do for her. Support is appropriate when people are facing a crisis, when they're venturing into frightening territory, when they attempt constructive changes and yet feel uncertain about these changes, and when they're struggling to rid themselves of old patterns that are limiting. Leaders should remember that too much support can send the message that people are unable to support themselves.

Blocking.   Group leaders have the responsibility to block certain activities of group members, such as questioning, probing, gossiping, invading another's privacy, breaking confidences, and so forth. The skill is to learn to block counterproductive behaviors without attacking the personhood of the perpetrator. This requires both sensitivity and directness. Some examples of behavior that need to be blocked are:

· **Bombarding others with questions.** Offenders can be asked to make direct statements out of their questions.
· **Gossiping.** If a member talks *about* another member in the room, the leader can direct the person to speak directly to the person being spoken about.
· **Storytelling.** If lengthy storytelling occurs, a leader can intervene and ask the person to say how all this relates to present feelings and events.
· **Breaking confidences.** A member may inadvertently talk about a situation that occurred in another group or mention what so-and-so did in a prior group. This should be stopped by the leader in a firm but gentle manner.
· **Invasion of privacy.** If a person pushes another, probing for personal information, this behavior must be blocked by the group leader.

Diagnosing.   Diagnostic skills involve more than labeling behavior, identifying symptoms, and figuring out what category a person falls into. They include the ability to appraise certain behavior problems and choose the appropriate intervention. For example, a leader who diagnoses a client as deeply angry must consider the safety and appropriateness of encouraging the client to "let out your pent-up rage." Leaders also need to develop the skill of determining whether a particular group is indicated or contraindicated for a member, and they need to acquire the expertise necessary to make appropriate referrals.

Reality Testing.   A group is a place where participants can safely explore new alternatives that open up for them and where they can test the reality of some of their plans. Consequently, group leaders should be aware of the importance of encouraging members to appraise their alternatives realistically. If a man spontaneously decides to quit his job, the leader can encourage him to think about what the ramifications are and what other possibilities are open to him. If an adolescent decides to drop out of school, she can be directed to explore what the decision may mean in terms of her future.

The leader can best foster reality testing by having the other members give feedback on how realistic they consider the person's plans to be. It is important, however, that the leader caution group members not to tell the person what to do but rather to offer what they see as the possible outcomes of taking various alternative routes.

Evaluating.   A crucial leadership skill is evaluating the ongoing process and dynamics of a group. After each group session it is valuable for the leader to evaluate what happened, both within individual members and among the members, and to think about what interventions might be used next time with the group. Leaders need to get in the habit of asking themselves questions such as: What changes are resulting from the group? What are the therapeutic and antitherapeutic forces in the group?

The leader must also teach participants how to evalute, so that they can appraise the movement and direction of their own group. Once the group has evaluated a session or series of sessions, its members can decide what, if any, changes need to be made. For example, during an evaluation at the close of a session the leader and the members are in agreement that the group as a whole has been passive. The leader might say: "I feel the burden of initiating and sense that you're waiting for me to do something to energize you. I'm challenging each of you to examine your behavior and to evaluate to what degree you're personally responsible. Then please think about what, specifically, you're willing to do to change this group."

Terminating.   Group leaders must learn when and how to terminate their work with both individuals and groups. They need to develop the ability to tell when a group session should end, when an individual is ready to leave a group, and when a group has completed its work, and they need to learn how to handle each of these types of termination. The skill of terminating a single session or a whole group involves (1) providing the members with suggestions for transferring what they've learned in the group to the environment they must return to, (2) creating a climate that will encourage members to make contracts to do work between sessions or after the group, (3) preparing people for the psychological problems they may face on leaving a group, (4) arranging for a follow-up group, (5) telling members where they can get additional therapy, and (6) being available for individual consultation at the termination of a group. Follow-up and evaluation activities are particularly important if the leader is to learn the impact of the group as a therapeutic agent.

■■ An Integrated View of Leadership Skills

Some counselor-education programs focus mainly on developing counseling skills and assessing competencies, whereas other programs focus more on the personal qualities, described earlier, that underly these skills. Ideally, training programs for group leaders give due weight to both of these aspects. We agree with Ritter's (1984) conclusion that there is enough evidence to retain both group experiences (designed for enhancing growth and awareness) and skill-training programs as a basic part of preparing group counselors. In the next chapter, when professional standards of training group counselors are described, we will go into more detail about the specific areas of knowledge and skill competencies that group workers need.

In concluding this section we want to acknowledge that you are likely to feel somewhat overwhelmed when you consider all the skills that are necessary for effective group leadership. It may help to remember that, as with other areas of life, you will become frustrated if you attempt to focus on all aspects of this field at once. You can expect to gradually refine your leadership style and gain confidence in using these skills effectively.

Several points need to be emphasized about the skills we have discussed. First, they can best be thought of as existing to various degrees, rather than on an all-or-nothing basis. They can be highly developed and used in a sensitive and appropriate manner, or they can exist to only a minimal extent. Second, these skills can be learned and constantly improved through training and supervised experience. Participating in a group as a member is one good way to acquire a sense of what a group is about. Leading or co-leading a group under supervision is another excellent way to acquire and refine leadership skills. Third, the skills are not separate and discrete entities; they overlap a great deal. Active listening, reflection, and clarification are interdependent, as are interpreting and diagnosing. Hence, by developing certain skills, a leader automatically improves others. Finally, these skills cannot be divorced from the counselor's personhood, for the choice of which skills to develop and use is an expression of the leader's personality.

The Co-Leadership Model

■■ The Basis of Co-Leadership

Many who are involved in the education and training of group leaders have come to favor the co-leadership model of group practice. There are a number of advantages to this practice for all concerned: for the group members, who can gain from two leaders in a group; for the co-leaders, who can learn from each other; and for supervisors, who can work closely with the co-leaders during their training. Although we prefer the co-leadership model, we do not want to give the impression that all groups must conform to this technique. Many leaders work alone and do so effectively.

We like the co-leadership model both for leading groups and for train-ing and supervising leaders. In conducting training workshops with students in the university, we continually hear how they value working with a partner, especially if this is their first time in leading a group. As we discussed earlier, group leaders preparing to meet their first group experience self-doubt, anxiety, and downright trepidation! The task seems far less monumental if they meet their new group with a co-leader whom they trust and respect. In our in-service training work-shops for group workers we find value in having the participants gain practice in co-leading a group as we observe them. Then, during our feedback to them, we frequently ask these co-leaders to talk with each other about how they felt as they were co-leading and what they think about the session they have just led. The feedback between these co-leaders can be both supportive and challenging. They can make con-structive suggestions about each other's style, and the process of ex-changing perceptions can enhance their ability to function effectively as co-leaders. This model continues to work well for all concerned.

In our own leading of groups and workshops we usually work as a team. Although each of us has independent professional involve-ments (including leading groups alone at times), we very much enjoy co-leading and continue to learn from each other, as well as from the colleagues we work with.

The choice of a co-leader is important. If the two leaders are incom-patible, their group is bound to be negatively affected. For example, ongoing power struggles between co-leaders will have the effect of di-viding the group. If co-leaders are in continual conflict with each other, they are providing a poor model of interpersonal relating. This conflict typically leads to unexpressed hostility within the group, which gets in the way of effective work. We are not suggesting that co-leaders will never have conflicts. What is important is that they work out any dis-putes in a decent and direct manner, for doing so can model ways of coping with interpersonal conflict effectively.

We believe that the basis for selecting a co-leader should be mutual respect. Two or more leaders working together will surely have their differences in leadership style, and they will not always agree or share the same perceptions or interpretations. If there is mutual respect and trust between them, however, they will be able to work cooperatively instead of competitively, and they will be secure enough to be free of the constant need to prove themselves.

It is not a coincidence that those we lead with are also our closest friends. When several of us work together as a team in leading a work-shop (or presenting as a panel at a convention), we often receive feed-back about our style of interacting with one another. For example, peo-ple at times comment that our personality and stylistic differences complement one another. They observe enthusiasm, playfulness, a willingness to openly disagree, an absence of competition, and a liking and respect for one another. The point we want to make is that the way we work as a team has a definite impact on the people we work with.

It is not essential that you be best friends with your co-leader. What you need is a good working relationship, which comes about through taking time to talk with each other. Although we take delight in our personal and professional relationship, we are also willing to engage in the hard work necessary for a successful team. This relationship reflects our belief that it is essential that co-leaders get together regularly to discuss any matters that may affect their working as a team. We emphasize discussing how we are feeling in regard to our personal life as well as talking about specific group purposes and making plans for an upcoming group. Further, we tell co-leaders in training to arrange to spend time together both before and after each group session in order to evaluate their leadership and the group's progress, as well as to make plans for future sessions.

■■ Advantages of the Co-Leadership Model

Having acknowledged our clear preference for co-leading groups, we will now present a summary of what seem to us the major advantages of using the co-leadership method.

1. Leader "burn-out" can be reduced by working with a co-leader. This is especially true if you are working with a draining population, such as psychotics who often simply get up and leave, who hallucinate during sessions, and who may be withdrawn or be acting out. In such groups one leader can attend to certain problem members while the other attempts to maintain the work going on in the group.

2. If intense emotions are being expressed by one or more members, one leader can pay attention to those members while the other leader scans the room to note the reactions of other members, who can later be invited to share their feelings. Or, if appropriate, the co-leader can find a way to involve members in the work of someone else. Many possibilities exist for linking members together, for facilitating interaction between members, and for orchestrating the flow of a group when co-leaders are sensitively and harmoniously working as a team.

3. If one leader must be absent because of illness or professional reasons, the group can proceed with the other leader. If one of the co-leaders is especially drained on a given day or is temporarily experiencing some emotional pain, the co-leader can assume primary leadership, and the leader having problems can feel less burdened with the responsibility to "be there" for the group members. In such a case it may be appropriate for the co-leader to state to the group that he or she is going through some difficulties personally, without feeling the necessity to go

into great detail. Again, this provides sound modeling for the members, for they can see that group leaders are not beyond dealing with personal problems. Furthermore, by announcing that he or she does not want to accept full leadership responsibility for a given session, the leader is likely to feel freer and may be much more present simply for having said this.

4. If one of the leaders has been strongly affected by the sessions, he or she can explore feelings of anger, depression, or the like in some detail with the co-leader after the session ends. The co-leader can be used as a sounding board, can check for objectivity, and can offer useful feedback. There is no problem of breaking confidentiality in such instances, for the co-leader was also present at the session. However, we do want to emphasize that it is often necessary for leaders to express and deal with such feelings in the session itself, especially if they were aroused in the group setting. For example, if you are aware that you are perpetually annoyed by a given member, you might need to deal with your annoyance as a group matter. In certain cases a group member's concerns might touch your own "unfinished business," and you might explore your personal issues in the session. This is a time when a competent and trusted co-leader is especially important.

5. An important advantage of co-leading emerges when one of the leaders is affected by another member to the degree that countertransference is present. Countertransference can distort a leader's objectivity so that he or she may not be able to work effectively. For example, your co-leader may typically react with hostility or some other intense feeling to one member who is seen as a problem. Perhaps you are better able to make contact with this member, and so you may be the person who primarily works with the member. You can be of valuable assistance by helping your co-leader talk about, and perhaps even resolve, some irrational reactions and attachments toward a certain member.

■■ Disadvantages of the Co-Leadership Model

Even with a co-leader you choose, one you respect and like, there are likely to be occasional disagreements. This difference of perspective and opinion need not be a disadvantage or a problem in co-leadership practices; it can be healthy for both of you, because you can keep yourself professionally alert through constructive challenges and differences. Moreover, if you deal with your differences or conflicts constructively during the session (rather than pretending they do not exist), you are providing excellent modeling on how to work with conflicts. Most of the disadvantages in co-leading groups have to do with poor selection of a co-leader, random assignment to a co-leader, or failure of the co-leaders to meet regularly:

1. Problems can occur if co-leaders rarely meet with each other. The results are likely to be a lack of synchronization or even a tendency to work at cross purposes instead of toward a common goal. For example, we've observed difficulties when one group leader thought that all leader intervention should be positive, supportive, and invitational, whereas the other leader functioned on the assumption that members need to be pushed and directly confronted and that they should bring up issues that are difficult for them to talk about. The group became fragmented and polarized as a result of the incompatible leadership styles. The main problem was that the leaders did not take the time to discuss their differences.

2. Related to the above issue is the matter of competition and rivalry. For example, one leader may have an exaggerated need to have center stage, to be dominant at all times, to be perceived as the one in control; such a leader might even actively put down the co-leader. Obviously, such a relationship between co-leaders is bound to have a negative effect in the group. In some cases members may develop negative reactions toward groups in general, concluding that all that ever goes on in them is conflict and jockeying for power.

3. If co-leaders do not have a relationship built on trust and respect or if they do not value each other's competence, they may not trust each other's interventions. Each leader may insist on following his or her own hunches, convinced that the other's are not of value.

4. If one leader colludes with members against the other leader, this will be detrimental. For example, assume that Sue confronts a male leader with strong negative reactions and that his co-leader (a woman) joins Sue in expressing her reactions and even invites the members to give feedback to the co-leader. This can result in a division within the group, with members taking sides about who is "right." This is especially a problem in cases where one leader has not previously given negative reactions to the other and now uses the situation as a chance to "unload" feelings.

5. Co-leaders who are involved in an intimate relationship with each other can get into some problematic situations if they attempt to use time in the session to work on their own relationship struggles. Although some in the group may support the co-leaders' "working on their issues" in the group, the members are likely to resent these co-leaders for abdicating their leadership functions.

Although we are advocates of the co-leadership model, we think that it is important that the two leaders have some say in deciding to work as a team. Otherwise, there is a potential for harm for both the group members and the co-leaders. Careful selection of a co-leader and time devoted to meeting together are essential. We encourage those who co-lead groups to spend some time both before *and* after each session discussing their reactions to what is going on in the group as well as their working relationship as co-leaders.

Trends in Group Work

There is a clear trend in the United States toward specialized groups for specialized populations. When we give workshops in various states, we are struck with the range of these structured groups. Groups seem to be offered for almost any imaginable problem, and they are limited only by a leader's interest, enthusiasm, and creativity. These groups tend to be of relatively short duration and to have an educational and a therapeutic focus. Perhaps one reason for this trend is the increased pressure that mental-health practitioners feel to be accountable. Consumers are demanding more evidence that a counselor's methods are indeed working. They seem to be less interested in loosely structured or unfocused groups that merely promise self-actualization and growth experiences.

Another trend is toward increased awareness of ethical, professional, and legal issues relevant to group work. In line with this interest, the Association for Specialists in Group Work has published *Ethical Guidelines for Group Leaders* (ASGW, 1980) and *Professional Standards for Training of Group Counselors* (ASGW, 1983). Several textbooks have chapters or sections that address the ethical and legal issues special to group work (see Corey, Corey, & Callanan, 1984; Hopkins & Anderson, 1985; Rosenbaum, 1982; Van Hoose & Kottler, 1985). Malpractice awards to clients who felt that they had been treated unprofessionally and irresponsibly have increased the anxiety level of many mental-health professionals. When groups reached their zenith in the 1960s and the 1970s, there were some excesses in the name of "experimentation." Group practitioners who are aware of ethically questionable practices are attempting to improve the reputation of groups by designing ethical and legal safeguards. This issue will be explored in depth in the next chapter.

Cross-cultural counseling has made important contributions to group work. In addition to recognizing and respecting cultural differences, practitioners are highlighting the unique strengths of various cultures. Most graduate programs now require a course in cultural and ethnic diversity, and students receive specialized training in cross-cultural counseling both in their course work and as a part of their supervised fieldwork and internship.

A review of programs at various universities reveals a trend toward combining experiential and didactic components in training group leaders. Some programs stress the systematic development of skills, others emphasize acquiring theoretical knowledge, and still others work toward the personal development of the group counselor. Reddy

(1985) contends that the most critical aspect of training group specialists is helping them look at their own dynamics through an experiential model. We fully support the view that effective group workers need training and education in both the cognitive and emotional dimensions.

Finally, in a review of patterns and trends, Zimpfer (1984b) asserts that group work has come to be accepted as the treatment of choice for certain clients and particular settings. He concludes that the tendency in group work is toward greater variety in the choice of interventions, toward more growth-inducing approaches, and toward conceiving of group participants as collaborators in treatment rather than as passive receivers.

Exercises

There are exercises at the end of each of the chapters in Parts One and Two. These exercises can be done on your own or in class in small groups. The goal is to provide you with an opportunity to experience some of the techniques, issues, group processes, and potential problems that can occur at the various stages of a group's development.

We suggest that you read over all the suggested exercises at the end of each chapter and then focus on those that appeal to you the most or those that seem to have the most potential for clarifying issues for you.

For those of you who are leading a group for the first time, we encourage you to complete these exercises both before you begin leading and then again toward the end of the semester. This comparison will give you a basis for seeing how your attitudes and ideas may evolve with experience.

■■ Attitude Questionnaire on Group Leadership

Below are some statements concerning the role and functions of a group leader. Indicate your position on each statement, using the following scale:

1 = strongly agree
2 = slightly agree
3 = slightly disagree
4 = strongly disagree

_____ 1. It is the leader's job to actively work at shaping group norms.
_____ 2. Leaders should teach group members how to observe their own group as it unfolds.
_____ 3. The best way for a group leader to function is by becoming a participating member of the group.

_____ 4. It is generally wise for leaders to reveal their private life and personal problems in groups they are leading.

_____ 5. A group leader's primary task is to function as a technical expert.

_____ 6. It is extremely important for good leaders to have a definite theoretical framework that determines how they function in a group.

_____ 7. A group leader's function is to draw people out and make sure that silent members participate.

_____ 8. Group leaders influence group members more through modeling than through the techniques they employ.

_____ 9. It is generally best for the leader to give some responsibility to the members but also to retain some.

_____ 10. A major task of a group leader is to keep the group focused on the here and now.

_____ 11. It is unwise to allow members to discuss the past or to discuss events that occurred outside of the group.

_____ 12. It is best to give most of the responsibility for determining the direction of the group to the group members.

_____ 13. Group leaders should limit their self-disclosures to matters that have to do with what is now going on in the group.

_____ 14. If group leaders are basically open and engage in disclosing themselves, transference by members will not occur.

_____ 15. A leader who experiences countertransference is not competent to lead groups.

_____ 16. Group leaders should develop a personalized theory of leadership based on ideas drawn from many sources.

_____ 17. To be effective, group leaders must recognize their reasons for wanting to be group leaders.

_____ 18. Part of the task of group leaders is to determine specific behavioral goals for the group participants.

_____ 19. A group leader's theoretical model has little impact on the way people actually interact in a group.

_____ 20. If group leaders have mastered certain skills and techniques, it is not essential for them to operate from a theoretical framework.

_____ 21. Group leaders who possess personal power generally dominate the group and intimidate the members through this power.

_____ 22. There is not much place for a sense of humor in conducting groups, because group work is serious business.

_____ 23. Group leaders should not expect the participants to do anything that they, as leader, are not willing to do.

_____ 24. In groups with co-leaders there is the potential that the members will play one leader against the other like children playing one parent against the other.

_____ 25. For co-leaders to work effectively with each other, it is essential that they share the same style of leadership.

_____ 26. In selecting a co-leader it is a good idea to consider similarity of values, philosophy of life, and life experiences.

_____ 27. If co-leaders do not respect and trust each other, there is the potential for negative outcomes in the group.

_____ 28. Those who co-lead a group should be roughly equal in skills, experiences, and status.

_____ 29. Co-leaders should never openly disagree with each other during a session, for this may lead to a division within the group.

_____ 30. The group is bound to be affected by the type of modeling that the co-leaders provide.

We suggest that, after you have completed this self-inventory, your class break into small groups to discuss the items.

■■ Self-Assessment of Group-Leadership Skills

Review the section on group-leadership skills, and ask yourself to what degree you have mastered the skills described. Rate yourself on the following self-assessment scale for group leaders, and then discuss with a small group of class members why you rated yourself as you did. With your group explore specific things you might do to develop these skills.

Rate yourself from 1 to 5 on the following items:

1 = I am very poor at this.
5 = I am very good at this.

_____ 1. **Active listening.** I am able to hear and understand both direct and subtle messages.

_____ 2. **Reflecting.** I can mirror what another says without being mechanical.

_____ 3. **Clarifying.** I can focus on underlying issues and assist others to get a clearer picture of some of their conflicting feelings.

_____ 4. **Summarizing.** When I function as a group leader, I'm able to identify key elements of a session and to present them as a summary of the proceedings.

_____ 5. **Interpreting.** I can present a hunch to someone concerning the reason for his or her behavior without dogmatically telling what the behavior means.

_____ 6. **Questioning.** I avoid bombarding people with questions about their behavior.

_____ 7. **Linking.** I find ways of relating what one person is doing or saying to the concerns of other members.

_____ 8. **Confronting.** When I confront another, the confrontation usually has the effect of getting that person to look at his or her behavior in a nondefensive manner.

_____ 9. **Supporting.** I'm usually able to tell when supporting another will be productive and when it will be counterproductive.

_____ 10. **Blocking.** I'm able to intervene successfully, without seeming to be attacking, to stop counterproductive behaviors in the group such as gossiping, storytelling, and intellectualizing.

_____ 11. **Diagnosing.** I can generally get a sense of what specific problems members have without feeling the need to label people.

_____ 12. **Evaluating.** I appraise outcomes when I'm in a group, and I make some comments concerning the ongoing process of any group I'm in.

_____ 13. **Facilitating.** I'm able to help others openly express themselves and work through barriers to communication.

_____ 14. **Empathizing.** I can intuitively sense the subjective world of others in a group, and I have the capacity to understand much of what others are experiencing.

_____ 15. **Terminating.** At the end of group sessions I'm able to create a climate that will foster a willingness in others to continue working after the session.

▪▪ Evaluation of Group Leaders

The following evaluation form can be used in several ways. Group leaders can use it as a self-evaluation device, supervisors can use it to evaluate group leaders in training, group leaders can evaluate their co-leader with it, and group members can use it to evaluate their leader. These rating scales can be used by leader trainees at several points during a course. The self-evaluation forms can pinpoint progress made and areas needing further work.

Rate the leader from 1 to 5 on the following items.

1 = to an extremely low degree
5 = to an extremely high degree

_____ 1. **Support.** To what degree does the group leader allow group members to express their feelings?

_____ 2. **Interpretation.** To what degree is the group leader able to explain the meaning of behavior patterns within the framework of a theoretical system?

_____ 3. **Confrontation.** To what degree is the group leader able to actively and directly confront members when they are engaging in behavior that is inconsistent with what they are saying?

_____ 4. **Modeling.** To what degree is the group leader able to demonstrate behaviors that he or she wishes members to emulate and practice both during and after the session?

_____ 5. **Assignment.** To what degree is the group leader able to direct the members to improve on existing behavior patterns or to develop new behaviors before the next group session?

_____ 6. **Referral.** To what degree is the group leader able to make available to members someone who is capable of further assisting them with personal concerns?

_____ 7. **Role direction.** To what degree is the group leader able to direct members to enact specific roles in role-playing situations?

_____ 8. **Empathy.** To what degree does the group leader demonstrate the ability to adopt the internal frame of reference of a group member and communicate to the member that he or she is being understood?

_____ 9. **Self-disclosure.** To what degree does the group leader demonstrate a willingness and ability to reveal his or her own present feelings and thoughts as it is appropriate to the group-counseling situation?

_____ 10. **Initiation.** To what degree is the group leader able to get interaction going among members or between leader and member?

_____ 11. **Facilitation.** To what degree is the group leader able to help members clarify their own goals and take steps to reach these goals?

_____ 12. **Diagnosis.** To what degree is the group leader able to identify specific areas of struggle and conflict within each member?

_____ 13. **Following through.** To what degree is the group leader able to follow through to reasonable completion work with a member in an area the member has expressed a desire to explore?

_____ 14. **Active listening.** To what degree does the group leader actively and fully listen to and hear the subtle messages communicated by group members?

_____ 15. **Knowledge of theory.** To what degree does the group leader demonstrate a theoretical understanding of group dynamics, interpersonal dynamics, and behavior in general?

_____ 16. **Application of theory to practice.** To what degree is the group leader able to appropriately apply a given theory to an actual group situation?

_____ 17. **Perceptivity and insight.** To what degree is the group leader able to sensitively and accurately extract the core meanings from verbal and nonverbal communications?

_____ 18. **Risk taking.** To what degree is the group leader able to risk making mistakes and to profit from mistakes?

_____ 19. **Expression.** To what degree is the group leader able to express thoughts and feelings directly and clearly to members?

_____ 20. **Originality.** To what degree does the group leader seem to have synthesized a personal approach from a variety of approaches to group leadership?

_____ 21. **Group dynamics.** To what degree is the group leader able to help a group of people work together effectively?

_____ 22. **Cooperation as a co-leader.** To what degree is the group leader able to work cooperatively with a co-leader?

_____ 23. **Content orientation.** To what degree is the group leader able to help group members focus on specific themes in a structured group experience?

_____ 24. **Values awareness.** To what degree is the group leader aware of his or her own value system, aware of the members' value systems, and able to avoid imposing his or her values on the members?

_____ 25. **Flexibility.** To what degree is the group leader able to change approaches—to modify style and technique—to adapt to each unique working situation?

_____ 26. **Awareness of self.** To what degree is the group leader aware of his or her own needs, motivations, and problems, and to what degree does the leader avoid exploiting or manipulating members to satisfy these needs?

_____ 27. **Respect.** To what degree does the group leader communicate an attitude of respect for the dignity and autonomy of members?

_____ 28. **Caring.** To what degree does the group leader communicate an attitude of genuine caring and concern for members?

_____ 29. **Techniques.** To what degree is the group leader knowledgeable about techniques and able to use them well and appropriately to help members work through conflicts and concerns?

_____ 30. **Ethical awareness.** To what degree does the group leader demonstrate awareness of and sensitivity to the demands of professional responsibility?

2

Ethical and Professional Guidelines for Group Leaders

Focus questions · **Introduction** · **Professional competence and training** · The issue of leader competence · Professional standards for training of group counselors · Training and personal experience · **Ethical issues in group membership** · Involuntary membership · Informed consent · Freedom to withdraw from a group · Psychological risks for members · **Confidentiality** · **Community and legal standards** · Legal liability and malpractice · Legal safeguards for group practitioners · **Uses and abuses of group techniques** · **The role of the leader's values in the group** · **Summary of ethical principles for group leaders** · **Where to go from here** · ASGW's Ethical Guidelines for Group Leaders · Resources for further reading · **Exercises**

Focus Questions

1. What will an ethical group leader be sure to tell prospective members about a group?
2. What is your position on the issue of group leaders' providing individual therapy for members? What are some advantages and disadvantages of this practice?
3. What are some measures you might take as a leader to ensure confidentiality in your group?
4. What psychological risks do you think are associated with group membership? How can these risks be minimized?
5. What legal issues might you consider in setting up a group? Can you think of some legal safeguards to help you avoid becoming embroiled in a malpractice suit?
6. What education and training do you think a person needs in order to be a competent leader?
7. What kind of experience and supervision would you like to receive as a part of your program in group leadership?
8. What is your position on the issue of private psychotherapy for group leaders? Should group membership be part of a leader's background?
9. What is your position on using techniques that encourage the release of aggression?
10. What are some of the ethical rules that group leaders should follow in their practice?

■■

Introduction

For those who are preparing to become group leaders, a thorough grounding in ethical considerations is as essential as a solid base of psychological knowledge and skills. Our aim in this chapter is to highlight what we consider to be the ethical issues of central significance to group workers. Both professionals and paraprofessionals must be thoroughly familiar with their field's ethical standards. They must also learn to make ethical decisions, a process that can be taught both in group courses and in supervised practicum experiences.

It is our position that group leaders eventually develop their own ethical codes to guide their practice. In making such a statement we are not suggesting that absolute freedom should be the rule. We're not implying that leaders are free to choose any set of rules merely on the basis that it "feels right." Your practice should be guided by established principles that have clear implications for group work. We've selected certain ethical guidelines from professional organizations that we think have the most relevance for group leadership: *Ethical Standards*, by the American Association for Counseling and Development (AACD, 1981); *Ethical Guidelines for Group Leaders*, by the Association for Specialists in Group Work (ASGW, 1980); *Ethical Principles of Psychologists*, by the American Psychological Association (APA, 1981); *Guidelines for Psychologists Conducting Growth Groups*, by the American Psychological Association (APA, 1973); *Code of Ethics*, by the National Association of Social Workers (NASW, 1979); *Standards for the Private Practice of Clinical Social Work*, (NASW, 1981); *Code of Ethics for Certified Clinical Mental Health Counselors*, by the American Mental Health Counselors Association (AMHCA, 1980); and *Code of Professional Ethics*, by the American Association for Marriage and Family Therapy (AAMFT, 1975).

Although professionals should know the ethical code of their specialization and be aware of the consequences of practicing in ways that are not sanctioned by the appropriate professional organization, such codes alone are not adequate for professional leadership of groups. In many situations leaders will need to make wise decisions that are not simple and clear. Functioning within the broad guidelines of established ethical codes will be a beginning, but you will have to base your practice on sound, informed, and responsible judgment. To do this, experience in leading groups is essential, yet it alone is also not enough. You will learn much by consulting with colleagues, by getting continued supervision and training during the early stages of your development as a leader, by doing what is necessary to keep up with recent trends, and by attending relevant conventions and workshops.

Some beginning group leaders burden themselves with the expectation that they should always know the "right" thing to do for every possible situation. In contrast, we expect that you will gradually refine your positions on the issues we raise in this chapter, a process that demands a willingness to remain open and to adopt a self-critical attitude. We do not think that these issues are resolved once and for all; they take on new dimensions as you gain experience as a group leader.

We decided to place this chapter early in the book because the guidelines that we discuss here pertain to all phases of a group's development as well as to each special group population. In the chapters that follow we will return to some of these guidelines, and we will explore ethical and professional issues that especially pertain to a particular period in the group's history or to conducting various types of group.

Professional Competence and Training

Group leaders must provide only services and use techniques for which they are qualified by training and experience. Leaders have the responsibility of accurately representing their competence to the participants in their groups. They should also recognize the need for continuing education and be open to new procedures and changes in the field. Although we encourage group leaders to think of creative ways of reaching diverse populations, we also emphasize the need for adequate training and supervision in leading such groups. Those who lead groups that are clearly beyond the scope of their preparation are not only practicing unethically but also opening themselves up to legal action.

Because various professions have differing training and educational standards for group work and because specializations call for various skills, we will not try to specify an "ideal program" that would produce competent group leaders. Rather, we'll outline several general areas of professional experience that we consider basic in the development of the capable leader.

■■ The Issue of Leader Competence

Who is qualified to lead groups? What are some criteria by which to determine the level of competence of group leaders? How can leaders recognize their limits?

Concerning the issue of who is qualified to lead groups, several factors must be considered. One is the type of group. Different groups require different leader qualifications. Some professionals who are highly qualified to work with college students are not competent to lead children's groups. There are professionals who are trained to lead personal-growth groups but who lack either the training or the experience necessary to administer group therapy to an outpatient population. Some may be very successful with groups for alcoholics or drug addicts yet be unequipped to lead couples' groups or to work with families. So we can restate the basic question as: Who is qualified to lead *this type* of group with *this type* of population?

There are many ways of becoming a professional group leader. Some of the fields of study that prepare people to lead therapeutic groups are:

· counseling psychology
· clinical psychology
· psychiatry
· educational psychology

· school counseling
· marriage and family counseling
· clinical social work
· pastoral psychology or pastoral counseling
· child and adolescent psychology
· rehabilitation counseling
· community mental-health counseling
· human services

Other disciplines that can help prepare professionals for group work are sociology and philosophy. Course work in personality theory, human growth and development, abnormal psychology, clinical techniques, theories of counseling, and vocational and career development can also be helpful. The main point is that no one discipline has a monopoly when it comes to offering valuable information and training to potential group leaders. Each type of therapeutic group calls for a different type of training and experience. We think it is appropriate for group leaders to have a mixed background; it adds depth to their group work. Thus, group leaders who work with children might do well to have training in both general psychology and marital and family counseling.

During the professional education of counselors who hope to work as group leaders, at least one course in the theory and practice of group counseling is essential. Unfortunately, it is not uncommon to find only one such survey course available to students in a master's degree program in psychology or counseling.

Another issue related to competence is that of licenses, degrees, and credentials. In our judgment the training that leads to the attainment of such certification is usually valuable, but degrees alone do not indicate that a person is a qualified leader. A person may hold a Ph.D. in counseling psychology and be licensed to practice psychotherapy yet not be equipped, either by training or by personality, to practice *group* work. At the same time, we can conceive of a paraprofessional, without a degree or a license, who could competently lead or co-lead certain types of therapeutic groups. This issue becomes even more complicated and serious when we consider the number of unqualified people who call themselves experts or who consider themselves qualified to lead any type of group, without benefit of formal training. There are those who organize and conduct intensive encounter groups or marathons merely on the basis of their attendance at a few such sessions as participants. These are the leaders who can bring psychological harm to group members.

Group leaders need to recognize their limitations. Toward this end, they might well ask themselves:

· What kinds of client am I capable of dealing with?
· What are my areas of expertise?

· What techniques do I handle well?
· How far can I safely go with clients?
· When should I consult another professional about a client?
· When should I refer a client to someone else?

Professional group leaders know their limitations and recognize that they can't lead all kinds of group or work with all kinds of client. They familiarize themselves with referral resources and don't attempt to work with a client they're not trained to work with. Furthermore, a responsible leader is keenly aware of the importance of continuing his or her education. Even a licensed and experienced professional will attend conventions and workshops, take courses, seek consultation and supervision, and get involved in special training programs from time to time.

Truly competent group leaders also have an awareness of the reasons for most of the activities they suggest in a group. They are able to explain to their clients:

· the theory behind their group work
· their goals in the group
· the relationship between the way they lead the group and their goals
· ways to evaluate how well the goals are being met

Effective group leaders try to conceptualize the group process and to relate their operations to this model. They continually refine their techniques in light of their model. This does not mean that they rigidly adhere to one specific approach. As we've pointed out, a leader may synthesize several group models into a personalized approach.

■■ Professional Standards for Training of Group Counselors

In its *Professional Standards for Training of Group Counselors*, the ASGW (1983) sets out *knowledge competencies, skill competencies,* and suggested supervised clinical group *experience* for leaders.* In the area of *knowledge competencies,* the ASGW takes the position that the qualified group leader has demonstrated specialized knowledge in the following aspects of group work:

· the major theories of group counseling, including their differences and common concepts
· the basic principles of group dynamics and the key ingredients of group process

* Adapted from *Professional Standards for Training of Group Counselors* (ASGW, 1983) and reproduced by permission of the ASGW, a division of the American Association for Counseling and Development, 5999 Stevenson Avenue, Alexandria, VA 22304.

- one's own strengths and weaknesses, values, and other personal characteristics that have an impact on one's ability to function as a group leader
- ethical and professional issues special to group work
- updated information on research in group work
- the facilitative and debilitative roles and behaviors that group members may assume
- the advantages and disadvantages of group work and the situations in which it is appropriate or inappropriate as a form of therapeutic intervention
- the characteristics of group interaction and counselor roles involved in the stages of a group's development

In the area of *skill competencies,* the ASGW contends that qualified group leaders should be able to demonstrate a mastery of the following skills:

- being able to screen and assess the readiness of clients to participate in a group
- having a clear definition of group counseling and being able to explain its purpose and procedures to group members
- diagnosing self-defeating behaviors in group members and being able to intervene in constructive ways with members who display such behaviors
- modeling appropriate behavior for group members
- interpreting nonverbal behavior in an accurate and appropriate manner
- using skills in a timely and effective fashion
- intervening at critical times in the group process
- being able to make use of major techniques, strategies, and procedures of group counseling
- promoting therapeutic factors that lead to change both in a group and within an individual
- being able to use adjunct group procedures, such as homework
- being able to work effectively with a co-leader
- knowing how to effectively bring a group session to a close and how to terminate a group
- using follow-up procedures to maintain and support group members
- using assessment procedures to evaluate the outcomes of a group

In the area of *clinical practice,* the ASGW specifies the following types of supervised experience in group work:

- critiquing of group tapes
- observing group counseling sessions
- participating as a member in a group
- co-leading groups with supervision

· practicum experience—leading a group alone with critical self-analysis of performance as well as a supervisor's feedback
· internship—practice as a group leader with on-the-job supervision

■■ Training and Personal Experience

It is essential for prospective group leaders to undergo extensive training. There are three types of experience that we highly recommend as adjuncts to a training program and that we feel are invaluable to the person who seeks to become a competent group leader: personal (private) psychotherapy, group therapy, and participation in a training group.

Personal Psychotherapy for Group Leaders.   Should group leaders have individual therapy before or during their internship period? Should this experience be required, or merely strongly recommended? What is the rationale for expecting leadership candidates to experience their own personal therapy? What are the possible values of such an experience?

Our strong conviction is that it is the ethical and professional responsibility of those who plan to become group therapists to seek private therapy before they attempt to become therapists of others. During the course of their sessions, it is hoped, they will come to a greater understanding of their motivation to become leaders of therapeutic groups. They can also explore the biases that might hamper their receptiveness to clients; any unfinished business that might lead to distortions in their perceptions of group members; their philosophy of life—which directly relates to the way they view human beings—and the need they may have to impose this philosophy on clients; other needs that might either facilitate or inhibit the group process; current conflicts; and their character (aspects of their personhood such as courage, enthusiasm, integrity, honesty, and caring) and the impact their character traits will have on others. In short, group therapists should demonstrate the courage to do for themselves what they expect members in their groups to do—expand their awareness of self and of how that self affects others. The rationale here is that a group counselor cannot effectively assist clients to explore in depth conflicts that the counselor has not recognized in himself or herself. We are not implying that therapists must have experienced every personal problem of the clients they work with, but they must have the courage to honestly search within themselves and face what they find.

Self-Exploration Groups for Group Leaders.   We have discovered that participation in a self-exploration group (or some other type of therapeutic group) is an extremely valuable adjunct to a group leader's internship training experiences.

Beginning group leaders typically experience some anxiety regarding their adequacy, and their interactions with group members frequently lead to a surfacing of unresolved past or current problems. We think it is inappropriate for group leaders to use the group they're responsible for leading as a place to extensively examine their own problems. Leaders who find themselves doing this should join a therapeutic group as a member and use that group for continuing their growth. Besides being of therapeutic value, such a group can be a powerful teaching tool for the intern. Group leaders have said that exploring their own struggles in a group setting gives them the capacity to empathize with others. One of the best ways for leaders to learn how to assist members in their struggles is by working themselves as members of a group.

Training Groups for Group Leaders.   In addition to participating in a therapeutic group as a member, the beginning group leader must, we believe, join a training group—that is, a group of leader trainees. The training group can lead to insights and awareness without becoming a therapy group. The interns can learn a great deal about their response to criticism, their competitiveness, their need for approval, their jealousies, their anxieties over being competent, their feelings about certain members of the group they lead, and their power struggles with co-leaders or members of their group. These are but a few of the issues that are appropriate for work in a training group.

There is a subtle difference between a training group and a therapeutic group: the focus of a training group is on the skills necessary for efficient intervention. New group leaders can become aware of values and attitudes they hold that influence their leadership style. For example, leaders who have an exaggerated need for approval may avoid being confrontive, may assume a passive stance, or may become inappropriately supportive in their groups. Their need for approval thus hampers their potential effectiveness by preventing them from effectively encountering others. Another example is the person who is attracted to being a group leader primarily by the power inherent in this position. This person's exaggerated need to control and direct others and to inspire the adulation of the group members may lead to mechanical use of a repertoire of techniques designed to impress the group participants with the therapist's prowess. Styles such as these can be detected and worked with during the sessions of a training group. Examples of questions that a supervisor might raise with the members of a training group are:

1. What were you feeling and thinking when your group sat silently for 10 minutes? How did you deal with this silence? What do you suppose it meant?
2. How did you feel when Jim, one of your group members, openly challenged you on your qualifications to lead a group of college students, many of whom are older than you are?

3. Why did you keep pushing Sally to "work," when she had given several indications that she would rather be left alone?
4. Do you think that there was adequate closure for your group today? Did you allow yourself enough time to summarize what had happened in your group?
5. What did you feel when your co-leader openly disagreed with your perception of George, a group member?
6. Do you think you were confrontive enough with John when he continued with his long-winded storytelling? Why did you allow him to go on as long as you did?
7. Your group today seemed very lethargic, and several members finally stated that they were bored. What do you think was contributing to this situation? How do you and your co-leader feel about the way you dealt with the group's lethargy?
8. For several weeks you seem to have been extremely quiet in your group, and your co-leader has been assuming all of the leadership responsibility. What thoughts run through your mind as you work with your co-leader? Are you satisfied with your participation level?
9. How did you feel when you invited Sue to participate in an exercise and she flatly refused, saying "No, I won't role-play, because that seems phony to me"? Did you like your response to her?

Ethical Issues in Group Membership

■■ Involuntary Membership

Obviously, voluntary participation is an important beginning point for a successful group experience. The members must want something for themselves, and they must be receptive. They will make significant changes only to the extent that they actively participate. Unfortunately, all groups are not composed of clients who have chosen to be in a group. In some mental-health facilities the main therapeutic vehicle is group therapy, sometimes as often as three times weekly. People from all wards may be required to attend these sessions. This situation is somewhat akin to compulsory education: people can be forced to attend but not to learn.

For those group leaders who work in institutions in which the policy is to require group treatment, the group members should at least be given the opportunity to ventilate their feelings about this requirement. Perhaps many are reluctant to become involved because of misinformation about or stereotyped views of the nature of therapy. They may not trust the group leaders or the process involved. They may think that group therapy is a form of indoctrination. Perhaps they view themselves as healthy and the members of the group as ill. Most likely, many of them are frightened and have reservations about opening themselves up to others. They may be very concerned about other's gossiping or maliciously using information against them. Perceptive leaders will deal with these issues openly, and, although they may not be able to provide the members with the option of dropping out of the group, they can provide the support necessary to enable the members to fully come to grips with their fears and resistances. The members can also be given the freedom to decide how to use the session time. Group leaders can assure members that the degree to which they participate is up to them—that they may remain silent if they wish and that it's up to them to decide what personal topics they will discuss and what areas they will keep private. In other words, they should be clearly informed that they have the same rights as the members of any group, with the exception of the right not to attend.

The issue of mandatory group participation becomes particularly thorny for students enrolled in programs designed to train counselors or paraprofessionals. Increasingly, colleges and universities that offer degrees in counseling and other human services are requiring participation in either individual or group therapy as an integral part of these degree programs. The rationale for requiring personal counseling for these students is that the students need to be aware of their own motivations, needs, and problems before they attempt to counsel others. There are some faculty members and students who oppose the requirement on the ground that any form of counseling should be initiated by the client; they believe that *mandatory counseling* is a contradiction in terms.

Some guidelines can be established. If counseling is a requirement, then the university should provide it for the students. Private and public institutions alike should make psychological services available, either free or at rates adjusted to student income. It is unethical for schools to require therapy and then suggest that the students pay professors on campus for this service. Understandably, students may question the motivation of professors who support this requirement and then encourage students to become their clients. Furthermore, conflict of interest is a consideration when a student is also a client of a professor.

We have found that most serious students who are sincerely interested in becoming professionally qualified as group leaders are very willing to invest themselves in membership in a therapeutic group. The quality of the group experience is highly related to the degree of acceptance by the students. If a therapeutic group is offered as a resource for the personal development of counselors and if students are given the freedom to determine their goals and the structure of the experience, most students will be eager for a group and will appreciate such a resource. Those who are highly defensive and antagonistic are the ones who may need to reexamine their commitment to becoming counselors.

In examining the ethics of requiring group participation for students in counseling programs, we think that another question should be asked: Is it ethical for group leaders to consider themselves qualified to lead groups if they've never been group members themselves? We strongly endorse participation in a group as part of a leader's training. Learning from books and lectures is important but has its limitations; certain skills can be learned only through experimentation. Struggling with trusting a group of strangers, risking vulnerability, receiving genuine support from others, feeling joy and closeness, and being confronted are all vital learning experiences for future group leaders. If for no reason other than because it provides a deep understanding of what clients face in groups, we think that group experience for leaders is indispensable.

The *Ethical Standards* of the AACD (1981) state that forms of learning that are aimed primarily at self-understanding and personal growth should generally be voluntary; if this type of experience is required as part of the educational program, prospective students should be informed before entering the program. In those cases where the program offers or requires a group experience that involves personal disclosures and involvement, the AACD guideline is that the leader must have no administrative, supervisory, or evaluative authority over the participant.

Although we can see the rationale of the last part of this guideline, we do not fully concur with the AACD's position. One of us (Jerry Corey) is a university professor who specializes in teaching group courses, such as Practicum in Group Leadership. The course is taught in such a manner that students get a balanced experience of didactic material on group process and theories of group, opportunities to lead and co-lead self-directed groups where they can apply what they are learning, supervised experience in group leadership, experiential learning involving working on their own personal issues in a group, and supervision sessions that are therapeutic as well as educational. Thus, in a single course the students are exposed to a variety of ways of learning about groups, both cognitive and experiential. Like most other courses, this one makes use of traditional grading and evaluation procedures. We cite this class as an example of the many group-leadership courses that typically combine academic learning with opportunities for personal learning. One way many educators attempt to minimize the conflict entailed in being both a professor and a counselor is to avoid grading students on their participation in the experiential activities that are part of the course.

■■ Informed Consent

In general, participation in groups is voluntary in that people are not forced either to join the group or, once they are in the group, to participate in activities if they choose not to. As we have explained, however, this is not always the case. Providing adequate information to prospective group members so that they are able to make informed choices about their participation is essential for both voluntary and involuntary groups. Especially in those cases where group participation is mandatory, much effort needs to be directed toward clearly and fully informing members of the nature and goals of the group, group procedures that will be used, the rights of members to decline certain activities, the limitations of confidentiality, and how active participation in the group may have an effect on them personally. For example, in a state mental hospital in which we serve as consultants, groups are the basic form of treatment for "those incompetent to stand trial" and "mentally disordered sex offenders." Further, patients' release from the institution depends in part on their cooperation in treatment and rehabilitation, which includes participation in regular group-therapy sessions. In cases such as these, informed consent implies that leaders explore with the members during a screening or orientation session what the group process consists of and that they be careful to ascertain whether the members understand what may be involved in the group process.

The matter of informed consent is related to leaders' making the members aware of their rights (as well as their responsibilities) as group participants. Thus, in mandatory groups or in required groups that emphasize self-disclosure and personal involvement, leaders are advised to take special care in discussing what the members have a right to expect. The guidelines that follow, of course, are not restricted to involuntary groups; each point applies equally to groups composed of voluntary participants. Those who join a group have a right to expect:

- a clear statement regarding the purpose of the group, the procedures to be used, and the leader's policies and ground rules
- a statement of the education and training of the leader
- clarification of what services can and cannot be provided within the group
- a discussion of both the rights and responsibilities of being a group member
- reasonable safeguards to minimize the potential risks and hazards of the group
- respect for member privacy
- freedom from undue group pressure or coercion from either members or leaders to participate in exercises or to disclose matters they are unwilling to discuss
- protection against either verbal or physical assaults
- notice of any research involving the group, any observations of the group through one-way mirrors, or any audio or video taping of group sessions

· full discussion on the limitations of confidentiality, including a statement from the leader concerning how information acquired during
group sessions will be used outside the group structure

■■ Freedom to Withdraw from a Group

A difficult, and crucial, question is: Once members make a commitment
to be a part of a time-limited and closed group, do they have the right to
leave the group at any time they choose? The ASGW's (1980) position on
this issue is: "Group leaders shall inform members that participation is
voluntary and that they may exit from the group at any time."

Although this is a generally accepted position, we hold a somewhat
different view (see Corey, Corey, Callanan, & Russell, 1982b). We are not
in favor of forcing members to remain in a group regardless of the
circumstances, but neither do we emphasize to prospective members
that they have the freedom of exit whenever they choose. Instead, during the individual screening interview and the orientation session we
take great care to inform prospective members about the nature of the
group. In time-limited, closed groups we also stress to participants the
importance of a careful commitment to carrying out their responsibilities. Our position is that anyone who decides to withdraw from a group
has a responsibility to the other members and to the leader to at least
explain his or her reasons for wanting to leave. The member could be
encouraged to take time to consider whether to stay in the group as well
as to think honestly about the factors that led to the decision to leave.

If a person leaves without this careful consideration and explanation,
the consequences could be negative to the members remaining as well
as to the departing member. Some members may feel burdened with
guilt and may blame themselves for saying or doing the "wrong" thing
that contributed to an individual's decision to quit; the person who
leaves may be stuck with negative feelings that could have been resolved with some discussion. With a commitment to discuss the factors
related to leaving, there is an opportunity for everyone concerned to
express and explore unfinished business. It is critical, however, that
neither the leader nor the other members subject the individual to undue pressure to remain if the person ultimately chooses to leave.

■■ Psychological Risks for Members

The forces at work in a therapeutic group are powerful ones. They can
be constructive, effecting positive change, but their unleashing always
entails some risk. It is essential that group leaders inform prospective
members of some of the risks; leaders must not assume that the participants are aware of them. Leaders must also make serious attempts to
reduce the risks. Members of a group may be subjected to scapegoating,

group pressure, breaches of confidence, inappropriate reassurance, and hostile confrontation. The group process may even precipitate a crisis in a member's life. A person may enter a group feeling relatively comfortable and leave feeling vulnerable and defenseless. Areas of personal conflict may be exposed for the first time, causing much pain and leading to a new self-awareness that is difficult to cope with. A person's outside life may be drastically affected, for family members may have adverse reactions to changes. Participants may be left, at the conclusion of a group, in no better condition than when they began the group; they may even feel less equipped than ever to cope with the demands of daily life.

These hazards should be discussed with the participants during the initial session, and the leader should examine with the group how these dangers can be avoided. For example, a leader of a group for women who have been victims of incest might say: "As you begin to uncover painful memories of your childhood and the abuse that took place, you may feel more depressed and anxious for a time than before you entered this group. It is very important to talk about these feelings in the group, especially if you have thoughts about quitting." Group leaders should also help members explore the concerns they have about translating what they are learning in the group to their everyday life. Some groups—short-term intensive workshops, in particular—may arouse strong, previously hidden feelings, and it is important that people be given the means of understanding, or even resolving, the issues that are behind these feelings. Participants sometimes leave a group with conflicting feelings, wanting to continue with individual or group counseling yet afraid of going further. In a follow-up session these members can get the support they need in order to be able to examine the ambivalence and decide what to do.

Sometimes, rather than being unaware of the dangers of participating in a group, members invent dangers of their own and are very fearful. For example, some members believe that, if they allow themselves to feel their pain, they'll go crazy or sink into a depression so deep they won't be able to climb out of it. Some are convinced that, if they give up their self-control, they won't be able to function. Others are frightened of letting others know them, because they think they'll be rejected. There are those who are reluctant to experience their anger, because they fear physically hurting another. Such fears should be explored early, so that the members can determine how realistic they are and, it is hoped, put some of them to rest.

Not only do certain risks need to be identified and dealt with in the group, but safeguards against these risks also need to be established. It should be stressed by the leader that group members have the right to decide for themselves what to explore and how far to go. Group leaders must be alert to group pressure and block any attempts of members to get others to do something they choose not to do. Members can be invited or asked rather than ordered to participate in certain exercises or techniques. Group members should be assured that they have the option of declining to participate in group activities they find extremely threatening. Direct expression of aggression could result in another person's getting physically hurt. Therefore, we ask members to release feelings of anger in a symbolic way. Symbolic actions, such as beating a pillow, can be just as valuable as direct actions. It is essential that group leaders learn how to cope effectively with whatever may arise as the result of an exercise. It may be easy to provoke someone into experiencing rage, but it is another matter to know what to do when this person releases some long-standing controls.

After a group experience—particularly an intensive weekend or week-long experience—participants may make rash decisions that affect not only their own life but also the lives of members of their family. What the individual may see as the result of newfound spontaneity or decisiveness may be due merely to a burst of energy generated by the group. For example, a woman who has been married for 20 years and who becomes aware in the group of her extreme alienation from her husband may leave the group with a resolve to get a divorce. The group leader should caution her of the danger of making decisions too soon after the group. If this woman has changed in the group, she may be able to relate to her husband differently; if she acts too soon, she may not give this a chance to happen. It is not the leader's responsibility to stand in the way of members' decisions, but it is the leader's responsibility to warn members against acting on a "group high."

At this point we summarize some of the other possible risks in therapeutic groups. Later in the book we will expand our treatment of the issue by developing guidelines for making the participants aware of risks and for preparing the members in a way that will reduce the chances of their having a negative experience.

1. Self-disclosure is sometimes misused by group members. This issue will be dealt with at greater length in a later chapter, but we do want to mention that action needs to follow self-disclosure. The group ethic has sometimes been misunderstood as the more disclosure, the better. Privacy can be violated by indiscriminate sharing of one's personal life. Self-disclosure is an essential aspect of any working group, but this disclosure is a means to the end of fuller self-understanding and should not be glorified in its own right, at the expense of follow-through.

2. Some of the disclosures made during a session may not remain in the group. Confidentiality is an issue that needs continual emphasis in any group, but even when this is done, the possibility remains that members will talk about what they've heard in the group.

3. Scapegoating may occur in a group, particularly if group leaders do not intervene when they see members "ganging up" on one particu-

lar group member. When confrontation occurs, we find it useful to ask the person doing the confronting to state what reactions he or she is having to the person being confronted. This usually stops the person from merely throwing judgmental labels at another.

4. The danger of inadequate leadership is a by-product of the growth of the group movement. Some people attend a few weekend workshops as participants and then decide, with very little additional experience, to lead groups of their own. Because they experienced a "high," they decide that groups are the answer for any seeker of self-fulfillment. Lacking adequate training or experience, they hastily gather a group together, without bothering to screen members or even prepare members for the particular group. Such leaders can do extensive damage and, in the process, cause participants to close themselves off from the possibility of seeking any type of therapy or counseling in the future.

The *Ethical Guidelines for Group Leaders* (ASGW, 1980) specify that leaders have the responsibility to provide information and discuss the possible risks of participating in groups. The guideline is: "Group leaders shall stress the personal risks involved in any group, especially regarding potential life-changes, and help group members explore their readiness to face these risks."

As we've suggested, it is not realistic to expect that all personal risks can be eliminated, and to imply this is to mislead prospective members. What is essential is that members be made aware of the major risks, that they have an opportunity to discuss their willingness and ability to deal with them, and that as many safeguards as possible be built into the structure of the group. For example, if members experience chronic depression, severe anxiety attacks, periods of confusion and crisis, and lack of clarity regarding the effects of the group experience on them, they should have somewhere to turn for further professional assistance. This is true both during the course of the group and once the group has been terminated.

Often the "risks" and "terrible things" that some people associate with groups are really misconceptions about the purpose of groups. In conjunction with exploring potential risks, we make it a practice to separate facts from fantasy by discussing with members any preconceptions they may have brought with them to a group.

Confidentiality

One of the central ethical issues in group work is confidentiality. It is especially important because the group leader must not only keep the confidences of members but also get the members to keep one another's confidences.

In certain group situations confidentiality becomes especially critical and also more difficult to maintain. This is true of groups in institutions, agencies, and schools where the group members know and have frequent contact with one another and with one another's associates outside of the group. In an adolescent group in a high school, for example, great care must be exerted to ensure that whatever is discussed in the group session is not taken out of the group. If some members gossip about things that happened in the group, the group process will come to a halt. People are not going to reveal facts about their personal life unless they feel quite sure that they can trust both the leader and the group members to respect their confidences.

The group leader should emphasize the importance of confidentiality at various stages of the group's evolution. During the individual screening interview this issue should be stressed, and it should be clarified at the initial group sessions. At appropriate times during the course of a group the leader should remind the members of the need for not discussing identities or specific situations connected with the group. The leader should point out that confidences can be broken by carelessness as well as by malicious gossip. If at any time any member gives indications that confidentiality is not being respected, the leader should explore this matter with the group as soon as possible.

We do expect that members will want to talk about their group experiences with significant people in their life. We caution them, however, about breaking others' confidences in this process. We tell them to be careful not to mention others who were in the group or to talk about what others said and did. Generally, members do not violate confidentiality when they talk about *what* they learned in group sessions. But they are likely to breach confidentiality when they talk about *how* they acquired insights or what they actually did in a group. For example, David becomes aware that he solicits women to take care of him, only to resent them for treating him like a child. He may want to say to his wife "I realize that I often resent you for the very thing that I expect you to do." It is not necessary that he describe the particular exercise, involving several women in the group, that led to his insight. If David talks about these details, out of context, he runs the risk that he may be misunderstood and that he may inappropriately reveal other members' personal work.

Group leaders may be tested by some members of the group. For instance, a group counselor may tell the participants of a group in a juvenile correctional institution that whatever is discussed will remain in the group. The youths may not believe this and may in many subtle ways test the leader to discover whether in fact he or she will keep this promise. For this reason, it is essential that group leaders not promise to keep within the group material that they may be required to disclose. Counselors owe it to their clients to specify at the outset the limits on confidentiality. For instance, a counselor working with children may be expected to disclose some information to parents if the parents insist on it, or a leader of a group of parolees may be expected to reveal to the members' parole officers any information they acquire in the group concerning certain criminal offenses. A group leader should let the members know that he or she may be required to testify against them in court unless the leader is entitled to privileged communication. In general, licensed psychologists, psychiatrists, and licensed clinical social workers are legally entitled to privileged communication. At the present time school counselors in 20 states and licensed counselors in 7 states are also entitled to privileged communication. This means that these professionals cannot break the confidence of clients unless (1) in their judgment, clients are likely to do serious harm to themselves or to others; (2) clients are gravely disabled; (3) child abuse of any kind is suspected; or (4) clients give specific written permission.

A particularly delicate problem is safeguarding the confidentiality of minors in groups. Parents may inquire about what their child discusses in a group, and it is the responsibility of the group leader to inform them in advance of the importance of confidentiality. Parents can be told about the purpose of the group, and they can be given some feedback concerning their child, but care must be taken not to reveal specific things that the child mentioned. One way to provide feedback to parents is through a session involving one or both parents, the child, and the group leader.

Group leaders have some general guidelines for what disclosures they should and should not make about what occurs in group sessions. The AACD's (1981) caution to group counselors is that they must set a norm of confidentiality regarding all group participants' disclosures. However, they do specify exceptions: "When the client's condition indicates that there is clear and imminent danger to the client or others, the counselor must take reasonable personal action or inform responsible authorities. Consultation with other professionals must be used where possible."

In basic agreement with the above position is the APA's (1981), which asserts that psychologists have a primary obligation to respect the confidentiality of information obtained in the course of their work. This position is qualified by the principle that psychologists "reveal such information to others only with the consent of the person or the person's legal representative, except in those unusual circumstances in which not to do so would result in clear danger to the person or to others. Where appropriate, psychologists inform their clients of the legal limits of confidentiality."

There are some other ramifications of confidentiality that group leaders would do well to consider. Following are some guidelines concerning the issue of confidentiality:

· When working with minors or with clients who are unable to give voluntary and informed consent, it is essential that the professional exert special care to protect the client's welfare (APA, 1981).
· It is a wise policy to ask participants to sign a contract in which they agree not to discuss or write about what transpires in the sessions or talk about who was present.
· Professionals who obtain personal material during the course of their work and then use this in writing or in lectures do so after they have obtained prior consent to do so or adequately disguise all identifying information (AACD, 1981; AMHCA, 1980; APA, 1981).
· It is essential that group leaders become familiar with the local and state laws that will have an impact on their practice. This is especially true in cases involving child molestation, neglect or abuse of the elderly and children, or incest.

Community and Legal Standards

Most professional organizations affirm that practitioners should be aware of the prevailing community standards and of the possible impact on their practice of deviation from these standards. Specifically, there are several guidelines for ethical practice in this area of which group workers should be aware:

· Leaders will avoid inappropriate personal relationships with members, both during the group and in any later professional involvement (ASGW, 1980).
· Sexual conduct between clinical mental-health counselors and clients is in violation of ethical standards (AMHCA, 1980).
· Psychologists do not exploit their professional relationships with clients, supervisees, and students sexually or otherwise; psychologists do not condone or engage in sexual harassment; sexual intimacies with clients are unethical (APA, 1981).
· Dual relationships with clients that could impair professional objectivity (such as sexual intimacies with any client) must be avoided (AACD, 1981).
· In providing psychological or counseling services to clients, professionals (clinical mental-health counselors, psychologists) do not violate or diminish the legal and civil rights of their clients (AMHCA, 1980; APA, 1981).

The last guideline implies that professionals who work with groups need to be familiar with the legal ramifications of group work. Those leaders who work with groups of children, adolescents, and certain involuntary populations are especially advised to learn the laws restricting group work. Issues such as confidentiality, parental consent, informed consent, protection of member welfare, and civil rights of institutionalized patients are a few areas in which group workers must be knowledgeable. Since most group leaders do not possess detailed legal knowledge, it is a good idea to obtain some legal information concerning group procedures and practices. Awareness of legal rights and responsibilities as they pertain to group work protects not only the clients but also group leaders from needless lawsuits arising from negligence or ignorance.

■■ Legal Liability and Malpractice

Group leaders who fail to exercise due care and act in good faith are liable to a civil suit. Professionals leading groups are expected to practice within the code of ethics of their particular profession and to abide by legal standards. Practitioners are subject to civil liability for not doing right or for doing wrong to another. If group members can prove that personal injury or psychological harm is due to a group leader's failure to render proper service, either through negligence or ignorance, then this leader is open to a malpractice suit. Negligence consists of departing from the standard and commonly accepted practices of others in the profession.

The following are some of the most frequent causes of malpractice actions against mental-health professionals:

· violating a client's right to privacy
· causing physical injuries through the use of group exercises
· striking or physically assaulting a client as a treatment technique
· engaging in sexual relations with a client
· misrepresenting one's professional training
· providing birth control or abortion information to a minor
· prescribing and administering drugs inappropriately
· failing to exercise reasonable care before a client's suicide
· failing to warn and protect a potential victim of a client who has made threats

■■ Legal Safeguards for Group Practitioners

The key to a group leader's avoiding a malpractice suit is maintaining reasonable, ordinary, and prudent practices. Below are some guidelines for group leaders that are useful in translating the terms *reasonable, ordinary,* and *prudent* into concrete actions. Many of these suggestions are from the comprehensive textbook *The Law and the Practice of Human Services* (1984), by Woody and his associates. Other references that we have found of value include *Legal Liability in Psychotherapy* (B. M. Schutz, 1982), *The Counselor and the Law* (Hopkins & Anderson, 1985), *Ethical and Legal Issues in Counseling and Psychotherapy* (Van Hoose & Kottler, 1985), and *Law and Ethics in Counseling* (Hummel, Talbutt, & Alexander, 1985).

· Follow the practice of adequately informing group participants about the group process, including policies and procedures that govern your practice.
· Develop written informed-consent procedures at the outset of a group. Using contracts, signed by both the leader and the members, is an example of such a procedure.
· Obtain written parental consent when working with minors.
· Have a clear rationale for the techniques you employ in group sessions. Be able to intelligently and concisely discuss the theoretical underpinnings of your procedures.
· Have a clear standard of care that can be applied to your services, and communicate this standard to the members.
· Seek consultation from colleagues or supervisors in cases involving difficult legal and ethical issues.
· Avoid becoming entangled in social relationships with group members.
· Be aware of those situations in which you legally *must* break confidentiality.
· If you work for an agency or institution, have a contract that specifies the employer's legal liability for your professional functioning.
· Abide by the policies of the institution that employs you. If you disagree with certain policies, first attempt to find out the reasons for them. Then see if it is possible to work within the framework of institutional policies. Realize that you do not always have to agree with such policies to be able to work effectively. If you have strong disagreement with policies and if they interfere with your ability to do your job, then do what you can to get them changed, or consider resigning.
· Practice within the boundaries of your local and state laws. (There are several books in the reading list at the end of this chapter that deal with law and ethics in counseling.)
· Create reasonable expectations about what a group can and cannot do, and avoid promising members magical cures.
· Make it a practice to assess the general progress of a group, and teach members how to evaluate their individual progress toward their own goals.
· Be alert to when it is appropriate to refer a group member for another form of treatment, as well as when group therapy might be inadvisable.

- Incorporate ethical standards in your practice of group work. You might want to give the members of your groups a copy of the ASGW's *Ethical Guidelines for Group Leaders* (1980) and discuss relevant guidelines at appropriate times during the course of a group.
- Take steps to keep up with theoretical and research developments that have a direct application to group work. Update your group-leadership skills. Compare your knowledge, skill, and supervised experiences in group work against the ASGW's *Professional Standards for Training of Group Counselors* (1983), which we described earlier in this chapter.
- Carry malpractice insurance. Students are not protected against malpractice suits. (If students join the AACD, they not only receive the benefits of this professional organization but are also entitled to participate in the liability insurance program.)

Uses and Abuses of Group Techniques

Participants in many groups engage in a variety of nonverbal exercises, ranging from touching others affectionately to fighting. Some of these activities are falling backward and trusting to be caught by a partner, arm wrestling, pushing and shoving, fighting with bataccas (soft, felt-covered clubs), wrestling, beating pillows, holding a person down, milling around with eyes closed and making body contact, touching and caressing, and massaging.

Regarding the use of aggressive exercises, we think group leaders have a responsibility to use caution. Release of anger on a symbolic object is recommended. Group leaders should be equipped to cope with powerful feelings, including uncontrolled aggression, that can be triggered by certain role-playing activities. As a general rule, leaders should not introduce a technique that will encourage the aggressive expression of anger unless they have confidence that they can handle the consequences, both physical and psychological. As we and our colleagues have stated elsewhere, the concern here is not simply for the physical safety of the group members. Those members who have held in emotions for many years, perhaps out of a fear of negative consequences if they expressed their feelings, would have their fears tragically reinforced if they were to lose control and harm themselves or someone else. We generally avoid involving the entire group in physical techniques, for reasons of safety. We employ such techniques, especially those that are likely to arouse strong emotions, with members with whom we have established a trusting relationship (Corey, Corey, Callanan, & Russell, 1982a).

Concerning the nonaggressive physical techniques, such as touching and embracing, the following precautions are suggested: First, it is important that members choose to participate in touching exercises and that those who have reservations have the option of abstaining. People should be reminded, however, that forcing themselves to do something that makes them uncomfortable may be the only way of overcoming their discomfort. Second, group leaders and members should not simulate affection. It should be expressed only when it is felt; otherwise, members may come to distrust any affectionate gesture as a form of role playing.

Group leaders should use discretion in introducing nonverbal exercises. It is also important to intervene if members attempt to coerce or pressure a reluctant member into participating. The participants should have an opportunity to share their reactions to the activities.

The following are some guidelines we use in our practice to avoid abusing techniques in a group:

· Techniques have a therapeutic purpose and are grounded in some framework.
· They are used to promote a client's further self-exploration.
· Techniques are not used to stir up emotions but rather to work therapeutically with emotional issues the client initiates. Techniques can help members experience feelings that are hidden or merely beginning to emerge.
· Techniques are not used to cover up the group leader's discomfort or incompetence.
· They are introduced in a sensitive and timely manner.
· They are abandoned if they prove ineffective.
· Members are given the option of whether to participate in certain techniques; they are not ordered to participate, but invited.

It is important that leaders use techniques that they have some knowledge about, preferably those that they have experienced personally or have received supervision in using. The relevant ASGW (1980) guideline is: "Group leaders shall not attempt any technique unless thoroughly trained in its use or under supervision by an expert familiar with the intervention."

Group practitioners should be aware of what a technique might potentially lead to as well as being able to deal with intense emotional outcomes. For example, we have observed student leaders with a reading knowledge of guided fantasy techniques who decided to introduce them in their groups. They were surprised and unprepared to work therapeutically with the emotions released in some members. It would be unrealistic for us to expect that leaders should always know *exactly* what will result from an intervention, but they should be able to cope with unexpected outcomes.

The Role of the Leader's Values in the Group

Your values are a fundamental part of the person you are. Thus, they cannot help but influence how you lead a therapeutic group. You can increase your effectiveness as a leader by becoming aware of the values you hold as well as the subtle and direct ways in which you might influence the people in your groups.

We see the function of the leader as challenging members to discover what is right for them, not persuading them to do what he or she thinks is right. You need not always express your personal views on value-laden situations during a session, but if members ask about your views, little is gained by refusing to express them. We are particularly inclined to tell members about our values in cases where there is a conflict, rather than blandly acceding or pretending that no difference of opinion exists. Expressed values are less likely to interfere with the process in a group than values that are concealed. In certain cases it might be necessary to refer clients to someone else because the conflict inhibits the leader's objectivity.

We have heard leaders comment that they would not want to make known their personal values concerning religion, abortion, child rearing, extramarital affairs, and other such controversial areas because of the fear of swaying members to blindly accept their values. It is our position that leaders cannot simply remain neutral in value-laden areas.

Consider for a moment the example of a man who is struggling with the decision of whether to file for a divorce. He tells the group that he is not sure he is willing to risk the loneliness he fears he'll experience as a divorced man, yet he feels stuck in an unsatisfying marriage and sees little hope for things to change for the better. Surely the values you have as a leader will influence how you relate to him. Nevertheless, it is one thing to challenge him to look at all his alternatives before making his decision and to use the group to help him explore these alternatives, and quite a different matter to persuade him (or to enlist the group to give him advice) to do what you (or they) think he should do. Your own values might include staying with the marriage at all costs, or they might include divorcing if one is unhappy. The key point is that it is not your role as leader to make this man's decision for him.

The ASGW's (1980) guideline on the role of the leader's values is: "Group leaders shall refrain from imposing their own agendas, needs, and values on group members." The critical word for us is *imposing*. We see a big difference between *im*posing and *ex*posing one's values. In the former case, the leader is pushing a given set of values and not respecting the right of the members to find their own way; in the latter case, the members are free to challenge their own thinking against that of the leader, and they can still make choices for themselves. It is important for group leaders to be aware that extremely needy and high dependent members may feel a pressure to please the leader at all costs and hence assume the leader's values automatically. This is a useful issue to explore in the sessions.

Summary of Ethical Principles for Group Leaders

A mark of professional group leadership is establishing a set of guiding principles. What follows is not a rigid set of policies but rather guidelines that we think will help group leaders clarify their own values and encourage them to take a position on some basic professional issues. We have struggled with these issues in our work with groups, and these guidelines make sense to us. We fully realize that other group leaders will have to develop principles that are appropriate for them. Our aim in presenting these guidelines is to stimulate you to think through a code of conduct that will guide you in making sound decisions as a leader.

1. It is good for leaders to reflect often on their personal identity. They can think about their needs and behavior styles and about the impact of these factors on group participants. They need to have a clear idea of what their roles and functions are in the group, and they need to communicate this idea to the group members.

2. Leaders need to have a clear idea of the type of group they're designing. This means that they must be able to express the purpose of the group and the characteristics of the people who will be admitted.

3. Group leaders must develop a means of screening that will allow them to differentiate between suitable and unsuitable applicants.

4. It is a group leader's responsibility to ask a potential group member who is undergoing psychotherapy or intensive counseling to consult his or her therapist before becoming involved in a group.

5. Prospective group members can be told what is expected of them as members and encouraged to develop contracts that call for them to satisfy these expectations. In other words, members can be told that they will be expected to develop concrete personal goals, make appropriate self-disclosures, experiment with new interpersonal behaviors, examine their interpersonal style in terms of the impact they have on others, express their feelings and thoughts, actively listen to others and attempt to see the world through their eyes, show respect for others, offer genuine support, engage in confrontation of others as a way of developing an honest relationship with them, and be willing to experiment with new behaviors outside of the group.

6. It is important that prospective participants be made aware of the types of technique that will be employed and of the types of exercise that they may be asked to participate in. They should be made aware of the ground rules that will govern group activities.

7. Group leaders should avoid undertaking a project that is beyond the scope of their training and experience. Furthermore, they might write a statement of their qualifications to conduct a particular group and make it available to the participants. In a situation where an experienced clinician and a student intern are co-leading a group, this fact should be made clear to the group. This kind of team can be of value to the group as well as to the intern if this difference in leadership experience is not kept hidden. Of course, it is essential that co-leaders meet regularly to discuss any problems that come up in their leading together.

8. Leaders must make clear at the outset of a group what the focus will be. For example, some groups have an educational focus, and so a didactic approach is used. Other groups have a therapeutic focus, and these take an emotive/experiential tack. Some groups have a developmental focus, with the aim being to get members to fully utilize their potential, whereas other groups are more remedial in nature and stress treatment of disabling symptoms or elimination of faulty behavior patterns. Participants need to be fully aware of the primary focus of the group they are about to enter.

9. Group leaders can protect group members' right to decide what to share with the group and what activities to participate in. Group leaders should be sensitive to any form of group pressure that violates the self-determination of an individual and to any activity, such as scapegoating or stereotyping, that unfairly undermines a person's sense of self.

10. It is good for group leaders to develop a rationale for using the group exercises they do and to be able to verbalize this rationale. Further, group leaders should use only those exercises that they are competent to employ. It is best if leaders have experienced as group members the techniques they use.

11. Every attempt should be made to relate practice to theory. Leaders need to keep themselves informed about research findings relating aspects of group process to certain outcomes and use this information to increase the effectiveness of their group practice. It is also essential to be thoroughly grounded in a number of diverse theoretical orientations as a basis for creating a personalized style of leading groups. Unless leaders have a clear belief about the way to function in groups and about how groups work, they lack a basis for using methods that flow from various theoretical approaches.

12. Group leaders should avoid exploiting the members of their groups. There is a tendency on the part of some members to glorify and

idealize the group leader and to lessen their own power in the process. Ethical group leaders do not take advantage of this tendency and manipulate the participants. They don't enter into sexual relationships with group members, for to do so would be to misuse their power—to exploit clients in the service of their ego needs. Nor should group leaders keep clients in groups too long and thus promote dependency. Because of their own financial or psychological needs, some leaders may keep members in a group far beyond the time that it is therapeutically useful.

13. The psychological and physical risks involved in group participation can be pointed out to members before they enter and also when appropriate during the course of a group.

14. The importance of confidentiality should be stressed to members before they enter a group, during the group sessions when relevant, and before a group terminates. The limits of confidentiality need to be discussed at the beginning of a group.

15. Although leaders should, when it is appropriate, be open with the group about their values, they should avoid imposing their values and beliefs on clients, respect their clients' capacity to think for themselves, and be sure that members give one another the same respect. Members often impose their values on others by telling them what to do under the guise of being helpful.

16. Group leaders should be alert for symptoms of psychological debilitation in group members, which may indicate that participation in the group should be discontinued. Referral resources should be made available to people who need or desire further psychological assistance.

17. It is important that group leaders not just allow but actually encourage participants to discuss their functioning in the group and their reactions to their experiences in the group. Time can be set aside at the end of each session for members to express their thoughts and feelings about that session.

18. It is a good idea to prepare participants for the negative responses they are likely to encounter when they try to transfer their group learning to their daily life. Such problems make useful material for exploration in the group, and members are able to learn specific ways of dealing with setbacks.

19. It is an excellent practice to schedule follow-up sessions so that members are able to see how others in their group have done and so that the leader has a basis for evaluating the impact of the group experience. Individual sessions may sometimes be of value for members who feel a need to confer with the leader after a group has ended. These sessions can point the way to continued growth experiences.

20. Group leaders have a professional responsibility to develop some method of evaluation to determine the effectiveness of the procedures they use. Accountability is one way of subjecting the leader's proce-

dures to some form of scrutiny. Through at least informal research efforts, leaders are in a better position to make informed judgments concerning the effectiveness of their leadership style.

This chapter is not intended to increase your anxiety level or make you so careful that you avoid taking any risks. Leading groups is a risky as well as a professionally rewarding venture. You are bound to make mistakes from time to time. Making mistakes is not necessarily fatal, but what is essential is that you be willing to acknowledge them. It is a disservice to treat group members as though they were fragile and, thus, never challenge them. We hope you won't be frozen with anxiety over needing to be all-knowing at all times. What we do encourage you to do is remain willing to ask yourself throughout your professional career *what* you are doing and *why* you are doing it. Ethical decision making is not a matter of seeking ready-made answers that are immune to questioning and revision. It is a never-ending process.

Where to Go from Here

This chapter is merely an introduction to the ethical and professional issues in group work. Those of you who wish to do additional reading in the areas of training of group workers, ethical standards, and legal issues will find a resource guide in this section.

Below we present a portion of the *Ethical Guidelines for Group Leaders* adopted by the ASGW (1980). We will be discussing many of these guidelines in more detail as they pertain to the various stages of a group's development.

■■ ASGW's Ethical Guidelines for Group Leaders*

A. RESPONSIBILITY FOR PROVIDING INFORMATION ABOUT GROUP WORK AND GROUP SERVICES

A-1.   Group leaders shall fully inform group members, in advance and preferably in writing, of the goals in the group, qualifications of the leader, and procedures to be employed.

A-2.   The group leader shall conduct a pre-group interview with each prospective member for purposes of screening, orientation, and, insofar as possible, shall select group members whose needs and goals are compatible with the established goals of the group; who will not impede the group process; and whose well-being will not be jeopardized by the group experience.

* Copyright © 1980 by the Association for Specialists in Group Work. Reprinted by permission.

A-3. Group leaders shall protect members by defining clearly what confidentiality means, why it is important, and the difficulties involved in enforcement.

A-4. Group leaders shall explain, as realistically as possible, exactly what services can and cannot be provided within the particular group structure offered.

A-5. Group leaders shall provide prospective clients with specific information about any specialized or experimental activities in which they may be expected to participate.

A-6. Group leaders shall stress the personal risks involved in any group, especially regarding potential life-changes, and help group members explore their readiness to face these risks.

A-7. Group leaders shall inform members that participation is voluntary and that they may exit from the group at any time.

A-8. Group leaders shall inform members about recording of sessions and how tapes will be used.

B. RESPONSIBILITY FOR PROVIDING GROUP SERVICES TO CLIENTS

B-1. Group leaders shall protect member rights against physical threats, intimidation, coercion, and undue peer pressure insofar as is reasonably possible.

B-2. Group leaders shall refrain from imposing their own agendas, needs, and values on group members.

B-3. Group leaders shall insure to the extent that it is reasonably possible that each member has the opportunity to utilize group resources and interact within the group by minimizing barriers such as rambling and monopolizing time.

B-4. Group leaders shall make every reasonable effort to treat each member individually and equally.

B-5. Group leaders shall abstain from inappropriate personal relationships with members throughout the duration of the group and any subsequent professional involvement.

B-6. Group leaders shall help promote independence of members from the group in the most efficient period of time.

B-7. Group leaders shall not attempt any technique unless thoroughly trained in its use or under supervision by an expert familiar with the intervention.

B-8. Group leaders shall not condone the use of alcohol or drugs directly prior to or during group sessions.

B-9. Group leaders shall make every effort to assist clients in developing their personal goals.

B-10. Group leaders shall provide between-session consultation to group members and follow-up after termination of the group, as needed or requested.

■■ Resources for Further Reading

1. Training of Group Leaders

For those interested in standards for the training and education of group leaders, as well as basic issues relating to leader competence, we recommend the following: *Professional Standards for Training of Group Counselors* (ASGW, 1983); *Guidelines for the Training of Group Psychotherapists* (American Group Psychotherapy Association, 1978); *Current Practice in the Training of Group Psychotherapists* (Dies, 1980); *Description of a Practicum Course in Group Leadership* (Corey, 1981); *In-Service Training for Group Leaders in a Prison Hospital: Problems and Prospects* (Corey, Corey, & Callanan, 1981); *Theory and Practice of Group Counseling* (Corey, 1985), Chapter 2; *Group Counseling: Theory and Process* (Hansen, Warner, & Smith, 1980), Chapter 16; *Methods of Group Psychotherapy and Encounter* (Shapiro, 1978), Chapter 7; and *The Theory and Practice of Group Psychotherapy* (Yalom, 1985), Chapter 17.

2. Ethical Issues

Concerning ethical standards in group work, we recommend the following: *Guidelines for Psychologists Conducting Growth Groups* (APA, 1973); *Ethical Standards* (AACD, 1981); *Ethical Principles of Psychologists* (APA, 1981); *Ethical Guidelines for Group Leaders* (ASGW, 1980); *Code of Ethics for Certified Clinical Mental Health Counselors* (AMHCA, 1980); *Ethical Leader Practices in Sensitivity Training for Prospective Professional Psychologists* (Bass & Dole, 1977); *Group Procedures: Purposes, Processes, and Outcomes* (Diedrich & Dye, 1972), Part 5; *Group Counseling: A Developmental Approach* (Gazda, 1984); *Ethical and Legal Issues in Counseling and Psychotherapy* (Van Hoose & Kottler, 1985); *Professional Issues* (Zimpfer, 1976); *The Counselor and the Law* (Hopkins & Anderson, 1985), Chapters 2 and 3; *Developmental Groups for Children* (Duncan & Gumaer, 1980), Chapter 1; *Ethical and Legal Issues in Group Psychotherapy* (Pinney, 1983); *Ethical Problems of Group Psychotherapy* (Rosenbaum, 1982); and *Training Group Leaders in Ethical Decision Making* (Gumaer & Scott, 1985).

Issues and Ethics in the Helping Professions (Corey, Corey, & Callanan, 1984) contains many topics of relevance to the group worker. This book is a combination of textbook, manual, and resource guide, with open-ended cases and many situations relating to ethical and professional issues that affect the practice of group counseling. Chapter 8 deals with ethical issues special to group work. Two other sources that contain separate chapters on the ethics of group practice are *Theory and Practice of Group Counseling* (Corey, 1985) and *Group Techniques* (Corey, Corey, Callanan, & Russell, 1982b). See also *A Casebook of Ethical Guidelines for Group Leaders* (Corey, Corey, & Callanan, 1982), which is designed as an instructor's resource manual for this book and is also available for students. It contains many case vignettes geared to the ASGW's (1980) guidelines.

3. Legal Issues

Although we are not aware of any books that deal strictly with legal issues in group work, we recommend that group leaders consult books such as the following for some additional information: *The Law and the Practice of Human Services* (Woody & Associates, 1984); *Legal Liability in Psychotherapy* (B. M. Schutz, 1982); *Ethical and Legal Issues in Counseling and Psychotherapy* (Van Hoose & Kottler, 1985); *The Counselor and the Law* (Hopkins & Anderson, 1985); *School Law for Counselors, Psychologists, and Social Workers* (Fischer & Sorenson, 1985); and *Law and Ethics in Counseling* (Hummel, Talbutt, & Alexander, 1985).

Exercises

1. It comes to your attention that certain group members have been gossiping about matters that came up in a high school group you're leading. Do you deal with the offenders privately, or in the whole group? What do you say?

2. Assume that you are about to begin leading a high school counseling group and that the policy of the school is that any teacher or counselor who becomes aware that a student is using drugs is expected to report the name of the student to the principal. How do you cope with this situation?

3. You are conducting a self-exploration group with children in a family clinic. The father of one of the children in your group meets with you to find out how his child is doing. What do you tell him? What do you not tell him?

4. Assume that you are a private practitioner who wants to co-lead a weekend assertiveness-training workshop. How would you announce your workshop? How would you screen potential members? What kind of person would you exclude from your workshop, and why?

5. You are employed as a counselor in the adolescent ward of a county mental hospital. As one of your duties you lead a group for the young people, who are required to attend the sessions. You sense resistance on the part of the members. What are the ethical problems involved? How do you deal with the resistance?

6. Assume that you are asked to lead a group composed of involuntary clients. Since their participation is mandatory, you want to take steps to clearly and fully inform them of procedures to be used, their

rights and responsibilities as members, your expectations of them, and matters such as confidentiality. If you were to write up an "informed consent document," what would you most want to put into this brief letter?

7. A member in a group you are leading comes to you after one of the group sessions, saying: "I don't want to come back next week. It doesn't seem like we're getting anywhere in here, because all that ever goes on is people putting each other down. I just don't trust anyone in here!" She has not said any of this in the sessions, and the group has been in progress for five weeks. What might you say or do? Would you simply let her know that she has the "freedom of exit"? Would you attempt to persuade her to stay in the group?

8. Consider some of the following areas where your values and those of the members might clash. Consider how you might respond in each of these situations that could arise in your group:

- A woman discloses how excited she is over a current affair and then wonders if she should continue staying with her husband.
- Same situation as above, only the client is a man.
- An adolescent relates that his life feels bland without drugs.
- A pregnant 16-year-old is struggling with the decision of whether to have an abortion or give up her baby to an adoption agency.
- A chronically depressed man talks about suicide as his way out of a hopeless situation.

Distinguish between stating what your values are and imposing your values on members.

9. Consult the section on resources for further reading that precedes these exercises. Several students can form a panel and, after doing some reading on a particular ethical or professional issue of interest, present ideas to the class.

Group Process: Stages of Development

■■ The stages in the life of a group do not generally flow neatly and predictably in the order described in these chapters. In actuality, there is considerable overlap between stages, and once a group moves to an advanced stage, it is not uncommon for it to stay at a plateau for a time or to temporarily regress to an earlier stage. Similarly, the fact that certain tasks have been accomplished in a group, such as working through conflicts, does not mean that new conflicts will not erupt. Groups ebb and flow, and both members and leaders need to pay attention to the factors that affect the direction a group takes.

Knowing about typical patterns in the evolution of a group will give you a valuable perspective. You will be better able to predict problems and to intervene in appropriate and timely ways. Knowledge of the critical turning points in a group lets you help the participants mobilize their resources so that they can successfully meet the tasks facing them at each stage.

3

Forming a Group

Focus questions · **Introduction: Where to begin** · Developing a proposal for a group · Working within the system · **Attracting and screening members** · Announcing a group and recruiting members · Screening and selection procedures · How to choose which group to join · **Practical considerations in forming a group** · Group composition · Group size · Frequency and duration of meetings · Length of group · Place for group meetings · Voluntary versus involuntary membership · Open versus closed groups · Building evaluation into group work · **Uses of a pregroup meeting** · Clarifying leader and member expectations · Setting up basic ground rules · Exploring the advantages and limitations of groups · Dealing with misconceptions · An integrated approach to pregroup preparation: Research findings · **Co-leader issues at the pregroup stage** · **How we prepare for groups** · **Exercises** · Exercise in group planning · Interviewing exercises

Focus Questions

1. What issues do you think leaders should consider in organizing a group?
2. How would you go about drafting a written proposal for a group, and how would you "sell" your idea to the agency or institution where you work?
3. How would you announce your group and recruit members? What are some practical ways you can think of to get a group started?
4. What criteria would you use to screen and select members for a group? If you decided to exclude someone who had applied, how would you handle this matter?
5. If you were conducting individual interviews to select group participants, what are some questions you would most want to ask?
6. How would you explain to a potential member the risks and benefits involved in groups? What are some ways of minimizing the psychological risks?
7. What are some misconceptions that you think people have concerning the nature and functioning of groups?
8. What are some advantages of a preliminary session in which potential members can determine whether a given group is for them? How would you want to make use of this first meeting?
9. What are the major ethical considerations in organizing and forming a group?
10. Do you have different attitudes about forming a voluntary group than you do regarding an involuntary one?

■■

Introduction: Where to Begin

We cannot overemphasize the importance of the preparatory period in the formation of a group. Careful attention to pregroup concerns is crucial to the outcome of a group. Thus, leaders will spend time wisely by thinking about what kind of group they want and by getting themselves psychologically ready for it. The more clearly you can state your expectations, the better you will be able to plan and the more meaningful will be the experience for the participants. We have found that a lack of careful thought and planning will show up later in a variety of problems that lead to confusion and unnecessary floundering of the participants. In planning a group, one must begin by clarifying the rationale for it. This entails drafting a detailed proposal.

■■ Developing a Proposal for a Group

Many good ideas for groups are never put into practice because they are not developed into a clear and convincing plan. If you are going to create a group under the auspices of an agency, you will probably have to explain your proposed goals and methods. The following questions are the kind you should consider in preparing your proposal:

1. What type of group will it be? A personal-growth group or one designed to treat people with certain disorders? Long-term or short-term?
2. Whom is the group for? For a particular population, such as college students or married couples? For people seeking something specific, such as help with a personal problem?
3. What are your goals for this group? That is, what will members gain from participating in it?
4. Why do you feel that there is a need for such a group?
5. What are the basic assumptions underlying this project?
6. Who will lead or co-lead the group? What are his or her qualifications?
7. What screening and selection procedures will be used? What is the rationale for using these particular procedures?
8. How many members will be in the group? Where will the group meet? How often? How long will each meeting last? Will new people be allowed to join the group once it has started?
9. How will the group members be prepared for the group experience? What ground rules will be established by the leader at the outset?
10. What kind of structure will the group have? What techniques will be used? Why are these techniques appropriate?
11. How will you handle the fact that people will be taking some risks by participating in the group? What will you tell the members about these risks, and what will you do to safeguard members from unnecessary risks? Will you take any special precautions with participants who are minors?
12. What evaluation procedures do you plan? What follow-up procedures?
13. What topics will be explored in this group? To what degree will they be determined by the group members and to what degree by the leader?

14. What do you expect to be the characteristics of the various stages of the group? What is the function of the leader at each stage? What might the problems be at each stage, and how will the leader cope with them?

Summary Checklist for a Proposal.   Five general areas form the basis of a sound and practical proposal.

1. **Rationale.** Do you have a clear and convincing rationale for your group? Are you able to answer questions that might be raised?
2. **Objectives.** Are you clear about what you most want to attain and how you will go about this? Are your objectives specific, measurable, and attainable within the specified time?
3. **Practical considerations.** Is the membership defined? Are the meeting time, frequency of meetings, and duration of the group practical and possible?
4. **Procedures.** Are specific procedures indicated to meet the stated objectives? Are these procedures appropriate, realistic, and practical for the given population?
5. **Evaluation.** Does your proposal contain strategies for evaluating how well the stated objectives were met? Are your evaluation methods objective, practical, and relevant?

■■ Working within the System

If you hope to have your proposal accepted by both your supervisors in an agency and the potential members, it is essential that you develop the skills necessary to work within the system. In order to get a group off the ground you will need to be sensitive in negotiating with the staff of the institution involved. In all clinics, agencies, and hospitals there are power issues and political realities that need to be addressed. You may become excited about organizing groups only to encounter resistance from your co-workers or your administrators. You may be told, for example, that only psychologists, social workers, and psychiatrists are qualified to lead groups. The rest of the staff may be as cynical as you are inspired about the prospects of doing groups in your setting. Some of your colleagues may be jealous of your efforts, especially if you have successful groups. They may feel that you are taking "their" clients away from them.

The representatives of institutions need to be educated about the potential value, as well as realistic limitations, of groups for their clients. It is helpful to be able to predict some of the major concerns that administrators and agency directors are likely to have about the proposal you submit. For example, if you are attempting to organize a group in a public high school, some timid administrators may be anxious about parental complaints and potential lawsuits. If you are able to appreciate their concerns and speak directly to ethical and legal issues, you stand a better chance of getting your proposal accepted. If you are not clear in your own mind about what you hope to accomplish through group work or how you will conduct the meetings, the chances are slim that a responsible administrator will endorse your program. If you have not thought through some questions that you are likely to be asked about your proposal, you are setting yourself up for defeat. A few examples of questions that we've been asked as we were presenting a group proposal include:

· How will this institution be covered legally in the event of a lawsuit?
· Will the program be voluntary, and will the parents of minors give written consent?
· What will you do in the event that this group proves psychologically disruptive to some of the members?
· Are you prepared to deal with potential attacks from parents or from community members?

At the various stages of our professional development we have developed group proposals for such diverse situations as elementary and secondary schools; community colleges; teacher-training and counselor-training departments of several universities; church-related groups; mental hospitals for elderly and psychotic patients; a state mental hospital for mentally disordered sex offenders; workshops in foreign countries for mental-health professionals; a mountain resort community operated through the continuing education programs of several universities; and a variety of groups in private practice. With all the above examples except for private practice, we have found that a clear and organized written proposal (followed up by a person-to-person presentation) is the key to getting our ideas translated into the reality of a group in action.

Attracting and Screening Members

■■ Announcing a Group and Recruiting Members

Assuming that you have been successful in getting a proposal accepted, the next step is to find a practical way to announce your group to prospective participants. How a group is announced influences both the way it will be received by potential members and the kind of people who will join. Although professional standards should prevail over a commercialized approach, we have found that personal contacts with potential members are one of the best methods of recruiting members.

Professional issues are involved in publicizing a group and recruiting members. The American Psychological Association's *Guidelines for Psy-*

chologists Conducting Growth Groups (1973) and the Association for Specialists in Group Work's *Ethical Guidelines for Group Leaders* (1980) state that prospective members should have access to the following information (preferably in writing):

· a statement of the group's purpose and goals
· the techniques and procedures that may be used, especially any specialized or experimental activities in which members may be expected to participate
· the education, training, and qualifications of the group leader
· the fees and any other related expenses
· a statement of whether follow-up service is included in the fee
· a realistic statement of what services can and cannot be provided
· the personal risks involved in the group
· the use of any recording of sessions
· the division of responsibility between the leader and the participants

In writing announcements it is best to give an accurate picture of the group and to avoid making "promises" about the outcomes of the group and raising unrealistic expectations. As we've indicated, making direct contact with the population that is most likely to benefit from the group is an excellent way to follow up printed announcements. These personal contacts, which can include distributing printed information to those interested, lessen the chances that people will misunderstand the purposes and functioning of the group.

Another effective method of announcing and recruiting for a group is to inform your agency colleagues. They can then refer clients to you who are appropriate for the particular group. It is possible that they can also do the preliminary screening, including giving written information on the group to potential members with whom they have contact. Involve your co-workers as much as possible in every phase of organizing your group.

■■ Screening and Selection Procedures

The *Ethical Guidelines for Group Leaders* developed by the ASGW (1980) state:

> The group leader shall conduct a pre-group interview with each prospective member for purposes of screening, orientation, and, in so far as possible, shall select group members whose needs and goals are compatible with the established goals of the group; who will not impede the group process; and whose well-being will not be jeopardized by the group experience.

The above guideline raises several questions: What kind of screening method should be used? How can you determine who would be best suited for the group and who might have a negative impact on the group process or would be likely to be jeopardized by the experience? How can you therapeutically deal with those candidates who for whatever reason are not included in the group?

The type of group should determine the kind of members accepted. A person who can work well in a group that meets once a week for an hour and a half might not be ready for an intensive weekend marathon group. Psychotic individuals would probably be excluded from a personal-growth workshop yet might benefit from a weekly group for outpatients at a mental-health center. The question that needs to be considered is: Should *this* particular person be included in *this* particular group at *this* time with *this* group leader?

Preliminary Screening Sessions. We endorse screening procedures that include a private session between the candidate and the leader. During the private session the leader might look for evidence that the group will be beneficial to the candidate. Some questions to consider are: Is this person motivated to change? Is this a choice of the individual or of someone else? Why this particular type of group? Does he or she understand what the purposes of the group are? Are there any indications that group counseling is contraindicated for this person at this time?

Group applicants should be given the opportunity, at their private session, to interview the group leader. They should be invited to ask questions concerning the procedures, basic purposes, and any other aspect of the group. This questioning is important as a means not only of getting information but also of developing a feeling of confidence in the group leader, which is necessary if productive work is to take place. In other words, we believe that screening should be a two-way process and that potential members should be encouraged to form a judgment about the group and the leader. Given enough information about the group, a member can make a better informed decision about whether to enter it.

In addition to the private screening session a pregroup session for all of the candidates is extremely valuable. At a preliminary session the leader can outline the reason for the group and the topics that might be explored. This introduction can be most helpful for people who are uncertain whether they want to invest themselves in this group. Potential members can meet one another and begin to explore the potential of the group.

We admit that screening and selection procedures are subjective and that ultimately the intuition and judgment of the leader are crucial. We are concerned that candidates benefit from a group but even more concerned that they might be psychologically hurt by it or might drain the group's energies excessively. Certain members, while remaining unaffected by a group, sap its energy for productive work. This is particularly true of hostile people, people who monopolize, extremely aggressive people, and people who act out. The potential gains of including certain of these members must be weighed against the probable losses to the group as a whole. We also believe that group counseling is contraindicated for individuals who are suicidal, extremely fragmented or acutely psychotic, sociopathic, facing extreme crises, highly paranoid, or extremely self-centered.

A leader needs to develop a system for assessing the likelihood that a candidate will benefit from a group experience. Factors that must be taken into consideration are the level of training of the leader, the proposed makeup of the group, the setting, and the basic nature of the group. For example, it might be best not to accept a highly defensive individual into an ongoing adolescent group, for several reasons. A group may be too threatening for a person so vulnerable and may lead to increased defensiveness and rigidity, or such a person may have a counterproductive effect on group members who want to do serious work.

In some cases it may not be practical and realistic to conduct individual interviews, and alternatives will have to be relied on. One alternative is group screening sessions. This method saves time and also has the advantage of providing an idea of how each person reacts to a group situation. The pregroup session can also be used for screening; once members meet one another in a group situation, they can better decide if they want to make a commitment to the group.

Personal contact is always best. For example, we offered a personal-growth group in Europe in which it was unrealistic to screen members privately on a personal basis. We did provide the person who had agreed to organize this group with a detailed letter that described relevant information about the workshop. In several personal contacts with the sponsor we discussed our philosophy of group work, the central purposes of the workshop, and who would most benefit from it. In spite of our efforts to spell out the nature of the group and to prepare those who would attend, we met with considerable opposition from some members, who asserted that the group was not what they had envisioned. This experience reinforced our belief in the value of screening and detailed preparation done in a personal way.

There are other instances when screening may not be practical or even possible. If you work in a county facility or a state hospital, the chances are that you will simply be assigned a group. The basis for assigning members could be their diagnosis or the ward they are on. Even if you are not able to select members for your group, you can make at least brief individual contact with them to prepare them. You will also have to devote part of the initial sessions to preparation, for many of the members may not have the faintest idea why they are in the group or how the group might be of any value to them. In open groups, whose membership changes as some clients leave and new ones are added, it is a good practice to meet individually with incoming members so that you can orient them.

Assessing and Choosing Members.   We are often asked the questions: "How do you decide who will best fit into the group, who will most benefit from it, and who is likely to be harmed by the experience? If you decide to exclude a person from the group, how do you handle this in a tactful and therapeutic manner?" As a group leader you must make the ultimate decision to include or exclude certain members. Because the groups that we typically offer are voluntary, one factor we look for during the interview is the degree to which a candidate wants to make some changes and is willing to expend the necessary effort. We consider whether a group seems the appropriate method of intervention to accomplish the desired changes. We also weigh heavily how much the candidate seems to want to become a member of this group, especially after he or she is given information about it.

We sometimes find ourselves reluctant to let certain people into a group in spite of their desire to join. As we've mentioned, we do pay attention to our intuitions concerning a person, so in the last analysis our screening and selection process is a subjective one. There can be a variety of reasons that would lead us to exclude a person, but whatever our reservations might be, we generally discuss them with the prospective member. At times, after we've discussed our concerns, we see matters differently. At other times we simply are not with a clear conscience able to admit a person.

If we do not accept people, we tend to stress how the group might not be appropriate for them and, in some cases, how they would not be appropriate for the group. We strive to break the news in a manner that is honest, direct, and sensitive and that helps those who are being rejected remain open to consider other options. For example, we might determine that a highly defensive and extremely anxious person who is very frightened in interpersonal relationships is likely to benefit from a series of individual counseling sessions before being placed in a group situation. We would explain our rationale and encourage the person to consider accepting a referral for an appropriate type of intervention. In other words, we do not close the door on people we exclude from a group with no explanation, nor do we convey that there is something intrinsically wrong with them because they were not included in this particular group.

When we do in-service training workshops for group leaders in various agencies and institutions, many leaders tell us that they don't screen people for their groups. They cite any number of reasons: they don't have the time; they don't have much voice in choosing group members, because people are simply assigned to a group; they don't really know how to determine who will or will not benefit or will be negatively influenced by a group experience; they cannot see why screening is really important; they don't want to play the role of expert in deciding who will be included or excluded; or they don't want to make a mistake by turning away people who might gain from a group. In response, we emphasize that we see screening not as a highly objective and scientific process but as a rough device for getting together the best clientele for a given group. As we mentioned earlier, our view of screening entails a dialogue with the prospective members—it is an opportunity to give information to them and to orient them to the group, and it is a way to help them share in the decision of whether it is appropriate for *them* to become involved in *this* type of group, with *this* leader, at *this* time.

During the screening and selection interviews, as well as in your general announcements, it is well to educate the public on how best to select a group. If people are to make an informed decision about a group, they need information and guidelines. Because people often wonder what to look for in selecting a group, we've prepared the following section, aimed at informing consumers.

▪▪ How to Choose Which Group to Join

Potential members often ask how they can make an informed decision about joining a particular group. Although there are no guarantees that the group one picks will be the right one, a consumer can make a wise choice by considering the following suggestions:

1. Do not join a group just because someone you know thinks you should. Decide for yourself whether you want to be a member of a particular kind of group.

2. Check with others who know the group leader before you make your decision. Although some reports may be biased (either positively or negatively), feedback from people who have participated in one of the leader's groups can be particularly valuable.

3. Before you join a group, interview the group leader. Many leaders will want a private session with a prospective client to determine the person's readiness for a group. By the same token, it is reasonable for the prospective client to want to know about the personal and professional qualifications of the person who leads the group. If the therapist is indignant over such a request, you should probably avoid this person's group. If you do speak to the leader, try to decide whether he or she inspires your trust.

4. Questions such as the following can be asked of a group leader:

· What is the purpose of your group?
· What are the responsibilities of the leader and of the members?

- What do you see as the risks of participation, and what safeguards do you take to minimize the risks?
- What results do you see in your groups?
- What techniques do you use?
- Is there an opportunity for individual sessions?
- What is your background and training?
- What experience do you have in leading groups?
- Are you licensed as a therapist? If not, what are your qualifications as a group practitioner?
- What theoretical model do you use?

5. Ask the leader about matters such as fees, the structure of the group, the method of deciding when a member should quit the group or when the group should be terminated, and follow-up procedures.

6. Be cautious about responding to advertisements or to brochures and pamphlets circulated in the mail. Referrals from agencies, from professionals, and most of all from clients who have been in the leader's groups should guide you in selecting a group.

7. The size of the group is another factor to consider. Groups of more than 16 or fewer than 5 members are best avoided (except for children's groups, which may have fewer than 5 members). If a group is very small, there are not enough interaction possibilities. If a group is very large, group cohesion is hard to establish, and even a highly qualified leader may have trouble monitoring the interaction. For a group as large as 16, there should be at least two leaders.

Practical Considerations in Forming a Group

■■ Group Composition

The composition of a group must depend on what type of group it is. The solution to the problem of heterogeneity versus homogeneity is found in the goals of a particular group.

In general, for a specific target population with given needs, a group composed entirely of members of that population is more appropriate than a heterogeneous group. Consider a group composed entirely of elderly people. It can focus exclusively on the specific problems that characterize their developmental period, such as loneliness, isolation, lack of meaning, rejection, deterioration of the body, and so forth. The similarity of the members can lead to a great degree of cohesion, which in turn allows for an open and intense exploration of this life crisis. Members can express feelings that have been kept private, and their life circumstances can give them a bond with one another.

Examples of other homogeneous groups are Alcoholics Anonymous, Recovery Inc., Parents without Partners, and Weight Watchers. It is common to hear people claim that, unless one has actually experienced what it is like to be, for example, an alcoholic, one cannot fully understand, and thus cannot help with, an alcoholic's unique problems. We don't accept the premise that, in order to have a therapeutic impact on a client, the group leader must have experienced every problem of the client. It is important only that group leaders be able to identify with the feelings of clients—their loneliness, fear, and anxiety. When a specific problem exists, however, group cohesion can help, and so homogeneity, which facilitates cohesion, is appropriate.

A case can sometimes be made, however, for combining people from different populations in a single group. In one of her "Death and Dying" seminars, Dr. Elisabeth Kübler-Ross shared her dream of having children on every hospital ward for the elderly. She maintained that this would give the elderly a chance to share their life and experiences with children and to get the meaning from life that comes from taking care of children. The children would benefit by getting the opportunity to experience older people. Thus, a combination of these two age groups could have some unique therapeutic results for members of both.

Sometimes a microcosm of the outside social structure is desired, and in that case a heterogeneous group is, of course, called for. Personal-growth groups and certain therapy groups tend to be heterogeneous. Members can experiment with new behavior and develop interpersonal skills with the help of feedback from a rich variety of people in an environment that represents out-of-group reality.

■■ Group Size

What is a desirable size for a group? The answer depends on several factors: the age of the clients, the experience of the leader, the type of group, and the problems to be explored. For instance, a group composed of elementary school children might be kept to 3 or 4, whereas a group of adolescents might be made up of 6 to 8 people. For a weekly ongoing group of adults, about 8 people with one leader may be ideal. A group of this size is big enough to give ample opportunity for interaction and small enough for everyone to be involved and to feel a sense of "group."

■■ Frequency and Duration of Meetings

How often should a group meet? For how long? Should a group meet twice weekly for one-hour sessions? Or is an hour and a half to two hours once a week preferable? With children and adolescents it may be better to meet more frequently and for a shorter period, to suit their attention span. If the group is taking place in a school setting, the meeting times can correspond to regularly scheduled class periods. For groups of college students or relatively well-functioning adults, a two-hour weekly session might be preferable. This two-hour period is long enough to allow some intensive work yet not so long that fatigue sets in. You can choose any frequency and duration that suit your style of leadership and the type of people in your group. For an inpatient group composed of lower-functioning members, it is desirable to meet on a daily basis for 45 minutes. Because of the members' psychological impairments it may not be realistic to hold their attention for a longer period. Even for higher-functioning inpatient groups it is a good practice to meet several times a week, but these groups might be scheduled for 90 minutes. (An excellent description of inpatient therapy groups for both higher-level and lower-functioning clients is provided by Irvin Yalom in his 1983 book *Inpatient Group Psychotherapy*.)

■■ Length of Group

What should the duration of a group be, and is it wise to set a termination date? We believe that with most groups a termination date should be announced at the outset, so that members will have a clear idea of the time limits under which they are working. Our college groups typically run about 15 weeks—the length of a semester. With high school students the same length seems ideal, for it is long enough for trust to develop and for work toward behavioral changes to take place but not so long that the group seems to be dragging on interminably. One of our colleagues has several closed groups in his private practice that last 16 weeks. After a few meetings he schedules an all-day session for these groups, which he finds adds greatly to their cohesion. When the group comes to an end, those who wish to join a new group have that option. The advantages of such an arrangement are that the time span allows for cohesion and productive work and that members can then continue practicing newly acquired interpersonal skills with a new group of people. Perhaps a major value of this type of time-limited group is that members are forced to realize that they do not have forever to attain their personal goals. At different points in this 16-week group the members are challenged to review their progress, both individually and as a group. If they are dissatisfied with their own participation or with the direction the group is taking, they have the responsibility to do something to change the situation.

Of course, there are some groups composed of the same members who meet for years. Such a time structure allows them to work through issues in some depth and to offer support and challenge to make life changes. These ongoing groups do have the potential for fostering dependency, and thus it is important that both the leader and members evaluate the impact of the group on the members' daily living.

■■ Place for Group Meetings

Where should the group hold its meetings? Many places will do, but privacy is essential; the members must feel that they will not be overheard by people in adjoining rooms. Groups often fail because of their physical setting. If they are held in a day hall or ward full of distractions, productive group work will not occur. We like a group room that is not cluttered up with chairs and tables and that allows for a comfortable seating arrangement. We prefer a setting that enables the group to sit in a circle. This arrangement lets all the participants see one another and allows enough freedom of movement that the members can spontaneously make physical contact. It is a good idea for co-leaders to sit across from each other. In this way the nonverbal language of all members can be observed by one leader or the other, and a "we-versus-them" atmosphere can be avoided.

■■ Voluntary versus Involuntary Membership

Obviously, the most desirable group is composed of clients who are motivated to change and committed to working. Realistically, some of your groups will be made up of people who are sent to you. In such cases, providing members with information about the group, teaching them how to participate, and orienting them to the basic procedures of group process are essential. It is usually helpful to let the members know that, although they don't have much choice about attending, they *can* decide how they will spend their time in the group. Discussing with members various ways in which they can use their time profitably increases the chances that the group will be meaningful.

■■ Open versus Closed Groups

Open groups are characterized by changing membership. The group continues, and as certain members are ready to leave, new members are admitted. *Closed groups* typically have some time limitation, and members are expected to remain in the group until it ends; new members are not added. Should a group be open or closed? There are some advantages to incorporating new members as others leave, for this can provide stimulation. There can be a lack of cohesion, however, particularly if too many clients drop out or too many new ones are introduced at once. Therefore, we prefer to bring in new members one at a time as an opening occurs. One colleague who co-leads open groups in an agency stresses reviewing of the ground rules with each incoming member. Rather than taking group time each time a new person is included, he covers the rules with the new member as part of the intake interview.

He also asks other members to teach the new member about a few of the guidelines in an attempt to have them take more responsibility for their own group. If members are dropped and added sensitively, these changes do not necessarily interfere with the cohesiveness of the group.

In some settings, such as mental-health wards in state hospitals or certain day-treatment centers, group leaders do not have a choice between an open and a closed group. Because the membership of the group changes almost from week to week, continuity between sessions and cohesion within the group become difficult to achieve. Nevertheless, Yalom (1983) maintains that cohesion is possible, even in cases where members attend only once or a few times. He provides detailed guidelines for making these groups a valuable experience.

One of our colleagues regularly conducts several open groups in a community mental-health agency. He finds that trust and cohesion do occur in most of these groups, for even though the membership does change somewhat over a period of time, there is a stable core of members. When new members join, they agree to attend for at least six sessions. Also, members who miss two consecutive meetings without a valid excuse are not allowed to continue. These practices increase the chances for continuity.

■■ Building Evaluation into Group Work

If you do group work in a community agency or an institution, you may be required to demonstrate the efficacy of your treatment approach. Federal and state grants typically stipulate measures for accountability. Thus, it is essential in most settings that you devise procedures for assessing the degree to which clients benefit from the group experience. Such evaluation can also help you sharpen your leadership skills.

There is no need to be intimidated by the idea of incorporating a research spirit into your practice. Nor do you have to think exclusively in terms of rigorous empirical research. One alternative to traditional scientific methods is evaluation research, which aims at gathering data that can be useful in making improvements within the structure of a group. *Member-specific measures* are used to assess changes in attitudes and behaviors of individual clients. It is possible to develop your own devices for evaluating the degree to which members attain their goals. *Group-specific measures* assess the changes that are common to all members of the group, such as increased self-awareness, decreased anxiety, and improved personal relationships. Many of these measures are available in standardized form, or you can adapt them to suit your needs. (The problems of combining research and practice are addressed in some detail in Chapter 7.)

Uses of a Pregroup Meeting

We suggested earlier that a preliminary meeting of all those who were thinking of joining the group was a good follow-up to screening and orientation interviews as well as a useful device when individual interviews were impractical. We think that such a pregroup session provides an excellent way to prepare members and to get them acquainted with one another. This session also provides the members with more data to decide if they are willing to commit themselves to what would be expected of them.

At this initial session the leader can explore the members' expectations, clarify the goals and objectives of the group, discuss procedural details, impart some information about group process, and answer members' questions. The structuring of the group, including the specification of procedures and norms, should be accomplished early in the group's history. Some of this structuring should have been done during the individual intake session, but a continuation of it should be the focus of the first session. Some procedural issues also need to be explored at this initial session. Group counselors should either establish ground rules or ask the group to do so.

Research Findings on Pregroup Preparation.   Members who receive such pregroup preparation generally benefit more from a group experience than do those who are unprepared (Borgers & Tyndall, 1982; LeCluyse, 1983; Muller & Scott, 1984). Such members tend to have an increased faith in the group, more awareness of appropriate group behavior and roles, and lower levels of anxiety. They show increased openness and have a greater willingness to disclose themselves and to give and receive feedback (Bednar, Melnick, & Kaul, 1974; LeCluyse, 1983; Yalom, 1983).

■■ Clarifying Leader and Member Expectations

The pregroup session is the appropriate time to encourage members to express the expectations they are bringing with them to the group. We typically begin by asking: "What are your expectations for this group? What did you have in mind when you signed up?" This usually gives us a frame of reference for how the members are approaching the group, what they want from it, and what they are willing to give to it to make it a success.

We also share *our* expectations by giving the members an idea of why we designed the group, what we hope will be accomplished, and what we expect of ourselves as leaders and them as members. This is a good time for leaders to reemphasize and clarify what they see as their responsibilities to the group and to further discuss the members' rights and responsibilities. Leaders can explain what services they can and cannot realistically provide within the particular structure offered—for example, private consultations or follow-up sessions.

Research Findings.   Members who understand what behaviors are expected of them tend to be more successful (Stockton & Morran, 1982). Research suggests that pretraining increases the chance of successful outcomes because it lessens the intense anxiety that often marks the initial sessions (Bednar, Melnick, & Kaul, 1974). Yalom (1983) maintains that group leaders can do a great deal to prevent the unnecessary anxiety that results when a client is thrown into an ambiguous therapy situation. Leaders can avoid such ambiguity by making clear to the members their goals, their methods of achieving these goals, and the role behavior they expect.

■■ Setting Up Basic Ground Rules

The pregroup session is the appropriate place to establish some procedures that will facilitate group process. Some leaders prefer to present their own policies and procedures, in a nonauthoritarian manner, whereas other leaders tend to place the major responsibility on the group members to come up with procedures that will assist them in attaining their ends. Whatever approach is taken, some discussion of ground rules will be necessary.

Ethical Guidelines for Group Leaders (ASGW, 1980) can help group leaders establish minimum ground rules and ethical standards. Some of these standards state, for example, that group leaders:

· shall not condone the use of alcohol or drugs directly prior to or during group sessions
· shall protect members by defining clearly what confidentiality means, why it is important, and the difficulties involved in enforcing it
· shall inform members that participation is voluntary and that they may exit from the group at any time
· shall protect member rights against physical threats, intimidation, coercion, and undue peer pressure.
· shall discuss with members the risks involved in group participation, especially regarding life-changes, and help members explore their readiness to face these risks

As we have seen, confidentiality is a crucial issue in groups. Ideally, this issue is discussed during the individual interview, but because it is so important to the functioning of a group, you cannot stress it too often. At the pregroup session it is a good idea to state that confidentiality is not an absolute and that there are restrictions. Depending on the type of group and the setting, leaders may not be able to guarantee that all member disclosures will be kept within the group. Limitations to confidentiality apply especially to groups with children and adolescents, groups with parolees, groups composed of involuntary populations such as criminals and sex offenders in an institution, and groups of psychiatric patients in a hospital or clinic. This last category, for example, should be informed that certain things they say in the group may go into their hospital chart, which will be available for other staff members and their own doctor to read. They should be informed of what kinds of information might be recorded in the chart and who will have access to it. What is essential is that leaders clearly and openly specify what they can and cannot promise to their clientele. Then the members can decide what and how much they will disclose. This kind of leader honesty about confidentiality will go a long way toward establishing the trust that is absolutely necessary for a working group. You are referred back to Chapter 2 for a further discussion of confidentiality.

In addition to the ground rules mentioned there are other issues to explore with your group at the first (or an early) session. These include policies about tardiness; attendance; smoking and eating during sessions; bringing friends to a session; written parental permission, in the case of minors; socializing outside of the group with other members; getting involved intimately with other members; and member rights and responsibilities. You will not be able to fully discuss all of the policies and procedures that you deem essential to the smooth functioning of your group in one or two sessions, yet knowing what your position is on these matters will be an asset when they arise at some point in the development of the group.

▪▪ Exploring the Advantages and Limitations of Groups

We typically devote some time at the pregroup session, to a discussion of both the advantages and the limitations of therapeutic groups. This can be done by pointing out how group methods have specific applicability to this particular group and how the members can use what they learn in their everyday life. Some of the cautions about groups should also be mentioned.

Advantages. Therapeutic groups have certain distinct advantages over other intervention strategies. A few of the values of group work are:

1. Participants are able to explore their style of relating to others and to learn more effective social skills.

2. The group setting offers support for new behavior and encourages experimentation. Members can try out new behaviors and decide whether they want to incorporate them into their outside life.

3. There is a re-creation of the everyday world in some groups, particularly if the membership is diverse with respect to age, interest, back-

ground, socioeconomic status, and type of problem. When this occurs, a member has the advantage of contacting a wide range of personalities, and the feedback received can be richer and more diverse than that available in a one-to-one setting.

4. Certain factors that facilitate personal growth are more likely to be present in groups. For instance, members have the opportunity to learn about themselves through the experience of others; to experience emotional closeness and caring, which encourage meaningful disclosure of self; and to identify with the struggles of other members.

Limitations.   Following are a few of the limitations to the effectiveness of therapeutic groups:

1. Groups are not "cure-alls." Unfortunately, some practitioners and participants view groups as the exclusive means of changing people's behavior. Worse yet, some hope that a brief and intense group experience can remake people's lives. Counseling and therapy are difficult forms of work, and we believe that shortcuts are not necessarily fruitful.

2. There is often a subtle pressure to conform to group norms and expectations. Group participants sometimes unquestioningly substitute group norms for norms they unquestioningly acquired in the first place.

3. Some people become "hooked" on groups and make the group experience an end in itself. Instead of using their group as a laboratory for human learning and a place where they can learn behavior that will facilitate their day-to-day living, they stop short, savoring the delights of the group for its own sake.

4. Not all people are suited to groups. The idea that groups are for everybody has done serious harm to the reputation of the group movement. Some people are too suspicious, too hostile, or too fragile to benefit from a group experience. Some are psychologically damaged by attending certain groups. Before a person is accepted into a group, the factors need to be carefully weighed by both the counselor and the client to increase the chances that the person will benefit from such an experience.

5. Some people have made a group a place to ventilate their miseries and be rewarded for baring their soul. Unfortunately, some use groups as a vehicle for expressing their woes, in the hope that they will be understood and totally accepted, and make no attempt to do what is necessary to effect substantial change in their life.

▪▪ Dealing with Misconceptions

Some myths about groups need to be critically appraised at the pregroup meeting, for these misconceptions regarding the purpose and functioning of groups can lead people to conclude that the disadvantages far outweigh the advantages. What follows are some key myths and the facts to debunk them.

· "The group is a place to get emotionally high." If people leave a group feeling high, then this might be considered frosting on the cake, but we don't see this as the main reason for participating in groups. Participants need to be aware that a "high" may change to a "low" when they encounter difficulty being the way they were in the group in their real life. In the group they may have received positive feedback and support for daring to change. When they return home, they may well meet with resistance and antagonism when they deviate from old and familiar ways. Others may have an investment in keeping them as they were, because that way they're more predictable and more easily controlled. The depression that so often follows the feeling of being able to conquer the world is a reality that participants need to examine.

· "The goal of a group is to leave it feeling close and loving toward everyone in the group." The genuine closeness that can be achieved in an intensive group can be the result of shared struggles, and the worth of this emotional bond is not to be discounted. However, the basic purpose of a group is not to create a loving bond among all the members. Rather, intimacy should be considered a by-product of meaningful work in a group.

· "Groups are places where people tear you down and then don't rebuild you." We frequently hear people express the fear that they will leave the group defenseless and not have the resources to recover. This belief relates to the issues of confrontation and scapegoating. Our hope is that people can learn that rigid defenses are not always necessary and that they can safely remove unnecessary walls that separate them from others. When people become more authentic, even though they may become vulnerable, they discover a core of strength within themselves. We certainly don't support the approach of some groups, in which ruthless attacks are seen as a desirable way of stripping away a person's defenses.

· "Groups make people more miserable and unhappy, because their problems surface." To some extent this is true. When people face the truth about their life, pain and conflict may be the result. However, we don't think that people must remain fixated in this unhappy condition. Once people recognize those aspects of themselves or their environment that are contributing to this misery, they can take some decisive steps to change. Continued group counseling or individual therapy can be useful in assisting people to work through the personal conflicts that surface in the group.

· "Groups practice a form of brainwashing." Instead of merely accepting the dictates or suggestions of others, successful group members acquire an increased ability to look within themselves for their own answers to the present and future problems life poses. Groups are neither places to dispense cheap advice nor means of indoctrinating people into agreement with a particular philosophy of life. Hopefully, the leaders and members can challenge a person to reexamine his or her own philosophy without imposing their beliefs on that person.

· "Only people who are sick seek groups." There is a misconception that all therapy or counseling, either individual or group, is designed to cure people of mental and emotional illness. It is true that some groups are aimed at helping a disturbed population discover some relief; but there are also many groups for developmental purposes—groups designed to help people recognize their potential and remove blocks to personal growth. Healthy people can use the group experience as an aid in viewing themselves more honestly and critically and seeing themselves as others see them. There is a wide variety of groups that focus on a well population and use therapy for preventive as well as remedial purposes.

· "Groups are artificial and unreal." Some criticize groups on the ground that they operate in an unreal context. We believe that a group setting can be more real than so-called real life in the sense that people shed many of the pretenses that characterize their everyday interactions. Certain aspects of this experience may seem artificial, but if the participants can discover ways of putting into practice what was learned in a group, the real value of the experience is undeniable. That some groups never transcend an artificial level does not necessarily mean that what is experienced in all groups is artificial.

· "Group pressure forces people to lose a sense of identity." Although it is true that group pressure can be used in destructive ways, this pressure can also be used constructively. Some pressure is almost inevitable, for there are expectations to be honest, to get involved personally, to interact with people in the group in direct and open ways, and to reveal oneself. What is important is how leaders and members deal with the basic pressure that is part of a group experience. Pressure does not have to be viewed as something that "cracks a person" and forces submission; rather, it can be seen as a challenge for members to face and work through conflicts they might otherwise avoid.

■■ An Integrated Approach to Pregroup Preparation: Research Findings

Borgers and Tyndall (1982) describe three ways of preparing members for a group experience: cognitive learning, vicarious experiencing, and behavioral practice. With cognitive methods, members acquire basic factual information and performance information. Vicarious experiencing includes the use of tape recordings, videotapes, and films to model desired group behavior. Behavioral practice involves members' engaging in structured activities. Borgers and Tyndall conclude: "Perhaps the most valuable pregroup preparation consists of a combination of these approaches and would ideally be fitted to the individual client after considering such factors as risk-taking propensity, interpersonal sensitivity, and level of cognitive functioning" (1982, p. 111). Their conclusions are supported by research. Studies have consistently shown that groups receiving both instruction and modeling do better than those receiving only one treatment or neither (Stockton & Morran, 1982).

For his long-term outpatient groups, Yalom (1983) provides an overview of the interpersonal theory of therapy and shows members that many of their current problems are linked with past personal relationships. He also clears up misconceptions about group therapy by teaching members how to involve themselves in active and responsible ways in the group sessions. In sum, he shows them how group therapy can be a rich arena for learning more about their interpersonal style and how they can use the group as a place to acquire and to practice more effective interpersonal skills. For his short-term inpatient groups, Yalom modifies his approach to preparation, because most hospital stays are too short to allow for much pretraining. Instead, he does this preparation as an initial part of the therapy group. He invites members who have been in the group for a time to join him in the orientation process for newcomers.

In concluding this discussion of the preliminary session, let us caution against bombarding the members with too much information at the initial meeting. Some topics, such as risks, misconceptions about groups, extragroup socializing, and so forth, could be dealt with as these issues come up in the course of the group sessions.

It should be emphasized that the research literature supports the value of systematically preparing members for a group experience. Many groups that get stuck at an early developmental stage do so because the foundations were poorly laid at the outset. What is labeled as "resistance" on the part of group members is often the result of failure on the leader's part to adequately explain what groups are about, how they function, and how members can become actively involved.

Co-Leader Issues at the Pregroup Stage

If you are co-leading a group, the central issue at this early stage is that you and your co-leader have equal responsibility in forming the group and getting it going. Both of you need to be clear as to the purpose of the group, what you hope to accomplish with the time you have, and how you will meet your objectives. Cooperation and basic agreement between you and your co-leader will be essential in getting your group off to a good start.

This cooperative effort might well start with your meeting to develop a proposal, and ideally both of you will present it to whoever has the authority of accepting your joint proposal. This practice ensures that designing and originating the group is not solely one leader's responsibility. This shared responsibility for organizing the group continues with the various tasks that we've outlined in this chapter. You and your co-leader will be a team when it comes to matters such as announcing and recruiting for membership; conducting screening interviews and agreeing on whom to include and exclude; agreeing on basic ground rules, policies, and procedures and presenting them to the members as a co-leading team; and sharing in the practical matters that must be handled to form a group.

It may not always be possible to share equally in all the responsibilities. Although it is *ideal* that both leaders interview the applicants, time constraints may make this impractical. Tasks may have to be divided, but as much as possible both leaders should be involved in what is necessary to make a group a reality. If one leader does a disproportionate share of the work, the other can easily develop a passive role in the leadership of the group once it begins.

If co-leaders do not know each other or if they don't have much sense of how each works professionally, they are likely to get off to a poor start. Simply walking into a group cold, without any initial planning or acquaintance with your co-leader, is to invite future problems. We have a few suggestions that co-leaders can consider before the initial session:

1. Make the time to at least get to know something about each other personally and professionally before you begin leading together.
2. Talk about your theoretical orientation and how each of you perceives groups. What kind of group work has each of you experienced? What ways will your theory and leadership style influence the direction the group takes?
3. Does either of you have any concerns or reservations about leading with the other? What might get in your way with each other? How can you use your separate talents productively as a team? How can your differences in leadership style have a complementary effect and actually enhance the group?
4. Each of you can talk about your own strengths and weaknesses, with implications for how they will affect your leading together. With this knowledge you may be able to forestall some potential problems.
5. For the two of you to work together well as a team you should be in agreement on the ethical aspects of group work. What does each of you consider to be unethical practice, and are there differences? The ethical issues touched on both in this chapter and in the preceding chapter need to be discussed.

Although these suggestions do not represent all the possible areas that co-leaders can explore in getting to know each other, they do provide a basis for focusing on significant topics.

How We Prepare for Groups

Because we believe that involvement, enthusiasm, inventiveness, and caring are important in group leaders, we try to be physically and psychologically ready for every new group or workshop we lead. We have found that, in order to avoid becoming programmed group leaders or programming a certain course for our groups, we must spend some time away from our daily routines thinking about the group that will shortly be convening.

Whether the group is a weekend workshop of skills training for counselors and teachers, a couples group, or a week-long intensive personal-growth group, we generally arrange to spend a day or at least several hours together before we begin. Not only is it important for us to reflect on the goals and structure that we would like a particular workshop to have, it is also important for us to talk about ourselves with each other. How are things between us? Are there any sources of friction between us that might interfere with the progress of the group? Do we feel good enough about ourselves and each other to devote our energy to the demanding tasks of group leadership, or will our unspoken conflicts drain off our vitality and energy? Are we feeling nurtured by each other and excited by the prospect of working together?

Our summer residential workshops come after a busy school year, and so we feel a need to shift gears and become psychologically ready for them. Sometimes at the end of spring we realize that we've both been so involved with the demands of our separate projects that we've neglected to make contact with each other or failed to resolve certain grievances between us. Even though we may not work through all of our conflicts, we do attempt to air our grievances so that our needs will be known to each other.

We don't want to give the impression that a husband and wife who lead groups together must present an ideal image of togetherness and self-actualization. We find that being ourselves, with our individual problems and interpersonal differences, doesn't necessarily block our effectiveness in leading groups. In fact, by being honest with each other and our groups about our strengths and limitations, we're able to provide a model of behavior that facilitates group movement. However, we do mean to emphasize that our job is taxing; it requires our full attention. We can't afford to divert energy to an unspoken resentment between us. If there were a crisis in our relationship, it would be very difficult for us to function effectively and be there fully for the group. And we don't believe we would be justified in using the group time for our therapy. To bring our unfinished business into a group we were leading and attempt to work it through would be to unfairly burden the group. If there are major difficulties or differences between us, we evaluate the wisdom of attempting to co-lead at that particular time.

We believe not only that our relationship should be in good shape but also that we must feel in good psychological shape as individuals. If we're feeling ineffectual, overworked, overtired, unappreciated, depressed, highly anxious, or in a state of personal crisis, then our effectiveness as leaders will be seriously diminished. We know how much physical and emotional energy leading an intensive group workshop generally takes, and if we're not personally nourished before the group, the danger exists that, lacking the energy to lead, we'll only use the group to satisfy our own needs. But if we feel ready when we enter a group, we derive additional energy from our giving and receiving. The questions we ask ourselves before we begin a new group are:

· Am I really looking forward to beginning this group?
· Do I feel alive and enthusiastic?
· How personally effective have I been feeling lately?
· Have my projects been rewarding?
· Are there certain internal conflicts that are haunting me and that need to be resolved before I attempt to work therapeutically with others?
· Am I liking the quality of my own life and the direction it's taking, or am I dissatisfied with the choices I've made?
· Am I willing to do for myself what I might be encouraging group members to do?
· Am I willing to face myself honestly, accept what I see, make decisions to change, and act on my decisions?

Before most of the groups for adults that we do, we ask the members to write a paper telling about significant aspects of themselves, about their personal goals for the group, and about the nature of the personal struggles that they hope to explore in the group. This writing exercise not only helps the group members get a clear focus on the areas they most want to understand and change but also provides us with their subjective view of what they want for themselves from this group. As we read these papers, we look for common themes and give some thought to how we might work with these topics. We do not bring up specific issues or break confidentiality as we are working in the group by saying "In your paper you wrote . . ." Instead, we encourage members to initiate the kind of work they want to do; they take responsibility for what they will explore.

Most of all, we want to be looking forward to the experience at the initial session. We hope to direct our full attention to effectively and creatively leading a group, and we find that preparing ourselves pays off for both the group and ourselves.

Exercises

■■ Exercise in Group Planning

Select a particular type of group (personal-growth, counseling, or other) and a target population (children, adolescents, or adults). Keeping in mind the type of group you've selected, answer the following questions. The purpose of the exercise is to give you an idea of the questions you need to ask yourself while planning your group.

1. What is your role in this group?
2. What do you most want to occur in your group? State your purposes simply and concretely.
3. Would you form a contract with your group, and, if so, what would be the essence of the contract? Would you expect each member to develop a contract?
4. Mention a few ground rules or policies you feel would be essential for your group.
5. How can you determine whether you have the skills necessary to lead this particular type of group?
6. What is the focus of your group? (Is it didactic? experiential? remedial? developmental?)
7. Would you accept only volunteer group members? Why or why not?
8. What characteristics would people have to have to be included? What is the rationale?
9. What procedures and techniques would you use in your group? Are your procedures practical? Are they related to the goals and the population of the group?
10. What evaluation methods might you use to determine the effectiveness of your approaches? Are your evaluation procedures appropriate to the purposes of your group?

■■ Interviewing Exercises

1. Screening-Interview Exercise.   One person in the class volunteers to play the role of a group leader conducting a screening interview for members for a particular type of group. The group leader conducts a 10-minute interview with a potential member, played by another class member. Then the prospective client tells the group leader how he or she felt and what impact the group leader made. The group leader shares his or her observations about the prospective group member and tells whether the person would have been accepted into the group, and why or why not. This exercise can be repeated with another client so that the group leader can benefit from the feedback and try some new ideas. Several students can experience the role of the interviewer and the role of the interviewee. It is essential that feedback be given so that people can improve their skills in conducting screening interviews. The rest of the class can offer feedback and suggestions for improvement after each interview.

2. Group-Member Interview.   We have recommended that prospective group members examine the leader somewhat critically before joining a group. This exercise is just like the preceding one, except that the group member asks the questions of the leader, trying to learn things about the leader and the group that will allow a wise decision about whether to join. After 10 minutes the leader shares observations and reactions, and then the member tells whether he or she would join this leader's group and explains any reservations. Again, the class is invited to make observations.

4

Initial Stage of a Group

Focus questions · Introduction · **Helping members get the most from a group experience** · Guidelines for members · Teaching can be overdone · **Group characteristics at the initial stage** · Some early concerns · Initial resistance · Self-focus versus focus on others · Trust versus mistrust · **Identifying and clarifying goals at the initial stage** · Some general goals for group members · Helping members define goals · The contract as a method of setting personal goals · **Group-process concepts at the initial stage** · Group norms · Group cohesion · **Creating trust: Leader and member roles** · The importance of modeling · Attitudes and actions leading to trust · **Leader issues at the initial stage** · The division of responsibility · The degree of structuring · Opening and closing group sessions · **Exercises**

103

1. What are some guidelines you might offer to help members get the most from a group experience?
2. What ways can you think of to assist members in creating trust in the leader and among themselves? What role do you see yourself as having in establishing trust during the initial stages of a group?
3. What are some specific ways to help members identify and clarify their goals for group participation?
4. If you were meeting with your co-leader during the early stage of a new group, what are some topics you'd most want to discuss?
5. What sort of resistance behaviors might you encounter during the first few sessions?
6. What group norms, or standards, would you most want to establish?
7. What are some ways to help a group develop cohesion at the first few meetings?
8. What are a few things you would attend to in opening each group session?
9. What ideas do you have for effectively bringing each session to closure?
10. How much structuring do you think is helpful for a group to accomplish its tasks? To what degree might you assume the responsibility for providing structure in a group you lead or co-lead?

■■

Introduction

This chapter, on the initial stage, contains many examples of teaching members about how groups function. We describe the characteristics of a "young" group, explore the topic of establishing goals early in the life of a group, and discuss the formation of group norms and the beginnings of group cohesion. Also treated are the roles of the leader and members in creating trust, leader skills in opening and closing group meetings, and leader responsibility for providing a structure that will help members attain their goals.

Helping Members Get the Most from a Group Experience

Some behaviors and attitudes facilitate the establishment of a cohesive and productive group—that is, a group in which meaningful self-exploration takes place and in which honest and appropriate feedback is given and received. We begin orientation and member preparation during the preliminary session, but we typically find that time allows only an introduction to ways in which members can get the most from their group experience. Consequently, during the initial phase of the group's evolution we devote some time to teaching members the basics of group process, especially how they can involve themselves as active participants. We emphasize that they will benefit from the experience in direct proportion to how much they invest of themselves, both in the group and in practicing on the outside what they are learning in the sessions.

The following guidelines are not something that we present as a lecture in one sitting. We allocate time to discuss these topics as they occur naturally within the sessions. Because the teaching is an outgrowth of what is going on in the group, the participants are more receptive to learning about how groups function and how they can best participate.

We encourage you to use these guidelines as a catalyst for thinking about your own approach to preparing members. Reflecting on this material may help you develop an approach that suits your own leadership style and your personality and that is appropriate for the groups you lead. Although the following suggestions are written from the leader's point of view, they are directed to the members. Examples are taken from our own groups.

■■ Guidelines for Members

Learn to Help Establish Trust.   Participants often wait for some other person to take the first risk or to make some gesture of trust. Members can enhance their experience in the group by helping to create a trusting climate. They can do this, paradoxically, by revealing their lack of trust. Members can gain from initiating a discussion that will allow genuine trust to develop.

Example: Harold was older than most of the other group members, and he feared they would not be able to empathize with him, that he would be excluded from activities, that he would be viewed as an outsider a parent figure—and that he would not be able to open up. After he daringly disclosed these things, many members gave Harold honest feedback concerning his courage in revealing his mistrust. His disclosure, and the response to it, stimulated trust in the entire group by making it clear that it was OK to express fear. Instead of being rejected, Harold was accepted and appreciated, for he was willing to make a real part of himself known to the rest of the group.

Express Persistent Feelings.   There are times when members keep their feelings of boredom, anger, or disappointment a secret from the rest of the group. It is most important that persistent feelings related to the group process be aired. We often make statements to members such as: "If you are feeling detached and withdrawn, let this be known" or "If you are experiencing chronic negative feelings toward others in this group, don't keep these feelings to yourself."

   Example: In a group of adolescents that met once a week for 10 weeks, Margaret waited until the last session to disclose that she didn't trust either the members or the leader, that she was angry because she felt pressured to participate, that she was scared to express what she felt because she might look foolish, and that she really didn't know what was expected of her as a group member. She had had these feelings since the initial sessions but had withheld them from the group. Had Margaret expressed her feelings earlier, they could have been explored and, possibly, resolved. As it was, she left the group feeling that she had accomplished nothing.

Beware of Misusing Jargon.   It is unfortunate that the group movement offers another way of being phony. Some people learn a new language that can remove them from their experiencing. Take, for example, phrases such as "I can really relate to you," "I want to get closer to my feelings," "I get good vibes from you," "I'd like to stop playing all these games with myself," "Let me be in the present moment," and "I have to be spontaneous." If terms such as *relate to*, *get closer to*, and *vibes* aren't clearly defined and reserved for certain circumstances, the quality of communication will be poor. People who learn to use this vague language may deceive themselves into thinking that they are self-actualized. What a refreshing experience it is to talk with people who have had no group experience and who are able to say in plain English what it is they want and why they decided to get involved in a group.

   We encourage members to use descriptive language by asking them what they mean by "really relating to that" or by asking them to clarify what feelings they want to express. When members speak in very vague terms and use group slogans, we are likely to ask them to imagine that they are talking with a foreigner who has little command of English, or to repeat what they said in terms that a 10-year-old child could understand.

Related to misusing jargon is the way members' use of language sometimes distances them from themselves and from others. For example, when people say "I can't" instead of "I won't," or when they use many qualifiers in their speech ("maybe," "perhaps," "but," "I guess"), we ask them to be aware of how they are contributing to their powerlessness by their choice of words. This practice also applies to the use of a generalized "you" or "people" when "I" is what is meant. The more members can assume responsibility for their speech, the more they can reclaim some of that power they have lost through impersonal modes of expression.

Decide for Yourself How Much to Disclose.   Group members are sometimes led to believe that the more they disclose about themselves, the better. They are asked not to think about the need for privacy. Though self-disclosure is an important tool of group process, it is up to each participant to decide what aspects of his or her life to reveal. This principle cannot be stressed too much in groups, for the idea that one will have to tell everything contributes to the resistance of many people to becoming participants in a group.

The most useful kind of disclosure is unrehearsed. It expresses present concern and may entail some risk. As participants open up to a group, they fear how what they reveal will be received by the other members. Self-disclosure that is appropriate can open doors of self-knowledge and can encourage other members to open up.

Further, as members make themselves known, they provide others with an opportunity to care about them. If certain members decide to keep themselves mysterious, others have little basis for developing a meaningful relationship with them. One way that people grow is by letting others know who they are, in everyday life as well as in a group. Those members who are willing to share their thoughts and feelings are taking active steps toward the building of trust within the group.

However, members should be cautioned of the dangers of "paying membership dues" by striving to drop the biggest secret. Self-disclosure is not a process of "letting everything hang out" and of making oneself psychologically naked. It helps to let members know time and again that they are responsible for deciding what, how much, and when they will share personal conflicts pertaining to their everyday life.

Example: In a weekly group in an agency, Luis, a minority client, did not want to talk about his sexual relationship with his wife. One of the cultural values he grew up with was to keep such personal concerns private. Luis did talk about how difficult it was for him to identify what he felt, let alone express feelings to others. Although he did not feel comfortable in discussing sexuality, he was willing to share with the group his difficulties in letting himself experience feelings of sadness, compassion, jealousy, and fright. Luis did not want to go through life as an unfeeling person. Other group members respected him for his willingness to tell them why he was not ready to talk about his sexual relationship. Because of this understanding that he felt from other members, he was encouraged to share more of his feelings of fear and sadness.

Be an Active Participant, Not an Observer.   A participant might say: "I'm not the talking type. It's hard for me to formulate my thoughts, and I'm afraid that I don't express myself well, so I usually don't say anything in the group. But I listen attentively to others, and I learn by observing. I really don't think I have to be talking all the time to get something out of these sessions." Although it is true that members can learn by observing interactions and reacting nonverbally, their learning will tend to be limited compared with what they could get if they became contributing members. If they assume the stance of not contributing, others will never come to know them, and they can easily feel cheated and angry at being the object of others' observations.

Another way some members keep themselves as passive observers on the fringe of group activity is by continually saying "I have no real problems in my life at this time, so I don't have much to contribute to the group." We attempt to teach these members to share their reactions to their experience in the group as well as to let others know how they are being perceived. Members who choose to share little about events outside of the group can actively participate by keeping themselves open to being affected by others in the group. Leaders can contribute to group cohesion by helping those members who feel they have nothing to contribute recognize that they are depriving fellow members if they do not at least share how they are reacting to what others are saying.

Example: When Thelma was asked what she wanted from the group, she replied: "I haven't really given it that much thought. I figured I'd just be spontaneous and wait to see what happens." As the sessions progressed, Thelma did learn to let the other members know what she wanted from them. Instead of being a passive observer, without any clear goals, who would be content to wait for things to happen to her, she began to take more initiative. She showed that she wanted to talk about how lonely she felt, how desperate and inadequate she frequently felt, how fearful she was of being weak with men, and how she dreaded facing her world every morning. As Thelma learned to focus on her wants, she found that she could benefit from her weekly sessions.

Expect Some Disruption of Your Life.   Participants in therapeutic groups should be given the warning that their involvement may complicate their outside life for a time. As a result of group experiences, members tend to assume that the people in their life will be both ready and willing to make significant changes. It can be shocking for members to discover that others thought they were "just fine" the way they were, and the friction that results may make it more difficult than ever to modify old, familiar patterns. Therefore, it is important for members to be prepared for the fact that not everyone will like or accept some of the changes they want to make. Perhaps some relationships will be discontinued and some new ones formed.

Example: Ron came away from his group with the awareness that he was frightened of his wife, that he consistently refrained from expressing his wants to her, and that he related to her as he would to a protective mother. He feared that, if he asserted himself with her, she would leave. In the group he not only became disgusted with his dependent style but also decided that he would treat his wife as an equal and give up his hope of having her become his mother. Ron's wife did not cooperate with his valiant efforts to change the nature of their relationship. The more assertive Ron became, the more disharmony there was in his home. While he tried to become independent, his wife struggled to keep their relationship the way it was; she was not willing to change.

Realize that You Don't Have to Be Sick to Benefit from a Group.   It is not uncommon to find members questioning the value of the group and being somewhat skeptical about its ability to help them. Some people shy away from involvement in counseling groups because they believe that groups are only for people with severe emotional problems. Members should be taught that a minor "tune-up" is possible without a major overhaul. Groups can offer the opportunity to examine how past decisions influence one's present life. The group can provide the challenge and support necessary for evaluating one's direction.

Example: Sharon was hesitant to involve herself fully in her group, because she accepted the notion that any kind of therapy is for people with serious emotional and mental disorders. Gradually, through the example of fellow group members, she found that struggling for change is not sick but, rather, courageous. She then felt freer to use the group as a place to try out new behavior, and she became open to working with internal blocks that were preventing her from forming close ties with those she cared about.

Expect to Discover Positive Aspects of Yourself.   A common fear about therapy is that one will discover how "rotten," how unlovable, how empty, how hopeless, or how powerless one is. More often than not, though, people in groups begin to realize that they're lovable, that they can control their own destiny, and that they have talents they never knew about. Groups need not be devoted exclusively to the reliving of pain and to intense struggle; they can also be happenings of great joy. For instance, many participants experience an inner strength, discover a real wit and sense of humor, create moving poetry or songs, or dare for the first time to show a creative side of themselves that they have kept hidden from others and from themselves. A group experience, then, can show people a positive, even ecstatic, dimension of themselves.

Example: One member expressed the positive side of the group experience when he said: "I have learned that there are lots of beautiful rose bushes with pretty roses, and on those bushes are thorns. I'd never trade the struggle and pain I had to go through to appreciate the joy of smelling and touching those roses. Both the roses and the thorns are a part of life."

Listen Closely and Discriminatingly.   Group members should listen carefully to what the other members say about them, neither accepting it wholesale nor rejecting it outright. Members should listen discriminatingly, deciding for themselves what does and what doesn't apply to them.

Example: In an adolescent group Jack received feedback that he was seductive and controlling. Members told him that, when the focus was not on him, he would attempt to draw attention to himself. Jack became defensive and angry and denied that he acted that way. He could have been asked by the leader or members to think over the feedback before so rigorously rejecting it.

Pay Attention to Consistent Feedback.   A person may get similar feedback from many people in different groups yet may still dismiss it as invalid. Although it is important to discriminate, it is also important to realize that a message that has been received from a variety of people is likely to have a degree of validity.

Example: In several groups Dan heard people tell him that he looked bored, distant, and detached. The other members felt that Dan was present partially—bodily—but that he was psychologically removed from the group. Each time he heard this, Dan insisted that his behavior in the group was different from his behavior in outside life—that on the outside he felt close to people and was interested and involved. It seems unlikely that someone could be so different in the two areas, however, and he might have done well to pay attention to the fact that so many people were saying the same thing.

Don't Categorize Yourself.   During the initial stage of a group, members often present themselves to the other members in terms of a role, one that they dislike but at the same time appear to cling to. For instance, we've heard people introduce themselves as "the group mother," "a hard-ass," "the fragile person who can't stand confrontation," and "the one in this group whom nobody will like." There are times when a person who views himself or herself as a "hard-ass" would like to be different. What is important is for people not to fatalistically pin labels on themselves and for the group not to fulfill the expectations and thereby even further convince members that they are what they fear. It may be helpful for group leaders to remind themselves and the members of how certain participants can be pegged with labels such as "the monopolist," "the storyteller," "the intellectualizer," "the withdrawn one," "the obsessive/compulsive one," and so on. People may exhibit behaviors that characterize them in one way or another, and it is appropriate to confront them with this during the group. But this confronting can be done without cementing people into rigid molds that become very difficult to shatter.

Example: Roz presented herself to the group as withdrawn and fragile. She made a contract requiring her to speak out and at least act as though she were strong. In this way she was able to put on the shelf an old image she had clung to and to experiment with behavior associated with other images.

Other Suggestions for Group Members.   Some additional guidelines that we bring up early in a group as they seem appropriate are briefly listed below:

· Be willing to do work both before and after a group. Consider keeping a journal as a supplement to the group experience. Create homework assignments as a way of putting in-group learning to practice in everyday living.
· Develop self-evaluation skills as a way of assessing your progress in the group. Examples of questions you might ask are: "Am I contributing to the group? Am I satisfied with what is occurring in the sessions? If not, what am I doing about it? Am I using in my life what I am learning in my group?"
· Spend time in clarifying your own goals by reviewing specific issues you want to explore during the sessions. This can best be done by thinking about specific changes you want to make in your life and by deciding what you are willing to do both in and out of the group to bring about these changes.
· Concentrate on making personal and direct statements to others in your group; avoid giving advice, making interpretations, and asking impersonal questions. Instead of telling others how they are, let them know how they are affecting you.
· Realize that the real work consists of what you actually do outside of your group. Consider the group a means to an end, and give some time to thinking about what you will do with what you are learning. Expect

some setbacks, and be aware that change may be slow and subtle. Do not expect one group alone to renovate your entire life.

■■ Teaching Can Be Overdone

As much as we've been stressing the value of teaching members about how groups function, we want to add that too much emphasis on teaching group process can have a negative influence in several ways. All the spontaneous learning can be taken out of the group experience if members have been told too much of what to expect and have not been allowed to learn for themselves. Moreover, it is possible to foster a dependency on leader structure and leader direction.

Our hope, as the group progresses, is that members will increasingly be able to function with less intervention from the leader. There is a delicate balance between providing too much structuring and failing to give enough structure and information, which results in confusion. Perhaps what is especially important is that the leader be aware of factors such as group cohesion, group norms, and what is occurring within the group at any given point; then the leader can decide whether it would be productive to discuss certain issues.

Group Characteristics at the Initial Stage

■■ Some Early Concerns

During the early stage of a group the central process is orientation and exploration. Members are getting acquainted, learning how the group functions, developing spoken and unspoken norms that will govern group behavior, exploring their fears and hopes pertaining to the group, clarifying their expectations, identifying personal goals, and determining if this group is a safe place. This stage is characterized by members' expressing negative feelings as well as positive ones. The manner in which the leader deals with these feelings determines the degree of trust that can be established in the group.

It is common at the initial sessions to see considerable tentativeness and a lack of clarity concerning what the participants hope to get from a group experience. Members tend to present the aspects of themselves that they think others will accept, for they are concerned about questions such as:

· Will I be accepted or rejected in here?
· Can I really say what I feel, or do I have to couch my words carefully so that others won't be offended?
· How will this group be any different from my interactions in daily situations?

· Am I like other people in here?
· Will I feel pressured and pushed to perform?
· What will these sessions be like?
· What risks will I take in here?

Because most members are uncertain about the norms and expected behavior of the group situation, there are moments of silence and awkwardness. Some may be impatient to "get things moving" and say that they feel like an airplane on the runway ready to take off. If the leader provides little structure, the level of anxiety is likely to be high because of the ambiguity of the situation. In this case there will probably be considerable floundering and requests from members for direction. Members will say: "What are we supposed to be doing in here?" "Why don't we get down to business?" "I really don't know what we should be talking about."

If someone does volunteer a problem for discussion, chances are that members will be oriented toward problem solving. Rather than encouraging the person to fully explore a struggle, some members are likely to offer suggestions and what they consider as helpful advice. Though this may at first appear to some as progress, participants will soon tire of ready-made solutions to every problem posed.

Eventually, negative feelings may surface over a number of situations: some are angry at the lack of direction and being allowed to simply "waste time"; some are growing impatient with those who are quick to tell others what to do; some are bored with social chit-chat; some are resentful that a few are doing "all the talking" while others "say nothing"; and some are hostile over seemingly trivial matters. Regardless of what is triggering any negative feelings, it is crucial that leaders be sensitive to these reactions and encourage members to express them openly. If leaders react defensively or cut off the exploration of negative feelings, then a norm is being established that only positive feelings are acceptable. Trust can be lost or gained by the manner in which the leader handles the initial expression of any negative feelings. A member may be saying something like the following to himself or herself: "I'll take a chance and say what I am thinking, and then I'll see how this leader and others in here respond. If they are willing to listen to what I don't like, perhaps I can trust them with some deeper feelings."

■■ Initial Resistance

During the initial phase of a group the members typically appear rather resistant. In some cases the participants are highly suspicious of the group leader, fearing being manipulated. The participants may doubt that counseling groups can be of any real value in helping them solve their problems. Some clients will not believe that they have the freedom to talk about whatever they want, and they may sit back and wait, almost expecting to be lectured to.

Leaders need to be aware of cultural factors and how they influence one's readiness to participate in a group. Members may be seen as "resistant" when they are only being true to their cultural heritage. Such members may be operating on the value that it is distasteful to talk publicly about private matters such as sexuality, family problems, and religious convictions. A group leader can help such members by being aware of their cultural context and at the same time respectfully challenging them to consider modifying their values enough to allow them to explore personal issues. An important leadership function is assisting members in understanding how some of their initial resistance to self-disclosure relates to their cultural conditioning.

Regardless of the type of group, some initial resistance is to be expected in the early stage, even if people are eager to join. This resistance can be manifested by griping about the place of meeting or focusing on what appear to be inconsequential matters. What members do talk about is likely to be less important than what is kept inside them—their real fears about being in this group at the moment. Because resistance often arises from fearful expectations, putting these fears to rest at the outset will benefit the whole group.

What are some fears that clients typically experience? The following anxieties are not uncommon:

· I'm afraid I'll look stupid.
· What if I find I'm abnormal?
· Will I tell too much about myself?
· Will I be accepted by the group?
· What if I find out what I'm really like?
· What if everyone rejects me?
· I'm afraid I'll be withdrawn and passive.
· I fear being hurt.
· What if the group attacks me?
· I'm afraid of seeing my problems magnified.
· What if I become dependent on the group?
· What if I find out things about myself that I can't cope with?
· Will I physically hurt someone if I'm really open to my feelings?
· What if I go crazy?
· What will my spouse feel/think if I talk about him/her?
· What if I'm asked to do something I don't want to do?
· What if I stutter and shake?

Because we recognize that anxieties exist, we begin by encouraging the members to openly share and explore them. It sometimes helps in the building of a trusting atmosphere to ask people to split up into pairs and then to join pairs and make groups of four. In this way members can choose others with whom to share their expectations, get acquainted, discuss their fears or reservations, and so forth. For some reason, talking with one other person and then merging with others is far less threatening to most participants than talking to the entire group. This subgroup approach seems to be an excellent icebreaker, and when the entire group gets together again, there is generally a greater willingness to interact.

It is vital that participants be allowed to express their concerns and anxieties openly. If encouragement to face these issues is lacking, group process gets bogged down by unspoken agendas (issues that affect the way the group is progressing but are not openly discussed). Time and again, we have observed groups getting stuck because of personal reactions that were concealed. Hidden agendas have a devastating effect on a group; the norm of being closed, cautious, and defensive replaces the norm of being open. If the participants cannot be open about their reactions to the group, including any reservations they may have, it is highly unlikely that they will feel free enough to reveal personal matters pertaining to out-of-group conflicts.

Members are testing the waters at the early sessions to see if their concerns are taken seriously and if this group is a safe place to express what they think and feel. If their reactions, positive or negative, are listened to with respect and acceptance, they have a basis to begin dealing with deeper aspects of themselves. A good place for leaders to start dealing with members' resistance is by listening to members' fears and encouraging full expression of them.

■■ Self-Focus versus Focus on Others

One characteristic we observe in members of most beginning groups is a tendency to talk about others and to focus on people and situations outside of the group setting. At times storytelling participants will deceive themselves into believing that they are really working, when in fact they are resisting speaking about and dealing with their own feelings. They may talk about life situations, but there is a tendency to focus on what other people in their life are doing to cause them difficulties. Skilled group leaders help such members examine their own reactions to others. Leaders do this by teaching participants that they are responsible for their own problems and that they are free to make choices.

During the initial phase of a group the demanding job is to get the group members to focus on themselves. Of course, trust is a prerequisite for this openness about oneself. When members deviate from a self-focus and use a focus on others as a method of resisting deeper exploration of self, leaders should remind them of the value of focusing on themselves. Leaders need to learn to confront members who are using this defense in such a manner that the members will not defensively close themselves off from what the leader or other members are saying. For example, a leader might say: "I'm aware that you are talking a lot about several important people in your life. They are not here, and we won't be able to work with them. But we *are* able to work with your feelings and reactions toward them." An awareness of proper timing is essential; the readiness of a client to accept certain interpretations or observations must be considered. Leaders must be skilled not only in helping people recognize that their focus on others is defensive but also in giving them the courage to work through their resistance.

■■ Trust versus Mistrust

The issue of trust versus mistrust is one of the most basic issues in group process. If a basic sense of trust and security is not established at the outset, serious problems can be predicted. People can be said to be developing trust in one another when they can express their feelings, no matter what they are, without fear of censure; when they are willing to decide for themselves specific goals and personal areas to explore; when they focus on themselves, not on others; and when they are willing to risk disclosing personal aspects of themselves.

In contrast, a lack of trust is indicated by an undercurrent of hostility and suspicion and an unwillingness to talk about these feelings. Other manifestations of lack of trust are participants' taking refuge in being abstract or overly intellectual and being vague about what they expect from the therapeutic group. Before a climate of trust is established, people tend to wait for the leader to decide for them what they need to examine. Any disclosures that are made tend to be superficial and rehearsed, and risk taking is at a low level.

Identifying and Clarifying Goals at the Initial Stage

One of the major tasks of the initial stage is to establish both group goals and individual goals. Examples of general group goals include creating a climate of trust and acceptance within the group, promoting the sharing of oneself in significant ways, and encouraging the taking of risks in the group. It is essential that these group goals (and norms, which we will discuss later) be explicitly stated, understood, and accepted by the members early in the group. Otherwise, considerable conflict and confusion are certain to occur at a later stage. What follows are some general goals that are common to most therapeutic groups and some examples of member goals for specialized groups.

■■ Some General Goals for Group Members

Although the members must decide for themselves the specific goals of a group experience, there are some broad goals:

- to increase self-esteem
- to accept the reality of one's limitations
- to decrease behavior that prevents intimacy
- to learn how to trust oneself and others
- to become freer and less bound by external "shoulds" and "musts"
- to increase self-awareness and thereby increase the possibilities for choice and action
- to learn the distinction between having feelings and acting on them
- to free oneself from the inappropriate early decisions that keep one less than the person one could or would like to be
- to recognize that others struggle too
- to clarify the values one has and to decide whether and how to modify them
- to be able to tolerate more ambiguity—to learn to make choices in a world where nothing is guaranteed
- to find ways of resolving personal problems
- to increase one's capacity to care for others
- to become more open and honest with selected others
- to deal with one another in a direct manner in the here-and-now group situation
- to provide support and challenge for others
- to confront others with care and concern
- to learn how to ask others for what one wants
- to become sensitive to the needs and feelings of others
- to provide others with useful feedback

The above goals are only general ones, and they must be narrowed down to apply to what each member expects to gain from group participation. What follows are a few examples of member goals for specialized groups:

- **Goals for an incest group:** to assist people in talking about incidences of incest; to discover common feelings of anger, hurt, shame, and guilt; to work through unfinished business with the perpetrator.
- **Goals for disabled people:** to express anger, grief, and resentment about the disability; to learn to deal with the reduced privacy caused by the disability; to learn to work with the limitations imposed by the handicap; to establish a support system.
- **Goals for a substance-abuse group:** to help the abuser confront difficult issues and learn to cope with life stresses more effectively; to provide a supportive network; to learn more appropriate social skills.

· **Goals for elderly people:** to review life experiences; to express feelings over losses; to improve members' self-image; to continue finding meaning in life.
· **Goals for acting-out children:** to accept feelings and at the same time learn ways of constructively expressing them and dealing with them; to develop skills in making friends; to channel impulses into constructive behavior.

Regardless of the type of therapeutic group, it is important to consider some methods of assisting participants in developing concrete goals that will give them direction.

■■ Helping Members Define Personal Goals

Participants are typically able to state only in broad terms what they expect to get from a group. For instance, Carol, who says that she'd like to "relate to others better," needs to specify with whom and under what conditions she encounters difficulties in her interpersonal relationships. She also needs to learn to state concretely what part of her behavior she needs to change. The leader's questions should help her become more concrete. With whom is she having difficulties? If the answer is her parents, then what specifically causes her problems with them? How is she affected by this? How does she want to be different with them? With all this information the leader has a clearer idea of how to proceed with this participant.

It should be mentioned that defining goals is an ongoing process, not something that is done once and for all. As members gain more experience, they are in a better position to know what they want from a group, and they also come to recognize additional goals that can guide their participation. Their involvement in the work of other members can act as a catalyst in getting them to think about ways in which they can profit from the group experience. Once members have a general idea of what they want to get from being a group member, establishing a contract is one excellent way for them to be more precise in their personal goals.

■■ The Contract as a Method of Setting Personal Goals

We believe that the contract is a very useful device for helping people achieve their personal goals in a group. Basically, a contract is a statement by the group member of what he or she is willing to do, both during group sessions and outside of them. The purpose of the contract is to specify what problems the member wants to explore and what behaviors he or she is willing to change. It is a way of encouraging the member to think about the group and about his or her role in it. In the contract method the group member assumes an active and responsible stance. Of course, contracts can be open-ended; that is, they can be modified or replaced as appropriate. Contracts can be used in most of the types of group discussed in this book.

Contracts and homework assignments can be combined fruitfully. In Carol's case a beginning contract could commit her to observe and write down each time she experiences difficulties with her parents. If Carol discovers that she usually walks away at times of conflict with them, she might pledge in a follow-up contract to stay in one of these situations rather than avoiding it.

As another example, consider a woman in an assertiveness-training group who decides that she would like to spend more time on activities that interest her. She might make a contract that calls for her to do more of the things she would like to do for herself, and she might assign herself certain activities to be carried out during the week as experiments. At the next group session she would report the results. Partly on the basis of these results, she could decide how much and in what ways she really wants to change. Then she could do further work in the group toward her chosen ends.

Group-Process Concepts at the Initial Stage

Group process, as we have said, involves stages groups tend to go through, each characterized by certain feelings and behaviors. Initially, as the members get to know one another, there is a feeling of anxiety. Each waits for someone else to begin the work. Tension, hostility, or even boredom build up. Someone may attack the leader or another member. Then, if things go well, the members learn to trust one another and the leader and begin to openly express feelings, thoughts, and reactions. These are the types of element that constitute the group process. Included under the rubric *group process* are activities such as establishing norms and group cohesion, learning to work cooperatively, establishing ways of solving problems, and learning to express conflict openly. We'll now discuss in depth two of these group-process concepts—group norms and group cohesion—that are especially important during the initial stage. *Group norms* are the shared beliefs about expected behaviors that are aimed at making groups function effectively. *Group cohesion* is a sense of togetherness, or community, within a group. A cohesive group is one in which there are incentives for remaining in the group and a feeling of belongingness and relatedness among the members.

▪▪ Group Norms

Norms and procedures that will help the group attain its goals can be developed during the early stage. If the norms—standards that govern behavior in the group—are vague, then valuable time will be lost, and tensions will arise over what is appropriate and inappropriate. It needs to be mentioned, however, that there are implicit (or unspoken) norms as well as those that are explicitly stated.

Implicit norms may develop because of preconceived ideas about what takes place in a group. Members may assume, for example, that groups are places where everything must be said, with no room for privacy. Unless the leader calls attention to the possibility that members can be self-disclosing and still retain a measure of privacy, members might misinterpret the norm of openness and honesty as a policy of complete openness, with no secrets.

Implicit norms may also develop because of leader modeling. If a leader curses and uses abrasive language, members are more likely to adopt this pattern of speech in their group interactions, even though the leader has never expressly encouraged people to talk in such a manner.

Another example of an implicit norm pertains to changes in members' everyday life. If an unassertive member reports that he is being perceived as more assertive at work, he might receive applause from the group. Even though behavior change outside of the group is not specifically stated as a norm, this implicit norm can have a powerful effect on shaping the members' responses and behaviors. Implicit norms do affect the group. They are less likely to have an adverse influence if they are made explicit.

The following norms are examples of standards of behavior that are common in many groups; we usually attempt to foster them in the groups we lead:

1. Members are expected to attend regularly and show up on time. When members attend sessions only sporadically, the entire group suffers. Members who regularly attend will resent the lack of commitment of those who miss sessions.

2. Members are encouraged to be personal and share meaningful aspects of themselves—to talk about themselves, communicate directly with others in the group, and in general become active participants.

3. A usual norm is that members give feedback to one another. Members can evaluate the effects of their behavior on others only if others are willing to state how they are affected. It is important for members not to withhold their perceptions and reactions but rather to let others know what they perceive.

4. One norm is focusing on feelings and expressing them, rather than talking about problems in a detached and intellectual manner.

5. A common norm is to focus on here-and-now interactions within the group. *Immediacy* refers to being genuine in one's relationships; as this relates to groups, there is an emphasis on expressing and exploring conflicts within the group. Immediacy is called for when there are unverbalized thoughts and feelings about what is happening in a session, particularly if these reactions are having a detrimental effect on group process in any way. There is little need to dwell in the group on the details of how members behave in various social situations, because this becomes apparent in the here and now of group interaction. Thus, one of the leader's tasks is to ask questions such as: "How is it for you to be in this group now? With whom do you identify the most in here? What are some of the things that you might be rehearsing to yourself silently? Whom in this room are you most aware of?" The leader can also steer members into the here and now by asking them to reveal what they think and feel about what is going on in the group.

6. Many groups operate on the norm that members will bring into the group personal problems and concerns they are willing to discuss. Members can be expected to spend some time before the sessions thinking about the out-of-group matters that they want to work on during group time. This is an area in which unspoken norms frequently function. For example, in some groups the participants might get the idea that they are not good group members unless they bring personal issues from everyday life to work on during the sessions. Members might get the impression that it is not acceptable to focus on here-and-now matters within the group itself and that they should be willing to work on other problems.

7. Providing therapeutic support is another norm of groups. Ideally, this support facilitates both an individual's work and group process as well, rather than distracting members from self-exploration. But some leaders can implicitly "teach" being overly supportive or by their modeling can demonstrate a type of support that has the effect of short-circuiting painful experiences that a member is attempting to work through. Leaders who are uncomfortable with intense emotions (such as anger or the pain associated with past memories) can actually collude with members by fostering a pseudosupportive climate that prevents members from fully experiencing and expressing intense feelings of any kind. Some groups are so supportive that challenge and confrontation are ruled out. An unverbalized norm in this area is the focus on positive feelings and expressing only favorable reactions; members can get the idea that it is not acceptable to express any criticism, even if it is constructive.

8. The other side of the norm of support is providing members with challenges to look at themselves. Confrontation is the process that involves expressing in a direct and caring manner a challenge for a member (or a leader) to look at some discrepancy between what he or she is

saying and doing. Members need to learn how to confront in such a way that others are most able to listen nondefensively. For example, early in our groups we establish a norm that it is not acceptable to dismiss another in a hostile and labeling way, such as saying "You're an idiot!" Instead, we teach members to directly and cleanly express the anger they are feeling, avoiding name calling. Members are asked to express the source of their anger, including what led up to their feelings. In contrast, some leaders model harsh confrontations, and members soon pick up the unexpressed norm that the appropriate way to relate to others in this group is with attacks. Some groups even specialize in confrontation, on the assumption that the only way people change is by having their defenses stripped away through unrelenting verbal attacks.

9. Groups can operate by either a norm of exploring personal problems or a norm of problem solving. For example, in some groups as soon as members bring up situations that they'd like to understand better, they are bombarded by suggestions on how they can "solve" these problems. The fact of the matter is that in many of these instances solutions are not possible, and what members most need is an opportunity to talk about what they are feeling.

10. Members can be taught the norm of listening without thinking of a quick rebuttal and without becoming overly defensive. Although we don't expect people to merely accept all the feedback they receive, we do ask them to really hear what others say to them and to seriously consider these messages—particularly those messages that are repeated consistently.

The above are merely a few examples of norms. The important point is that the group's norms be discussed as the group unfolds and develops. Many groups become bogged down because members are unsure of what is expected of them. For instance, a member may want to intervene and share her perceptions while a leader is working with an individual in the group, but she may be inhibited because she is not sure whether she should interrupt the group leader at work. Another member may feel an inclination to support a fellow group member at the time when that member is experiencing some pain or sadness but may refrain because he is uncertain whether his support will detract from the other's experience. Another member who is bored, session after session, might keep this feeling to herself because she is not sure of the appropriateness of revealing it. Perhaps if she were told that it is permissible to experience, and valuable to express, boredom, she might be more open with her group and, consequently, less bored.

If group norms are clearly presented and if the members see the value of them and cooperatively decide on some of them, then these norms will be potent forces in the shaping of the group.

∎∎ Group Cohesion

During the early stage of a group the members do not know one another well enough for a true sense of community to be formed. There is an awkwardness and a period of becoming acquainted. Though the participants talk about themselves, it is likely that they are presenting more of their public self rather than deeper aspects of their private self. Genuine cohesion typically comes after groups have struggled with conflict, have shared pain, and have committed themselves to taking significant risks, which are some of the characteristics of the working stage. But the foundations of cohesion can begin to take shape at the initial stage.

Some indicators of this initial degree of cohesion are cooperation among members; a willingness to show up for the meetings and be punctual; an effort to make the group a safe place, including talking about any feelings of lack of trust or fears of trusting; support and caring, as evidenced by being willing to listen to others and accept them for who they are; and a willingness to express reactions to and perceptions of others in the here-and-now context of the group interactions. Real cohesion is not a fixed condition arrived at automatically; rather, it is an ongoing process of solidarity that members earn. Group cohesion can be developed, maintained, and increased in a number of ways, some of which are described below.

1. Trust must be developed during the early stage of a group. One of the best ways of building trust is to create a group climate characterized by respect for the opinions and feelings of the members. It is essential that members openly express their feelings concerning the degree of trust they experience in their group. An opportunity can be provided at the outset for members to share their reservations, and this open sharing of concerns will pave the way for productive work. (The creating of trust will be discussed in detail in the next section.)

2. If group members share meaningful aspects of themselves, they both learn to take risks and increase group cohesiveness. By modeling— for instance, by sharing their own reactions to what is occurring within the group—group leaders can encourage risk-taking behavior. When group members do take risks, they can be reinforced with sincere recognition and support, which will increase their sense of closeness to the others.

3. Group goals and individual goals can be jointly determined by the group members and the leader. If a group is without clearly stated goals, animosity can build up that will tend to lead to the fragmentation of the group.

4. Cohesion can be increased by inviting (but not forcing) all members to become active participants. Members who appear to be passive or withdrawn can be invited to express their feelings toward the group.

These members may be silent observers for a number of reasons, and these reasons ought to be examined openly in the group.

5. Cohesion can be both established and increased by the sharing of the leadership role by all members of the group. In autocratic groups all the decisions are made by the leader. A cooperative type of group is more likely to develop when members are encouraged to initiate discussion of issues they want to explore. Also, instead of fostering a leader-to-member style of interaction, group leaders can foster member-to-member interactions. This can be done by inviting the members to respond to one another, by encouraging feedback and sharing, and by searching for ways to involve as many members as possible in group interactions.

6. Conflict is inevitable in groups. It is desirable for group members to recognize sources of conflict and to deal openly with it when it arises. A group can be strengthened by acceptance of conflict and by the honest working through of differences.

7. Group attractiveness and cohesion are related; it is generally accepted that the greater the degree of attractiveness of a group to its members, the greater the level of cohesion. Thus, ways of increasing the attractiveness of the group are important. If the group deals with matters that interest the members, if the members feel that they are respected, and if the atmosphere is supportive, the chances are good that the group will be perceived as attractive.

8. Members can be encouraged to disclose their ideas, feelings, and reactions to what occurs within their group. The expression of both positive and negative reactions should be encouraged. If this is done, an honest exchange can take place, which is essential if a sense of group belongingness is to develop.

Creating Trust: Leader and Member Roles

■■ The Importance of Modeling

We've alluded to the establishment of trust as a central task for the initial stage of a group. It is not possible to overemphasize the significance of the leader's modeling and the attitudes expressed through the leader's behavior in these early sessions. In thinking about your role as a leader, you might ask yourself questions such as these: Do you feel energetic and enthusiastic as you approach your group? Do you trust yourself in your leadership, and are you able to inspire confidence? To what degree do you trust the group members to work effectively with one another? Are you able to be psychologically present in the group sessions, and are you willing to be open about your own reactions to what is going on in the group?

It is our opinion that your success in creating a climate of trust in the groups you lead has much to do with how well you've prepared both yourself and the members for the group. If you've given careful thought to why you are organizing the group, what you hope to accomplish, and how you'll go about meeting your objectives, the chances are greatly increased that you'll inspire trust and confidence in the members. They will see your willingness to think about the group as a sign that you care about them. Furthermore, if you've done a good job with the pregroup issues (such as informing members of their rights and responsibilities, giving some time to teaching group process, and preparing the members for a successful experience), this shows the members that you are taking your work as leader seriously and that you are interested in their welfare. Such attention can go a long way toward the establishment of trust.

The person who you are, and especially the attitudes about group work and people that you demonstrate by the way you behave in the sessions, may be the most crucial factor in building a trusting community. You teach most effectively through your example. If you trust in the group process and have faith in the members' capacity to make significant changes in themselves, they are likely to see value in this group as a pathway toward personal growth. If you listen nondefensively and respectfully and are able to convey that you value members' subjective experience, they are likely to see the power in active listening. If you are genuinely willing to engage in appropriate self-disclosure, you will foster honesty and disclosure among the members. If you are truly able to accept others for who they are and avoid imposing your values on them, your members learn valuable lessons about accepting people's right to differ and to be themselves. In short, what you model through what you do in the group is one of the most potent ways to teach members how to relate to one another constructively.

If you are co-leading a group, you and your co-leader have ample opportunities to model a behavioral style that will promote trust. For example, if the two of you function harmoniously with a spontaneous give and take between you, members will feel more trusting in your presence. If your relationship with your co-leader is characterized by respect, authenticity, sensitivity, and directness, the members are learning about the value of such attitudes and behaviors. Furthermore, the way in which you and your co-leader interact with the members contributes to or detracts from the level of trust. For example, if one co-leader's typical manner of speaking with members is sharp, short, critical, and sarcastic, the members will quickly pick up this leader's lack of respect for them and tend to become closed or resistant. Therefore, it is wise for co-leaders to examine each other's style of interacting.

It is a mistake to assume that as a leader or a co-leader you have sole responsibility for the development and maintenance of trust. The level of trust is engendered by your attitudes and actions, yet it also depends to a large degree on the level of investment of the members. If they want very little for themselves, if they are unwilling to share enough of themselves so that they can be known, if they simply wait passively for you to "make trust happen," and if they are unwilling to take risks in the sessions, then trust will be slow to develop. In the last analysis, however, the tone set by your leadership will influence their willingness to disclose themselves and to take those steps necessary to establish trust.

■■ Attitudes and Actions Leading to Trust

We value Carl Rogers' emphasis on the "facilitative dimensions of the therapeutic relationship," and we see certain attitudes and actions as either enhancing or inhibiting the level of trust in a group. We present now some of the dimensions that lead to the establishment of trust.

Attending and Listening.   Careful attending to the verbal and nonverbal messages of others is necessary for trust to occur. If genuine listening and understanding are absent, there is no basis for connection between members. If members feel that they are heard and deeply understood, they are likely to trust that others care about them.

There are numerous ways in which both leaders and members demonstrate a lack of attending, including not focusing on the speaker but thinking of what to say next; asking many closed questions that have the effect of probing for information; doing too much talking and not enough listening; giving advice readily instead of encouraging the speaker to explore a struggle; paying attention only to what people say explicitly and thus missing what they express nonverbally; and engaging in selective listening (hearing only what one wants to hear).

We don't think that most group members naturally possess listening skills, nor do they have the skills necessary for responding effectively to what they perceive. Therefore, teaching basic listening and responding skills is a part of the trust process. Pay attention to whether members feel they are being listened to with understanding. If they don't feel that they are, why should they speak about matters that are deeply personal? Why should they reveal themselves to those who do not care?

Empathy.   Empathy is the ability to tune into what others are subjectively experiencing and to understand their world through their eyes. When people experience this understanding without critical judgment, they are more likely to reveal their real concerns, for they believe that others understand and accept them as they are. This kind of nonjudgmental understanding is vitally related to trust.

Leaders can help members develop greater empathy by pointing out behaviors that block this understanding, such as responding to others with pat statements, not responding to others at all, questioning inappropriately, telling others how they should be or should feel, responding with critical judgment, and being defensive.

Empathy is an avenue of demonstrating support. For example, Judy benefits when others are able to understand her. If she talks about going through an extremely painful divorce, Clyde can let her know the ways in which he identifies with and understands her pain. Though their circumstances are different, he empathizes with her pain and is willing to share with her his feelings of rejection and abandonment when his wife left him. What helps Judy is Clyde's willingness to tell her about his struggles rather than providing her with quick answers. Instead of giving her ready-made solutions or offering her reassurance, he helps her most by sharing his life with her.

Genuineness and Self-Disclosure.   Genuineness implies a congruence between a person's inner experience and what he or she projects externally. Applied to your role as a leader, genuineness means that you don't pretend to be accepting when internally you are critical, you don't give out fake responses, you don't rely on behaviors that you think will surely win approval, and you avoid hiding behind a professional role of leader. Through your own authenticity, you offer a model to members that inspires them to be real in their interactions.

Related to being real is the matter of self-disclosure. As a leader you can invite members to make themselves known by letting others in the group know you. As we have pointed out before, this does not have to entail an indiscriminate sharing of your private life with the participants. You can reveal your thoughts and feelings that are related to what is going on within the group. If you are authentic and appropriately self-disclosing and if you avoid hiding behind defenses, there is an encouragement for the rest of the group to be open about their concerns.

Respect.   Respect is shown by what the leader and the members actually do, not simply by what is said. Attitudes and actions that demonstrate respect include avoiding critical judgments, avoiding reducing people to a mere label, looking beyond self-imposed or other-imposed labels, expressing warmth and support that is honestly felt, being genuine and risking being oneself, and recognizing the rights of others to be different from you. If people receive this type of respect, they are supported in their attempts to talk about themselves in open and meaningful ways.

Nancy may express her fear of being judged by others and talk about how she is reluctant to speak because of this fear of criticism. Members are not offering her respect when they too quickly reassure her that they like her just as she is and that they would not judge her. It would be more helpful to encourage Nancy to explore her fear of being judged, both in past situations and in the group situation. It is important to let

Nancy's feelings stand and to work with them, rather than discounting them.

Confrontation.   A crucial factor in the development of trust is the way confrontations are handled in the sessions. Confrontation can be an act of caring that takes the form of an invitation for members to examine some discrepancy between what they are saying and what they are doing or between what they say and some nonverbal cues they manifest. If confrontations are made in an abrasive and "hit-and-run" fashion and if the leader allows people to be verbally abusive, trust is greatly inhibited. Leaders can teach members directness coupled with sensitivity, which results in their seeing that confrontation can be handled in a caring yet honest manner. Challenging members is just as important as supporting them, for a timely challenge can inspire them to look at aspects of themselves that they have been avoiding. Whereas hostile attacks have the result of closing people up by making them defensive, caring confrontations can actually increase the trust in a group. Members learn that they can express even negative feelings in a way that respects those they are confronting.

An example of a caring confrontation follows. Claire is very willing to speak on everything and constantly brings herself in on others' work. An ineffective confrontation is "I want you to be quiet and let others in here talk." An effective confrontation is: "Claire, I appreciate your willingness to participate and talk about yourself. However, I'm concerned that I have heard very little from several others in the group, and I want to hear from them, too." The leader might also ask others in the group why they are so willing to let Claire do most of the talking.

Trust as an Ongoing Issue.   The attitudes and behaviors described above have an important bearing on the level of trust that is established within a group. Although trust is the major task to be accomplished at the initial stage of a group's development, it is a mistake to assume that, once trust has been established, it is taken care of for the duration of that group. We want to emphasize that trust ebbs and flows, and new levels of trust must be established as the group progresses toward a deeper level of intimacy. A basic sense of trust and safety is essential for the movement of a group beyond the initial stage, but this trust will be tested time and again and take on new facets in later stages.

Leader Issues at the Initial Stage

Early in the history of a group it is especially important to think about the balance of responsibility between members and the leader (or co-leaders) as well as the degree of structuring that is optimal for the group. Related to structuring is the way you choose to open and close group sessions. If you are working with a co-leader, discussing these issues is essential. Divergent views are bound to have a negative impact on the group.

For example, if you assume the majority of the responsibility for keeping the group moving and your co-leader assumes almost no responsibility, on the ground that the members must decide for themselves what to do with group time, then the members will sense this division and are bound to be confused by it. Similarly, if you function best with a high degree of structure in groups and your co-leader believes that any structuring should come from the members, this difference of opinion might have a detrimental effect on the group.

For these reasons, it is wise to select a co-leader who has a philosophy of leadership that is compatible with yours, though this does not mean that both of you need to have the same style of leading. You can have differences that complement each other; it is when these differences lead to fragmenting the group that problems occur.

■■ The Division of Responsibility

A basic issue that leaders must consider is responsibility for the direction and outcome of the group. If a group proves to be nonproductive, is this due to a lack of leader skill, or does the responsibility rest with the group members?

One way of conceptualizing the issue of responsibility is to think of it in terms of a continuum. At one end is the leader who assumes a great share of the responsibility for the direction and outcomes of the group. Such leaders tend to have the outlook that, unless they are highly directive, the group will flounder. They tend to see their role as that of the expert, and they actively intervene to keep the group moving in ways they deem productive. A disadvantage of this form of leadership is that it robs the members of the responsibility that is rightfully theirs; if members are perceived by the leader as not having the capacity to take care of themselves, they soon begin to live up to this expectation by being irresponsible, at least in the group.

Leaders who assume an inordinate degree of responsibility not only undermine members' independence but also burden themselves. If people leave unchanged, such leaders see it as their fault. If members remain separate, never forming a cohesive unit, these leaders view this as a reflection of their lack of skill. If the group is disappointed, they feel disappointed and tend to blame themselves, believing that they didn't do enough to create a dynamic group. This style of leadership is draining, and leaders who use it may eventually lose the energy required to lead groups.

At the other end of the responsibility continuum is the leader who proclaims: "I am responsible for me, and you are responsible for you. If you want to leave this group with anything of value, it is strictly up to you. I can't do anything for you—make you feel something or take away any of your defenses—unless you allow me to." This type of leadership frequently characterizes leaders of some personal-growth groups. It is not our preferred style. When people are together for a period of time in an intensive group, they need some protection, and we feel that it is irresponsible for the leader not to provide it.

Ideally, each leader will discover a balance whereby he or she accepts a rightful share of the responsibility but does not usurp the members' responsibility. This issue is central, because a leader's approach to other issues (such as structuring and self-disclosure) hinges on his or her approach to the responsibility issue. The leader's personality is involved in the determination of the amount of responsibility he or she will assume and what, specifically, this responsibility will include.

■■ The Degree of Structuring

The proper question is not *whether* a group leader should provide structure but, rather, *what degree* of structure. Like responsibility, structuring exists on a continuum. The leader's theoretical orientation, the type of group, and the membership population are some of the factors that determine the amount and type of structuring employed.

Balance at the Initial Stage.   Providing therapeutic structuring is particularly important during the initial stage of a group, when members are typically confused about what behavior is expected in the group and are therefore anxious. Structure can be both useful and inhibiting in a group's development. Too little structure results in members' becoming unduly anxious, and although some anxiety is productive, too much can inhibit spontaneity.

Although leaders may be particularly active during the early phase of a group, it is important that they encourage members to assume an increasing role. Too much structuring and direction can foster leader-dependent attitudes and behavior. The members may wait for the leader to "make something happen" instead of acting themselves.

Yalom (1983) sees the basic task of the group leader as providing enough structure to give a general direction to the members yet avoiding the pitfalls of fostering dependency. His message for leaders is to structure the group in a fashion that facilitates each member's autonomous functioning. An example of fostering dependency on the leader would be encouraging members to speak only when they are invited to do so by the leader. By contrast, the leader can encourage members to bring themselves into the interactions without being called on.

We do not subscribe to a passive style of group leadership, for we do not simply wait and let the group take any direction it happens to go in.

By providing some structure we give group members the opportunity to experiment with new levels of awareness and to build new forms of behavior from this awareness. During the initial stage our structure is aimed at helping members identify and express their fears, expectations, and personal goals. For example, we often use dyads, go-arounds, and structured questions as ways of making it easier for members to talk to one another about current issues in their life. After talking to several people on a one-to-one basis, as you have seen, members find it easier to talk openly in the entire group. The rationale underlying the leadership activity that we provide is to help members focus on themselves and the issues they most want to explore in the group.

Research on Structuring.   Research indicates the value of an initial structure that builds supportive group norms and highlights positive member interactions. This therapeutic structure must be carefully monitored throughout the life of a group, rather than limiting the evaluation process to the final stage. Structuring that offers a coherent framework for understanding the experiences of individuals and the group process will be of the most value. When goals are clear, when appropriate member behaviors are identified, and when the process is structured to provide a framework for change, then members tend to engage in therapeutic work more quickly (Dies, 1983b). In agreement with the findings of Dies, another summary of the research indicates that leader direction during the early phases of a group tends to facilitate the development of cohesion and the willingness of members to engage in risk taking by making themselves known to others and by giving others feedback (Stockton & Morran, 1982).

Bednar, Melnick, and Kaul (1974) developed a group model that shows the value of some type of structure for group process and outcome. In their formulation, as the cohesion increases, members gradually begin to feel safer in sharing themselves in meaningful ways, in giving feedback, and in providing support and challenge to others. Their general model specifies the following sequence: initial ambiguity and anxiety, increased structure through specific instructions, increased risk taking, increased group cohesion, and increased personal responsibility.

Research-Based Guidelines for Leaders.   There are some guidelines for providing therapeutic structure in your groups; they underscore many of the major points that we have developed in this and the previous chapter. What follows is an adaptation of some of the conclusions of research on short-term groups, as summarized by Dies (1983b):

· Be aware that direct instruction, or teaching, tends to facilitate a group's development during the early stages.

· Introduce an initial structure to build supportive group norms and foster the establishment of trust.
· Once the basic norms are established and the therapeutic potential of the group is developed, the degree of structure can be lessened. Less-directive structure is appropriate during the later stages as the group members assume increased direction of their group.
· Use more structured interventions with clients whose level of personal functioning restricts their capacity to interact in socially competent ways.
· Employ active leadership, yet at the same time use interventions that encourage members to assume increased responsibility.
· Develop and maintain a task-oriented focus by helping members develop and stick to clear goals.
· Help members understand the value of disclosing themselves, of providing feedback to one another, and of providing a balance between support and confrontation, by giving them a clear rationale for such group behaviors.
· Acknowledge what members do by providing positive reinforcement. Make statements more often than asking questions of members. Provide concrete feedback that describes specific behavioral characteristics, and teach members to do the same.
· Model directness by speaking *to* members instead of talking *about* them.
· Structure initial sessions in a way that will help members acquire a clear framework for understanding experiences that occur within the group.
· Use interpretations that help members generalize from how they behave in the here and now of the group situation to their problems in everyday living. Discuss with members the value of experimenting outside of the group with new interpersonal behaviors.

In summary, some degree of structuring exists in all groups. It is not possible to have an "unstructured" group, for even this is a form of structure. The art is to provide structuring that is not so tight that it robs the group members of the responsibility for finding their own structure.

▪▪ Opening and Closing Group Sessions

An important aspect of structuring involves the procedures leaders use in opening and closing group sessions. Such skills are very important throughout the group process; we discuss them here because we believe you must be aware of this essential aspect of group leadership from the very beginning. We suggest that you refer back to this discussion as you read about subsequent stages.

Guidelines for Opening Sessions.   We have observed that many leader trainees do not pay attention to how they open group sessions. Such leaders are all too ready to focus on the first person who speaks, staying with this person for an undue time because at least someone is speaking. There is often no attempt to link the coming session with the last session, and there is no checking with each member to determine how the members want to use the time for this particular session. If a session simply begins abruptly, it may be difficult to involve many of the members in productive work for that session.

We've emphasized in our workshops the value of learning the skills necessary for introducing each session in an effective way. For groups that meet on a regular basis, such as each week, we suggest some of the following procedures to open each session:

1. Members can be given at least a brief opportunity to share what they did in the way of practice outside of the group since the last session. This also encourages them to do some thinking and practicing outside of the sessions in a variety of situations.

2. We find it useful to have each member briefly state what he or she wants from the upcoming session. A quick go-around is all that is needed for the members to identify and declare issues they are interested in pursuing; in this way an agenda can be developed that is based on some common concerns. If several members say that they are having difficulties in talking with their spouse, for example, the leader can then bring members together in working on communication problems.

3. In many groups the participants will be asked to think of homework assignments as a way of applying to daily life what they are learning in the group. Some may want to talk about problems they are experiencing in translating their learning from group into everyday situations. This can then be the basis for work that will take place in that session of the group.

4. The participants may have unresolved feelings about the previous session, or they may have given thought to that session during the week. If members do have unresolved feelings about a prior session and don't mention this, chances are that hidden agendas will develop and block effective work. Therefore, it's a good practice to give members an opportunity to bring up for discussion some earlier session.

5. The leader might also have afterthoughts about the previous session. You could begin some sessions by letting the group know what you were thinking during the week about how the group is progressing. This is especially appropriate when you are seeing certain problems emerging or if you think that the group is getting stuck. Your self-disclosure can lead the way for members to be open with their reactions to what is or is not going on in the sessions.

   Although we don't want to suggest that you memorize certain lines to
open a session, we'd like to suggest some comments that convey the
spirit of what we see as important material for leading into a session.
Consider some of these lines, and let them serve as catalysts that can be
a part of your own leadership style. At different times we've opened a
session with remarks such as:

· How is each of you feeling about being here today?
· Before we begin today's session, I'd like to ask each of you to take a few
  minutes to silently review your week and think about anything you
  want to tell us.
· Did anyone have any afterthoughts about last week's session?
· As a way of beginning tonight, let's have a brief go-around and have
  each of you say what you'd most like to be able to say by the end of this
  session.
· Could each of you briefly complete this sentence: "Today I'd like to get
  actively involved by . . ."
· What were you thinking and feeling before coming to the group?
· Whom are you most aware of in this room right now, and why?

Guidelines for Closing Sessions.   Just as important as opening a session is the way you bring a meeting to closure. Too often a leader will
simply announce that "time is up for today," with no attempt to summarize and integrate and with no encouragement for members to practice certain skills. Some time, if even only 10 minutes, should be set
aside to give participants an opportunity to reflect on what they liked or
did not like about the session, to mention what they hope to do outside
of the group during the week, to express how they feel about what they
did or did not do, and so forth. Attention to closing ensures that consolidation of learning will take place.
   For groups that meet weekly, it is important to summarize at the
close of each session what occurred in that session. At times, it is useful
for the leader to stop the group halfway through the session and say: "I
notice that we have about an hour left today, and I'd like to check out
how each of you feels about what you've done so far today. Have you
been as involved as you want to be? Are there some issues you'd like to
explore before this session ends?" This does not need to be done routinely, but sometimes such an assessment during the session can help
the members focus their attention on problem areas, especially if the
leader senses that the members are not doing and saying what they
need to do or say.
   In closing a weekly group session, consider the following guidelines.

   1. It is good for clients to leave a session with some unanswered
questions. We think it's a mistake to try to ensure that everyone leaves
feeling comfortable. If clients leave feeling that everything is nicely

closed, they will probably spend very little time during the week reflecting on matters raised in the group.

2. Some statement from the members concerning their level of investment of energy is useful. If clients report boredom weekly, they can be asked what they're willing to do to relieve their boredom.

3. Members can be asked to tell the group briefly what they're learning about themselves through their relationships with other members of the group. The participants can briefly indicate some ways in which they've changed their behavior in response to these insights. If participants find that they would like to change their behavior even more, they can discuss with the leader contracts and homework assignments they can do before the next session.

4. Members can be asked whether there are any topics, questions, or problems they would like to explore in the next session. This creates a link between one session and the next. By prompting the members to think about the upcoming session, it also indirectly encourages them to stick to their contracts during the week.

5. Members can be asked to give one another feedback. Especially helpful is positive feedback concerning what is actually observed. For instance, if Hal's voice is a lot more secure, others may want to let him know that they perceive this change. Of course, feedback on what members are doing to block their strengths is also very helpful.

As we did for opening sessions, we present the following comments for you to consider in closing a session:

· What was it like for you to be in this group tonight?
· What would each of you be willing to do outside of the group this week to practice some of the new skills you are acquiring?
· I'd like a quick go-around to have everyone say a few words on how this group is progressing so far and make any suggestions for change.
· Before we close tonight, I'd like to share with you some of my reactions and observations of this session.

By developing skills in opening and closing sessions, you increase the possibility of continuity from meeting to meeting. Such continuity can lead to translating insights and new behaviors from the group into daily life and, along with encouragement and direction from your leadership, can facilitate the participants' ongoing assessment of their level of investment for each session.

If you work with a co-leader, the matter of how the sessions are opened and closed should be a topic for discussion. A few questions for exploration are: Who typically opens the sessions? Do the two of you agree on when and how to bring a session to closure? With 5 minutes left in the session, does one leader want to continue working, whereas the other wants to attempt some summary of the meeting? Do both of you pay attention to unfinished business that might be left hanging toward the ending of a session? Although we are not suggesting a mechanical division of time and functions in beginning and ending sessions, we do think it is worth noting who tends to assume this responsibility. If one leader typically opens the session, members may be likely to direct their talk to this person. In our groups, one of us may open the session, while the other elaborates and makes additional remarks. In this way spontaneous give-and-take between co-leaders can replace an approach characterized by "Now it's your turn to make a remark."

Exercises

1. Initial-Session Exercise.   For this exercise, ten students volunteer to play group members at an initial group session, and two people volunteer to play co-leaders. We suggest that the co-leaders begin by giving a brief orientation explaining the group's purpose, the role of the leader, the rights and responsibilities of the members, the ground rules, group-process procedures, and any other pertinent information they might actually give in the first session of a group. The members then express their expectations and fears, and the leaders try to deal with them. This lasts for approximately half an hour, and the class members then describe what they saw occurring in the group. The group members describe how they felt during the session and offer suggestions for the co-leaders. The co-leaders can discuss with each other the nature of their experience and how well they feel they did, either before any of the feedback or afterward.

2. Introducing-Yourself Exercise.   This exercise consists of telling the class what you would tell a group about yourself if you were the group leader. About four people volunteer, and each person is given 5 minutes. When this is completed, the four talk among themselves first, and then the class offers input regarding the impact made by each person.

3. Exercise for the Beginning Stage of a Group.   This exercise can be used to get group members acquainted with one another, but you can practice it in class to see how it works. The class breaks into dyads. Select a new partner every 10 minutes, and each time you change partners, consider a new question or issue. The main purpose of the exercise is to get members to contact all of the other members of the group and to begin to reveal themselves to others. We encourage you to add your own questions or statements to our list.

· Discuss your reservations about the value of groups.
· What do you fear about groups?

· What do you most want from a group experience?
· Discuss how much trust you have in your group. Do you feel like getting involved? What are some things that contribute to your trust or mistrust?
· Decide which of the two of you is dominant. Does each of you feel satisfied with his or her position?
· Tell your partner how you imagine you would feel if you were to co-lead a group with him or her.

4. Exercise in Meeting with Your Co-Leader.   Select a person in your class with whom you might like to co-lead a group. Explore with your partner some of the following dimensions of a group during the initial stage:

· How would both of you assist the members in getting the most from this group? Would you be inclined to discuss any guidelines that would help them be active members?
· How would the two of you attempt to build trust during the initial phase of this group?
· How much structuring would each of you be inclined to do early in a group? Do both of you agree on the degree of structure that would help a group function effectively?
· Whose responsibility is it if the group flounders? What might you do if the group seemed to be lost at the first session?
· What are some specific procedures that each of you might use to help the members define what they want to get from their group?

5. Brainstorming about Ways of Creating Trust.   In small groups, explore as many ideas and ways you can think of that might facilitate the establishment of trust in your group. What factors do you think are likely to lead to trust? What would it take for *you* to feel a sense of trust in a group? What do you see as the major barriers to the development of trust?

5

Transition Stage of a Group

Focus questions · **Introduction** · **Characteristics of the transition stage** · Anxiety · Defensiveness and resistance · The struggle for control · Conflict · Challenges to the group leader · Confrontation · **The leader's reactions to resistance** · **Problem behaviors and difficult group members** · Silence and lack of participation · Monopolistic behavior · Storytelling · Questioning · Advice giving · Band-Aiding · Hostile behavior · Dependency · Acting superior · Seductive behavior · Socializing · Intellectualizing · Emotionalizing · **Dealing with transference and countertransference** · How members may view the leader · Guidelines for leaders · **Effective leadership: Research findings** · Support versus confrontation · Guidelines for creating therapeutic member relationships · **Co-leader Issues at the transition stage** · **Exercises** · Self assessment · Exercises and questions for exploration

139

1. If your group consisted of members much like yourself, what do you imagine it would be like to lead it?
2. What reasons can you think of for a lack of participation by group members? Have you been a nonparticipating member in any group?
3. Have you been in a group with people who monopolize? What was the effect on you?
4. What might you say (as a group leader or a member) to a person who told anecdotes about his or her past?
5. What guidelines can you think of for effectively confronting others in a group? How can you challenge them in a caring way and not increase their defensiveness?
6. What is the distinction between giving advice and giving feedback? Do you think giving advice is ever warranted? If so, when?
7. What distinction is there between smoothing things over and giving genuine support?
8. How might you, as a leader, deal with a member's hostility?
9. What member behavior would you find most difficult to deal with as a leader?
10. If you have been in a group before, did you experience any resistance in either yourself or others? How was it handled? Did conflicts surface in the group? If so, how were they managed?

■■

Introduction

Before groups progress to a working stage, they typically go through a transitional phase. During this phase, groups are generally characterized by anxiety, defensiveness, resistance, the struggle for control, member conflicts, conflicts with or challenges to the leader, and various patterns of problem behaviors. In order for a group to move to a working stage, these problems must be recognized and dealt with effectively. Some groups remain stuck at the transitional stage because resistance

is bypassed or because conflict is smoothed over and left as an undercurrent that destroys open group interaction.

Because a group's ability to move forward is dependent on the ability
and willingness of both members and leader to face and work with
various forms of resistance, it is essential that leaders fully understand
the dynamics of a group during the transition period. What follows is a
discussion of typical characteristics of a group during the transition
stage.

Characteristics of the Transition Stage

■■ Anxiety

Anxiety during the transition stage is high. The sources of this anxiety
are within individuals and within the group itself. For example, Christie
expresses anxiety due to internal factors: "I'm really afraid to go any
further for fear of what I'll find out about myself." However, when
Sunny says "I'm afraid to speak up in here because several people are so
judgmental," her anxiety is due to external factors as well as internal
ones: she is inhibited by what others in the group think of her and how
they are liable to judge her.

Anxiety also relates to one's fears of looking foolish, of losing control,
of being misunderstood, of being rejected, and of not knowing what is
expected. As the participants come to more fully trust one another and
the leader, they become increasingly able to share their concerns, and
this openness lessens their anxiety about letting others see them as
they are.

■■ Defensiveness and Resistance

Group participants need to test the leader and other members before
the group can move from the transition phase to the working phase. It is
essential that the leader encourage an openness in which the members
express their hesitations and anxieties.

During the transition phase, participants are torn between wanting to
stay safe and wanting to risk getting involved. Often they are wise to
show some resistance. It is foolish for a leader to think that a group will
gather and effortlessly begin intensive work. Resistance needs to be
respected, which means the leader does not chastise a reluctant member but explores the source of the resistance. Both leader and members
must understand the meaning of resistance.

If leaders do not respect the members' resistances, they are really not
respecting the members themselves. For example, Betty reveals some
painful material and then suddenly stops and says that she doesn't want

to go on. In "going with" the resistance, the leader asks her what is stopping her. Betty indicates that she is afraid of losing people's respect. The issue now becomes her lack of trust in the group, rather than a painful personal problem. If the leader proceeds in this manner, Betty is more likely to eventually talk openly about personal matters. If the leader ignores her initial resistance by pushing her to open up, she will probably become increasingly defensive and resistant.

Not every instance of a member's unwillingness to participate fully can be accurately labeled "resistance." Sometimes members' unwillingness to cooperate is the result of factors such as an unqualified leader, an aggressive and uncaring leadership style, a failure to prepare members to participate in the group, and so on. Leaders need to accurately appraise whether the source of resistance is members' fears or ineffective leadership. Simply labeling a member "resistant" is to entrench this resistance even more deeply. A leader who shows willingness to explore and understand members' resistive behavior increases the likelihood of cooperation and risk taking.

If group members keep fears inside themselves, all sorts of avoidances are bound to occur. Although leaders cannot pry open members and force them to discuss the fears that could inhibit their participation, they can sensitively invite members to recognize some of these common fears.

The Fear of Making a Fool of Oneself.   People often worry about looking foolish if they step out of roles that are familiar to them. For example, Mike disclosed that he had held back from saying much because he did not want to take the chance of being seen as a fool. Therefore, he decided to enter in only when he was extremely sure of himself; at other times he found it safer to take the course of censoring and endlessly rehearsing his "performances."

The Fear of Rejection.   We often hear participants say that they are reluctant to bring up issues they want to talk about because of their fear of being rejected. Jim repeatedly came back to his fears that people would not want anything to do with him. Finally, he mustered the courage to challenge this fear. He saw that by not taking action he would learn little, so he made the decision to risk doing something that might bring rejection.

The Fear of Emptiness.   Sometimes members fear that, if they do get involved and explore issues they've kept tucked away, they'll discover that they are merely hollow and empty, that there is nothing in them that anyone could like or value. Janice expressed this fear, yet she continued in spite of her fears. She realized that, even if she did find that she was empty, she could begin a process of creating a different kind of existence for herself. She chose not to let her fear prevent her from looking at her life.

The Fear of Losing Control. Debby expressed her fear that she might open up some potentially painful areas and then be left without closure. She was anxious about "opening up Pandora's box," as she put it. She wondered: "Will I be able to stand the pain? Maybe it would be best if things were just left alone. If I started crying, I might never stop! Even though I might get support in the group, what will I do when I'm on my own if I'm stuck with this pain?" Members like Debby can learn that there is a difference between being left hanging with unfinished business in a group and bringing up a particular conflict that can be resolved.

The Fear of Self-Disclosure. Members often fear self-disclosure, thinking that they will not be able to control what and how much they reveal. Some members may feel pressured to open up as part of the "admission dues" for being what they consider an acceptable member. It often helps to reinforce emphatically to members that they can make themselves known to others and at the same time retain their privacy. As we explained in Chapter 4, it is their choice to determine what and how much they share. When they recognize that they are responsible for what they tell others about themselves, participants tend to be less fearful of self-disclosure.

Some Other Fears. A variety of other fears are often expressed by members:

· The leaders and members intimidate me, making me want to retreat.
· I'm afraid that I'll get too dependent on the group and that I'll rely on others to solve my problems for me.
· I often fear that I'll go crazy if I let myself feel.
· I'm uncomfortable with touching, and I fear that I'll be expected to touch and be touched even though I don't want to.
· I'm worried that I'll take too much group time by talking about my problems, that I'll bore people, and that they'll just tune me out.

Though it is not realistic to expect that all these fears can be eliminated, we do think that members can be encouraged to face their fears. Leaders can help create a trusting climate in which members will feel free enough to test their fears and put the unrealistic ones to rest. If members decide to be open about the fears that stop them from talking about themselves and if this can be done relatively early in a group, a good foundation of trust is created that will enable them to deal constructively with other personal issues as the group evolves.

▪▪ The Struggle for Control

Struggles over control issues are common at the transition stage. Characteristic group behaviors include competition, rivalry, jockeying for position, jealousies, challenges to the leadership (or lack of it), and discussions about the division of responsibility and decision-making procedures. Participants' main anxieties relate to having too much or too little responsibility. In order to deal constructively with these control issues, members must bring them to the surface and talk about them. If the here-and-now problems are ignored, the group will be inhibited by a hidden agenda.

▪▪ Conflict

Conflict often carries a negative connotation, as people sometimes assume that it is indicative of something intrinsically wrong and to be avoided at all costs. When there are conflicts within a group, both the leader and the members often want to avoid them rather than spending the time necessary to work through them. However, since conflict is inevitable in all relationships, including groups, it is the avoidance (rather than the facing) of conflict that makes it destructive. Unexplored conflict is typically expressed in defensive behavior, hostility, indirectness, and a general lack of trust. It is especially crucial in the transition stage that conflict be managed effectively. If conflict is handled successfully, the level of trust will increase. Thus, a primary task of leaders is to teach members the value of working through conflicts in a constructive way.

A conflict within one group is expressed by Diane when she says "There are some people in here who never say anything." Jeff immediately replies, defensively, "Not everybody has to be as talkative as you." Sylvia joins in, sarcastically, "Well, Diane, you talk so much that you don't give me a chance to participate!" Bert's contribution is: "I wish you would all be nicer to one another and stop this arguing. This isn't getting us anywhere."

Unproductive interventions by the leader might be: "I agree with you, Bert, and I wish people would knock it off!" "Diane, you're right. There are too many people in here who blend into the woodwork. I wish everyone would take as many risks as you do!" Such remarks increase the members' defensiveness and entrench resistance.

The emerging conflict can be dealt with constructively if the leader's interventions have the purpose of exploring the underlying dynamics of what has been said and of what is *not* being said. More constructive interventions include: "I agree with you, Bert, that right now we're not getting anywhere. But I don't want people to stop talking, because we need to get to the bottom of what all this means." Turning to Diane, the leader could make any of the following statements: "How are you affected by all these reactions?" "Who in particular do you want to hear from?" "What does it do to you when people don't say anything?" "What do you imagine that these people may be saying about you to themselves?"

Diane's original statement is a defensive and chastising remark to the group in general. The group reacts with appropriate defensiveness. The leader is attempting to get Diane to be more specific about how she is affected by people whom she sees as being silent. There is a refocusing on Diane's difficulty with the group. The conflict finds resolution when Diane lets people know that she is afraid that they are judging her when they say very little, that she is interested in how they perceive her, or that she is concerned for them and wonders how they experience the group. Chances are that this conflict would not have come about if Diane had made such statements to begin with. For example, had Diane said to Sylvia, "I notice that you're quiet, and I often wonder what you think of me. I don't like it when you don't say much, because I'm really interested in what you have to say." Such a statement reflects more accurately what is going on with Diane than does her punitive remark. It is important for the leader not to cut off the expression of conflict but to facilitate more direct expression of feeling and thinking among the members.

Cohesion and authentic positive feelings within a group typically increase after negative feelings are recognized and expressed, for venting such feelings is one way of testing the freedom and trustworthiness of the group. The participants soon discover whether this group is a safe place to disagree openly and whether they will be accepted in spite of their negative feelings. When conflict is constructively dealt with, the participants learn that their relationships are strong enough to withstand an honest level of challenge.

■■ Challenges to the Group Leader

Although leaders may be challenged throughout the duration of a group, they are more often confronted both personally and professionally during the transition stage. For example, several members may complain about not getting the "right" type of leadership, thereby challenging the leader's competency. It is a mistake for leaders to assume that every confrontation is an attack on their integrity. Instead, they need to examine nondefensively what is being said in order to differentiate between a *challenge* and an *attack*. How they respond to members' confrontations has a bearing on how trusting the participants will be in the future in expressing themselves to the leaders.

If Art says to the leader "I'm bored in here, and I wish you'd do more to make this a better group," a nontherapeutic reply is "Do you think you could do it better yourself?" By contrast, therapeutic replies might include: "Tell me more about what you'd like from me or what you'd like me to do differently." "Say more about what's missing for you in this group." "What could you continue to do to make this a more meaningful group for you?" (By saying what he does, Art has already taken the first step in changing the situation for himself.) It is not necessary that the leader quickly comply with Art's demand to conduct the group differently. What is essential is that the leader listen nondefensively and promote a full expression of Art's dissatisfaction. The leader is not willing to assume the total responsibility for Art's boredom. She explores with him their mutual responsibility to make this a meaningful and productive group, and she invites others to express their reactions to what she has said.

Though challenges may never be comfortable to the leader, it is important to recognize that these are often the members' significant first steps toward becoming independent. The way the group leader responds to challenges such as Art's has a powerful effect on the members' willingness to continue to take risks and to trust. Leaders can be good role models if they respond openly and avoid becoming defensive with the members.

▪▪ Confrontation

Our view of a therapeutic group includes both support and challenge. At times, people see confrontation as a negative act with destructive potential. Because of this connotation, confrontation is sometimes avoided at all costs. By contrast, we think that people cease being effective catalysts to others' growth if all they offer is support and empathy. If carried to excess, such an "understanding" attitude can be counterproductive. Groups that focus almost exclusively on positive feedback and strengths too often do not challenge participants to take a deeper look at themselves. If members limit their responses to supportive ones, they fail to provide people with information on the way they are perceived and how they affect others.

We think leaders have a responsibility to teach members what confrontation is and is not and how to challenge others in constructive ways. We see confrontation *not* as (1) tearing others down carelessly, (2) hitting others with negative feedback and then retreating, (3) committing an act of hostility aimed at hurting others, (4) telling others what is basically wrong with them, or (5) assaulting others' integrity. Ideally, we see confrontation as an invitation for participants to look at some aspect of their interpersonal style or their life to determine if they want to make changes.

Our approach to group practice entails providing members with guidelines for appropriate and responsible confrontation, which include the following:

1. Members should know why they are confronting.
2. Confrontations should not be dogmatic statements concerning who or what a person is.
3. The person being confronted is likely to be less defensive if told what effect he or she has on others rather than simply branded with a label or judgment.
4. Confrontations are more effective if, instead of being global generalizations about a person, they focus on specific, observable behaviors.
5. One of the purposes of confrontation is to develop a closer and more genuine relationship with others.
6. Sensitivity is an important element of effective confrontation; it is useful for the person doing the confronting to imagine being the recipient of what is said.
7. Confrontation should give others the opportunity to reflect on the feedback they receive before they are expected to act on it.
8. Those confronting would be wise to ask themselves if they are willing to do for themselves what they are asking others to do.

The quality of the confrontations that occur in a group is an index of how effective a group is. The more cohesive a group is, the more challenging and risking members can be. Groups that disintegrate under challenge are based on a false sense of cohesion.

To make the issue of confrontation more concrete, we present the following examples. The first statements illustrate ineffective confrontation; they are followed by effective confrontations.

· "You're always so judgmental, and you make me feel inadequate." This could be changed to: "I feel uncomfortable with you because I'm afraid of what you think of me. Your opinion is important to me. I don't like it that I often feel inadequate when I'm with you."
· "You're a phony! You're always smiling, and that's not real." An effective confrontation is: "I find it very difficult to trust you, because often when you say you're angry, you're smiling. This makes it hard for me to get close to you."
· "You aren't getting anything from this group. All you ever do is sit and observe. We're just interesting cases for you." An effective challenge would be: "I'd like to get to know you. I'm interested in what you think and feel, and sometimes I worry that you see me as an interesting case. I'd like to change the way I feel around you."
· "If I were your husband, I'd leave you. You're full of venom, and you'll poison any relationship." A more effective statement is: "I find it very difficult to be open with you. Many of the things you say really hurt me and distance me from you, and I want to strike back. It would be hard for me to be involved in an intimate relationship with you."
· "You do nothing but play games." A more concrete and effective statement is: "Most of what you're doing in here appears dramatic to

me. When you cry, I'm bothered, because it's not easy for me to feel compassionate. I'd like to talk to you more about this."

In each of the ineffective statements the people being confronted are being told how they are, and in some way they are being discounted. In the effective statements the members doing the confronting are revealing their perceptions and feelings about the other members and how they are being affected by them.

The Leader's Reactions to Resistance

As we have seen, a central characteristic of the transition stage is resistance, which manifests itself in many forms of member behavior. As a leader, it is essential that you not only learn to recognize and deal with the members' resistance but also become aware of your own reactions to resistance. A mistake that we commonly observe when we supervise group leaders is their tendency to focus on "problem members" or difficult situations, rather than on their own dynamics and how they are affected personally when they encounter a "resistant group." Typically, leaders have a range of feelings: being threatened by what they perceive as a challenge to their leadership role; anger over the members' lack of cooperation and enthusiasm; feelings of inadequacy to the point of wondering if they are qualified to lead groups; resentment toward several of the members, whom they label as some type of "problem"; and anxiety over the slow pace of the group, with a desire to stir things up so that there is some action.

One of the most powerful ways to intervene when you are experiencing some strong feelings over what you perceive to be resistance is to deal with your own feelings and possible defensive reactions to the situation. If you ignore your reactions, you are leaving yourself out of the interactions that occur in the group. Furthermore, by giving the members your reactions, you are modeling a direct style of dealing with conflict and resistance, rather than bypassing it. Your own thoughts, feelings, and observations can be the most powerful resource you have in dealing with defensive behavior. When you share what you are feeling and thinking about what is going on in the group—in such a way as not to blame and criticize the members for deficiencies—you are making it possible for the members to experience an honest and constructive interaction with you.

We hope that you will keep these thoughts in mind as you read the next section, which deals with problem behaviors and difficult group members.

Although it is understandable that, as leaders, you will want to learn how to handle problem members and the disruption of the group that they can cause, the emphasis should be on actual *behaviors* rather than labels. It is helpful to consider each of the following problem behaviors as a manifestation of resistance that most participants display at one time or another during the history of a group.

Problem Behaviors and Difficult Group Members

We think it is important to describe specific behaviors that interfere with the establishment of a cohesive and productive group, but as we have said, we want to resist the temptation to characterize any member as "the monopolist," "the group nurse," "the assistant therapist," "the calculator," and so on. Certain problems inherent in such labeling have already been discussed. In addition, placing a fixed label on a participant represents a failure to take into account what the person is besides that behavior. Although a man may exhibit overly supportive behavior, he is surely more than a "group nurse." And even though a woman is prone to intellectualizing and storytelling, she is surely more than just an "avoider." With this caution, we will now describe member behaviors that are counterproductive to group functioning.

■■ Silence and Lack of Participation

Silence and withdrawal are two forms of behavior that most group leaders must eventually learn to deal with. Even though the silent and withdrawn member does not interfere verbally with group functioning, this behavior may constitute a problem for both the member and the group. The danger is that quiet or withdrawn members will go unnoticed and that their pattern of silence may indicate a problem.

Some silent group members may argue that their lack of verbal participation is not an index of their involvement. They may maintain that they are learning by listening and by identifying with others' problems. These members may say that they "don't feel like talking just to hear themselves talk" or that, when they have something important to contribute, they'll do so. Group leaders should encourage these members to discuss their silence in the group. There are many reasons for nonparticipating behavior, and these should be explored. Some of the reasons are:

· the feeling that one doesn't have anything worthwhile to say
· the feeling that one shouldn't talk about oneself or that one should be seen and not heard
· fear of looking foolish; not knowing the appropriate thing to say or do
· fear of certain members in the group or of the authority of the group leader

· resistance, particularly if the person doesn't really want to be a member of the group
· uncertainty about how the group process works
· fear of being rejected or of being accepted
· lack of trust in the group; fear of leaks of confidentiality

It is important that members not be attacked for their silence but instead be invited to participate. Also, group leaders must be careful to avoid consistently calling on a silent person, for in this way the member is relieved of the responsibility of initiating interaction. A "game" can be made of drawing out the person, and this can lead to resentment on the part of both the rest of the group and the silent member and frustration on the part of the leader who perpetuates this behavior.

Silent members can be invited to explore what their silence means. For example, is this the way they are outside of the group as well? How does it feel for them to be in this group? Do they want to do anything about becoming verbally active participants? The rest of the group can participate in this discussion, for group members generally do have reactions to nonparticipating members. They may feel cheated that they know so little of that person, or they may resent that the person is observing them as they risk and reveal themselves. If there are several silent members in a group, the verbally active members may become less revealing because they don't trust those who aren't revealing also.

Silent members can be taught that others will not know of their involvement unless they express it in words. The leader may ask such members to make a contract to speak at every session, sharing with the group at some point how they responded to the session that day. Another way for the leader to handle this behavior is to ask the relatively silent members at the end of a session whether they got from the session what they wanted. If they indicate that there were some things they wanted to talk about but that time ran out before they got a chance, then they can make a contract to be the first on the agenda at the next group meeting.

A useful group technique is to ask people who feel that they are not active participants to form an inner circle within the group. Those who identify themselves as active participants sit in an outer circle. The members of the inner circle are then instructed to talk among themselves about how they feel in the group, what their fears and concerns are, and in what ways they want to change their behavior. After a time, the members of the outer group can take the inner circle and react to what they've heard. In this way the entire group is involved in the discussion of the issue of participation/nonparticipation. If certain members remain extremely silent or withdrawn and chronically have a draining effect on a group, the group leader can meet with them privately to discuss the reasons for the silent behavior and the advisability of their staying in the group.

▪▪ Monopolistic Behavior

At the other end of the participation continuum is the person who exhibits a high degree of self-centeredness by monopolizing the activities of the group. This person is continually "identifying with others"—that is, taking others' statements as openings for detailed stories about his or her own life. Through compulsive, self-centered chattering, this person prevents others from getting their share of group time.

During the beginning stages of a group, members may be relieved that someone else is going first, but they soon tire of hearing the same person over and over. As meetings continue, the group generally becomes less tolerant of the person who monopolizes, and unless these feelings of annoyance are dealt with early, they may be bottled up and then released in an explosive way. For this reason it is essential that the monopolizing person be gently challenged to look at the effects of such behavior on the group. Ideally, members will let the person know how they feel about his or her continually stepping into the spotlight. If the group does not take this initiative, the group leader might ask "I wonder why so many of you seem to be willing to let Ralph take up so much group time?"

The person who monopolizes should not be silenced by mandate. Instead, his or her behavior should be examined in the group. The person is sending messages with monopolizing antics, and these messages can be productively analyzed. For example, Ralph initially seemed very charming. He seemed to reveal personal aspects of himself, he readily made suggestions to others, he could identify with most who spoke, he became an "assistant therapist" by questioning and interpreting, he told detailed stories of his past, and most of his behavior was an expression of the message "Please notice me and like me." The group leader intervened firmly but gently with: "You seem desperate to get people's attention, yet you seem to not want us to really get to know you and your feelings. How would it be if we talked about how your behavior in here may be an extension of the way you are outside of the group, so that you can see whether this behavior is really working for you?"

▪▪ Storytelling

Self-disclosure is frequently misunderstood by some group members to mean a lengthy recitation about their life, past and present. If they are confronted about continually relating their detailed history, they sometimes express resentment, maintaining that they are risking disclosing themselves. In teaching group process, leaders need to differentiate between pseudodisclosure, which is merely talking about oneself or about others and life situations, and disclosure of what a person is thinking and feeling now. During the beginning stages of a group the leader may allow some storytelling, for people who are new to groups frequently need to hear facts about others or to share some of their own past. However, if storytelling behavior becomes a familiar style (either for the whole group or for one member), the leader should recognize this and deal with it. The following examples illustrate how storytelling can be handled.

Richard would, almost predictably, bring the group up to date each week on developments in his marriage. He focused on details of his wife's behavior during the week, but he rarely described his own feelings or behavior. Since Richard was the spouse who was in the group, the leader pointed out, it was him the group was interested in. As Richard and the group looked more at this behavior, it became obvious to him that this was his way of avoiding talking about himself. He thus made a contract to talk about his reactions and not to talk about his wife in the group each week.

Sandra typically told every detail of her earlier experiences, but even though the group knew a lot about the events in her past, they knew very little about how she felt about what she had experienced. Like Richard, she felt that she was open in sharing her private life with the group; and, like Richard's group, her group wanted to know more about how she responded to her life situations. The group leader told her that he was "losing Sandra" in all of the details. He let her know that he was indeed interested in knowing her but that the information she was offering was not helping him to do so.

Storytelling can be any form of talking about out-of-group life that leaves the person telling the story unknown. Feedback from the group given directly, without judgment, can assist the person to speak in personal terms and keep the focus on feelings, thoughts, and reactions.

▪▪ Questioning

Another counterproductive form of behavior in the group is interrogation. Some members develop a style of relating that involves questioning others, and they intervene at inappropriate times, asking why a person feels a certain way. People who habitually ask questions should be helped to see that this may be a way of hiding, of remaining safe and unknown in a group. And they should be taught that the people to whom the questions are addressed typically lose the intensity of any emotion they may have been experiencing; questions tend to direct people to thinking and away from feeling.

If members can be made to understand that questions not only intrude on others but also keep the questioner's feelings about others disguised, there is a good chance that change will occur. Practice for behavior change might consist of trying to make only direct statements. For example, Marie could be invited to say what prompted her to ask a question. If she had asked another member why he was so quiet, the leader could encourage her to say what was going on with her before she asked the question. She may tell the leader "I noticed that Jim hardly says anything in here, and I'm interested in Jim and would like to get to know him." In such a statement, Marie discloses her investment in her question without putting Jim on the spot. Questions often arouse defensiveness, whereas personal statements are less likely to do so.

■■ Advice Giving

A problem behavior that is related to questioning is advice giving. It is one thing to offer a perception or opinion to other members and quite another to tell people what they should feel or what they should or shouldn't do. The advice giving may be subtle: "You shouldn't feel guilty that your parents divorced, because that was their decision and not something you made them do." Although this is true, the point is that the young woman does feel guilty and believes that, if it had not been for her, her parents might still be married. It does not serve the best interest of the woman to advise her not to feel guilty. She has to resolve this feeling for herself. The man who had a need to tell her that she shouldn't feel guilty could profit from examining his own motives for wanting to remove the guilt. What does this mean about him? At this point the focus might be shifted to the advice giver, and the meaning of his giving such advice might be explored.

Advice giving can be less subtle. Pam has been considering not only leaving her husband but also leaving her two teenage daughters with him. She is confused, and though she thinks she wants to live alone, she feels somewhat guilty. Robin intervenes: "Pam, you owe it to yourself to do what you want to do. Why should you be stuck with your kids? Why not let him take them? Pam, if I were you, I'd leave both my kids and my husband, get an apartment, and take that job as an interior decorator." This type of behavior raises a lot of questions about Robin. What are her values and possible unresolved problems? Why does she feel a need to straighten Pam out? Wouldn't it be better for Robin to talk about herself instead of trying to be helpful by deciding what is best for Pam? The group might now focus on Robin's need to provide others with a pat solution. Robin might learn about what she is getting from giving others advice.

Advice giving has the tendency to interrupt the expression of thoughts and feelings and to increase dependency. If Pam were given enough time to explore her conflict more fully, she would be better able to make her own decision. In essence, an abundance of advice tells her that she is not capable of finding her own way, and it conditions her to become more dependent on others for direction. In our opinion, this is not a positive outcome of a therapeutic group. Even if the advice given is helpful and sound, in the long run it does not teach Pam the process of finding her own solutions to new problems as they occur.

A related behavior is displayed by members who want to assist the leader. They ask questions, probe for information, freely give advice, and focus more on others in the group than on themselves. This issue must be dealt with, because it will create resentment among the other members as well as the leader. Recognizing this behavior as a possible defense, or form of resistance, the leader can sensitively block it by pointing out to such members that they are depriving themselves of maximum benefit from the group by paying more attention to others than to themselves.

▪▪ Band-Aiding

Related to the advice-giving style is the style that some adopt of trying to soothe wounds, lessen pains, and keep people cheerful. This behavior is sometimes manifested by a person who complains of how negative the group is and who wants to focus more on the positive side. The following are two examples of "Band-Aiding."

Jack is finally able to feel his sadness over the distance between his sons and himself, and he sobs in the group as he talks about how much he wants to be a better father. Before Jack can have a cathartic cry, Randy puts his hands on Jack's shoulders and tries to reassure him that he's not such a bad father, because at least he lives with his kids. Randy may want to make Jack feel better so that he (Randy) will feel more comfortable.

Jan reveals her memories of the loneliness, rejection, and fright she felt when she had an abortion as an adolescent. She is reliving the loneliness that she felt earlier. Louise moves across the room and holds Jan and tries as best she can to take Jan's lonely feelings away. What has Jan provoked in Louise? Why does Louise need to protect Jan from the intensity of her pain? Far too often people fail to see the therapeutic value in the release of pain.

There is a real difference between behavior that is Band-Aiding and behavior that is a genuine expression of care, concern, and empathy. Where there is real caring, the interests of the people who are experiencing the pain are given paramount importance. Sometimes it is in people's interest to allow them to experience the depths of their pain; ultimately, they may be better off for having done so. They can be supported after they've had the chance to intensely experience their pain. Band-Aiding is pseudosupport, designed primarily to aid the one who is supporting. Finding it too difficult to witness another's pain, the supportive one attempts to distract the other. Like questioning and advice giving, Band-Aiding needs to be examined at some point for its meaning to the person who performs it.

■■ Hostile Behavior

Hostility is difficult to deal with in a group, because the person who expresses hostility often works indirectly. Hostility can take the form of caustic remarks, jokes, sarcasm, and other "hit-and-run" tactics. Members can express it by missing group sessions, by coming late, by acting obviously bored and detached, by leaving the group, by being overly polite, and the like. Extremely hostile people are not generally good candidates for a group, because they are so defensive that they will not acknowledge their fears. In addition, extreme hostility can have a devastating effect on the group climate. People are not going to make themselves vulnerable if there is a good chance that they will be ridiculed or in some other way devalued.

One way to deal with the person who behaves in a hostile way is to request that he or she listen without responding while the group members tell how they are being affected by that individual. It is important that the members not be allowed to dump their own feelings of hostility, however. Instead, they can describe how they feel in the group with the hostile person and what they would like the person to do differently. Then it should be ascertained what the hostile individual wants from the group. Hostile behavior may be a manifestation of fear of getting intimate or of a limited capacity for vulnerability. If the fears underneath the hostility can be brought to the surface and dealt with, the hostility may decrease.

One notable manifestation of hostility is passive/aggressive behavior. This behavior characteristically involves the element of surprise: the person confronts and then quickly retreats. The confrontation has a sharp and cutting quality, and the person attacking withdraws, leaving the attacked person stunned.

For example, Karl, who has a good relationship in the group with Linda, suddenly calls her a "castrating female." Before she has a chance to express her surprise, hurt, and anger, he tells Linda that he sees his wife in her, and it isn't really her he is upset with. Karl has attempted to take back what he said, yet Linda is still stuck with her hurt feelings. On an intellectual level Linda may understand that Karl is transferring his reactions to her, but on an emotional level she is hurt and has become distrustful of him. Even though it makes sense on an intellectual level, Linda needs some time to recover emotionally. Eventually, Karl acknowledges that he indeed had some negative feelings toward Linda personally, not just as his symbolic wife. He quickly wanted to retreat when he saw that Linda had responded strongly.

▪▪ Dependency

Group members who are excessively dependent typically look either to the group leader or to the other members to direct them and take care of them. Dependency is manifested in a variety of behaviors in the group, such as exclaiming that one couldn't live without one's wife (or husband, or parents, or children), presenting oneself as stupid so that others will provide one with answers, and playing helpless.

A special variety of the dependency syndrome is the "yes, but" style of interaction. The person requests help, and the group gives feedback, perhaps pointing out options that the person had not considered. Without even allowing this input to register, the individual replies with a "Yes, but . . ." Consider Donald, 25 years old and living with his mother. He has been complaining that his mother constantly harasses him, treating him like a child, reminding him to take his vitamins, telling him to do his homework, admonishing him that he should not stay out too late, and on and on. The group members soon tire of listening to his litany of complaints, and the following exchanges occur:

Maria: If things are as bad as you say, why do you stay at home? Wouldn't it be a good idea to leave?

Donald: Yes, but I don't have a job, and I'm broke.

Jim: If you don't like the way your mother treats you, wouldn't it help to let her know?

Donald: Yes, but my mother would just disintegrate if I were to confront her.

The essential point is that dependent people are not helped by being allowed to lure others into the trap of giving pity. They can't use advice, because no matter what is suggested, they can show why it will fail. The starting point for helping dependent people is to refuse to reinforce the helpless position by refusing to fill the dependency needs. At the same time, the leader should help such people realize the means they use to keep themselves dependent.

In confronting Donald with his dependent behavior, the leader could work toward getting him to recognize the ways in which he is continuing his dependency. She might say: "Donald, I've noticed in several sessions now that you seem to provoke people into helping you. You complain that your mother is treating you like a child, but I wonder how you solicit this kind of response from your mother also." As an alternative, she might say: "Do you really want to change, or do you think you're waiting for your mother to change? When will *you* begin to be different with your mother?" Or the leader could ask Donald to list all the possible reasons for being afraid of leaving home.

Leaders sometimes foster dependency in their clients. They have an exaggerated need to be wanted and needed, and they feel a sense of importance when participants rely on them. This is an example of the leader's unmet psychological needs interfering with the therapeutic outcome of a group. There are many other reasons that leaders collude with members to form a dependent alliance, some of which include:

· The leader may need the economic rewards from the members' attendance.
· The group may be filling the leader's unmet needs for a social life.
· Some leaders have a need to be parental in the sense of directing others' lives.
· Leaders may rely on their groups as the sole source of feeling appreciated and recognized.
· Leaders may feel useful when participants tell them how much they need them.
· Leaders may attempt to work through their own unresolved conflicts by using the group.

These examples show how the personality of the leader cannot be separated from what sometimes appears as problem behavior within the group. The behaviors of leader and members have a reciprocal effect.

■■ Acting Superior

Some group members take a superior tone. They may be moralistic or may even send the message "I'm cured, and I'm here to observe the rest of you." Such people can find no personal problems to explore but are very willing to listen to others and even to offer them compassion. They may antagonize others with comments such as "I can identify with you, because at one time I was where you are." In the condescending tone is the message "I really don't need anything for myself, and there are no problems in my life; I'm perfectly content now." A group leader can legitimately challenge such comments by asking the members what they want from the group. A teaching point for the entire group is that it is more helpful to someone in pain to share one's own struggle than to offer solutions.

"Superior" behavior tends to have the same effect on a group as hostility. It freezes up participants, for they don't want to expose their weaknesses to someone who's perfect.

■■ Seductive Behavior

The person using seduction is attempting to manipulate others in the group in order to avoid any genuine encounter. Seductive behavior can take many forms, including some of the behaviors already mentioned. Four types of seductive behavior are:

- **Quiet seduction.** This involves trying to get others to draw one out. The game element consists of the individual's underlying belief that, "if people really care about me, they'll come and reach out to me first."
- **Active seduction.** This involves trying to get intimacy instantly, to get acceptance without earning it. The person tells others what they want to hear, touches others a lot, suggests all sorts of "touching" exercises, and is scared of genuine intimacy.
- **Playing fragile.** Individuals may pretend they're so fragile that, if confronted, they'll be devastated.
- **Sexual seduction.** Members may be very sexually provocative and then be angry and hurt when others respond to them in a sexual manner.

▪▪ Socializing

When members socialize outside of the sessions, group cohesion can be increased. Members can extend what they are learning in their group to the informal gatherings. Such meetings can also be useful in challenging members to follow through with their plans and commitments. For some populations, such as an inpatient group for the elderly, this can be the only network of support.

Meetings outside the group can also be a form of resistance, however, and can therefore work against cohesion. This is especially true when participants talk about group matters but refuse to discuss these issues in the group. Other signs that indicate counterproductive socializing include the forming of cliques and excluding of certain members from such gatherings; the forming of romantic involvements without a willingness to share these in the group; a refusal to challenge one another in the group because of a fear of jeopardizing friendships; and an exclusive reliance on the group as the source of social life.

When socializing outside of the sessions hampers group progress, it is essential that the issue be openly examined by the group. The leader can ask the members if they are genuinely concerned about developing the kind of group that will function effectively. Members can be helped to see that forming cliques and making pacts to keep information out of the regular sessions do not lead to a productive and cohesive group.

▪▪ Intellectualizing

It is a mistake to see groups as places where people are allowed to have only "gut reactions" and where only immediate feelings are valued. We contend that thoughtful analysis is a necessary part of group process, but it should be integrated with feeling. When group members discuss in a very detached way, as though out of intellectual interest, topics that

for most people are emotionally loaded, they can be said to be intellectualizing. Intellectualizing is a defense against feelings. Most people use
this defense at times; it is when it comes to characterize a person's
behavior that it becomes a problem.

It is important for people who intellectualize to be made aware of
what they're doing. Some Gestalt awareness techniques can be useful in
helping such people more directly experience the emotions associated
with the events they talk about. Individuals can be directed to reexpe-
rience events, perhaps via role playing. Group leaders need to be alert,
however, when dealing with intellectualizing. As with other counterproductive styles, there is obviously some defensive purpose being
served. Leaders ought to ask themselves whether they're competent to
deal with what would be revealed should the defenses be stripped away.

■■ Emotionalizing

Groups are typically seen as a place to focus on emotions. Although this
is a valuable aspect of group work, members who constantly express a
wide range of intense emotions can sometimes be displaying a form of
resistance. Lori is triggered by everyone's emotions, and her responses
manage to draw attention to herself. Perhaps she believes that the only
way to be productive in the group is to be highly cathartic and, consequently, to be seen by the leader as a "good" member. She can be
deceiving herself in thinking that she is "really working" because she
cries so easily and frequently. This can also serve as a defense, because
others are likely to hesitate in confronting her. In Lori's case it is not so
much a matter of her being sad. Instead, her issues are wanting attention from people—wanting to be liked, accepted, and approved of. Her
emotionalism is an indirect way of getting what she wants. The leader
needs to be sensitive in determining when catharsis is an expression of a
genuine struggle and when it is a form of resistance and, therefore,
counterproductive.

Dealing with Transference and Countertransference

As we've mentioned earlier, it is essential for leaders to be aware of their
own dynamics when leading groups and to recognize how their unresolved personal issues can feed into problematic behaviors in members.
To understand this interplay, it is useful to consider the issues of transference and countertransference.

Transference consists of the feelings that clients project onto the therapist. These feelings usually have to do with relationships the clients
have experienced in the past, and when they're attributed to the therapist, they're not realistic. Countertransference refers to the feelings that

are aroused in the therapist by clients—feelings that, again, have more to do with unresolved conflict in a past relationship than with any feature of the present relationship.

■■ How Members May View the Leader

Regardless of the value a leader puts on exploring transferences, he or she should be aware of the kinds of feelings toward and expectations about their leader that members have. Unless these feelings are dealt with in the group, meaningful work may never occur. Participants do have an image of the group leader, and at times this includes unrealistic expectations. We'll now describe some of the more common ways clients may initially perceive a group leader.

The Expert.   Some members enter a group because they're seeking direction and help. What they hope is that the therapist will "cure" them—offer them a recipe for happiness or give them some quality that they don't believe they can find in themselves. They obediently, respectfully, and hopefully place their trust in the leader, waiting to be shown the way. They hope to increase their self-confidence, to know themselves better, to become more assertive, to feel more intensely, to lose their fears, and to gain courage. If they don't move in this direction, they may tend to resent the leader for not doing his or her job.

The Authority Figure.   It is not uncommon for members, during the initial phases of a group, to timidly reveal how stifled they feel in the presence of the leader, whom they view as an authority figure. They say that they feel judged, that they feel inferior and insignificant when they're in the leader's presence, and that they don't see themselves as able to measure up to the leader's standards. These people may be psychologically bringing their parents with them into the group; how they feel toward the leader is much the way they've always felt toward their parents. By elevating the leader to a superior place, they discount their own worth. They cannot really enjoy, like, or respect the group leader as a person, for they have too much resentment and fear.

The Superperson.   Clients often view their therapist as a superbeing. It is inconceivable to them that leaders may feel inadequate at times, that their marriage may not be perfect, or that they do not have all the answers to human suffering. These clients are amazed if they discover that their leader is not a perfectly adjusted, self-actualized being. Perhaps they need to believe that the leader has "arrived" and that, therefore, they can also hope to do so.

The Friend.   Some clients resent the professional aspects of a client/ therapist relationship. Others experience jealousy over having to share "their" therapist with others. Some say that the office structure—appointments, fees, waiting room, and so on—interferes with the spontaneity they would like. It may be true that a leader can be a "therapist/ friend," one who cares for members and is involved with them. But it is not realistic for members to expect the therapist to be a friend. If clients rely too heavily on this therapeutic relationship for friendship, they may fail to develop friendships on the outside. The dynamics of making a friend out of a group leader are similar to the dynamics of making a parent out of the leader. Clients hope that the leader will care for them in a special way, that they will be approved of and even loved unconditionally, and that they will be seen as desirable.

The Lover.   Some group members want to convert the therapeutic relationship into a romantic one. They may attempt in many ways to attract and seduce the group leader. They may feel that, if they succeed in getting the leader's special attention, they will hold a special place in the group. Chances are that they'll be disappointed, because they're usually searching for love that they never received as a child or for love that they don't now receive from others. Thus, no matter what they experience with the leader, their expectations will not be fulfilled. Of course, seductive behavior often generates countertransference, which the group leader must deal with. This is true of all of the projections— whether a group leader is made into the expert, the authority figure, the superperson, the friend, or the lover. Unless the therapist is well aware of his or her own motivations and unresolved conflicts, there is a likelihood that the member/leader relationship will be antitherapeutic.

■■ Guidelines for Leaders

How can the group leader deal with transference? The answer is complex and depends on the circumstances under which the relationship develops. Following are some general guidelines:

First, the feelings should be brought out openly in the group. This also allows for consensual validation. In other words, if all the members see the leader as an aloof and distant expert, it may be that the leader indeed presents himself or herself that way and that this is not a transference situation.

Once the feelings are revealed, they can be explored like any other problem that a member chooses to deal with in the group. The best way for a member to resolve an "authority hang-up" is to confront the leader who represents this authority and to examine the intimidation experienced in the leader's presence. The member might simply talk about feelings toward the leader. In addition, the leader might assume the role of the person's father or some other authority figure. Roles can be reversed, the member becoming the parent and the leader becoming the member. This can be a useful feedback device; that is, the member can see how he or she is viewed by the leader. Also, while the member continues in the authoritarian role, the leader (or another group member) might take an assertive stance. In this way an alternative response to authority is offered. The members might now resume dialogue with the "parent/leader," this time experimenting with the more forceful position that was demonstrated. Still another approach to this problem would be to use the Gestalt empty-chair approach, in which the member plays out both parts, the underdog and the top dog. These are but a few illustrations of how transference problems can be worked out. The important elements are that (1) the feelings be recognized and expressed and (2) the feelings then be dealt with therapeutically.

A more delicate issue is how the leader can best deal with feelings toward a group member. Even in the Freudian tradition, which dictates that therapists spend years in analysis in order to understand and resolve blocked areas, countertransference is a potential problem. So it can be a very big problem for the beginning group leader. Some people are attracted to this profession because, on some level, they imagine that as a helper they will be respected, needed, admired, looked to as an expert, and even loved. Perhaps they have never experienced the acceptance and self-confidence in their ordinary life that they experience while "helping others." Such leaders are using groups to fulfill needs that would otherwise go unmet.

The issue of power is germane here, for as group members elevate the group leader to the level of expert, perfect person, or demanding parent, they also give away most of their power to the group leader. A self-aware therapist who is interested primarily in the client's welfare will not encourage the client to remain in an inferior position. The insecure leader who depends on the underdog position of clients for a sense of adequacy and power will tend to keep the group members powerless.

We do not want to convey the impression that it is inappropriate for leaders' needs to be met through their work. Nor are we suggesting that leaders should not feel powerful. In fact, we think that leaders who have none of their needs met through their work are in danger of losing their enthusiasm. What is crucial is that leaders do not exploit the members as a way of fulfilling these needs. The problem occurs when leaders put their own needs first or fail to be sensitive to those of the members.

Countertransference feelings are likely to develop in the romantic/sexual realm, particularly when an attractive group member indicates an attraction to a group leader. A group leader may never have felt attractive before becoming a leader; now he or she feels desirable. The danger is dependence on group members for this feedback.

Dealing with countertransference openly in a group can compound the complexities of group process by generating negative feelings toward the group leader. Nevertheless, at times it may be important that this be done. One of the advantages of working with a co-leader is that the partner can offer valuable feedback from an objective viewpoint and can help the other partner see things that had been blocked from awareness.

Group leaders in training may have the opportunity to explore with a supervisor feelings of attraction or repulsion toward certain members. Leaders who are conducting groups independently and who become aware of a pattern that indicates possible countertransference problems should seek consultation with another therapist or become a member of a group to work through these problems.

Three additional points need to be emphasized to leaders:

1. Don't be gullible and believe uncritically whatever group members tell you, particularly initially. It's easy to become enamored with feedback that tells you how helpful, wise, perceptive, attractive, powerful, and dynamic you are; don't be swept away by the unrealistic attributions of group members.

2. Don't be overly critical and thus discount genuine positive feedback. All members who see a leader as helpful or wise are not suffering from "transference disorders." Members can feel genuine affection and respect for group leaders. By the same token, just because a participant becomes angry with the leader does not mean that this person is transferring anger toward parents onto the leader. Participants can feel genuine anger and have negative reactions toward the group leader personally. It may be true that the leader radiates a distant, know-it-all manner, manipulates the group toward his or her own ends, or is seductive with certain members. In short, all feelings that members direct toward the group leader should not be "analyzed" as transferences to be "worked through" for the client's good. If a group leader hears consistent negative feedback, it is imperative that this feedback be seriously examined for its validity and, if deemed valid, acted on.

3. Recognize that not all of your feelings toward members can be classified as countertransference. Some leaders operate under the misconception that they should remain objective and care for all members equally. Such leaders expect themselves to be superhuman. Countertransference is indicated by exaggerated and persistent feelings that tend to recur with various clients in various groups. You can expect to enjoy some members more than others and to be sexually attracted to some members. Again, this is not some disease to be cured. What is important is that you recognize your own feelings for what they are and that you avoid emotional entanglements that are antitherapeutic.

Effective Leadership: Research Findings

Research has yielded considerable evidence of the importance of a positive therapist/client relationship. As the relationship between the leader and the members becomes less favorable, the amount of group tension increases, and the potential for therapeutic gain diminishes (Lieberman, Yalom, & Miles, 1973). The group leader's interpersonal skills, genuineness, empathy, and warmth are significant variables associated with effective group work.

As we discussed in Chapter 1, however, these and other personal characteristics by themselves are not sufficient for effective group outcomes. Simply because group leaders possess these personal attributes does not necessarily mean that they will be successful. Dies (1983b) maintains that the quality of interpersonal relationships *among group members* is more crucial to therapeutic change than the leader's relationship to individual members. Thus, the leader's central task is to create interpersonal norms such as openness, directness, respect, and concern for one another that will lead to therapeutic interactions among members.

∎∎ Support versus Confrontation

Forging an effective group necessitates achieving an appropriate balance between support and challenge. In our opinion, groups having either explicit or implicit norms limiting group interactions to supportive ones do not have the power to help people challenge themselves to take significant risks. We further think that those groups that "push" confrontation as a requisite for peeling away the defensive maneuvers of members are characterized by hostile and increasingly defensive interactions. The research reviews that describe negative outcomes in groups consistently cite aggressive confrontation as the leadership style with the highest risks (Lieberman, Yalom, & Miles, 1973; Yalom, 1985). Based on research findings, Dies (1983b) suggests that leaders should not engage in highly confrontive interventions until they earn the right to be confrontive, which is achieved primarily by building a trusting relationship with the members. Once the foundation of interpersonal trust is established, group members tend to be more open to challenge. Dies recommends that, because it takes time to create a supportive atmosphere, confrontive interactions are probably most appropriate at a later stage of a group's development.

We agree that there are dangers in confronting too soon and that leaders must earn the right to confront. Destructive confrontations, with an attacking quality, can lead to an entrenchment of resistance and tend to breed hostility and mistrust within the group. But we think that confrontation is appropriate even during the initial stages of a group, if it is done with sensitivity and in a respectful manner. In fact, the foundations of trust are often solidified by caring confrontations on the leader's part. Beginning with the early phase of the group the leader needs to model ways of providing appropriate support and challenge. To avoid challenging a group in its early phase, when this is what the group needs, is to treat the group members as though they were fragile. How leaders deal with conflict, resistance, anxiety, and defensiveness does much to set the tone of the group. In our view, members have a tendency to follow the leader's manner of confronting.

■■ Guidelines for Creating Therapeutic Member Relationships

In this section we present an adaptation of further guidelines for practice based on research summaries done by Dies (1983b), Stockton and Morran (1982), and Bednar and Kaul (1978):

· Strive for positive involvement in the group through genuine, empathic, and caring interactions with the members. Impersonal, detached, and judgmental leadership styles can create resistance and can thwart the development of trust and cohesion.
· Develop a reasonably open therapeutic style characterized by appropriate and facilitative self-disclosure. Be willing to share your own reactions and emotional experiences, especially as they relate to events and relationships within the group.
· Keep in mind that leader self-disclosure can have either a constructive or detrimental effect on group process and outcome, depending on specific factors such as the type of group, the stage of its development, and the content and manner of the disclosure.
· Help members make maximum use of effective role models, especially those members who demonstrate desirable behavior. Members can be encouraged to learn from one another. If you have a co-leader, model openness with him or her.
· Provide opportunities for all members to make maximum use of the resources within the group by teaching them skills of active participation in the group process.
· Intervene when a member is preventing others from using the group's resources by engaging in nonconstructive confrontations, hostility, and indirect exchanges. Help members deal with one another in direct and constructive ways.

We want to underscore our belief that leaders can do much to encourage members to give up some of their defensiveness by reacting to them with directness, honesty, and respect. Members are more likely to develop a stance of openness in a group that they perceive as being safe for them, and what leaders model has a lot to do with creating this therapeutic atmosphere.

Co-Leader Issues at the Transition Stage

As you can see, the transition stage is a critical period in the history of the group. Depending on how conflict and resistance are handled, the group can take a turn for better or for worse. If you are working with a co-leader, there are a few particular problems that can easily develop at this time. You can efficiently use the time you have for meeting before and after sessions to focus on your own reactions to what is occurring in the group.

· **Negative reactions toward one leader.** If members direct a challenge or express negative feelings toward your co-leader, it is as important to avoid taking sides with your co-leader in attacking members as it is to side with the members in ganging up against the co-leader. What is called for in such an instance is for you to nondefensively (and as objectively as possible) continue your leadership by facilitating a constructive exploration of the situation.

· **Challenge to both co-leaders.** Assume that several members direct negative feelings to both you and your co-leader, saying: "You leaders expect us to be personal in here, yet we don't know anything about you that is personal. You should be willing to talk about your problems if that is what you expect us to do!" In such a case, difficulties can develop if one of you responds defensively while the other is willing to deal with this confrontation from the members. Ideally, both co-leaders would be willing to talk about the confrontation objectively; if not, this would surely be a vital topic to discuss in the co-leaders' meeting outside of the group or during a supervision session. We don't want to convey the impression that all difficulties should be reserved for a private discussion with the co-leaders. As much as possible, matters that pertain to what is happening during sessions should be discussed with the entire group. The failure to do this can easily lead to a *you*-versus-*them* split within the group.

· **Dealing with problem behaviors.** We have discussed a variety of difficult members that you and your co-leader might have to confront. We want to caution against the tendency of co-leaders to chronically discuss what such members are doing or not doing and never explore how such behavior affects them as leaders. It is a mistake to dwell almost exclusively on strategies for curing problem members while ignoring the leaders' personal reactions to such problematic behaviors.

· **Dealing with countertransference.** It is not realistic to expect a leader to work equally effectively with every member. At times, ineffectiveness is due to countertransference reactions on the part of one of the leaders. For example, a male leader could have strong and irrational negative reactions to one of the women in the group. It may be that he is seeing his ex-wife in this member and responding to her in cutting ways because of his own unresolved issues over the divorce. When this occurs, the co-leader can be therapeutic for both the member and the leader who is being nontherapeutic. The co-leader can intervene during the session itself as well as exploring these inappropriate reactions with the other leader outside the session. Co-leaders who are willing to be objective and honest with each other can have a positive impact through this process of mutual confrontation.

Exercises

■■ Self-Assessment

Use the following self-assessment scale to determine your strengths and weaknesses as a group member. Rate yourself as you see yourself at this time. This inventory assumes that you have had some type of group experience. If you have not, you might rate yourself in terms of your behavior in the class you're now in. This exercise can help you determine the degree to which you may be either resisting or being a productive member in a group. If you identify specific problem areas, you can decide to work on them in your group.

After everyone has completed the inventory, the class should break into small groups, each person trying to join the people he or she knows best. Members of the groups should then assess one another's self-ratings.

Rate yourself from 1 to 5 on each of the following self-descriptions.

1 = This is almost never true of me.
5 = This is almost always true of me.

_____ 1. I'm readily able to trust others in a group.
_____ 2. Others tend to trust me in a group situation.
_____ 3. I disclose personal and meaningful material.
_____ 4. I'm willing to formulate specific goals and contracts.
_____ 5. I'm generally an active participant, as opposed to an observer.
_____ 6. I'm willing to openly express my feelings about and reactions to what is occurring within a group.
_____ 7. I listen attentively to what others are saying, and I'm able to discern more than the mere content of what is said.
_____ 8. I don't give in to group pressure by doing or saying things that don't seem right to me.
_____ 9. I'm able to give direct and honest feedback to others, and I'm open to receiving feedback about my behavior from others.
_____ 10. I prepare myself for a given group by thinking of what I want from that experience and what I'm willing to do to achieve my goals.

_____ 11. I avoid monopolizing the group time.
_____ 12. I avoid storytelling by describing what I'm experiencing now.
_____ 13. I avoid questioning other group members and instead make direct statements to them.
_____ 14. I'm able to be supportive of others when it is appropriate without giving pseudosupport.
_____ 15. I'm able to confront others in a direct and caring manner by letting them know how I'm affected by them.

■■ Exercises and Questions for Exploration

Many of the following exercises are ideally suited for small-group interaction and discussion. Explore the following questions from the vantage point of a group leader.

   1. Assume that various members make these statements:
· "I'm afraid of looking like a fool in the group."
· "My greatest fear is that the group members will reject me."
· "I am afraid to look at myself, because if I do, I might discover that I am empty."
· "I am reluctant to let others know who I am, for this is not something I have done before."

   With each of the above statements, what might you say or do? Can you think of any ways to work with members who express these fears?
   2. Imagine that you are leading a group that does not seem to want to get beyond the stage of "playing it safe." Member disclosures are superficial, risk taking is minimal, and the members display a variety of resistances. What might you do in such a situation? How do you imagine you'd feel if you were leading such a group?
   3. Assume that there is a good deal of conflict in a group you are leading. When you point this out to the members and encourage them to deal with these conflicts, most of them tell you that they don't see any point in talking about the conflicts they are having with one another because "things won't change." What might be your response? How would you deal with a group that seemed to want to avoid facing and working with conflicts?
   4. In a group that you are co-leading, you experience an attack on your leadership competence from several members. In essence, they give you the message that you are not doing things right and that they favor the other leader. How do you imagine you'd feel in such a situation? What do you think you'd do or say?
   5. In one of your groups there is a member (Betty) who rarely speaks, even if encouraged to do so. What are your reactions to the following leader interventions? (a) Ignore her. (b) Ask others in the group how they react to her silence. (c) Remind her of her contract involving the

responsibility to participate. (d) Ask her what keeps her from contributing. (e) Frequently attempt to draw her out. What are some interventions you would be likely to make?

6. One member, Herb, continually gives unsolicited advice every time a member brings up an issue for exploration. Other members finally confront him for playing "assistant therapist" and express their impatience with his ready-made answers for every problem. What kind of intervention would you be inclined to make? What would you want to say to Herb? to the others who confronted him?

7. Larry has a style of asking many questions of fellow group members. You notice that his questioning has the effects of distracting members and interfering with their expression of feelings. What are some things you might say to Larry?

8. Jill has a habit of going into great detail in telling stories when she speaks. She typically focuses on details about others in her life, saying little about how she is affected by them. Eventually, another member says to Jill: "I'm really having trouble staying with you. I get bored and impatient with you when you go into such detail about others. I want to hear more about you and less about others." Jill responds: "That really upsets me. I felt I have been risking a lot by telling you about problems in my life. Now I feel like not saying any more!" What interventions would you make at this point?

9. How do you think you'd react in situations characterized by transference toward you? How might you react if certain members responded to you as an expert? as an authority figure? as a superperson? as a friend? as a lover? as a parent?

10. From what you know of yourself, in what area(s) are you most likely to experience countertransference? If you found that your objectivity were seriously hampered in a group because of your own personal issues, what might you do?

6

Working Stage of a Group

Focus questions · Introduction · Progressing from the transition stage to the working stage · Characteristics of the working stage · Cohesion and universality · Group norms and behavior · Contrasts between a working group and a nonworking group · The nonworking group member · The working group member · Group process during the working stage · Choices to be made in the working stage · **Therapeutic factors that operate in groups ·** Hope · Willingness to risk and trust · Caring and acceptance · Power · Catharsis · The cognitive component · Commitment to change · Freedom to experiment · Humor · Confrontation · **Research implications for the working stage ·** Cohesion · Self-Disclosure · Feedback · **Co-leader issues during the working stage ·** Our leadership style · Topics for co-leader meetings · **Exercises**

1. What do you think are the major differences between a working and a nonworking group? between a working and a nonworking member?
2. How can a client who has gained insight into the reasons for a problem be helped to act on this insight?
3. What is your position on the values and limitations of catharsis in groups?
4. As a group leader, what do you think you can do to assist participants in making constructive choices about their behavior in the group?
5. What is your position on the use of techniques and exercises to facilitate communication and interaction?
6. What is your view of the "ideal" group member?
7. What are three major factors that you think account for change in individuals? How do groups have a "healing capacity" for the members?
8. What specific guidelines can you come up with to determine whether self-disclosure would be appropriate and facilitative for you as a leader?
9. What would you want to teach members during the working stage about giving and receiving feedback?
10. What guidelines might you give members of your groups on how to give and receive feedback?

■■

Introduction

As we've mentioned before, there are no arbitrary dividing lines that neatly compartmentalize a group into various phases; in actual practice there is a considerable overlapping of the stages. This is especially true of the movement from the transition stage to the working stage, for there is often a thin line between expressing conflicts and resistance, which is so characteristic of the transition stage, and working them through, which moves the group into a more advanced stage of development.

Many groups never evolve to a true working level. There are several reasons for this. Some open groups with changing membership may not have the opportunity to develop trust, cohesion, and continuity. Some closed groups that fail to master the major tasks of conflict management and dealing with resistance do not establish enough trust to allow members to reach a level of what they (or the leader) consider productive work. However, individuals may still benefit from a group even if it does not reach a working stage.

As we discussed earlier, conflict, resistance, and feelings of mistrust must be expressed and a commitment made to face and work through barriers that halt progress. In this chapter we examine the following questions:

· What are the characteristics of the working stage of groups?
· How does a leader facilitate a group's movement from the transition stage to the working stage?
· What are some of the therapeutic factors that operate in the working stage? What are some of the factors that influence change within an individual and a group, and how are these changes brought about?
· How are leader and member self-disclosures particularly important during the working stage?

Progressing from the Transition Stage to the Working Stage

In Chapter 5 we gave a description of a group in its transition stage. With a few examples, we now show how a leader's intervention can assist a group in transition to become a working one.

Example 1

Frank and Judy declare that not enough is happening in the group and that they are getting impatient. They are likely to back off if the leader responds defensively. Therapeutic interventions could be any of the following statements:

· "What would you like to see happening?"
· "I suggest that you tell each person one thing that you would like him or her to do in this group. By now you have some sense of many of the members in the group, so you could let them know what you'd like for or from them."
· "Since I am the leader of this group, you might have some reactions to the way I'm leading. Is there anything you need to say to me?"

These leader interventions are helping Frank and Judy go beyond complaining, explore the source of their dissatisfaction, and express what they would like to see happen. When Joe, another member, makes a hostile remark ("If you don't like it, leave the group"), the leader can bring it into this interaction. This could be accomplished by asking Joe to make some direct statements to Frank and Judy, instead of dismissing them. If the leader does not notice hostile remarks, they will have a negative impact on the group.

Example 2

Sunny's saying that she is afraid of talking about herself in the group is another opportunity for productive work. A good place to begin is with her admission that she feels judged; the leader can further Sunny's work by intervening in any of these ways:

· "Would you be willing to talk to one person in here who you think would judge you the most harshly? Why not tell that person all the things you imagine he or she would think about you?"
· "Perhaps you can go around the group and finish this sentence: If I let you know me, I'm afraid you would judge me by . . ."
· "Sunny, would you be willing to go around and make some judgmental comment to each person in the group?"
· "If you would be willing, I'd like to have you close your eyes and imagine all the judgments that people in here could possibly make about you. You don't need to verbalize what you imagine, but do let yourself feel what it is like to be judged by everyone in the group."

In each of these interventions is the potential for further exploration, which can assist Sunny in learning how she allows herself to be inhibited by her fear of others' judgments. If she follows any of these leader suggestions, she has a basis for actually working through her fears.

Example 3

Jennifer says that she never gets any attention in her group and that the leader gives everyone else priority over her. The leader does not waste time trying to persuade her that she is indeed important to him; rather, he listens to her perceptions and feelings. He then asks her to talk directly to the members whom she sees as getting more of his attention. She talks about her feelings about being pushed aside. The leader intervenes with: "I wonder if being in this group is anything like being in your family. Are there any ways in which you felt that you were not given attention at home, and are the feelings you are experiencing in here familiar to you?" This intervention can encourage Jennifer to work in greater depth on connecting up her past and present outside life with reactions she is having in the here-and-now context of her group.

Characteristics of the Working Stage

After the tentativeness of the initial stage and the expression of feelings and problems in the transition stage, the working stage is characterized by the commitment of members to explore significant problems they bring to the sessions and their attention to the dynamics within the group. In our groups we find that our degree of structuring and leadership is lower than during the initial and transition stages. By the working stage, participants have learned how to involve themselves in group interactions, rather than merely waiting to be invited into an interaction. In a sense there is a sharing of the group leadership functions, for the members are able to assume greater responsibility for the work that occurs in the group.

■■ Cohesion and Universality

A central characteristic of the working stage is group cohesion, which has resulted from members' willingness to become transparent with one another. If the conflicts and negative feelings of the earlier stages have been faced, the deep level of trust that has developed allows for a working-through process.

At the working stage the members are able to see commonalities, and they are struck by the universality of their life issues. For example, our growth groups are composed of a very wide mixture of people: they come from all walks of life, the age range is from 18 to 65 years, they represent various social and cultural backgrounds, and they have a variety of careers. Although in the earlier stages members are likely to be aware of their differences and at times feel separated, as the group achieves increased cohesion these differences recede into the background. Members comment more on how they are alike than on how they are different. A woman in her early 50s discovers that she is still striving for parental approval, just as a man in his early 20s is. A man learns that his struggles with masculinity are not that different from a woman's concern about her femininity.

The circumstances leading to hurt and disappointment may be very different from person to person or from culture to culture. But the resulting feelings have a universal quality. Although we may not speak the same language or come from the same culture, we are connected through our experiences of feelings of joy and pain. It is when group members no longer get lost in the details of daily experiences and instead share their deeper struggles on these universal human themes that a group is most cohesive. The leader can help the group achieve this level of cohesion by focusing on the underlying issues, feelings, and needs that the members seem to share.

This bonding provides the group with the impetus to move forward, for participants gain courage by discovering that they are not alone in their feelings. A woman experiences a great sense of relief when she discovers, through statements by other women, that she is not strange for feeling resentment over the many demands her family makes on her. Men discover that they can share their tears and affection with other men without being robbed of their masculinity. Other common themes evolving in this stage that lead to increased cohesion and trust are members' fears of rejection, feelings of loneliness and abandonment, feelings of inferiority and living up to others' expectations, painful memories associated with life events, guilt and remorse over what they have and have not done, discovery that their worst enemy often lives within them, need for and fear of intimacy, feelings about sexual identity and sexual performance, and unfinished business with their parents. This list is not exhaustive; it is merely a sample of the universal human issues that participants recognize and explore with one another as the group progresses. Earlier we discussed group cohesion as a foundation quality of the initial stage of a group. The cohesion that is characteristic of the working stage is a deeper intimacy that develops with time and commitment. This bonding is a form of affection and genuine caring that often results from sharing the expression of painful experiences.

■■ Group Norms and Behavior

During the working stage there is a further development and solidification of group norms that were formed in the earlier stages. Members are more aware of facilitative behaviors, and unspoken norms become more explicit. At this time the following in-group behaviors tend to be manifested:

· There is provision of both support and challenge; members are reinforced for making behavioral changes both inside and outside of the sessions.
· The leader employs a variety of therapeutic interventions, designed to further self-exploration, that lead to experimentation with new behavior and to changes.
· Members increasingly interact with one another in more direct ways; there is less dependence on the leader for direction and less eye contact directed toward the leader as the members talk.

· Control issues, power struggles, and interpersonal conflicts within the group are frequently the basis of discussion and tend to be explored on a deeper level. Members learn about how they deal with conflict in everyday situations by paying attention to how they interact with one another in the group.

· There is the development of a healing capacity within the group as members increasingly experience acceptance for who they are. There is less need to put up facades, for members are learning that they are respected for showing deeper facets of themselves.

Group cohesion, which is a primary characteristic of a well-functioning group, actually fosters action-oriented behaviors such as self-disclosure, the giving and receiving of feedback, discussion of here-and-now interactions, confrontation, and the translation of insight into action.

Though it is our opinion that cohesion is necessary for effective group work, cohesion alone is not sufficient. Some groups make an implicit decision to stop at the level of comfort and security and do not push ahead to new levels. Groups can reach a plateau unless members are willing to confront one another. In an effective group the cohesion that has developed marks the beginning of a lengthy working process.

In the next section we provide a further discussion of the factors that differentiate a working group from a nonworking one.

■■ Contrasts between a Working Group and a Nonworking Group

The following lists represent our view of some basic differences between productive and nonproductive groups. As you study the lists, think of any other factors you could add. If you are or have been in a group, think about how these characteristics apply to your group experience.

Working Group	Nonworking Group
Members trust other members and the leaders, or at least they openly express any lack of trust. There is a willingness to take risks by sharing meaningful here-and-now reactions.	Mistrust is evidenced by an undercurrent of unexpressed hostility. Members withhold themselves, refusing to express feelings and thoughts.
Goals are clear and specific and are determined jointly by the members and the leader. There is a willingness to direct in-group behavior toward realizing these goals.	Goals are fuzzy, abstract, and general. Members have unclear personal goals or no goals at all.

Working Group

Most members feel a sense of inclusion, and excluded members are invited to become more active. Communication among most members is open and involves accurate expression of what is being experienced.

There is a focus on the here and now, and participants talk directly to one another about what they're experiencing.

The leadership functions are shared by the group; people feel free to initiate activities or to suggest exploring particular areas.

There is a willingness to risk disclosing threatening material; people become known.

Cohesion is high; there is a close emotional bond among people, based on sharing of universal human experiences. Members identify with one another. People are willing to risk experimental behavior because of the closeness and support for new ways of being.

Conflict among members or with the leader is recognized, discussed, and often resolved.

Members accept the responsibility for deciding what action they will take to solve their problems.

Feedback is given freely and accepted without defensiveness. There is a willingness to seriously reflect on the accuracy of the feedback.

Nonworking Group

Many members feel excluded or cannot identify with other members. Cliques are formed that tend to lead to fragmentation. There is fear of expressing feelings of being left out.

There is a "there-and-then" focus; people tend to focus on others and not on themselves, and storytelling is typical. There is a resistance to dealing with reactions to one another.

Members lean on the leaders for all direction. There are power conflicts among members as well as between members and the leader.

Participants hold back, and disclosure is at a minimum.

Fragmentation exists; people feel distant from one another. There is a lack of caring or empathy. Members don't encourage one another to engage in new and risky behavior, so familiar ways of being are rigidly maintained.

Conflicts or negative feelings are ignored, denied, or avoided.

Members blame others for their personal difficulties and aren't willing to take action to change.

What little feedback is given is rejected defensively. Feedback is given without care or compassion.

Working Group
Members feel hopeful; they feel that constructive change is possible—that people can become what they want to become.

Confrontation occurs in such a way that the confronter shares his or her reactions to the person being confronted. Confrontation is accepted as a challenge to examine one's behavior and not as an uncaring attack.

Communication is clear and direct.

Group members use one another as a resource and show interest in one another.

Members feel powerful and share this power *with* one another.

There is an awareness of group process, and members know what makes the group productive or nonproductive.

Diversity is encouraged, and there is a respect for individual and cultural differences.

Group norms are developed cooperatively by the members and the leader. Norms are clear and are designed to help the members attain their goals.

There is an emphasis on combining the feeling and thinking functions. Catharsis and expression of feeling occur, but so does thinking about the meaning of various emotional experiences.

Group members use out-of-group time to work on problems raised in the group.

Nonworking Group
Members feel despairing, helpless and trapped, victimized.

Confrontation is done in a hostile, attacking way; the confronted one feels judged and rejected. At times the members gang up on a member, using this person as a scapegoat.

Communication is unclear and indirect.

Members are interested only in themselves.

Members or leaders use power and control *over* others.

There is an indifference or lack of awareness of what is going on within the group, and group dynamics are rarely discussed.

Conformity is prized, and individual and cultural differences are devalued.

Norms are merely imposed by the leader. They may not be clear.

The group relies heavily on cathartic experiences but makes little or no effort to understand them.

Group members think about group activity very little when they're outside the group.

■■ The Nonworking Group Member

Having described the characteristics of a working and nonworking group in general, we now move to specifics. In the previous chapter we examined a variety of problem behaviors, and what follows is a composite picture of a nonworking group member.

Barney has joined a weekly ongoing group because his wife thinks he needs such an experience. Although he agreed to sign up for the group, he had many doubts that it would help him. He was convinced that groups do more harm than good.

Barney keeps all his reservations to himself. For several group sessions he either says nothing or reacts in a hostile manner to many of the women. When several of them let him know that they are feeling distant and are having difficulties with him, he reacts sarcastically and defensively by saying: "Well, aren't you supposed to be honest in here? What's wrong with my saying that you girls are all alike?"

At one point, tears come to Barney's eyes, and he looks very scared. When the leader checks with him about what he is feeling, he replies: "Stop pushing me, and leave me alone. All you ever do is make people cry." After that he storms out of the room.

Barney often talks about his wife, blaming her for most of his misery. When the leader suggests a role-playing exercise in which he could talk directly to his "wife" in this room, Barney refuses by saying: "That's silly. I can't talk to Bertha [a group member], because she's not my wife." At times he comes late to sessions or misses a session, either having a "good" excuse or simply not giving any reason.

Several times, toward the end of a session, Barney begins what could become some meaningful work. The leader lets him know of her concern that time is running out and makes the observation that his waiting until the end seems to be a pattern. He brusquely responds: "You don't care about me the way you do about the rest of the people. I can't program my feelings."

Although in some sessions Barney says almost nothing and expects to be drawn out, at other times he interrupts others' work by giving them unsolicited advice and solutions to their problems. He then rambles on with stories about himself. When confronted on his behavior, Barney replies, aggressively, "When I don't talk, you criticize me, and when I do talk, you want to shut me up!" He makes no attempt to listen to any constructive feedback given to him, and he is always quick to take a defensive stance.

When conflict arises in the group, Barney is quick to note: "See, I was right. All groups ever do is tear people down." He is very able to stir up conflict in his group, yet he quickly retreats in a hit-and-run fashion. At one point he admits that he feels isolated in this group, as well as his outside life. But he is unable to see how his behavior contributes to his feelings of isolation.

In considering Barney's case, how might you deal with him? Which of his behaviors would cause you the most difficulty? Would you have let him into the group to begin with? On what basis would you have included or excluded him at the outset? Would you have excluded him later, after he had joined the group?

■■ The Working Group Member

Now we describe the combination of traits that we think makes for a working and productive group member. We encourage you to create your own profile of the ideal group participant. Our ideal member is a woman we'll call Sandy.

Sandy wants to participate in a weekly, ongoing counseling group. She wants to take a good look at herself, her marriage, her career goals, and her relationship with her son, and she wants to discover more ways of feeling alive. She has sought group counseling voluntarily. She is motivated to work, as evidenced by her willingness to spend time thinking about what she wants from her group sessions. She eventually forms a contract that guides her work in the group. She is specific about what she wants, and she is willing to explore her problems with the group.

Sandy is sometimes scared by her feelings, and she expresses these fears. For example, she sometimes doubts that she wants to stay with her husband, and she's willing to face this issue squarely. She has never told anyone of her need to control in her sexual relationship, yet in her group she deals with this need and considers relinquishing the control.

Sandy says what she feels, not what others in her group (including the therapist) might expect of her. She confronts both leader and members when she feels that something needs to be challenged, and she does so by bringing her own reactions into the confrontation. She avoids labeling or judging and instead speaks of how she is affected by what others are doing in the group. Sandy gives feedback when she has something to offer and gives support or affection when she genuinely feels this toward another member. She resists participating in activities that don't seem right for her, and she is not pressured into doing or saying something to please anyone but herself. During the group sessions she listens undefensively to what others tell her, and when she is given feedback, she doesn't try to rationalize her behavior. Instead, she considers the feedback seriously. Then she decides for herself how accurate others' perceptions of her are and what she will do with this information.

Sandy devotes time between sessions to reflecting on her involvement in the group, and she eventually makes decisions to change her behavior. She not only tries out new behavior-in her group but also risks applying what she has learned in the group to her daily affairs. In between sessions she reads books dealing with areas of struggle for her and keeps a daily journal. She brings into therapy any insights she has about herself or about the group. She commits herself to doing things actively outside her group, yet at times she doesn't live up to these contracts. If she feels that she's backsliding, she mentions this in her sessions. At this point she evaluates her contract and determines how realistic her expectations are. Sandy realizes that she's not perfect, yet she accepts herself.

■■ Group Process during the Working Stage

At the outset of this chapter we reiterated that the stages of groups cannot be neatly compartmentalized. It also needs to be emphasized that, even if groups reach a high level of productivity during the working stage, this achievement does not imply that the group will always remain at that level. The group may stay on a plateau for a time and then regress to an earlier developmental phase characterized by issues faced during the initial and transition stages. For example, trust can become an issue again, and it may need to be reestablished. Some members may have the tendency to close off and withdraw. The reasons for this lack of trust could be that intensive work threatens them, that they have doubts about the validity of what they have experienced, that they have second thoughts about how involved they want to remain, that they are frightened by the display of anger between members or the expression of painful experiences, or that they are anticipating the eventual ending of the group and are prematurely winding down.

As is the case with personal relationships in daily life, groups ebb and flow. Periods of stagnation can be expected, but if they are recognized, they can be challenged. Because groups are not static entities, both the leader and the members have the task of accurately assessing the group's ever-changing character, as well as its effectiveness.

■■ Choices to Be Made in the Working Stage

In discussing the initial stages of a group's evolution we described several critical issues, such as trust versus mistrust, the struggle for power, and self-focus versus focus on others. During the more intensive working period of a group, certain other key issues are at stake, and again the group as a whole must resolve the issues for better or worse. We now discuss each of the choices that the group must make at this stage. Remember that a group's identity is shaped by the way its members resolve these critical issues.

Disclosure versus Anonymity.   People can protect themselves through anonymity, yet the very reason many become involved in a therapeutic group is that they want to make themselves known to others and to come to know others in a deeper way than they have allowed themselves in their daily lives. If the group process is to work effectively, the participants must be willing to reveal themselves, for it is through self-disclosure that they begin to learn about themselves.

Individuals can decide to disclose themselves in a significant and appropriate way, or they can choose to remain hidden out of fear that if they were to reveal themselves to others they would be rejected.

Honesty versus Game Playing.   There are those who believe that in order to survive in the real world they must sacrifice their honesty and substitute deceit, game playing, and manipulation. They may say that in order to get ahead they have to suppress what they really think and feel, figure out what others expect from them, and then meet these expectations.

It is fundamental to the success of a therapeutic group that honesty prevail and that a person not have to be dishonest to win acceptance. If these conditions hold, participants can both be themselves and learn to accept the true selves of others. Group interaction can deteriorate into another form of game playing unless the participants choose to be honest with themselves and one another.

Spontaneity versus Control.   We hope that group participants will make the choice to relinquish some of their controlled and rehearsed ways and allow themselves to respond more spontaneously to events of the moment. We encourage spontaneity indirectly, by making clients feel that it's all right to say and do many of the things they've been preventing themselves from saying or doing. One problem is that members and leaders alike may push themselves to be spontaneous and thereby produce behavior that is contrived or rehearsed. Another problem could arise if members "do their own thing" at the expense of others.

Acceptance versus Rejection.   Throughout the course of a group the members must deal with the acceptance/rejection polarity. We sometimes hear a member say "I'd like to reveal more of myself and be more active than I have been, but I'm afraid that if I'm me in here, I'll be rejected." This fear can be explored, and those who feel this way can choose to take the risk of looking foolish and of not being universally accepted.

We find that many clients are frightened more by acceptance than by rejection. It's as though some say "If you accept me or love me or care for me, I won't know how to respond; I'll feel burdened with a debt to you."

We hope that group members will recognize their own role and responsibility in the creation of an accepting climate and come to understand that by contributing to a climate either of acceptance or of rejection they can help determine whether they as individuals will be accepted or rejected.

Cohesion versus Fragmentation.   Our conviction is that cohesion is largely the result of the group's choice to work actively at developing unifying bonds. Members do this mainly by choosing to make themselves known to others, by allowing caring to develop, by initiating meaningful work, and by giving honest feedback to others.

If a group chooses to remain comfortable or to stick with superficial interactions, there will be little group togetherness. If enough members choose not to express their fears, suspicions, disappointments, doubts, and so forth but rather to bury or avoid these reactions, fragmentation will result. Cohesion results from working with meaningful, painful problems as well as from the intimate sharing of humorous and joyous moments.

Responsibility versus Blaming.   In individual therapy the client must accept the responsibility for his or her behavior if any significant behavior changes are to take place. Likewise, group members must stop viewing themselves as victims of external factors, including other people, if they are to become more effective individuals.

At some point in therapy and group work, clients usually focus their anger on others, whom they blame for their unhappiness. But during the more intensive phases of group work, clients generally come to accept the fact that a blaming style will get them nowhere. What they need to realize is that they can change only themselves; then, others may change in response to their changes. When members stop blaming others, they find that they are in control and are more able to make changes in their life.

Therapeutic Factors That Operate in Groups

In this section we give attention to the special forces within groups that produce constructive changes. We've come to believe that a variety of forces within groups can be *healing*, or *therapeutic*, and that these forces are interrelated. We came up with the therapeutic factors listed below by reflecting on our experiences in leading groups and by reading the reports of hundreds of people who have participated in our groups. (We've always had the participants in our groups write follow-up reaction papers telling what factors they think were related to their changes in attitudes and behavior.) We are also indebted to other writers in the field of group work, especially Yalom (1983, 1985).

▪▪ Hope

Hope is the belief that change is possible—that one is not a victim of the past and that new decisions can be made. It is therapeutic in itself, for it gives members confidence that they have the power to choose to be different. Some people approach a group convinced that they are victims of external circumstances over which they have no control. In the group, however, they may encounter others who have struggled and found ways to assume effective control over their life. Seeing and being associated with such people can inspire a new sense of optimism that their life can be different.

Example: Pete, who was left paralyzed as a result of a motorcycle accident, spent most of his energies thinking about all that he could no longer do. With the encouragement of his physician he joined a rehabilitation group, where he met several people who had at one time felt as he was feeling. By listening to their struggles and the ways in which they had effectively coped with their disability, Pete found hope that he, too, could discover more effective ways of living his life.

▪▪ Willingness to Risk and Trust

Risking involves opening one's self to others, being vulnerable, and actively doing in a group what is necessary for change. This willingness to reveal one's self is largely a function of how much one trusts the other group members and the leader. Trust is therapeutic, for it allows people to show the many facets of themselves, encourages experimental behavior, and allows people to look at themselves in new ways.

Example: Jane expressed considerable resentment and hostility to the men in her group. Eventually, she took the risk of disclosing that as a child she had been sexually exploited by her stepfather. As she explored ways in which she had generalized her distrust of getting close to men in everyday life and in her group, she began to see how she was keeping men at a distance so that they would never again have the chance to exploit her. Finally, she made a new decision that all men would not necessarily hurt her if she allowed herself to get close to them. Had she been unwilling to risk making the disclosure in her group, it is unlikely that she would have made this attitudinal and behavioral change.

▪▪ Caring and Acceptance

Caring is demonstrated by listening and involvement. It can be expressed by tenderness, compassion, support, and even confrontation. If members sense a lack of caring, either from other members or from the leader, their willingness to drop their masks will be reduced. Members are able to risk being vulnerable if they sense that their concerns are important to others and that they are valued as persons.

Caring implies acceptance, a genuine support from others that says, in effect, "We will accept all of your feelings. You do count here. It's OK to be yourself—you don't have to strive to please everyone." Acceptance involves affirming each person's right to have and express his or her own feelings and values.

Caring and acceptance develop into empathy, a deep understanding of another's struggles. Commonalities emerge in groups that unite the members. The realization that certain problems are universal—loneliness, need for acceptance, fear of rejection, fear of intimacy, hurt over past experiences—lessens the feeling that one is alone. Through identification with others, moreover, one is able to see oneself more clearly.

Example: Bobby, who was in a group for children of divorce, finally began to talk about his sadness over not having his father at home anymore. Other children were very attentive. When Bobby said that he was embarrassed by his crying, two other boys told him that they also cried.

■■ Power

A feeling of power emerges from the recognition that one has untapped internal reserves of spontaneity, creativity, courage, and strength. In groups, personal power can be experienced in ways that were formerly denied, and people can discover ways in which they block their strengths. This power is not a power over others; rather, it is the sense that one has the internal resources necessary to direct the course of one's life.

Example: Carl, a recovering alcoholic, admitted that he felt powerful only when he drank. In addition to his Alcoholics Anonymous group he joined an assertion-training group, where he learned social skills that helped him to deal effectively with situations in which he had felt powerless. He found the courage to ask people directly for what he wanted from them, and he learned how to nonaggressively deny unreasonable requests made of him.

■■ Catharsis

The expression of pent-up feelings can be therapeutic because energy is released that has been tied up in withholding threatening feelings. This type of emotional release plays an important part in many kinds of group, and the expression of feeling can facilitate trust and cohesion. However, both group leaders and members sometimes make the mistake of concluding that mere catharsis implies "real work." Some disappointed members who do not have an emotional release are convinced that they are not really getting involved. Although it is often healing, catharsis by itself is limited in terms of producing long-lasting changes. Members need to learn how to make sense of their emotional experiences, and one way of doing this is by putting words to their intense emotions and attempting to understand them.

Example: Susan learned that she could experience both positive and negative feelings toward her mother. For years she had buried her resentment over what she saw as her mother's continual attempts to control her life. In one session Susan allowed herself to feel and to fully express her resentment to her mother in a symbolic way. The group leader assisted Susan in telling her mother, in role playing, many of the things that had contributed to her feelings of resentment. She felt a great sense of relief after having expressed these pent-up emotions. The leader cautioned her of the dangers of harshly confronting her mother in real life but also encouraged her to begin dealing directly, honestly, and sensitively with her mother.

■■ The Cognitive Component

As mentioned above, catharsis is even more useful if a person attempts to find words to explain the feelings expressed. Some conceptualization of the meaning of the intense feelings associated with certain experiences can give members the tools to make significant changes. Members who simply *experience* feelings often have difficulty in integrating what they learn from these experiences.

Both the affective and the cognitive components are needed and can be integrated in group work. Yalom (1983, 1985) cites substantial research evidence demonstrating that to profit from a group experience the members require a cognitive framework that will allow them to put their here-and-now experiencing into perspective.

■■ Commitment to Change

A resolve to change is also therapeutic in itself. If one is motivated to the point of becoming an active group participant, the chances are good that change will occur. This commitment to change involves a willingness to specify what changes are desired and to make use of the tools offered by group process to explore ways of modifying one's behavior.

■■ Freedom to Experiment

The group situation provides a safe place for experimentation with new behavior. Members are able to show facets of themselves that they often keep hidden in everyday situations. In the accepting environment of a group, a shy member can exhibit spontaneous behavior and be outgoing. A person who typically is very quiet might experiment with being more verbal in a group. After trying new behavior, members can gauge how much they want to change their existing behavior.

▪▪ Humor

Not everything that goes on in group has to be heavy and serious. Effective feedback can sometimes be given in a humorous way. Laughing at oneself can be extremely therapeutic. This requires seeing one's problems in a new perspective.

Example: Sarah, who dressed extremely seductively and acted sexually provocative, expressed pain over the fact that men saw her only as a "sexual object." A male member spontaneously dressed up as a woman and moved about in a seductive way in the group, saying "All you ever see is my body!" Everyone, including Sarah, broke into hysterical laughter. As silly as this may seem, this was powerful feedback to Sarah. She realized that her seductive ways distracted others from seeing other dimensions of her.

▪▪ Confrontation

Constructive confrontation is a basic part of the working group. A lack of confrontation results in stagnation. It is through acts of caring confrontation that members are invited to examine discrepancies between what they say and do, to become aware of potentials that are dormant, and to find ways of putting their insights into action. Done with sensitivity and caring, confrontation by others ultimately assists members to develop the capacity for the self-confrontation that they will need to apply what they have learned to the problems they face in their daily life.

Research Implications for the Working Stage

In this brief review of research findings we consider three more group-process variables as they are related to the working stage. We have selected *cohesion*, *self-disclosure*, and *feedback* because these factors have a central role in determining group productivity.

▪▪ Cohesion

A group characterized by a high degree of cohesiveness provides a climate in which members feel free enough to do meaningful work. Under these conditions, the members are likely to express what they feel and think, engage in significant self-exploration, and relate more deeply to others (Bednar & Kaul, 1978).

Yalom (1985) maintains that research evidence shows cohesion to be a strong determinant of positive group outcome. If members experience little sense of belongingness or attraction to the group, there is little likelihood that they will benefit from a group experience, and they may well experience negative outcomes (Lieberman, Yalom, & Miles, 1973).

How, then, is group cohesion developed? If a group is to be cohesive, its members must perceive it as a means to helping them achieve their personal goals. According to Yalom (1983), groups with a here-and-now focus are almost invariably vital and cohesive. By contrast, groups in which members engage in much "talking about" with a "there-and-then" focus rarely develop much cohesiveness.

Although cohesion is thought to be one of the most crucial factors related to group process and outcomes and in spite of vast amount of research on it, the literature provides some conflicting conclusions. This is not surprising, because the area has not been systematically studied. Rather than being a stable factor, group cohesion is a complex process (Bednar & Kaul, 1985; Stockton & Hulse, 1981). Bednar and Kaul imply that research on cohesion can be improved by giving specific information about the members and the leaders, the nature of the treatment, and the stage in the group at which cohesion is assessed.

■■ Self-Disclosure

The willingness to make oneself known to others is a part of each stage of a group, but at the working stage self-disclosure is more frequent and more personal. Although disclosure is not an end in itself, it is the means by which open communication occurs within the group. Through the process of self-disclosure, the participants experience a healing force and gain new insights that often lead to desired life changes. If disclosures are limited to safe topics, the group does not progress beyond a superficial level.

Self-Disclosure and the Group Member

Group members are able to deepen their self-knowledge through the process of disclosing themselves to others. If members share with others what they know about themselves, they develop a richer and more integrated picture of who they are, and they are better able to recognize the impact they have on others.

We tell the members of our groups that it is essential that they let others know who they are. Otherwise, they are likely to be misunderstood, because people tend to project their own feeling onto members who are mysterious. For example, Andrea thinks that Hal is very critical and judgmental of her. When Hal finally talks, he discloses that he is both attracted to and scared of Andrea. Self-disclosure entails revealing current struggles, unresolved personal issues, goals and aspirations, fears and expectations, hopes, pains and joys, strengths and weaknesses, and personal experiences. If members keep themselves anonymous and say little about themselves that is personal, it is difficult for others to care for them, since genuine concern implies knowledge of the person. Therefore, if members hope to be cared for, it is essential that they reveal themselves in significant ways to others. In group situations this disclosure is not limited to revealing personal concerns; it is equally important to disclose ongoing persistent reactions toward other members and the leader.

What Disclosure Is Not.   We've found that group participants frequently misunderstand what it means to be a self-disclosing person, equating disclosure with "letting it all hang out" without any discrimination. They may believe that the more they can dig up hidden secrets and drop them on the group, the more they are being disclosing. Below are some observations on what self-disclosure is *not.*

· Self-disclosure is not merely telling stories about one's past in a rehearsed and mechanical manner. The question needs to be asked: How does what I reveal have relevance to my present conflicts?
· In the name of being open and honest and as a result of the pressure of other group members, people often say more than is necessary for others to understand them. They confuse being self-disclosing with being open to the extent that nothing remains private, and as a result they may feel deprived of their dignity.
· Dumping every fleeting feeling or reaction on others is not to be confused with self-disclosure. Judgment is needed in deciding how appropriate it is to share certain reactions. However, persistent reactions are generally best shared. People can be honest without being tactless and insensitive.

Guidelines for Appropriate Member Self-Disclosure.   In our groups we suggest the following guidelines as a way of assisting participants in determining *what* and *when* self-disclosure is both appropriate and facilitative:

1. Disclosure needs to be related to the purposes and goals of the group.
2. If members have persistent reactions to certain people in the group, they need to bring these out into the open, especially if these reactions are inhibiting their level of participation.
3. Members must make the determination of what and how much they want others to know about them; they have to decide what they are willing to risk and how far they are willing to go.

4. Reasonable risks can be expected to accompany self-disclosure. If groups are limited by overly safe disclosures, the interactions become boring.
5. The stage of group development has some bearing on the appropriateness of self-disclosure. There may be certain disclosures that are too deep for an initial session but quite appropriate during the working stage.

Related to the issue of member self-disclosure are the place of leader self-disclosure and the impact such disclosures have on group process. We now turn to some guidelines designed to assist leaders in thinking about the kinds of disclosure that can have a facilitative effect on a group.

Self-Disclosure and the Group Leader

The key question here is not whether leaders should disclose themselves to the group but, rather, how much and when. What are the effects of leader disclosure on the group? What are the effects on the leader?

Some group leaders keep themselves mysterious. They're careful not to make themselves personally known to their group, and they strive to keep their personal involvement in the group to a minimum. Some do this because of a theoretical preference; they view their role as one of a "transference figure" on whom their "patients" can project feelings that they've experienced toward parents and other "authority figures." By remaining anonymous, the leader tends to limit the reactions of group members to projections. Through this re-creation of an earlier relationship, unresolved conflicts can be exposed and worked through.

Other reasons some group leaders don't reveal themselves personally are that they don't want to incur the risk of losing their "expert" image and that they don't want to be uncomfortable. They strive not to "contaminate" the "doctor/patient" relationship out of their stated concern that this will interfere with effective therapy. There are leaders who, in addition to keeping their personal life a secret, disclose very little concerning how they feel in the group or how they feel toward different members. Instead of sharing these reactions they intervene, making interpretations and suggestions, clarifying issues, acting as a moderator or coordinator, evaluating, and imposing structured exercises to keep the group moving. Admittedly, all of these functions are important, but it is both possible and desirable for leaders to get involved in these activities by revealing what they are experiencing.

What about the leaders at the other end of the continuum, whose ethic is, the more disclosure, the better? Inexperienced group leaders tend to make the mistake of trying too hard to prove that they're just as human as the members. They freely disclose details of their personal life and explore their current problems in the groups they lead. There are several rationales for such an approach. These leaders may have submitted to group pressure to stop acting like a leader and become more of a group member. The leader may desire to use part of the group time for his or her own development or need to make himself or herself known in a personal way to group participants. The leader may feel that it is unfair to expect members to disclose and risk unless the leader is also willing to do so. Although this reasoning has merit, it is important that group leaders not fall into the trap of pretending that there are no differences between the roles and functions of leaders and members. That there are differences in functions does not mean that one is more human than, or in some other way superior to, the other. It does mean that, even though group leaders can function as participants at times, their primary reason for being in the group is to initiate, facilitate, direct, and evaluate the process of interaction among members. If a leader is uncomfortable in the role of leader, perhaps this is an indication that he or she should be participating in a group as a full-fledged member.

What follows are four guidelines for your consideration in determining your own position on the issue of leader self-disclosure. We use these guidelines in our practice.

1. If group leaders determine that they have problems they wish to explore, they should seek their own therapeutic group, in which they can be fully participating members without the concern of how their work will affect the group. Group leaders have a demanding job and shouldn't make it even more difficult by confusing their role with that of the participants.

2. Leaders should ask themselves why they're disclosing certain personal material. Is it to be seen as "regular people," no different from the members? Is it to model disclosing behavior for others? Is it because they genuinely want to show private dimensions to the members? It may be therapeutic for group members to know the leader and the leader's struggles, but they don't need to know it in elaborate detail. For instance, if a member is exploring her fear of not being loved unless she is perfect, the therapist may reveal in a few words that she also wrestles with this fear. A sense of identification can be established in this way. At another time it may be appropriate for this leader to talk at greater length about how this fear is manifested in the way she leads groups, particularly if it is manifested in a feeling of pressure to be a good therapist and a fear of not being loved if the group is not helped. Again, the timing is crucial. Although this disclosure may be appropriate in the advanced stages of a group, sharing it initially may burden the participants with the fear that this leader is using the group for her own therapy.

3. Disclosure that is related to what is going on in the group is the kind that is most productive. For instance, any persistent feeling a group leader has concerning a member or what is happening or not happening is generally best revealed. If a leader feels annoyed at a member's behavior, it is advisable for the leader to let the member know this reaction. If a leader senses a general resistance in the group, it is best to talk openly about the resistance and about how it feels to experience it. Disclosure related to how a leader feels in the group is generally more appropriate than disclosure of personal material that is not relevant to the ongoing interaction of the group.

4. Group leaders have to ask themselves how much they want to reveal about their private life to the many people they deal with. We regularly co-lead couples' groups, weekend workshops, week-long marathons, and other groups and classes. Do we want to be open books for all of these people? Our position is that we do want to feel the freedom to function openly as people, but at the same time we want to preserve a measure of our privacy. At times, we've been confronted by group members for not revealing more of our personal struggles. They feel they know us as leaders, they say, but want to know more about us personally. We want to take into consideration the fact that in a given year we may be exposed to 200 different people in about 15 groups. If we told everything about ourselves to everyone, not only would we lose privacy, we would also lose spontaneity, for it would probably be impossible with this kind of repetition to maintain a fresh and unrehearsed style. We usually do, however, decide to disclose worries or preoccupations we have that might interfere with our ability to be present and to listen effectively to the members.

Research on Self-Disclosure

Like cohesion, self-disclosure cannot be studied and discussed in a simple way. The empirical base for self-disclosure in group counseling is somewhat limited, but it suggests a complex, multidimensional interaction between frequency of disclosure and other factors such as type of group and population, level of disclosure, and timing (Morran, 1982; Stockton & Morran, 1982).

After surveying the literature on leader self-disclosure, Dies (1983b) suggests that this behavior may have either a constructive or detrimental effect on group process and outcome, depending on specific factors such as the type of group, the stage of group development, and the content of disclosure. Group leaders who are willing to be open about their own reactions to what is going on within the group are more likely to foster the development of positive interpersonal relationships. But Dies adds the cautionary note that clients tend to expect the group leader to possess confidence and competence and to provide some initial structuring and direction. Clients may not want the leader to be too revealing of his or her own feelings, experiences, or conflicts early in the course of a group. Leaders who disclose more to meet their own needs than to meet the needs of the members may tend to be manipulative and thus to cause members to question leader capabilities. But leaders can facilitate interaction within the group by disclosing some of their personal reactions related to the here and now, because this type of information generally pertains directly to member opportunities for interpersonal learning (Morran, 1982).

Yalom (1983) stresses that leader self-disclosure must be instrumental in helping the *members* attain their goals. He calls for selective therapist disclosure that provides members with acceptance, support, and encouragement. For Yalom, group leaders who disclose here-and-now reactions, rather than detailed personal events from their past, facilitate the movement of the group.

Jourard (1968) suggests that the group leader is a strong determiner of how open and trusting the client will become. He maintains that the therapist is the leader in the therapeutic dance and that the client follows the leader. Jourard's studies (1971a, 1971b) led him to conclude that therapist self-disclosure begets client self-disclosure and that therapist manipulation begets countermanipulation on the client's part.

Although research and clinical evidence clearly point toward the desirability of encouraging the norm of member self-disclosure, these findings do not imply that more disclosure is always better. There is a curvilinear relationship between self-disclosure and optimal group functioning, with either too little or too much disclosure being counterproductive. Although self-disclosure should be encouraged, there needs to be a balance so that a single member does not lead the others by too great of a gap in terms of frequency and depth of disclosure (Yalom, 1985).

■■ Feedback

Feedback is the process by which members let one another know how they are affected by their behavior in group. If feedback is given honestly and with care, members are able to understand the impact they have on others and decide what, if anything, they want to change. One of the most important ways by which learning takes place in a group is through the willingness of members to give and to receive feedback.

Although feedback as a process in groups is given further consideration in the following chapter, we want to discuss some guidelines for effective feedback during the working stage. Following are some points that we emphasize in teaching members how to give and receive feedback:

· Give others feedback throughout the course of a group. In doing so, share with them how they affect you, rather than telling them how they are or judging them.
· Avoid giving global feedback, because it is of little value. Feedback that relates to specific behavior in the group provides a person with a source of independent validation that is difficult to make alone.
· Feedback must be timed well and given in a nonjudgmental way, or else the person receiving it is likely to become defensive and reject it.
· Concise feedback given in a clear and straightforward manner is more helpful than statements with qualifiers.
· In giving feedback concentrate on what you like about a person and the person's strengths as well as the difficulties you might be experiencing with him or her.

Members sometimes make a sweeping declaration such as "I'd like feedback!" If such individuals have said very little, it is difficult to give them many reactions. Members need to learn how to ask for specific feedback and how to receive it. There is value in listening nondefensively to feedback, really hearing what others want to say to us, and then considering what we are willing to do with this information. As the group progresses to a working stage, we typically see a willingness of members to freely give one another their reactions. Also, if members are concerned about how others are viewing them, they do tend to ask for these perceptions. The norm of asking for, receiving, and giving of feedback is one that needs to be established early in a group.

Example: Joseph joined a group because he found himself isolated from people. He was sarcastic with everyone in his group, a trait that quickly alienated others. Because the members were willing to tell him in a caring way that they felt put off and distanced by his sarcastic style, he was able to examine and eventually assume responsibility for creating the distance and lack of intimacy he typically experienced. With the encouragement of his group, he sought out his son, toward whom he felt much anger. He found that, when he let go of his sarcasm and talked honestly with his son, they felt closer to each other.

Research on Feedback

Although feedback is considered a major therapeutic factor, little has been done empirically to investigate the degree to which it is effective as a curative factor or the nature of its effectiveness (Morran, Robison, & Stockton, 1985).

Bednar and Kaul (1985) suggest that feedback can be considered along a number of dimensions, including its *valence* (the positive or negative nature of the message); *content* (either behavioral, which describes another member's behavior, or emotional, which describes the feelings of the person giving the feedback); *source* (public or anonymous); *form of delivery* (written or spoken); and *time reference* (here and now or there and then). Some research findings on these specific dimensions of feedback are listed below:

· Positive feedback is almost invariably rated as being more desirable, having greater impact, and leading to greater intention to change than negative feedback (Dies, 1983b; Morran & Stockton, 1980; Morran, Robison, & Stockton, 1985).
· Feedback that describes specific behaviors is rated by group members as more effective than interpretive or mixed feedback; behaviorally focused feedback generally has advantages over other forms (Stockton & Morran, 1980).
· Negative feedback seems to be more credible and helpful if it comes at a later phase of the group; it is more likely to be accepted when it has been preceded by positive feedback (Stockton & Morran, 1981).
· Leader feedback is generally of higher quality than member feedback, but it is not more readily accepted; feedback tends to be of higher quality and to be more accepted in later sessions than in earlier ones; and positive feedback is more accepted and of higher quality than negative feedback (Morran, Robison, & Stockton, 1985).

In summarizing the research findings, Morran, Robison, and Stockton (1985) report that feedback is most effective and most readily accepted when it focuses on observable behaviors, is unqualified, refers to specific and concrete situations, and describes the giver's reactions, rather than being evaluative or judgmental.

Co-Leader Issues during the Working Stage

■■ Our Leadership Style

When we co-lead groups or intensive workshops, we become energized if the group is motivated to work and to engage in meaningful self-exploration. In effective groups the members do the bulk of the work, for they bring up subjects they want to talk about and demonstrate a willingness to be known.

Between group sessions we devote time to discussing our reactions to group members, to thinking of ways of involving the various members in transactions with one another, and to exploring possible ways of assisting participants to understand their behavior in the group and to resolve some of their conflicts. We think that it is essential for us to look critically at what we are doing as leaders and examine the impact of our behavior on the group. It is also essential that we talk with each other about the process and dynamics of the group. If we find that we have differing perceptions regarding the group process, we discuss our differences. In this way we challenge each other, and we grow.

When a group seems very resistant and productive work seems to emerge very slowly, we may wonder whether we want to continue doing group work. At times like this we experience a sapping of our energies. If we have persistent feelings that the group is avoiding doing meaningful work, we will express these feelings and the perceptions they're based on to the group. We try to express honestly what we see occurring and how we are feeling as members of the group, but we avoid chastising the members and telling them that they're not meeting our expectations. At the same time, we challenge the group to assess its own processes. If resistance is the general rule in a group, it is imperative that we challenge the group to recognize the barriers that are standing in the way of effective work.

■■ Topics for Co-Leader Meetings

We cannot overemphasize the importance of meeting with one's co-leader throughout the duration of the group. Much of what we have suggested in earlier chapters as issues for discussion at these meetings also applies to the working stage. We will briefly consider a few other issues that are particularly relevant to the working stage.

Ongoing Evaluation of the Group. Co-leaders can make it a practice to devote some time to appraising the direction the group is taking and its level of productivity. If the group is a closed one with a predetermined termination date (say, 20 weeks), co-leaders would do well to evaluate the group's progress around the 10th week. This evaluation can be a topic of discussion privately *and* in the group itself. For example, if both co-leaders agree that the group seems to be bogging down and that members are appearing to lose interest in the sessions, they should surely bring these perceptions into the group so that members have the opportunity to look at their degree of satisfaction with their direction and progress.

Discussion of Techniques. It is useful to discuss techniques and leadership styles with a co-leader. One of the co-leaders might be hesitant to try any technique for fear of making a mistake, because of not knowing where to go next, or because of passively waiting for permission from the co-leader to introduce techniques. Such issues, along with any stylistic differences between leaders, are topics for exploration.

Theoretical Orientations. As we've mentioned earlier, it is not essential that co-leaders share the same theory of group work, for sometimes differing theoretical preferences can blend nicely. You can learn a lot from discussing theory as it applies to practice. Therefore, we encourage leaders to read, attend workshops and special seminars, and then discuss what they are learning with their co-leader. Doing so can result in bringing to the group sessions some new and interesting variations.

Self-Disclosure Issues.   Self-disclosure was discussed earlier in this chapter, but we want to add here the value of co-leaders' exploring their sense of appropriate and therapeutic leader self-disclosure. For example, if you are willing to share with members your reactions that pertain to group issues yet are reserved in disclosing personal outside issues, whereas your co-leader freely and fully talks about her marital situation, then members may perceive you as holding back. This is another issue you might discuss both in the group and privately with your co-leader.

Confrontation Issues.   What has been said above about self-disclosure also applies to confrontation. You can imagine the problems that could ensue from one leader's practice of harsh and unrelenting confrontations to get members to open up, if the other leader believes in providing support to the exclusion of any confrontation. One leader can easily be labeled as the "good guy" and the confronting one as the "bad guy." If such differences in style exist, they surely need to be talked about at length between the co-leaders if the group is not to suffer.

Exercises

1. What signs do you look for to determine whether a group has attained the working stage? Identify specific characteristics you see especially related to this stage.

2. Assume that you are leading a group with changing membership. Although there is a core of members who attend consistently, members eventually terminate, and new members join the group. What are the obstacles the members will have to deal with if this group is to reach a working stage? What are your ideas on ways to increase cohesion in this type of group? How would you handle the reality of members' terminating and new members' being assimilated into the group?

3. What guidelines would you offer to members on appropriate self-disclosure? How might you respond to the following statement made by a member, Carol? "I don't see why there is so much emphasis on telling others what I think and feel. I've always been a private person, and all this personal talk makes me feel uncomfortable." How might you deal with Carol if she were in a voluntary group? an involuntary group?

4. There are important differences between effective and ineffective confrontation. How would you explain this difference to group members? Think about how you might respond to a person who had been in your group for some time and who said: "I don't see why we focus so much on problems and on confronting people with negative feelings. All this makes me want to retreat. I'm afraid to say much, because I would rather hear positive feedback."

7

Ending a Group

Focus questions · Introduction · Tasks of the final
stage: Consolidation of learning · Working with a member's fears: Overview of the group's development · Interventions at the initial stage · Interventions at the
transition stage · Interventions at the working stage ·
Interventions at the final stage · **Termination of a member** · **Termination of the group experience** · Dealing
with feelings of separation · Dealing with unfinished
business · Reviewing the group experience · Practice
for behavioral change · Giving and receiving feedback
· Ways of carrying learning further · Some final considerations · **Evaluation of the group experience** · **Co-
leader issues as the group ends** · **Follow-up** · Postgroup
sessions · Individual follow-up interviews · **Combining research and practice in group work** · Guidelines
for group research · Resources for further reading ·
Exercises

1. If a member wants to leave a closed group before its termination, how should the leader handle the situation?
2. What activities are important during the closing phases of a group?
3. What questions might you as a leader ask members in order to determine how the group had affected them?
4. How might you deal with members' requests to continue a time-limited group that is approaching termination?
5. How important do you think it is to hold some type of follow-up session? What might you want the group to discuss at such a session?
6. How might you handle an individual's leaving an open group? How would you work a new member into the group?
7. What personal characteristics of yours could get in the way of helping members in your groups deal fully with separation and termination issues?
8. What specific methods and procedures would you use to help members review the group experience and make plans for using what they had learned in the group in everyday life?
9. What assessment techniques might you use at both the beginning and the end of a group? How can you build evaluation research into your group design?
10. What issues might you explore with your co-leader after a group terminates?

■■

Introduction

The initial phase of a group's development is extremely crucial, for participants are getting acquainted, basic trust is being established, norms are being determined that will govern later intensive work, and a unique group identity is taking shape. The final stages of group evolution are also vital, for members have an opportunity to clarify the meaning of their experiences in the group, to consolidate the gains they've made, and to decide what newly acquired behaviors they want to transfer to their everyday life.

In this chapter we discuss ways of terminating the group experience. We show how leaders can help members evaluate the meaning of their behavior in the group. Questions we explore are these: How can the members be encouraged to evaluate the degree of their satisfaction with each session? How can a group complete its unfinished business? How can the members best be prepared for leaving the group and carrying their learning into the real world? What are the difficulties in saying good-bye, and are they avoidable? Are there any ways of preparing the members to cope with their tendency to regress to old ways or to discount the meaning of their experience in the face of the outside world's pressures and skepticism? Are follow-ups necessary? If so, how should they be designed? How can leaders get participants to actively prepare themselves for a follow-up session? How can members and leaders evaluate the group experience?

We describe many tasks that need to be accomplished in the final stage of a group's history. The number of sessions devoted to reviewing and integrating the group experience is dependent on how long the group has been in existence. A group that has been meeting weekly for 2 years will need more time to bring closure to the group than one that has met for only 10 weeks. Whatever the type of group, adequate time should be set aside for integrating and evaluating the experience. There is a danger of attempting to cover too much in one final meeting, which can have the effect of fragmenting the group instead of leading to closure.

Tasks of the Final Stage: Consolidation of Learning

During the final stage of a group certain questions need to be raised: What has this experience meant? You have shared your struggles, but is this enough in itself? You have experienced and expressed emotions, but so what? What does all of this mean in terms of your living in the world? Where can you go from here?

The final phase in the life of a group is extremely critical, for this is when group members must consolidate their learning. It is a difficult time, because the members are aware that their community is about to dissolve, and they mourn the loss of it in advance. Sometimes the intensity tapers off during the final sessions, because participants, aware that their time together is limited, are reluctant to bring up new business to explore. It is important that the group leader focus on the feelings of loss that may permeate the atmosphere. These feelings need to be identified and explored, although they probably cannot be alleviated. Members must face the reality of termination and learn how to say good-bye.

If the group has been truly therapeutic, they will be able to extend and continue their learning outside, even though they may well experience a sense of sadness and loss.

As members sense that their group is approaching a termination point, there is a danger that they will begin to distance themselves from the group experience and thus fail to closely examine the ways in which their in-group learning might affect their out-of-group behavior. For this reason group leaders must learn to help members put into meaningful perspective what has occurred in the group. Typically, this is the phase in group work that is handled most ineptly by group leaders, partly owing to their lack of training for this difficult stage and partly because of their own resistance to termination. Avoiding acknowledging a group's termination may reflect discomfort on the leader's part in dealing with endings and separations. When termination is not dealt with, the group misses an opportunity to explore an area about which many members have profound feelings. Also, the potential for learning permanent lessons is likely to be lost if the leader does not provide a structure that helps members review and integrate what they have learned.

This discussion on the consolidation and termination phase applies to both closed groups (those with the same membership for the group's history) and to open groups (those with a turnover of members). In a closed group the members can be helped to review their individual changes and the evolving patterns from the first to the final session. Of particular value is having members give one another feedback on specific changes that were made from the outset of the group. Members in open groups can also be encouraged to review the highlights of their individual work, to give one another feedback, and to put their learning in perspective by looking at ways to apply in-group experiences to daily life.

Before continuing with the discussion of issues at termination, we want to provide an illustration of techniques in working with a particular member's fear. This example demonstrates differences in our interventions depending on what phase of development the group is in.

Working with a Member's Fears: Overview of the Group's Development

For the sake of the discussion, assume that Joan, a member of an ongoing group, says "I'm afraid people in here will think I'm foolish." Members often express a range of similar apprehensions, fearing that others will see them as stupid, egocentric, weird, evil, crazy, and the like. The techniques that we describe in working with Joan's particular fear of looking foolish can easily be applied to these other fears. The way we work with Joan differs according to the stage of development of the group and the relationship that we have established with the member.

▪▪ Interventions at the Initial Stage

During the initial phase our interventions are aimed at providing encouragement for Joan to say more about her fear of being seen as foolish and to talk about how this fear is affecting what she is doing in the group. We facilitate a deeper exploration of Joan's concern in any of the following ways:

- We encourage others to talk about any fears they have, especially their concerns over how they are being perceived by others. If Susan also says that she fears others' reactions, she can be asked to talk directly to Joan about her fears. (Here we are teaching member-to-member interaction.)
- After the exchange between Susan and Joan we ask "Do any of the rest of you have similar feelings?" (Our aim is to involve others in this interaction and to help Joan see that she is probably not alone in her fears.)
- Members who have fears that they would like to explore are invited to form a small inner group. We leave the structure open-ended, so that they can talk about whatever fears they are experiencing. (We assume that Joan is not alone, and we encourage others to identify with her in their own way. In a nonthreatening way we link Joan's work with others, and both trust and cohesion are being established.)

▪▪ Interventions at the Transition Stage

If Joan makes the statement "I'm afraid people in here will think I'm foolish" during the transition stage, we are likely to encourage her to identify ways in which she has already inhibited herself because of her fear. She can be asked to say how she experiences her particular fear in this group. Such an intervention demands more of her than our interventions at the initial stage. We ask her questions such as: "When you have that fear, whom in this room are you the most aware of?" "How have your fears stopped you in this group?" "What are some of the things you've been thinking and feeling but haven't expressed?" We also suggest to Joan that she speak to the people whom she feels most foolish around and tell them what she imagines they are thinking and feeling about her. In this way we get her to acknowledge her possible projections and to learn how to check out her assumptions. We also gather data that can be useful for exploration later in the group.

Group members can be brought into this interaction by inviting them to give their reactions to what Joan has just said. The interchange between Joan and other members can lead to further exploration. She has most likely created some distance between herself and others in the group by avoiding them out of fear of their negative reactions. By talking about her reactions to others, she is taking responsibility for the distance she has partially created. She can work out a new stance with those whom she has been avoiding.

What we have just described could occur during any stage. What makes this scenario more characteristic of the transition stage is the fact that members are beginning to express reactions and perceptions that they have been aware of but have kept to themselves.

■■ Interventions at the Working Stage

If Joan discloses her fear during the working stage, we look for ways to involve the entire group in her work. Members might acknowledge how they feel put off by Joan, how they feel judged by her, or how they harbor angry feelings toward her. By expressing feelings they have kept to themselves, they are moving out of the transition stage and into the working stage. Reactions and perceptions are acknowledged and owned, projections and misunderstandings are cleared up, and conflict is worked through. The group can get stuck in the transition stage if people do not go further and express reactions that have affected their level of trust. What moves the group into the working stage is the commitment of the members to work through an impasse.

We can use other techniques to help Joan attain a deeper level of self-exploration. One is to ask her to identify people in her life with whom she has felt foolish. This allows a way of connecting her past to her present struggles. We may then ask Joan to tell some members how she has felt toward significant people in her life. She might even let others in the group "become" these significant figures and say things to them that she has kept to herself. Of course, doing this may well serve as a catalyst for getting others to talk about their unfinished business with important figures in their life.

Other strategies we might use:

· Joan can role-play with a member who reminds her of her mother, who often cautioned her about making a fool of herself.
· Joan can write an uncensored letter to her mother, which she does not mail.
· By using role reversal, Joan can "become" her mother and then go around to each person in the room, telling them how they are foolish.
· She can monitor her own behavior between group sessions, taking special note of those situations in daily life in which she stops herself because of her fear of looking foolish.

- Using cognitive procedures, Joan can pay more attention to her self-talk and eventually learn to give herself new messages. Instead of accepting self-defeating messages, she can begin to say constructive things to herself. She can change her negative beliefs and expectancies to positive ones.
- Both in the group and in daily life, Joan can make a contract to forge ahead with what she wants to say or do, in spite of fears she may have about being seen as foolish.

■■ Interventions at the Final Stage

As can be seen, our interventions in working with Joan's fear are geared to the level of trust that has been established in the group, the quality of our relationship with her, and the stage of the group's development. In the later stage of a group we are inclined to emphasize the importance of her reviewing what she has learned, how she acquired these insights, and how she can continue to translate her insights into behavioral changes outside of the group. We hope that she has learned the value of checking her assumptions out with others before deciding that they are true. We challenge her to continue acting in new ways, even if this means putting herself in places where she runs the risk of looking foolish. By now she may have developed the personal strength to challenge her fears rather than allowing herself to be controlled by them.

Termination of a Member

The tasks to be accomplished with a person who is terminating membership in an open group include:

- announcing in advance within the group the person's intended departure, to assure the clearing up of any potential unfinished business
- allowing time for the departing member to prepare for termination
- giving an opportunity to others to say good-bye and to share their own reactions and give feedback
- assisting the member who is leaving to review what has been learned in the group and, specifically, what to do with this learning
- making referrals, when appropriate, such as couple therapy, family therapy, individual therapy, or another type of group therapy

At times, members may want to leave a group prematurely. Although one of the guidelines of the Association for Specialists in Group Work (1980) states that "members have the right to exit a group at any time," we earlier discussed our position on the possible negative impact of premature termination on both the group and the departing member.

Again, we want to emphasize the importance of the leader's having discussed all the ramifications of leaving prematurely. Once members announce their intention to quit the group, it is the task of the leader to provide an atmosphere in which it is safe to express the reasons for wanting to leave. Such members should be protected against being badgered by others to stay at all costs. What is essential is that the matter of leaving can be explored by all concerned. It is also a good policy for the leader to provide departing members with alternative sources of further help. We find that members rarely leave a group prematurely when they are encouraged in a nonthreatening way to fully explore their reasons for wanting to leave.

Termination of the Group Experience

■■ Dealing with Feelings of Separation

In discussing the initial phase we commented on the importance of leaders' encouraging members to express their fears and expectations about entering the group so that trust would not be inhibited. As members approach the ending of the group, it is equally essential that they be encouraged to express their reactions. They may have fears or concerns about separating, and leaving the group may be as anxiety producing for some as entering it. Some members are likely to be convinced that the trust they now feel in the group will not be replicated outside. A central task of the leader at this time is to remind the participants that the cohesion and trusting community they now have is the result of active steps they took. They need to be reminded that close relationships don't happen by accident; rather, they are the product of considerable struggle and commitment to work through personal conflicts.

Even if the participants realize that they can create meaningful relationships and build a support system outside of the group, they still may experience a sense of loss and sadness over the ending of this particular community. The members are likely to need encouragement in facing the fact that their group is terminating, and some mourning over this separation can be expected if the group has become a cohesive one. If this mourning is avoided, the members are deprived of a valuable experience in learning how to cope with feelings of grief and loss. In order to be able to facilitate members' expressions of their feelings over separation, the leader must recognize and be able to deal with his or her own feelings about the ending of the group. If the leader avoids dealing with feelings of sadness, the members will probably follow this example. A main task for leaders is to facilitate an open discussion of the feelings of loss and sadness that accompany the eventual termination of a very meaningful experience.

■■ Dealing with Unfinished Business

During the final phase of a group, time needs to be allotted for expressing and working through any unfinished business relating to transactions between members or group process and goals. Some intermember issues may not get fully resolved, but members should be encouraged to discuss them. For example, a member may say that she has held back because of reservations about the leader. Though there may not be enough time to work through her concern completely, it is still important to discuss it.

A member may have unfinished business with another member (or members) or with the leader. It may well be the member's responsibility for waiting too long to bring up such matters, and this member could be assisted in looking at some of the ways he or she got into the situation. Members may need help in bringing some closure to deeply personal issues they have raised and explored. It is not realistic to assume that all of the issues that were explored will have been worked through. If members are given this reminder a few sessions before the final meeting, they can then be motivated to use the remaining time to complete their own personal agenda. We often ask the question "If this were the last session of this group, how would you feel about what you have done, and what would you wish you had done differently?" This catalyst challenges the members to work on issues they may not have addressed up to this point and to try to complete any unfinished business they might have. In addition, the group may point out many areas where people could productively focus once they leave the group. In this way members can be prepared to continue working with these issues in further groups or in individual counseling.

■■ Reviewing the Group Experience

At the final stage of a group we place value on reviewing what members have learned throughout the sessions and how they learned these lessons. For example, a member could have learned that keeping his anger inside himself contributed to his feelings of depression and to many psychosomatic ailments. If in the sessions he practiced expressing his anger, instead of smiling and denying those feelings, he may have acquired important skills. It is helpful for this member to recall what he actually did to get others to take him seriously, for he could easily forget some hard-earned lessons.

Part of our practice for ending groups involves setting aside some time for all the participants to discuss matters such as what they've learned in the group, turning points for them, what they liked and did not like about the group, ways that the sessions could have had a greater impact, and the entire history of the group seen in some perspective. To make this evaluation meaningful, we encourage participants to be concrete. When members make global statements such as "This group has been fantastic, and I grew a lot from it" or "I don't think I'll ever forget all the things I learned in here," we assist them in being more specific. We might ask some of these questions: *How* has this group been important for you? In what ways has it been "fantastic"? What are a few of the things that you've learned that you'd most want to remember? When you say that you've "grown a lot," what are some of the changes you've seen in yourself?

One way to help members review concrete highlights of their experience is to ask them to take a few minutes to spontaneously recall moments they shared together. Members can be helped to briefly relive their initial reactions toward being in the group and to recall specific events. Each member can take several turns in completing the sentence "I remember the time when . . ." Recalling incidents of conflict and pain in the group as well as moments of closeness, warmth, humor, and joy can contribute to putting the group experience into perspective. Such turning points of the group can provide a conceptual framework needed to make sense of what has taken place.

■■ Practice for Behavioral Change

In groups that meet weekly there are many opportunities for practicing new behaviors during each group session. It is good to encourage members to think of ways in which they can continue such work between the sessions. They can carry out homework assignments and give a report in the next week's session of how well they succeeded with trying new ways of behaving in various situations. In this way the transfer of learning is maximized. During the final stage of a group we emphasize the value of such actual practice (both in group situations and in outside life) as a way of solidifying and consolidating one's learning. We rely heavily on role-playing situations and rehearsals for anticipated interactions, teaching participants specific skills that will help them make their desired behavioral changes. We encourage them to take action and try out new behavioral patterns with selected others outside the group, both while the group is going on and after termination.

During the final few sessions we typically focus participants on preparing themselves to deal with those they live and work with. We ask members to look at themselves and the ways in which they want to continue changing, rather than considering how they can change others. For example, if Carol would like her husband to show more interest in the family and be more accepting of her changes, we encourage her to tell her husband about *her* changes and about herself. We caution her about the dangers of demanding that her husband be different. In rehearsals and role-playing situations we typically ask members to state briefly the essence of what they want to say to the significant people in their life, so they do not lose the message they'd most want to convey. For example, a man rehearses telling his father that he loves him and would like closer contact with him.

Feedback from others in the group is especially helpful as the members practice for the behavioral changes they expect to make in their everyday situations. For example, if Carol appears apologetic, members may comment on ways she might be more assertive. If in role playing she lectures her husband on all the ways he is deficient, people can share with her how they would be affected if they were her husband. This preparation for dealing with others outside the group is essential if members are to maximize the effects of what they've learned. They can benefit by practicing new interpersonal skills, by getting feedback, by discussing this feedback, and by modifying certain behaviors so that they are more likely to bring about the desired changes once they leave the group.

■■ Giving and Receiving Feedback

Throughout the history of a group the members have been giving and receiving feedback, which has helped them assess the impact of their behavioral experiments on others. During the closing sessions, however, we like to emphasize a more focused type of feedback for each person. We generally begin by asking members for a brief report on how they've perceived themselves in the group, what the group has meant to them, what conflicts have become clearer, and what (if any) decisions they've made. Then the rest of the members give feedback concerning how they've perceived and felt about that person.

Here we want to point to a potential problem: too often people give only positive feedback at this time, particularly if they feel a closeness with the others and some misgivings about the termination of the group. Favorable comments may give a person a temporary lift, but we question their long-term value. We do value positive feedback and deem it important that members disclose what they see as strengths and what they like about other members. But we also like members to express doubts or concerns, in ways such as the following:

· My greatest fear for you is . . .
· My hope for you is . . .
· I hope that you will seriously consider . . .
· I see you blocking your strengths by . . .
· Some things I hope you will think about doing for yourself are . . .

We caution against global feedback that will be of little use to members in remembering how others saw them. Examples of feedback that is not too helpful include: "I really like you." "I feel close to you." "You are a super person." "I will always remember you." In contrast, feedback that members can remember and can think about is most useful in making changes. Following are examples of this specific type of feedback:

· "I hope you remember that the reason you and I felt distant from each other is that we both were scared of each other, yet we acknowledged this. What brought us closer is that we talked about our fears and our assumptions."
· "I like your ability to be direct and honest in giving feedback and at the same time to treat people with dignity."
· "Remember that people liked you much better when you stopped being sarcastic."
· "The times you gave advice, people tended to reject it. They responded more favorably to you when you shared your own struggles, rather than giving them solutions."
· "I hope you will remember how easy it was for me to respond to you when you stopped bombarding me with questions and instead started to make statements about yourself."
· "My fear for you is that you will forget that more often than not you are judging yourself more harshly than others."
· "Remember that when you started expressing your annoyances toward others in this group, you became much less hostile."

The feedback at the end of a group needs to be constructive and stated in such a manner that the individual is not left hanging. It is inappropriate for members to now unload stored-up negative reactions, for the member being confronted does not have a fair opportunity to work through this feedback.

During this feedback session we emphasize that participants can make some specific contracts in areas they want to explore further after the group ends. We suggest some type of group follow-up session at a later date, which gives the members added incentive to think about ways to keep some of their new decisions alive.

■■ Ways of Carrying Learning Further

Assisting members to carry their learning into action programs is one of the most important functions of leaders. It is our practice to routinely discuss with participants various ways they can use what they've learned in the group in other situations. For many members a group is merely the beginning of personal change. At the end of a member's first group experience she might say: "One of the most valuable things I am taking from this group is that I need to do more work on how I tend to invite people to walk all over me. Before this group I wasn't even aware of how passive I was. I let myself listen to what others had to say about how I affected them, and I really saw how I back away from any possible conflict. I intend to get some individual counseling, as well as join an assertion-training group, so that I can go further with what I've learned in here."

If a group has been successful, the ending stage is a *commencement;* members now have some new directions they can follow in dealing with problems as they arise. Furthermore, members acquire some needed tools and resources for continuing the process of personal growth. For this reason, discussing available programs and making referrals is especially timely as a group is ending. In this way the end of a group leads to new beginnings.

The Use of a Contract

One useful way to assist members in continuing the new beginnings established during the group is to devote time during one of the final sessions to writing contracts. These contracts outline steps that the members agree to take to increase the chance of their successfully meeting their goals once the group ends. It is essential that the members *themselves* develop their own contract and that the plan is not so ambitious that they set themselves up for failure. If the participants choose to, they can read their contract aloud, so that others can give specific suggestions for carrying it out. It is also of value to ask members to select at least one person in the group to whom they can report on their progress toward their goals. This arrangement not only is useful for encouraging accountability but also teaches people the value of establishing a support system as a way to cope with possible setbacks and discouragement.

Guidelines for Applying Group Learning to Life

As we discussed in Chapter 4, certain behaviors and attitudes increase the chances that meaningful self-exploration will occur in a group. At this time we suggest that you refer to the section that deals with guidelines on getting the most from a group experience. As members are entering a group and during the early phase, we teach them how to actively involve themselves. This teaching continues to some extent throughout the life of the group. At the final phase we reinforce some teaching points to help members consolidate what they have learned and apply their learning to daily life. Toward the end of a group the participants are likely to be receptive to considering how they can extend what they have learned. Although the following guidelines are written from the leader's point of view, they are directed to the members.

Realize that the Group Is a Means to an End.   Unfortunately, there are those who consider a group experience an end in itself; for them, the main payoffs are the social interaction within the group setting and the temporary excitement and closeness they feel during the sessions. Some use a group as a place to get their batteries charged, a place to get positive strokes and support, or a place to grab for intimacy. Although these experiences may be pleasant, the purpose of a group is to enable participants to make decisions about how they will change their outside life. Groups that are therapeutic encourage people to look at themselves, to decide whether they like what they see, and to make plans for change.

As a group approaches termination, a leader's task is to help members reflect on *what* they have learned and *how* they learned it. Members are then in a position to decide what they are willing to do about what they have learned about themselves.

Example: Marnie came to the group as a frightened, tough, isolated, hurt, and skeptical person. To survive her hurts, she had learned to suppress her need for others, and she prided herself on her independence. During the course of the group she demonstrated great courage by letting others become important to her. She allowed herself to be needy and to trust people and, finally, made a decision to at least share the pain of her isolation and loneliness. The point is that after the group she acted on what she had learned during the group—that some people can be trusted. She allowed herself to be loved by a few people outside of the group. She discovered that, although she could still make it alone, life was more fulfilling if she allowed herself to care for others and others to care for her.

Realize that Change May Be Slow and Subtle.   People sometimes expect change to come about automatically, and once they do make changes, they may expect them to be permanent. This expectation can lead to discouragement when temporary setbacks occur.

Example: In her group-therapy sessions Barbara decided that she would no longer allow herself to be controlled by her husband and children. She engaged in rehearsing and role playing, saw that she had become what she thought her husband expected, and eventually made a contract to change those behaviors that resulted in her feeling powerless. Later she reported to her group that she had regressed—that she seemed to be even more susceptible to being controlled. She didn't fulfill her contract, and she began losing hope that she would really change. It would have been helpful if she had realized that setbacks are a part of the growth process, that changing entrenched habits cannot be done quickly, and that she had in fact made many strides that she was not giving herself full credit for. Her expectations of overnight changes were unrealistic. More important than dramatic life-style changes are directional shifts in attitudes and behavior, for these subtle beginnings may be significant in the redecision and relearning processes.

Don't Expect One Group Alone to Renovate Your Life.   Those who seek a therapeutic group sometimes cling to unrealistic expectations. They expect rapid change; they want to be "cured" immediately. Group leaders need to emphasize that a single therapeutic experience, as potent as it may be in itself as a catalyst for significant change, is not sufficient to sustain many of the members' decisions. People spend many years creating a unique personality, with its masks, defenses, and games, and it takes time to establish constructive alternatives. People do not easily relinquish familiar defenses, for even though the defenses may entail some pain, they do work. The change process is just that—a process, not a product. Unfortunately, many group members see the group experience as a convenient shortcut to becoming their ideal "finished product."

Example: Betty, a very busy university professor, joined a weeklong group and said at the initial session: "I really think I need to clean up some personal problems that are interfering with my research, writing, and teaching. So I've set aside this week to get myself in psychological shape." She seriously thought that in a week she could see what her problems were, work through them, and be able to resume her work without the annoying distractions of personal conflicts. The leaders of the group reminded Betty that personal growth can't be made to proceed according to a schedule. They told her they hoped her expectations would change so that she wouldn't wind up disappointed.

Decide What to Do with What You've Learned.   At its best, a group will provide moments of truth during which clients can see who they are and how they present themselves to others. Ultimately, it is up to the members to do something with the glimpses of truth they gain.

Example: Linda became aware that she (not her husband) was primarily responsible for her misery and depression. Before her participation in the group she had blamed other people for her unhappiness. If only they would change, she thought, then I might taste happiness. In the group she came to accept that, if she waited for others to make her feel worthwhile, she might indeed be condemned to a hopeless existence; by accepting that only she could change things, she opened up options for redecisions. Regardless of what she decided to do, she now knew that she was not helpless. The realization that we do have choices and that we're responsible for how we live and what we experience through our decisions may well be the most valuable outcome of participation in a group.

Think for Yourself.   Many people seek therapy because they've lost the ability to find their own way and have become dependent on others to direct their life and take the responsibility for their decisions. When such people enter a group, they adopt a new standard (that of the group) as their own. Although they may shed some of their inhibitions, they are still not deciding on their own direction. They expect the group to decide for them, or they are sensitively tuned to being what the group expects them to be.

Example: Very soon after disclosing her unhappiness with her marriage, Shirley decided to leave her husband. This decision was reached after a weekend workshop. Some participants had felt that, since she said she didn't love her husband anymore, for her own good she should file for divorce. Shirley might ultimately have reached this decision anyway, but she appeared to act in haste and somewhat under the influence of what other members felt.

▪▪ Some Final Considerations

As our groups are coming to an end, we take the opportunity to remind participants of a number of concerns:

· We again comment on the importance of keeping confidentiality, even after the group has ended. We caution that confidences are often divulged unintentionally by members enthusiastically wanting to share with others the details of their group experience. We provide examples of how they can talk about the group without breaking confidences. A suggestion we offer is that members can tell others *what* they learned but should be careful about describing the details of *how* they learned something. It is when members discuss the "how" of their experience that they are inclined to inappropriately refer to other members.

· We have observed that even enthusiastic group members are not beyond forgetting and discounting what they have learned soon after the termination of their group. This is especially true if they leave a supportive group and go out into an environment that is not supportive or speaks disparagingly about the value of groups. For example, Dennis learned the value of being open and direct with people in the group. Later he tried this same approach with certain people at work, only to meet with resistance and hostility. Before the group ends, we ask members such as Dennis to imagine how they might discount the value of the lessons they have learned when they are faced with people who do not appreciate their changes. In the case of Dennis we might have said: "So talk out loud now about how honesty doesn't really work in everyday life. How might you convince yourself that the only place you can be direct and honest with people is in this group?" If people are able to foresee how they might minimize their hard-earned lessons, they are less likely to do so.

· Some type of rating scale can be devised to give the leader a good sense of how each member experienced and evaluated the group. There are also standardized instruments that can tap individual changes in attitudes and values. Such practical evaluation instruments can not only help the members make a personal assessment of the group but can also help the leader know what interventions were helpful and what aspects of the group were least helpful. A willingness to build evaluation into the structure of the group is bound to result in improving the design of future groups. Later in this chapter we will talk about combining research and practice.

Evaluation of the Group Experience

After a group ends, we often send out a questionnaire to the group members. The responses tell us whether we succeeded in our therapeutic efforts. The following is a sample questionnaire:

1. What general effect, if any, has your group experience had on your life?
2. What were the highlights of the group experience for you? some of its most meaningful aspects?
3. What were some specific things that you became aware of about your life-style, attitudes, and relationships with others?
4. What are some changes you've made in your life that you can attribute at least partially to your group experience?
5. Which of the techniques used by the group leaders had the most impact on you?
6. What perceptions do you have of the group leaders and their styles?
7. What problems did you encounter on leaving the group and following up on your decisions to change?
8. Have the changes that occurred as a result of your group experiences lasted? If so, do you think the changes are permanent?
9. What questions have you asked yourself since the group? Were questions of yours left unanswered by the group?
10. Did the group experience have any negative effects on you?
11. What individual or group experiences have you been involved in since this particular experience?
12. What effects do you think your participation in the group had on the significant people in your life?
13. Have there been any crises in your life since the termination of the group? How did they turn out?

14. How might your life be different now had you not experienced the group? Do you feel that you would have made any significant changes in your behavior?
15. Have you become more aware since the end of the group of the part you played in the group process?
16. If a close friend were to ask you today to tell in a sentence or two what the group meant to you, how would you respond?
17. In retrospect, are you skeptical about the value of the group process or about the motivations of other people in the group?
18. Since the group have you encouraged others to become involved in a group or in some other kind of growth experience?
19. What is the potential of this form of group experience for helping people change in a positive direction? What are its limitations? its risks? How would you recommend it be used? Do the potential gains outweigh the risks?
20. What are some other questions you think we should ask in order to get a complete picture of the meaning the group had for you? Do you have anything else to say about yourself and your experience either during or since the group?

We have found it difficult to assess the process and outcomes of groups by empirical procedures such as statistical measures of change. Although we have made attempts at objective assessment through various inventories given both before and after a group, we have not been impressed with these methods. None of the measures proved adequate to detect subtle changes in attitudes, beliefs, feelings, and behavior. Therefore, we have continued to rely on subjective evaluation measures:

· We conduct individual follow-up interviews with members or keep in contact with members; letters and telephone conversations have been substituted when person-to-person interviews were not feasible.
· We hold one or more postgroup meetings, which will be described in a later section.
· We ask members to complete brief questionnaires, such as the one above, to assess what they found most and least valuable in their group experience.
· We ask or require (depending on the type of group) that members keep process notes in a journal. On the basis of their journal notes, which are private, they write several reaction papers describing their subjective experience in the group as well as what they are doing outside the group. These reaction papers are given to us during the life of the group and after the group has terminated.

We have found that asking the members to write about their group experience has been very useful in evaluating our groups. And members have continued to report to us that they found the writing they did both during and after the group extremely valuable to them in consolidating what they learned and providing them with an ongoing account of what they were doing with what they learned. By writing, members are able to focus on relevant trends and the key things they are discovering about themselves. Through the use of journals, members have a chance to privately clarify what they are experiencing and to rehearse what they want to say to significant people. Their writing also gives them a chance to recall turning points in the group for them, helps them evaluate the impact of the group in retrospect, and gives them a basis for putting this experience into meaningful perspective.

Co-Leader Issues as the Group Ends

It is critical that co-leaders agree on termination. They need to be in tune with each other about not bringing up new material that can't be dealt with adequately before the end of the group. At times, certain members save up some topics until the very end, almost hoping that there will be no time to explore them. It could be tempting to one of the co-leaders to initiate new work with such a member; the other co-leader may be ready to bring the group to an end.

There are some other specific areas that you and your co-leader can talk about during the final stage to ensure that you are working together:

· Are there any members whom either of you is concerned about and any things you might want to say to certain members?
· Are there perceptions and reactions either of you has about the group that would be useful to share with the members before the final session?
· Are both of you able to deal with your own feelings of separation and ending? If not, you may collude with the members by avoiding talking about feelings pertaining to the termination of the group.
· Have both of you given thought to how you can best help members review what they've learned from the group and translate this learning to everyday situations?
· Do you have some plan to help the members evaluate the group experience? You can discuss evaluation approaches before the end of the group or plans for follow-up evaluation.

Once the group finally ends, we encourage co-leaders to meet to discuss their experience in leading with each other and to put the entire history of the group into perspective. What follows are some ideas that you might want to explore with your co-leader as a way to integrate your experiences and learnings.

· Discuss the balance of responsibility between the co-leaders. Did one co-leader assume primary responsibility for directing while the other followed? Did one leader overshadow the other?
· Was one co-leader overly supportive, and the other overly confrontive?
· How did your styles of leadership blend, and what effect did this have on the group?
· Did you agree on basic matters such as evaluation of the group's direction and what was needed to keep the group progressing?
· You can each talk about what you liked and did not like about leading with each other. You can benefit by a frank discussion of what each of you learned from the other personally and professionally, including weaknesses and strengths, skills, and styles of leading.
· It would be helpful to evaluate each other in addition to evaluating yourselves. Comparing your self-evaluation as a leader with your co-leader's evaluation of you can be of great value. What is especially useful is to be aware of certain areas needing further work; in this way each of you can grow in your capacity to lead effectively.
· You both can learn much from reviewing the turning points in the group. How did the group begin? How did it end? What happened in the group to account for its success or failure? This type of global assessment helps in understanding group process, which can be essential information in leading future groups.

Follow-Up

■■ Postgroup Sessions

A follow-up group session 3 to 6 months after the termination of a group can be an invaluable accountability measure. Since the members know that they will come together to evaluate their progress toward their stated goals, they are likely to be motivated to take steps to make changes. Participants can develop contracts at the final sessions that involve action between the termination and the follow-up session. Members often use one another as a support system. If they experience difficulties in following through on their commitments after the group, they can discuss these difficulties. It is a matter not so much of relying on one another for advice as of using the resources of the group for support.

At follow-up sessions the participants can share difficulties they have encountered since leaving the group, talk about the specific steps they have taken to keep themselves open for change, and remember some of the most positive experiences during the group itself. Follow-ups also give members a chance to express and possibly work through any afterthoughts or feelings connected with the group experience. The members report on whether and how they are using their expanded self-aware-ness in their relationships in the outside world. A member may have met with resistance or hostility from other people, and the group can reinforce the member's new style of behavior at a time when his or her will to change may be weakening.

We ask members at the follow-up session whether they are continuing to reach out for what they want. Are they taking more risks? What results are they getting from their new behavior? People frequently report: "The outside world isn't like this group. I've been honest with some people out there, and they don't know how to take me!" At this point we usually emphasize that people do need to be selective about whom to be completely honest with, because many people will resist directness and openness or will not desire intimacy. The follow-up can thus help the members become more realistic about their expectations.

A follow-up session offers us one more opportunity to remind people that they are responsible for what they become and that they must take risks in order to grow. We have found that some members make deci-sions at the follow-up session to seek further ways of challenging them-selves. Some may decide to enter either individual or group therapy, some will take a drama class, some will make the choice to return to college, some will get motivated to start a self-directed program to change certain behavior patterns, and so forth. Thus, the follow-up ses-sion provides a timely opportunity to discuss other avenues for contin-ued personal growth.

If you administered any pretests to assess beliefs, values, attitudes, and levels of personal adjustment, the postgroup meeting is an ideal time to administer some of these same instruments for comparison purposes. We support the practice of developing an assessment instru-ment that can be given before members join a group (or at the initial session), again at one of the final sessions, and finally at some time after termination. If you meet with the members on an individual basis to review how well they have accomplished their personal goals, these assessment devices can be of value in discussing specific changes in attitudes and behaviors.

Of course, follow-up group sessions are not always practical or possi-ble, for many reasons. Alternatives can be developed, such as sending a brief questionnaire to assess members' perceptions about the group and its impact on their life. Members can also be contacted for individual follow-up sessions.

▪▪ Individual Follow-Up Interviews

If entire group follow-up sessions are impractical, an alternative is one-to-one sessions with as many members as would like such a meeting. Though ideally it is a good practice to meet with each member, even if the session lasts only 15 minutes, we realize the practical problems in arranging these sessions. If you are working in private practice, in a school setting, or in an institution and if you see the members on a fairly regular basis, then such follow-up interviews may be realistic. In other cases, the members may never be seen again.

The individual screening interview at the pregroup stage is partly devoted to ascertaining why people would like to join a group, helping them identify some personal goals, and discussing their expectations. The postgroup interview can be used to determine the degree to which members have accomplished their stated goals and met their expectations. Participants can also discuss what the group meant to them in retrospect. In addition, this one-to-one interview provides an ideal opportunity to discuss referral resources, should they be indicated. In our opinion this practice is one of the best ways for a leader to evaluate the effectiveness of a group.

The individual follow-up sessions can be very informal, or they can be structured with a common set of questions that the leader asks of each member. Of course, members should be given latitude to say whatever they want and not merely answer questions. The questionnaire to evaluate a group experience that we presented earlier can apply to individual follow-up meetings as well. You can adapt your questions to the population of your group. The data from these individual sessions, especially if they are combined with a follow-up group session, give you valuable information to decide how future groups could be improved.

In open groups it is not feasible to arrange for group follow-up sessions, because the membership changes over a period of time. However, it is an excellent practice to schedule an individual follow-up session about a month after a member terminates. This gives both the member and the leader an opportunity to review significant turning points in the group as well as the ways the group experience has influenced the member's behavior.

Combining Research and Practice in Group Work

We end this chapter with a discussion of some of the problems and challenges of integrating research with group practice. There are increasing pressures from consumers and funders to demonstrate the value of our therapeutic strategies. This section suggests some practical ways to evaluate the process and outcomes of groups.

There is a gap between research and practice in group counseling, and closing it involves overcoming some major obstacles. Practitioners often view researchers as a "strange breed," preoccupied with trivial issues pertaining to group process and outcome. They are likely to dismiss research without weighing its potential contributions. Further, empirical findings are seldom reported in a way that encourages clinicians to translate research into practice (Dies, 1983b). Only a small percentage of group practitioners use research findings in any consistent manner or engage in research of their own. If this knowledge gap is to be bridged, practitioners and researchers must work cooperatively, accepting the dual role of practitioner/researcher (Morran & Stockton, 1985).

■■ Guidelines for Group Research

Because of their attitudes toward research, most group workers have not been willing to devote time to devise evaluative instruments as a part of their clinical practice. It is possible, however, to make systematic observation and assessment a basic part of the practice of group work. Instead of thinking exclusively in terms of rigorous empirical research, practitioners can begin to consider alternatives to traditional scientific methods. One such alternative is evaluative research, which is aimed at gathering and assessing data that can be of value in making decisions about programs and in improving the quality of professional service (Dies, 1983a). In group work, pure research should not be seen as the only type of inquiry that has value. Practitioners and researchers can choose to do good field research instead (Morran & Stockton, 1985).

In writing about the best of all possible research worlds, Yalom (1983) envisions a project in which the members would be randomly and strategically assigned to various types of therapy group and to a control group. Outcomes would be objectively determined, and correlations would be measured between the outcome and the nature of the group-therapy experience. Yalom adds that no such project has been or ever will be done, because the methodological problems are so overwhelming. He concludes that it is best to settle for studies that are less than perfect.

Morran and Stockton (1985) offer some specific suggestions for evaluating the process and outcomes of groups:

· Develop an ongoing program of study that can be modified to provide increasingly relevant data. This kind of evolving program offers the advantage that each round of data collection can serve as a pilot study for the next.
· Consider your research findings as merely a contribution to a cumulative knowledge base. Single studies need not yield final answers to research questions.
· Select a number of evaluative measures for data collection that are realistic in terms of time, expense, and logistics but that relate to the major process and outcome variables specific to your group.
· Select (or build) instruments that are sufficiently sensitive to differences in group outcomes. Use member-specific measures, group-specific measures, and global measures.

Member-specific measures offer the flexibility of detecting changes among members who have various individual goals. Since instruments of this type are seldom available in standardized form, it is necessary to develop self-rating scales, observer-rating scales, and other scales to evaluate the degree to which members achieve their own personal goals in a group experience.

Group-specific measures reflect the changes that are common to all the members of a group, such as decreased levels of anxiety, increased self-awareness, and improved personal relationships. Some of these group-specific measures are available in standardized form, or instruments can be adapted from the standard instruments.

Global measures, such as moral development, self-concept development, and interpersonal development, reflect changes in major areas of psychological functioning and may be of value when they are used in conjunction with the above two measures.

Group workers can seek out their research-oriented colleagues to help them devise instruments to investigate the process and outcomes of groups. There is real promise in such collaboration between colleagues with differing, but mutually complementary, perspectives (Dies, 1983a). This direction seems to offer hope that research findings can be translated into the actual practice of group work.

■■ Resources for Further Reading

Chapters 3–7 have discussed various implications for practice of research findings. Some of you may want to consult other sources that provide more detailed reviews of the research. We suggest the following sources: Bednar & Kaul (1978, 1985); Bednar, Langenbahn, & Trotzer (1979); Bednar & Lawlis (1971); Bednar, Melnick, & Kaul (1974); Colson & Horwitz (1983); Dies (1983a, 1983b); Dies & MacKenzie (1983); Kaul & Bednar (1978, 1985); Lieberman, Yalom, & Miles (1973); Morran (1982); Morran, Robison, & Stockton (1985); Morran & Stockton (1980, 1985); Stockton (1978, 1980); Stockton & Barr (1977); Stockton, Barr, & Klein (1981); Stockton & Hulse (1981, 1983); Stockton & Morran (1980, 1981, 1982); Weigel & Corazzini (1978); Yalom (1985); and Zimpfer (1981).

Exercises

We think that exercises are important as catalysts during the initial stages of a group and that, applied at appropriate times in the course of a group, they can intensify a person's experience. There are fewer exercises appropriate to the final stage of a group, but there are a few activities that we find useful at these times. Again, most of the exercises we suggest are suitable both for a classroom and for a counseling group.

1. Discounting Exercise. After a group the participants may find ways of discounting that experience, or old patterns may erupt and block the establishment of new behavior. When she left her group, Jane felt close to many people and decided that it was worth it to risk getting close. She tried this at work, was rebuffed, and began telling herself that what she had experienced in the group was not real. In this exercise you are asked to imagine all the things you might say to yourself to sabotage your plans for change. The idea is to openly acknowledge tendencies you have that will interfere with your establishing new behavior.

2. Feedback Exercises. A student sits in the center of the circle, and the members express their hopes and fears for the person. Or the class details which traits, attitudes, or behaviors will interfere with, and which will increase, the person's effectiveness as a group leader.

3. Group-Termination Exercise. Students take turns pretending that they are leaders and that the class is a group about to terminate. The idea is for students to consider how to prepare members for leaving a group.

4. Termination-Interview Exercise. A person in the class volunteers to become a group leader and to conduct an interview with a group member (also a volunteer) as though they had just completed a group experience together. For about 10 minutes the group leader interviews the client regarding the nature of his or her group experience. After the exercise the client reacts to the interview.

5. Future-Projection Exercise. During the last session, members can be asked to imagine that it is 1 year (or 5 years or 10 years) in the future, and the group is meeting in reunion. What would they most hope to be able to say to the group about their life, the changes they have made, and the influence the group had on them? What fears might they have concerning this reunion?

6. Remembering Exercise. It is helpful to simply share memories and turning points during the group's history. Members could be given the task of recalling, in free-association style, events and happenings that most stand out for them.

7. Working on Specific Contracts. During the final sessions members might formulate contracts that state specific actions they are willing to take to enhance the changes they have begun. These contracts can be written down and then read to the group. Others can give each member feedback and alternative ways of completing the contract.

8. Reviewing the Class Experience.   A useful exercise is to form small groups and discuss what you have learned about yourself up to this point that you think would either contribute to or detract from your effectiveness as a group leader. How willing have you been to take risks in this class? What have you learned about how groups best function (or what gets in the way of an effective group) through your experience in the class?

8

Group Process Reviewed

This brief chapter reviews the characteristics of each stage of a group's development, summarizes the major functions of members and the main tasks of the leader at each stage, and comments briefly on co-leadership practices. We also summarize some of the main points we have developed in Parts One and Two.

Pregroup Stage: Summary

■■ Member Functions and Possible Problems

It is important that members joining a group possess the knowledge necessary for making an informed decision concerning their participation. Members should be active in the process of deciding if a group is right for them. Following are some issues that pertain to the role of members at this stage.

· Members should know all the specifics about a group that might have an impact on them.
· Members need to learn how to screen the group leader to determine if this group with this particular leader is appropriate for them at this time.
· Members need to be involved in the decision to include or exclude them from the group.
· Members need to prepare themselves for the upcoming group by thinking about what they want from the experience and how they can attain their goals.
· Members can be given pretests, which can be either standardized instruments or devices designed by the leader, to assess values, perceptions, attitudes, and personal problems.

Problems can arise if potential members:

· are coerced into a group
· do not have adequate information about the nature of the group and thus do not know what they are getting themselves into
· are passive and give no thought to what they want or expect from the group

228

▪▪ Leader Functions

The main tasks of group leaders during the formation of a group include:

· developing a clearly written proposal for the formation of a group
· presenting the proposal to the proper authorities and getting the idea accepted
· announcing the group in such a way as to inform prospective participants
· conducting pregroup interviews for screening and orientation purposes
· making decisions concerning selection of members and composing the group
· organizing the practical details necessary to launch a successful group
· getting parental permission, if necessary
· preparing psychologically for leadership tasks, and meeting with the co-leader (if any)
· arranging for a preliminary group session for the purposes of getting acquainted, orientation to ground rules, and preparation of the members for a successful group experience

Initial Stage: Summary

▪▪ Stage Characteristics

The early phase of a group is a time for orientation and determining the structure of the group. At this stage:

· Participants test the atmosphere and get acquainted.
· Members learn the norms and what is expected, learn how the group functions, and learn how to participate in a group.
· Members display socially acceptable behavior. Risk taking is relatively low and exploration is tentative.
· Group cohesion and trust are gradually established if members are willing to express what they are thinking and feeling.
· Members are concerned with whether they are included or excluded, and they are beginning to define their place in the group.
· Negative feelings may surface as members test to determine if all feelings are acceptable.
· A central issue is trust versus mistrust.
· There are periods of silence and awkwardness; members may look for direction and wonder what the group is about.
· Members are deciding whom they can trust, how much they will disclose, how safe the group is, whom they like and dislike, and how much to get involved.

- Members are learning the basic attitudes of respect, empathy, acceptance, caring, and responding—all attitudes that facilitate trust building.

■■ Member Functions and Possible Problems

Early in the course of the group some specific member roles and tasks are critical to the shaping of the group:

- taking active steps to create a trusting climate
- learning to express one's feelings and thoughts, especially as they pertain to in-group interactions
- being willing to express fears, hopes, concerns, reservations, and expectations concerning the group
- being willing to make oneself known to others in the group
- being involved in the creation of group norms
- establishing personal and specific goals that will govern group participation
- learning the basics of group process, especially how to be involved in group interactions

Some possible problems that can arise are:

- Members may wait passively for "something to happen."
- Members may keep to themselves feelings of distrust or fears pertaining to the group and thus entrench their own resistance.
- Members may keep themselves vague and unknown, making meaningful interaction difficult.
- Members may slip into a problem-solving and advice-giving stance with other members.

■■ Leader Functions

The major tasks of group leaders during the orientation and exploration phase of a group are:

- teaching participants some general guidelines and ways to participate actively that will increase their chances of having a productive group
- developing ground rules and setting norms
- teaching the basics of group process
- assisting members in expressing their fears and expectations, and working toward the development of trust
- modeling the facilitative dimensions of therapeutic behavior
- being open with the members and being psychologically present for them
- clarifying the division of responsibility

· helping members establish concrete personal goals
· dealing openly with members' concerns and questions
· providing a degree of structuring that will neither increase member dependence nor promote excessive floundering
· assisting members to share what they are thinking and feeling about what is occurring within the group
· teaching members basic interpersonal skills such as active listening and responding
· assessing the needs of the group and facilitating in such a way that these needs are met

Transition Stage: Summary

■■ Stage Characteristics

The transitional phase of a group's development is marked by feelings of anxiety and defenses in the form of various resistances. At this time members are:

· concerned about what they will think of themselves if they increase their self-awareness, and concerned about others' acceptance or rejection of them
· testing the leader and other members to determine how safe the environment is
· struggling with wanting to play it safe versus wanting to risk getting involved
· experiencing some struggle for control and power and some conflict with other members or the leaders
· challenged with learning how to work through conflict and confrontation
· reluctant to get fully involved in working on their personal concerns because they are not sure others in the group will care about them
· observing the leader to determine if he or she is trustworthy
· learning how to express themselves so that others will listen to them

■■ Member Functions and Possible Problems

A central role of members at this time is to recognize and deal with the many forms of resistance. Tasks include:

· recognizing and expressing any negative feelings
· respecting one's own resistances but working with them
· moving from dependence to independence
· learning how to confront others in a constructive manner

· being willing to face and deal with reactions toward what is occurring in the group
· being willing to work through conflicts, rather than avoiding them

Some of the problems that can arise with members at this time are:

· Members may be categorized according to "problem types," or they may limit themselves with some self-imposed label.
· Members may refuse to express persistent negative feelings, thus contributing to the climate of distrust.
· If confrontations are poorly handled, members may retreat into defensive postures, and issues will remain hidden.
· Members may form subgroups and cliques, expressing negative reactions outside of the group but remaining silent in the group.

▪▪ Leader Functions

The major challenge facing leaders during the transition period is the need to intervene in the group in a sensitive and timely manner. The major task is to provide the encouragement and the challenge necessary for members to face and resolve conflicts and negative feelings that exist within the group and the resistances that stem from their defenses against anxiety. Groups need to move from a stage of conflict and confrontation to an effective level of relating. To meet this challenge, leaders have the following tasks:

· teaching members the value of recognizing and dealing fully with conflict situations
· assisting members to recognize their own patterns of defensiveness
· teaching members to respect resistance and to work constructively with the many forms it takes
· providing a model for members by dealing directly and tactfully with any challenges, either personal or professional
· avoiding labeling members as "problem types," but learning how to understand certain problem behaviors
· assisting members in dealing with any matters that will influence their ability to become autonomous and independent group members
· encouraging members to express reactions that pertain to here-and-now happenings in the sessions

Working Stage: Summary

▪▪ Stage Characteristics

When a group reaches the working stage, the central characteristics include the following:

· The level of trust and cohesion is high.
· Communication within the group is open and involves an accurate expression of what is being experienced.
· Leadership functions are likely to be shared by the group, in that members interact with one another freely and directly.
· There is a willingness to risk threatening material and to make oneself known to others; members bring to the group personal topics they want to discuss and understand better.
· Conflict among members is recognized and dealt with directly and effectively.
· Feedback is given freely and accepted and considered nondefensively.
· Confrontation occurs in a way in which those doing the challenging avoid slapping judgmental labels on others.
· Members are willing to work outside the group to achieve behavioral changes.
· Participants feel supported in their attempts to change and are willing to risk new behavior.
· Members feel hopeful that they can change if they are willing to take action; they do not feel helpless.

▪▪ Member Functions and Possible Problems

The working stage is characterized by the exploration of personally meaningful material. To reach this stage, members have certain tasks and roles, which include:

· bringing into group sessions issues that they are willing to discuss
· offering feedback and being open to feedback from others
· assuming some leadership functions, especially by sharing their personal reactions of how they are affected by others' presence and work in the group
· being willing to practice new skills and behaviors in daily life and to bring the results to the sessions
· offering both challenge and support to others and engaging in self-confrontation
· continually assessing their level of satisfaction with the group and actively taking steps to change their level of involvement in the sessions if necessary

Some problems that can arise with members at this time are:

· Members may form a collusion to relax and enjoy the comfort of familiar relationships and avoid challenging one another.
· Members may gain insights in the sessions but not see the necessity of action outside of the group to bring about change.
· Members may withdraw because of anxiety over others' intensity.

■■ Leader Functions

Some of the central leadership functions at this stage are:

· continuing to model appropriate behavior, especially caring confrontation, and disclosing ongoing reactions to the group
· providing a balance between support and confrontation
· supporting the members' willingness to take risks and assisting them in carrying this into their daily living
· interpreting the meaning of behavior patterns at appropriate times so that members will be able to engage in a deeper level of self-exploration and consider alternative behaviors
· assisting members to pay attention to and ask clearly for what they want from the group
· exploring common themes that provide for some universality and linking one or more members' work with others in the group
· focusing on the importance of translating insight into action; encouraging members to practice new skills
· promoting those behaviors that will increase the level of group cohesion
· paying attention to the intensification and further development of group norms
· being aware of the therapeutic factors that operate to produce change and intervening in such a way as to help members make desired changes in feelings, thoughts, and actions

Final Stage: Summary

■■ Stage Characteristics

During the final phase of a group the following characteristics are typically evident:

· There may be some sadness and anxiety over the reality of separation.
· Members are likely to pull back and participate in less intense ways, in anticipation of the ending of the group.
· Members are deciding what courses of action they are likely to take.
· There may be some fears of separation as well as fears about being able to carry over into daily life some of what was experienced in the group.
· There is likely to be some feedback; members may express their fears, hopes, and concerns for one another.
· Group sessions may be devoted partly to preparing members to meet significant others in everyday life. Role playing and behavioral rehearsal for relating to others more effectively are common.
· Members may be involved in evaluation of the group experience.

· There may be some talk about follow-up meetings or some plan for accountability so that members will be encouraged to carry out their plans for change.

∎∎ Member Functions and Possible Problems

The major task facing members during the final stage of a group is consolidating their learning and transferring it to their outside environment. This is the time for them to review and put into some cognitive framework the meaning of the group experience. Some tasks for members at this time are:

· dealing with their feelings about separation and termination
· preparing for generalizing their learning to everyday life
· offering feedback that will give others a better picture of how they are perceived
· completing any unfinished business, either issues they have brought into the group or issues that pertain to people in the group
· evaluating the impact of the group
· making decisions and plans concerning what changes they want to make and how they will go about making them

  Some possible problems that can occur at this time are:

· Members may avoid reviewing their experience and fail to put it into some cognitive framework, thus limiting the generalization of their learning.
· Due to separation anxiety, members may distance themselves.
· Members may consider the group an end in itself and not use it as a way of continuing to grow.

∎∎ Leader Functions

The group leader's central tasks in the consolidation phase are to provide a structure that allows participants to clarify the meaning of their experiences in the group and to assist members in generalizing their learning from the group to everyday life. Group leader tasks at this period include:

· assisting members in dealing with any feelings they might have about termination
· providing members an opportunity to express and deal with any unfinished business within the group
· reinforcing changes that members have made and ensuring that members have information about resources to enable them to make desired changes

- assisting members in determining how they will apply specific skills in a variety of situations in daily life
- working with members to develop specific contracts and homework assignments as practical ways of making changes
- assisting participants to develop a conceptual framework that will help them understand, integrate, consolidate, and remember what they have learned in the group
- providing opportunities for members to give one another constructive feedback
- reemphasizing the importance of maintaining confidentiality after the group is over
- administering some type of end-of-group assessment instrument to evaluate the nature of individual changes and to evaluate the strengths and weaknesses of the group

Postgroup Stage: Summary

■■ Member Functions and Possible Problems

After their group is terminated, the members' main functions are applying in-group learning to an action program in their daily life, evaluating the group, and attending some type of follow-up session (if practical). Some key tasks of the postgroup stage for members include:

- finding ways of reinforcing themselves without the support of the group
- keeping some record of their changes, including progress and problems, so that they can determine the long-term effects of their group experience
- finding ways of continuing with new behaviors through some kind of self-directed program for change
- attending an individual session, if it is scheduled, to discuss how well their goals were met, or attending a follow-up group session to share with fellow members what they have done with their group experience after termination

Some possible problems that can occur at this time are:

- If members have difficulty applying what they learned in the group to everyday situations, they might become discouraged and discount the value of the group.
- Members may have problems in continuing with new behaviors without the supportive environment of the group.
- Members may forget that change demands time, effort, work, and practice, and thus they may not use what they've learned.

▪▪ Leader Functions

The last session of the group does not imply that the leader's job is finished, for there are important considerations after termination. Follow-up and evaluation procedures should be implemented. Leaders have the following tasks after a group ends:

- offering private consultations if any member should need this service, at least on a limited basis to discuss a member's reactions to the group experience
- if applicable, providing for a follow-up group session or follow-up individual interviews, to assess the impact of the group
- finding out about specific referral resources for members who want or need further consultation
- encouraging members to find some avenues of continued support and challenge so that the ending of the group can mark the beginning of a search for self-understanding
- developing some type of organized approach to evaluating the results of the group
- assisting members to develop contracts that will enable them to make use of support systems among the group members and outside the group
- if applicable, meeting with the co-leader to assess the overall effectiveness of the group
- administering some type of postgroup assessment to determine the long-range impact of the group

---

Points to Remember: Summary

What follows is a list of basic concepts and guidelines that we hope you will remember.

1. Effective group leaders are those who are willing to develop and refine a theory of their own. Since each established group theory stresses a particular dimension of group process, we encourage a selective borrowing of concepts from each of them. What is important is that group leaders devote time to conceptualizing group process.

2. Although we have described various group techniques, we firmly believe that personality and character are the most important variables in the making of effective group leaders. Group techniques cannot compensate for the shortcomings of leaders who lack self-knowledge, who are not willing to do what they urge group members to do, or who are poorly trained. Character traits of effective leaders, in our view, include courage, willingness to model, presence, caring, a belief in group process, openness, nondefensiveness, personal power, endurance, a sense of

humor, imagination, and self-awareness. We ask you to think about your personal characteristics and to try to decide which will be assets and which liabilities to you as a group leader.

3. In addition to having certain personal characteristics, good group leaders are knowledgeable about group dynamics and have skills in group leading. We suggest that you make frequent use of the inventories we presented as a means of thinking about personal areas you might need to improve and competencies you might need to develop.

4. Group leaders are faced with the need to take a stand on a number of basic issues, including how much responsibility for what goes on in the group is the leader's and how much the group member's; how much and what type of structuring is optimal for a group; what kind of self-disclosure is optimal in a group; what the role and function of a group leader should be; and what the ratio of confrontation to support should be.

5. Ethical codes have been established by professional organizations such as the American Psychological Association, the American Association for Counseling and Development, the Association for Specialists in Group Work, and the American Group Psychotherapy Association. Thus, the ethical standards governing group practice are not decided by the group leader alone. Group leaders should familiarize themselves with these established codes of ethics and with the laws that may affect group practice. The latter are particularly important for leaders who are working with children or adolescents.

6. A solid academic background is desirable for group leaders, but also important is an internship experience in which trainees can get supervised experience leading and co-leading groups. Ongoing training groups, as well as personal-growth groups, are essential for group leaders in training. Personal psychotherapy (both individual and group) is also valuable for those who want to become group leaders.

7. In developing a proposal for a group, include the selection procedures you plan to use, the composition you plan for the group, and details such as where and when you will hold the group. We recommend an individual screening session for all applicants and a group presession. The initial stage of a group is crucial, for during this time the trust level is being established. During the first few meetings, issues such as who will wield the power in the group and whether the members will focus on themselves or others are being decided.

8. Group approaches to therapy have some distinct advantages over individual approaches, but they also have limitations. It is a mistake to think that groups are for everyone, and we believe that anyone who is designing a group should be able to state clearly why a group approach will be of value. Such a written rationale should include descriptions of the goals of the group, the means that will be used to accomplish these

goals, the role of the members, the leader's function and role, and the means that will be used to assess the outcomes.

9. There are psychological risks associated with participation in a group. We believe that it is the leader's job to mention these risks to the members and to develop means of minimizing the risks.

10. A therapeutic group is a means to an end. Participants can use the group to learn more about themselves, to explore their conflicts, to learn new social skills, to get feedback on the impact they have on others, and to try out new behaviors. The group becomes a microcosm of society, in which members can learn more effective ways of living with others.

11. Members should clarify their goals at the beginning of a group. Developing contracts will help them to do so, and doing homework assignments will help them attain these goals.

12. Leaders should develop guidelines for behavior in groups and teach them to the members. Some of the behaviors leaders should stress are keeping the group's activities confidential, taking responsibility for oneself, working hard in the group, listening, expressing one's thoughts and feelings, and applying what one learns in the group to daily life.

13. Some of the factors that operate in groups to produce positive changes in the participants are the hope, commitment to change, and willingness to risk and trust that the members bring to the group; the caring, acceptance, and empathy that the members offer one another; the intimacy that develops; the freedom to experiment; the opportunity to get feedback, to experience catharsis, and to learn interpersonal skills; the laughter that is often generated; and the sense of cohesiveness that develops.

14. Group members need to be prepared for the termination of their group experience. If members are to get the most from a group, they must focus on how they can apply what they've learned in the group to their life. If you want to determine the impact of a group you've led, we strongly suggest that you plan a follow-up session. This session will give the members the chance to share the experiences they've had since the termination of their group.

REFERENCES AND SUGGESTED READINGS
FOR PARTS ONE AND TWO*

American Association for Counseling and Development. (1981). *Ethical standards*. Alexandria, VA: Author.

American Association for Marriage and Family Therapy. (1975). *Code of professional ethics*. Claremont, CA: Author.

* American Group Psychotherapy Association. (1978). *Guidelines for the training of group psychotherapists*. New York: Author.

American Mental Health Counselors Association. (1980). *Code of ethics for certified clinical mental health counselors*. Alexandria, VA: Author.

American Psychological Association. (1973). Guidelines for psychologists conducting growth groups. *American Psychologist, 28*(10), 933.

American Psychological Association. (1981). Ethical principles of psychologists. *American Psychologist, 36*(6), 633–651.

Anchor, K. N. (1979). High- and low-risk self-disclosure in group psychotherapy. *Small Group Behavior, 10*, 279–283.

* Association for Specialists in Group Work. (1980). *Ethical guidelines for group leaders*. Alexandria, VA: Author.

* Association for Specialists in Group Work. (1983). *Professional standards for training of group counselors*. Alexandria, VA: Author.

Atkinson, D. R., Morten, G., & Sue, D. W. (1979). *Counseling American minorities*. Dubuque, IA: William C. Brown.

Axelson, J. A. (1985). *Counseling and development in a multicultural society*. Monterey, CA: Brooks/Cole.

Bascue, L. O. (1978). A conceptual model for training group therapists. *International Journal of Group Psychotherapy, 28*(4), 445–452.

Bass, S., & Dole, A. (1977). Ethical leader practices in sensitivity training for prospective professional psychologists. *Journal Supplement Abstract Series, 7*(2), 47–66.

* Books and articles marked with an asterisk are recommended for further study.

Bates, M. M., Johnson, C. D., & Blaker, K. E. (1982). *Group leadership: A manual for group counseling leaders* (2nd ed.). Denver: Love Publishing.

Battegay, R. (1983). The value of analytic self-experience groups in the training of psychotherapists. *International Journal of Group Psychotherapy, 33*(2), 199–214.

Bednar, R. L., & Kaul, T. J. (1978). Experiential group research: Current perspectives. In S. L. Garfield & A. E. Bergin (Eds.), *Handbook of psychotherapy and behavior change* (2nd ed.). New York: Wiley.

* Bednar, R. L., & Kaul, T. J. (1985). Experiential group research: Results, questions, and suggestions (3rd ed.). In S. L. Garfield & A. Bergin (Eds.), *Handbook for psychotherapy and behavior change* (3rd ed.). New York: Wiley.

Bednar, R. L., & Kaul, T. J. (in press). *Group theory and practice: A comparative review and analysis.* Columbus, OH: Merrill.

Bednar, R. L., Langenbahn, D. M., & Trotzer, J. P. (1979). Structure and ambiguity: Conceptual and applied misconceptions. *Journal for Specialists in Group Work, 4*(4), 170–176.

Bednar, R. L., & Lawlis, F. (1971). Empirical research in group psychotherapy. In A. E. Bergin & S. L. Garfield (Eds.), *Handbook for psychotherapy and behavior change.* New York: Wiley.

Bednar, R. L., Melnick, J., & Kaul, T. J. (1974). Risk, responsibility, and structure: A conceptual framework for initiating group counseling and psychotherapy. *Journal of Counseling Psychology, 21*, 31–37.

Beutler, L. E. (1983). *Eclectic psychotherapy: A systematic approach.* New York: Pergamon Press.

Bloch, S., Browning, S., & McGrath, G. (1983). Humour in group psychotherapy. *British Journal of Medical Psychology, 56*, 89–97.

Blum, D. J. S. (1983). Group leadership training: An inclusive model. *Journal for Specialists in Group Work, 8*(2), 76–85.

Blustein, D. L. (1982). Using informal groups in cross-cultural counseling. *Journal for Specialists in Group Work, 7*(4), 260–265.

Borgers, S. B. (1980). An examination of the use of contracts in groups. *Journal for Specialists in Group Work, 5*(2), 68–72.

Borgers, S. B., & Koenig, R. W. (1983). Uses and effects of modeling by the therapist in group therapy. *Journal for Specialists in Group Work, 8*(3), 133–138.

Borgers, S. B., & Tyndall, L. W. (1982). Setting expectations for groups. *Journal for Specialists in Group Work, 7*(2), 109–111.

* Brabeck, M. M., & Welfel, E. R. (1985). Counseling theory: Understanding the trend toward eclecticism from a developmental perspective. *Journal of Counseling and Development, 63*(6), 343–348.

Budman, S. H., & Bennett, M. J. (1983). Short-term group psychotherapy. In H. I. Kaplan & B. J. Sadock (Eds.), *Comprehensive group psychotherapy* (2nd ed.) (pp. 138–144). Baltimore: Williams & Wilkins.

Callis, R., Pope, S. K., & DePauw, M. E. (1982). *Ethical standards casebook.* Alexandria, VA: American Association for Counseling and Development.

* Cole, S. A. (1983). Self-help groups. In H. I. Kaplan & B. J. Sadock (Eds.), *Comprehensive group psychotherapy* (2nd ed.) (pp 144–150). Baltimore: Williams & Wilkins.

Collins, A. H., & Grobman, J. (1983). Group methods in the general hospital setting. In H. I. Kaplan & B. J. Sadock (Eds.), *Comprehensive group psychotherapy* (2nd ed.) (pp. 289–293). Baltimore: Williams & Wilkins.

Colson, D. B., & Horwitz, L. (1983). Research in group psychotherapy. In H. I. Kaplan & B. J. Sadock (Eds.), *Comprehensive group psychotherapy* (2nd ed.) (pp. 304–311). Baltimore: Williams & Wilkins.

* Conyne, R. K. (1984). Thoughts about the future of group work. *Journal for Specialists in Group Work, 9*(2), 66–67.

Corey, G. (1981). Description of a practicum course in group leadership. *Journal for Specialists in Group Work, 6*(2), 100–108.

Corey, G. (1982). Practical strategies for planning therapy groups. In P. Keller & L. Ritt (Eds.), *Innovations in clinical practice: A sourcebook* (Vol. 1). Sarasota, FL: Professional Resource Exchange.

Corey, G. (1983). Group counseling. In J. A. Brown & R. H. Pate (Eds.), *Being a counselor: Directions and challenges* (pp. 95–123). Monterey, CA: Brooks/Cole.

Corey, G. (1984). Ethical issues in group therapy. In P. Keller & L. Ritt (Eds.), *Innovations in clinical practice: A sourcebook* (Vol. 3). Sarasota, FL: Professional Resource Exchange.

* Corey, G. (1985). *Theory and practice of group counseling* (2nd ed.) and *Manual.* Monterey, CA: Brooks/Cole.

Corey, G. (1986a). *Case approach to counseling and psychotherapy* (2nd ed.). Monterey, CA: Brooks/Cole.

Corey, G. (1986b). *Theory and practice of counseling and psychotherapy* (3rd ed.) and *Manual.* Monterey, CA: Brooks/Cole.

Corey, G., with Corey, M. (1986). *I never knew I had a choice* (3rd ed.). Monterey, CA: Brooks/Cole.

Corey, G., Corey, M., & Callanan, P. (1981). In-service training for group leaders in a prison hospital: Problems and prospects. *Journal for Specialists in Group Work, 6*(3), 130–135.

* Corey, G., Corey, M., & Callanan, P. (1982). *A casebook of ethical guidelines for group leaders.* Monterey, CA: Brooks/Cole.

* Corey, G., Corey, M., & Callanan, P. (1984). *Issues and ethics in the helping professions* (2nd ed.). Monterey, CA: Brooks/Cole.

Corey, G., Corey, M., Callanan, P., & Russell, J. M. (1980). A residential workshop for personal growth. *Journal for Specialists in Group Work, 5*(4), 205–215.

Corey, G., Corey, M., Callanan, P., & Russell, J. M. (1982a). Ethical considerations in using group techniques. *Journal for Specialists in Group Work, 7*(3), 140–148.

* Corey, G., Corey, M., Callanan, P., & Russell, J. M. (1982b). *Group techniques.* Monterey, CA: Brooks/Cole.

Corey, M., & Corey, G. (in press). Experiential/didactic training and supervision workshop for group leaders. *Journal of Counseling and Human Service Professions.*

Davis, K. L., & Meara, N. M. (1982). So you think it is a secret. *Journal for Specialists in Group Work, 7*(3), 149–153.

Day, M. (1981). Process in classical psychodynamic groups. *International Journal of Group Psychotherapy, 31*(2), 153–174.

Diedrich, R. C., & Dye, H. A. (Eds.). (1972). *Group procedures: Purposes, processes, and outcomes.* Boston: Houghton Mifflin.

Dies, R. R. (1980). Current practice in the training of group psychotherapists. *International Journal of Group Psychotherapy, 30*(2), 169–185.

* Dies, R. R. (1983a). Bridging the gap between research and practice in group psychotherapy. In R. R. Dies & K. R. MacKenzie (Eds.), *Advances in group psychotherapy: Integrating research and practice* (pp. 1–26). New York: International Universities Press.

* Dies, R. R. (1983b). Clinical implications of research on leadership in short-term group psychotherapy. In R. R. Dies & K. R. MacKenzie (Eds.), *Advances in group psychotherapy: Integrating research and practice* (pp. 27–78). New York: International Universities Press.

* Dies, R. R. (1985). Research foundations for the future of group work. *Journal for Specialists in Group Work, 10*(2), 68–73.

* Dies, R. R., & MacKenzie, K. R. (Eds.). (1983). *Advances in group psychotherapy: Integrating research and practice.* New York: International Universities Press.

Duncan, J. A., & Gumaer, J. (Eds.). (1980). *Developmental groups for children.* Springfield, IL: Charles C Thomas.

Durkin, H. E. (1982). Change in group psychotherapy: Therapy and practice: A systems perspective. *International Journal of Group Psychotherapy, 32*(4), 431–440.

Egan, G. (1973). *Face to face: The small-group experience and interpersonal growth.* Monterey, CA: Brooks/Cole.

Egan, G. (1976). *Interpersonal living: A skills/contract approach to human-relations training in groups.* Monterey, CA: Brooks/Cole.

Egan, G. (1977). *You and me: The skills of communicating and relating to others.* Monterey, CA: Brooks/Cole.

Egan, G. (1986). *The skilled helper: A systematic approach to effective helping* (3rd ed.). Monterey, CA: Brooks/Cole.

Elbirlik, K. (1983). The mourning process in group therapy. *International Journal of Group Psychotherapy, 33*(2), 215–228.

Evans, N. J., & Jarvis, P. A. (1980). Group cohesion: A review and reevaluation. *Small Group Behavior, 11,* 359–370.

* Fischer, L., & Sorenson, G. P. (1985). *School law for counselors, psychologists, and social workers.* New York: Longman.

Forsyth, D. R. (1983). *An introduction to group dynamics.* Monterey, CA: Brooks/Cole.

Frank, J. D. (1979). Thirty years of group therapy: A personal perspective. *International Journal of Group Psychotherapy, 29*(4), 439–452.

Gartner, A., & Riessman, F. (1977). *Self-help in the human services.* San Francisco: Jossey-Bass.

* Gazda, G. (Ed.). (1981). *Innovations to group psychotherapy* (2nd ed.). Springfield, IL: Charles C Thomas.

* Gazda, G. M. (Ed.). (1982). *Basic approaches to group psychotherapy and group counseling* (3rd ed.). Springfield, IL: Charles C Thomas.

* Gazda, G. M. (1984). *Group counseling: A developmental approach* (3rd ed.). Boston: Allyn & Bacon.

Gazda, G. M. (1985). Group counseling and therapy: A perspective on the future. *Journal for Specialists in Group Work, 10*(2), 74–76.

* Gazda, G. M., & Mack, S. (1982). Ethical practice guidelines for group work practitioners. In G. M. Gazda (Ed.), *Basic approaches to group psychotherapy and group counseling* (3rd ed.). Springfield, IL: Charles C Thomas.

Glatzer, H. T. (1978). The working alliance in analytic group psychotherapy. *International Journal of Group Psychotherapy, 28*(2), 147–162.

Grotjahn, M. (1983). The qualities of the group psychotherapist. In H. I. Kaplan & B. J. Sadock (Eds.), *Comprehensive group psychotherapy* (2nd ed.). Baltimore: Williams & Wilkins.

* Gumaer, J., & Scott, L. (1985). Training group leaders in ethical decision making. *Journal for Specialists in Group Work, 10*(4), 198–204.

Hall, R. P., et al. (1986). Treatment for survivors of incest. *Journal for Specialists in Group Work, 11*(2), 85–92.

Hansen, J. C., Warner, R. W., & Smith, E. M. (1980). *Group counseling: Theory and process* (2nd ed.). Chicago: Rand McNally.

Hart, J. T. (1983). *Modern eclectic therapy: A fundamental orientation.* New York: Plenum.

Harvill, R., Masson, R. L., & Jacobs, E. (1983). Systematic group leader training: A skills developmental approach. *Journal for Specialists in Group Work, 8*(4), 226–232.

* Hopkins, B. R., & Anderson, B. S. (1985). *The counselor and the law* (2nd ed.). Alexandria, VA: American Association for Counseling and Development.

Huhn, R. P., Zimpfer, D. G., Waltman, D. E., & Williamson, S. K. (1985). A survey of programs of professional preparation for group counseling. *Journal for Specialists in Group Work, 10*(3), 124–133.

* Hummel, D. L., Talbutt, L. C., & Alexander, M. D. (1985). *Law and ethics in counseling.* New York: Van Nostrand Reinhold.

Hutchins, D. E., & Cole, C. G. (1986). *Helping relationships and strategies.* Monterey, CA: Brooks/Cole.

Johnson, D. W. (1986). *Reaching out: Interpersonal effectiveness and self-actualization* (3rd ed.). Englewood Cliffs, NJ: Prentice-Hall.

Johnson, D. W., & Johnson, F. P. (1982). *Joining together: Group theory and group skills* (2nd ed.). Englewood Cliffs, NJ: Prentice-Hall.

Johnson, N., & Johnson, S. C. (1980). A group counseling contract. *Journal for Specialists in Group Work, 5*(2), 93–97.

Jourard, S. M. (1968). *Disclosing man to himself.* New York: Van Nostrand Reinhold.

Jourard, S. M. (1971a). *Self-disclosure: An experimental analysis of the transparent self.* New York: Wiley.

Jourard, S. M. (1971b). *The transparent self* (rev. ed.). New York: Van Nostrand Reinhold.

* Kaplan, H. I., & Sadock, B. J. (Eds.). (1983). *Comprehensive group psychotherapy* (2nd ed.). Baltimore: Williams & Wilkins.

Kaul, T. J., & Bednar, R. L. (1978). Conceptualizing group research: A preliminary analysis. *Small Group Behavior, 9*, 173–191.

* Kaul, T. J., & Bednar, R. L. (1985). Experiential group research: Results, questions, and suggestions. In S. L. Garfield & A. Bergin (Eds.), *Handbook of psychotherapy and behavior change* (3rd ed.). New York: Wiley.

Kellerman, B. (Ed.). (1984). *Leadership: Multidisciplinary perspectives.* Englewood Cliffs, NJ: Prentice-Hall.

Kolb, G. E. (1983). The dream in psychoanalytic group therapy. *International Journal of Group Psychotherapy, 33*(1), 41–52.

Kottler, J. A. (1981). The development of guidelines for training group leaders: A synergistic model. *Journal for Specialists in Group Work, 6*(3), 125–129.

* Kottler, J. A. (1983). *Pragmatic group leadership.* Monterey, CA: Brooks/Cole.

* LeCluyse, E. E. (1983). Pretherapy preparation for group members. *Journal for Specialists in Group Work, 8*(4), 170–174.

Lerner, H. E., Horwitz, L., & Burstein, E. D. (1978). Teaching psychoanalytic group psychotherapy: A combined experiential-didactic workshop. *International Journal of Group Psychotherapy, 28*(4), 453–466.

Levine, B. (1979). *Group psychotherapy: Practice and development.* Englewood Cliffs, NJ: Prentice-Hall.

Libo, L. (1977). *Is there a life after group?* New York: Anchor Books.

* Lieberman, M. A. (1980). Group methods. In F. H. Kanfer & A. P. Goldstein (Eds.), *Helping people change* (2nd ed.) (pp. 470–536). New York: Pergamon Press.

* Lieberman, M. A., Borman, L. D., & Associates. (1979). *Self-help groups for coping with crisis.* San Francisco: Jossey-Bass.

* Lieberman, M., Yalom, I., & Miles, M. (1973). *Encounter groups: First facts.* New York: Basic Books.

Lifton, W. (1972). *Groups: Facilitating individual growth and societal change.* New York: Wiley.

Lubin, B., Lubin, A. W., Taylor, B. S., & Taylor, A. (1979). The group psychotherapy literature: 1978. *International Journal of Group Psychotherapy, 29*(4), 523–576.

Lubin, B., Reddy, W. B., Taylor, A., & Lubin, A. W. (1978). The group psychotherapy literature: 1977. *International Journal of Group Psychotherapy, 28*(4), 509–556.

Luft, J. (1984). *Group processes: An introduction to group dynamics* (3rd ed.). Palo Alto, CA: Mayfield.

MacKenzie, K. R., Alonso, A., & Rutan, J. S. (1979). The behavioral approach to group therapy. *International Journal of Group Psychotherapy, 29*(4), 453–470.

Mahler, C. A. (1969). *Group counseling in the schools.* Boston: Houghton Mifflin.

Mendelsohn, R. (1981). When groups merge: Transference and countertransference issues. *International Journal of Group Psychotherapy, 31*(2), 139–152.

Mendelsohn, V. A., & Mider, P. A. (1984). The modified drug-free therapeutic community as group therapy. *Journal for Specialists in Group Work, 9*(1), 14–20.

* Merritt, R. W., & Walley, D. D. (1977). *The group leader's handbook: Resources, techniques and survival skills.* Champaign, IL: Research Press.

Mintz, E. E. (1972). *Marathon groups: Reality and symbol.* New York: Avon.

Mintz, E. E. (1978). Group supervision: An experiential approach. *International Journal of Group Psychotherapy, 28*(4), 467–480.

Morran, D. K. (1982). Leader and member self-disclosing behavior in counseling groups. *Journal for Specialists in Group Work, 7*(4), 218–223.

* Morran, D. K., Robison, F. F., & Stockton, R. (1985). Feedback exchange in counseling groups: An analysis of message content and receiver acceptance as a function of leader versus member delivery, session, and valance. *Journal of Counseling Psychology, 32*, 57–67.

Morran, D. K., & Stockton, R. (1980). Effect of self-concept on group member reception of positive and negative feedback. *Journal of Counseling Psychology, 27*, 260–267.

* Morran, D. K., & Stockton, R. (1985). *Perspectives on group research programs. Journal for Specialists in Group Work, 10*(4), 186–191.

Mullan, H. (1979). An existential group psychotherapy. *International Journal of Group Psychotherapy, 29*(2), 163–174.

Mullan, H., & Rosenbaum, M. (1978). *Group psychotherapy: Theory and practice* (2nd ed.). New York: Free Press.

Muller, E. J., & Scott, T. B. (1984). A comparison of film and written presentations used for pregroup training experiences. *Journal for Specialists in Group Work, 9*(3), 122–126.

Napier, R. W., & Gershenfeld, M. K. (1981). *Groups: Theory and experience* (2nd ed.). Boston: Houghton Mifflin.

Napier, R. W., & Gershenfeld, M. K. (1983). *Making groups work: A guide for group leaders.* Boston: Houghton Mifflin.

National Association of Social Workers (1979). *Code of ethics.* Washington, DC: Author.

National Association of Social Workers (1981). *Standards for the private practice of clinical social work.* Washington, DC: Author.

National Training Laboratory Institute (1969). *Standards for the use of laboratory methods.* Washington, DC: Author.

Nicholas, M. W. (1984). *Change in the context of group therapy.* New York: Brunner/Mazel.

Nolan, E. (1978). Leadership interventions for promoting personal mastery. *Journal for Specialists in Group Work, 3*(3), 132–138.

O'Hearne, J. (1983). Nonverbal behavior in groups. In H. I. Kaplan & B. J. Sadock (Eds.), *Comprehensive group psychotherapy* (2nd ed.) (pp. 48–54). Baltimore: William & Wilkins.

Ohlsen, M. (1977). *Group counseling* (2nd ed.). New York: Holt, Rinehart & Winston.

Patterson, C. H. (1985). New light for counseling theory. *Journal of Counseling and Development, 63*(6), 349–350.

* Pedersen, P., Draguns, J., Lonner, W., & Trimble, J. (Eds.). (1981). *Counseling across cultures* (rev. ed.). Honolulu: University Press of Hawaii.

Pines, M. (1983). Psychoanalysis and group analysis. *International Journal of Group Psychotherapy, 33*(2), 155–170.

Pinney, E. L. (1983). Ethical and legal issues in group psychotherapy. In H. I. Kaplan & B. J. Sadock (Eds.), *Comprehensive group psychotherapy* (2nd ed.) (pp. 301–304). Baltimore: Williams & Wilkins.

Piper, W. E., Debbane, E. G., Bienvenu, J. P., & Garant, J. (1982). A study of group pretraining for group psychotherapy. *International Journal of Group Psychotherapy, 32*(3), 309–326.

Porter, K. (1980). Combined individual and group psychotherapy: A review of the literature 1965–1978. *International Journal of Group Psychotherapy, 30*(1), 107–114.

Reddy, W. B. (1985). The role of the change agent in the future of group work. *Journal for Specialists in Group Work, 10*(2), 103–107.

Ringler, K. E., Whitman, H. H., Gustafson, J. P., & Coleman, F. W. (1981). Technical advances in leading a cancer patient group. *International Journal of Group Psychotherapy, 31*(3), 329–344.

* Ritter, K. Y. (1984). Personality characteristics, training methods, and counseling effectiveness. *Journal for Specialists in Group Work, 9*(2), 77–84.

Roark, A. E., & Roark, A. B. (1979). Group structure: Components and effects. *Journal for Specialists in Group Work, 4*(4), 186–192.

Rogers, C. R. (1970). *Carl Rogers on encounter groups.* New York: Harper & Row.

Rose, S. D. (1977). *Group therapy: A behavioral approach.* Englewood Cliffs, NJ: Prentice-Hall.

Rose, S. D. (1980). *A casebook in group therapy: A behavioral-cognitive approach.* Englewood Cliffs, NJ: Prentice-Hall.

* Rosenbaum, M. (1982). Ethical problems of group psychotherapy. In M. Rosenbaum (Ed.), *Ethics and values in psychotherapy: A guidebook* (pp. 237–257). New York: Free Press.

Rosenbaum, M. (1983). Co-therapy. In H. I. Kaplan & B. J. Sadock (Eds.), *Comprehensive group psychotherapy* (2nd ed.) (pp. 167–173). Baltimore: Williams & Wilkins.

Rosenbaum, M., & Snadowsky, A. (1976). *The intensive group experience: A guide.* New York: Collier Macmillan.

Roth, D., & Covi, L. (1984). Cognitive group psychotherapy of depression: The open-ended group. *International Journal of Group Psychotherapy, 34*(1), 67–82.

* Rudestam, K. E. (1982). *Experiential groups in theory and practice.* Monterey, CA: Brooks/Cole.

* Ruiz, A. S. (1984). Cross-cultural group counseling and the use of the sentence completion method. *Journal for Specialists in Group Work, 9*(3), 131–136.

Rutan, J. S., & Alonso, A. (1982). Group therapy, individual therapy, or both? *International Journal of Group Psychotherapy, 32*(3), 267–282.

Rychlak, J. R. (1985). Eclecticism in psychological theorizing: Good and bad. *Journal of Counseling and Development, 63*(6), 351–353.

Sadock, B. J. (1983). Preparation, selection of patients, and organization of the group. In H. I. Kaplan & B. J. Sadock (Eds.), *Comprehensive group psychotherapy* (2nd ed.) (pp. 23–32). Baltimore: Williams & Wilkins.

Saravay, S. M. (1978). A psychoanalytic theory of group development. *International Journal of Group Psychotherapy, 28*(4), 481–508.

Schutz, B. M. (1982). *Legal liability in psychotherapy.* San Francisco: Jossey-Bass.

Schutz, W. (1967). *Joy: Expanding human awareness.* New York: Grove Press.

Schutz, W. (1971). *Here comes everybody: Bodymind and encounter culture.* New York: Harper & Row.

* Shapiro, J. L. (1978). *Methods of group psychotherapy and encounter: A tradition of innovation.* Itasca, IL: F. E. Peacock.

Silliman, B. D. (1979). Group leadership training: An evaluation of an entry-level model. *Journal for Specialists in Group Work, 4*(3), 123–130.

Silver, R. J., Lubin, B., Miller, D. R., & Dobson, N. H. (1981). The group psychotherapy literature: 1980. *International Journal of Group Psychotherapy, 31*(4), 469–526.

Silver, R. J., Lubin, B., Miller, D. R., & Dobson, N. H. (1982). The group psychotherapy literature: 1981. *International Journal of Group Psychotherapy, 32*(4), 481–554.

Silver, R. J., Lubin, B., Silver, D. S., & Dobson, N. H. (1980). The group psychotherapy literature: 1979. *International Journal of Group Psychotherapy, 30*(4), 491–538.

* Smith, D. (1982). Trends in counseling and psychotherapy. *American Psychologist, 37,* 802–809.

Soloman, L. N., & Berzon, B. (Eds.). (1972). *New perspectives on encounter groups.* San Francisco: Jossey-Bass.

* Stockton, R. (1978). Reviews and bibliographies of experiential small group research: Survey and perspective. *Small Group Behavior, 9,* 435–448.

* Stockton, R. (1980). The education of group leaders: A review of the literature with suggestions for the future. *Journal for Specialists in Group Work, 5*(2), 55–62.

Stockton, R., & Barr, J. (1977, February). *The experiential small group: An examination of process and outcome variables.* Paper presented at the Henry Lester Smith Conference on Educational Research, Bloomington, IN.

Stockton, R., Barr, J., & Klein, R. (1981). Identifying the group dropout: A review of the literature. *Journal for Specialists in Group Work, 6,* 75–82.

* Stockton, R., & Hulse, D. (1981). Developing cohesion in small groups: Theory and research. *Journal for Specialists in Group Work, 6*(4), 188–194.

Stockton, R., & Hulse, D. (1983). The use of research teams to enhance competence in counseling research. *Counselor Education and Supervision, 22*(4), 303–310.

Stockton, R., & Morran, D. K. (1980). The use of verbal feedback in counseling groups: Toward an effective system. *Journal for Specialists in Group Work, 5,* 10–14.

Stockton, R., & Morran, D. K. (1981). Feedback exchange in personal growth groups: Receiver acceptance as a function of valence, session, and order of delivery. *Journal of Counseling Psychology, 28,* 490–497.

* Stockton, R., & Morran, D. K. (1982). Review and perspective of critical dimensions in therapeutic small group research. In G. M. Gazda (Ed.), *Basic approaches to group psychotherapy and group counseling* (3rd ed.) (pp. 37–85). Springfield, IL: Charles C Thomas.

Stokes, J. P. (1983). Toward an understanding of cohesion in personal change groups. *International Journal of Group Psychotherapy, 33*(4), 449–468.

* Sue, D. W. (1981). *Counseling the culturally different: Theory and practice.* New York: Wiley.

Sue, D. W., Bernier, J. E., Durran, A., Feinberg, L., Pedersen, P., Smith, E. J., & Nuttall, E. V. (1982). Position paper: Cross-cultural counseling competencies. *Counseling Psychologist, 10*(2), 45–52.

* Van Hoose, W., & Kottler, J. (1985). *Ethical and legal issues in counseling and psychotherapy* (2nd ed.). San Francisco: Jossey-Bass.

Verny, T. R. (1975). *Inside groups: A practical guide to encounter groups and group therapy.* New York: McGraw-Hill.

Wachtel, A. B. (1983). Videotape and group psychotherapy. In H. I. Kaplan & B. J. Sadock (Eds.), *Comprehensive group psychotherapy* (2nd ed.) (pp. 173–176). Baltimore: Williams & Wilkins.

Weigel, R. G., & Corazzini, J. G. (1978). Small group research: Suggestions for solving common methodological and design problems. *Small Group Behavior, 9,* 193–220.

Weiner, M. F. (1983). The role of the leader in group psychotherapy. In H. I. Kaplan & B. J. Sadock (Eds.), *Comprehensive group psychotherapy* (2nd ed.) (pp. 54–63). Baltimore: Williams & Wilkins.

Wilborn, B. L., & Muro, J. J. (1979). The impact of structuring technique on group function. *Journal for Specialists in Group Work, 4*(4), 193–200.

Wolberg, L. R., & Aronson, M. L. (Eds.). (1983). *Group and family therapy.* New York: Brunner/Mazel.

Wong, N. (1983a). Combined individual and group psychotherapy. In H. I. Kaplan & B. J. Sadock (Eds.), *Comprehensive group psychotherapy* (2nd ed.) (pp. 73–83). Baltimore: Williams & Wilkins.

Wong, N. (1983b). Fundamental psychoanalytic concepts: Past and present understanding of their applicability to group psychotherapy. *International Journal of Group Psychotherapy, 33*(2), 171–192.

* Woody, R. H., & Associates (1984). *The law and the practice of human services.* San Francisco: Jossey-Bass.

* Yalom, I. D. (1980). *Existential psychotherapy.* New York: Basic Books.

* Yalom, I. D. (1983). *Inpatient group psychotherapy.* New York: Basic Books.

* Yalom, I. D. (1985). *The theory and practice of group psychotherapy* (3rd ed.). New York: Basic Books.

Zimpfer, D. G. (1976). Professional issues. In D. G. Zimpfer (Ed.), *Group work in the helping professions: A bibliography.* Washington, DC: Association for Specialists in Group Work.

Zimpfer, D. G. (1981). Follow-up studies of growth group outcomes: A review. *Journal for Specialists in Group Work, 6*(4), 195–210.

* Zimpfer, D. G. (1984a). *Group work in the helping professions: A bibliography.* Muncie, IN: Accelerated Development.

* Zimpfer, D. G. (1984b). Pattern and trends in group work. *Journal for Specialists in Group Work, 9*(4), 204–208.

Zimpfer, D. G. (1985a). Texts used most widely in preparation for group counseling. *Journal for Specialists in Group Work, 10*(1), 51–56.

Zimpfer, D. G. (1985b). Demystifying and clarifying small-group work. *Journal for Specialists in Group Work, 10*(3), 175–181.

Zimpfer, D. G., Waldman, D. E., Williamson, S. K., Huhn, R. P. (1985). Professional training standards in group counseling—idealistic or realistic? *Journal for Specialists in Group Work, 10*(3), 134–143.

Group Practice:
Some Specific Groups

■■ In Part Two our focus was on describing group process at the various stages of a group's history. In Part Three we describe the application of these concepts and practices to groups geared to various stages of human development, focusing on the special needs for each age population. We also discuss special considerations and implications for group leaders who work with children, adolescents, adults, and the elderly. In writing these chapters we have drawn on our own experiences and those of our colleagues; our goal is to describe how we set up these specialized groups and to share with you approaches that all of us have found useful.

For each separate age group, numerous specialized types of group are offered. For example, you may have a group for children of divorce, a group of acting-out children, or a group composed of terminally ill children. For adolescents, there are groups designed for working with alcohol and drug abuse and church groups to meet normal developmental needs. For adults, there are groups for single parents, for middle-aged people doing career planning, and for the physically handicapped. With the elderly population, you may find yourself leading a preretirement group or a theme-oriented personal-growth group. The types of group available for each of the four age groups are as many as there are special problems and needs. Of course, not all of them can be described in this book. We hope that the groups we do describe assist you in generalizing the ideas and practices to any specialized group you might lead.

Focus Questions and Exercises are not included in the chapters in Part Three, as these chapters are intended as illustrations of groups in action. Suggested Readings are given at the end of each chapter for readers who want to pursue any of these special group areas further.

9

Groups for Children

Introduction

This chapter begins with a discussion of Marianne Corey's group-counseling program for children in a school setting, which was part of her internship experience in graduate school. We will also describe a children's group that was led by a colleague who works in a community agency and a group for children from divorced families that was done by a colleague in North Carolina. The general group format set forth in this chapter can be applied to various other settings, such as private practice and public and private clinics. It is possible to apply many of the ideas in this chapter to groups that deal with a variety of special needs, including those of abused children, children of alcoholic families, and children with learning and behavioral disorders.

This chapter alone will not provide you with enough information to conduct your own groups with children. We hope, however, that it will stimulate you to continue learning about designing children's groups by doing further reading, attending specialized workshops, and arranging for supervised field experience.

A School Counseling Program*

The program I applied for was a federally funded project. After an interview I was hired by the director of a community counseling center, to whom I was then responsible. He assigned me to an elementary school.

Although my work for this project was very rewarding and proved to be an excellent learning experience, I suffered some frustration at first because I didn't know from one month to the next whether the project would remain in existence or whether I would soon be out of a job. I expended a great deal of energy worrying about the future of the project—a fact that affected my work with the children, although I wasn't aware of it at the time. After several weeks I contacted the principal of

---

* This section is written from the perspective of Marianne Corey.

my school and ascertained that I could continue working on a voluntary basis if the funding for the project were discontinued. Freed of my worry about the unpredictable effects of politics on the project, I was able to devote all of my energy to the children.

Another initial source of frustration was the fact that I had been given little instruction on what to do. I knew only that I would be working with elementary school children, ranging in age from 6 to 11, designated as problem children by their teacher or the principal; it was up to me to design a program that would improve the children's behavior in class. Ten to fifteen children would make up my case load, and I was to see each child at least once a week for about an hour, for a total of 24 visits.

To be referred to me, a child would have to be acting out his or her emotional disturbance in some way, such as through aggressive behavior. In this special program, passive and withdrawn children, as much in need of counseling as the children who were expressing their anger, were not likely to be included. If a child showed one of the following behaviors or attributes, he or she would be considered a candidate for referral:

· excessive fighting
· inability to get along with peers
· frequent hurting of other children
· violation of school rules
· poor attitude toward school
· stealing from school or from peers
· violent or angry outbursts
· neglected appearance
· hunger symptoms or frequent failure to bring lunch to school
· chronic tiredness
· lack of supervision at home
· excessive truancy

My job would be trying to deal with the problems underlying the child's behavior, thereby alleviating the child's school problems and preventing more serious problems from developing.

■■ The Initial Phase

Contact with School Personnel

Being fully aware that counselors are often mistrusted in schools, I set out to earn the trust of the teachers and administrators. The first thing I did, therefore, was meet with the principal and the teachers. I asked them what their expectations were of me and what they hoped the project would accomplish. I told them that I wanted to work closely

with them, providing feedback about the children, making specific recommendations, and getting their suggestions. I let them know that I
intended to work with the children individually and in groups and to
involve the parents in the treatment process, too. I explained that I
would have the children play with clay and puppets, tell stories, and
role-play—all activities that allow self-expression—during their contact with me.

Accordingly, I developed a program in which I was in continuous
contact with the children's teachers, principal, and parents. The teachers and the principal were very cooperative about meeting with me. I
also spoke frequently with the school psychologist, the school nurse,
and the school secretaries about particular children, gathering as much
information as I could. This information turned out to be most helpful.

The School Setting

The setting for my work with the children was not ideal. The school
was short on space (a new school was being built), and I was continually
looking for a place to meet with the children. When the weather allowed, I would often meet with them on the school lawn, because I
needed a place where they could explore, touch, talk loudly, shout if
they were angry, or give vent to any other emotions they were experiencing. If I took them off campus or did anything special with them, I
first obtained written permission from the parents and the school authorities, preferring to be extremely cautious in my dealings with this
public institution. Although I never had an ideal place to work, this did
not keep me from working effectively with the children, as we often
improvised together.

Since I didn't have my own office for much of the time, I had to call
for the children at their classrooms. This deeply concerned me. How
would the children react to being singled out? Would my special attention to them amid their peers affect them negatively? Fortunately, I
found the contrary to be true. The children responded very positively to
my coming to pick them up and were always ready to come with me,
even during recess time. Frequently, some of their classmates would ask
whether they could come see me, too.

Initial Contact with the Parents

After meeting with the school staff, who identified which children I
would be working with, I contacted the parents of each child. The parents knew before I visited them about my intended involvement with
their child, because I had asked the principal and the child's teacher to
contact them. During my initial contact I usually explained to the parents that I worked as a special counselor at the school and that their
child had been referred to me by the teacher, who had become con-

cerned about the child's behavior in class. This interview gave the parents a chance to get to know me and to ask me questions, and it gave me the chance to get the parents' permission to work with their child. At this time I gathered information regarding any difficulties the parents were having with the child and collected the data I needed in order to complete numerous forms. If parents became anxious over my probing or over the fact that *their* child had been singled out for counseling, I explained to them that, since teachers have to deal with so many children, they can't always provide all the attention a child needs. It would be my job, I explained, to provide this extra attention.

I had previously counseled only people who had requested my services; it was a new experience for me to be confronted by the suspicions of parents who had been informed that their child needed my services. But for the most part parents were willing to cooperate and gave their consent. In response to my question about any difficulties they might be experiencing with their child at home, which I asked in order to get clues to the child's behavior in school, the comments I received were guarded at first; they became much more open with time and frequent contacts. My aim was not to communicate in any way that they were "bad" parents, as this would certainly have aroused their defensiveness. The children were experiencing difficulties, and I wanted to solicit their help in assisting the children to work through these problems. By going into the child's home, I was able to get much information relating to the problems the child was exhibiting that would otherwise have been difficult, if not impossible, to obtain.

I told the parents that their children would be discussing with me problems related to school, home, and peers. I explained that I wished to keep as confidential as possible what the child and I would be exploring in our sessions; therefore, I explained, I would let them know in a general way how I was proceeding with the child but I would not reveal any of the specifics. The parents were agreeable to this. I also told the parents that I hoped to see them alone sometimes and sometimes together with their children. It was often difficult to schedule further contacts with parents, though, because every one of them was employed. Some parents I was unable to see again after my initial contact. However, I was able to make at least some additional contact with most parents.

Initial Contact with the Children

Before participating in this project, I had worked only with adults and adolescents who were able to express themselves verbally. During my initial (individual) contact with children, I relied very heavily on my verbal skills, expecting that they would be verbal with me in turn. But conversation with the children proved difficult. They were reluctant to initiate conversation, being accustomed only to answering questions. The children needed some structure and some guidelines to express themselves and an acknowledgement that it was difficult for them. Catalysts such as naming five things they liked and didn't like about school were helpful.

I introduced myself to them, stating that I was a special type of teacher called a counselor. I explained that their teacher was concerned about their behavior in class and that they would be talking with me several times a week—individually, as a group, and in their homes. I told them that we would be discussing problems they had in school, at home, or with their peers, and that we would talk about feelings.

I let the children know that I would be talking about them with their parents and teachers and that I would tell them when I made such contacts. Although I did consider much of what we would talk about in the group as confidential, I told them, I would discuss with their parents and teachers anything that would be important in helping them work through any of their difficulties. I felt strongly that it was just as important for a 6-year-old child to know that what he or she told me would be treated with confidentiality as it would be for a 60-year-old adult. Children's rights are too often violated, and their need for privacy, too often ignored. At this time I also let them know that they were not to talk to others about what fellow group members revealed; this was one of the rules we discussed again in the group sessions. I told them that they could talk about anything they wanted to in the group or with me but that they would not be allowed to hurt other children or destroy any property. I set up other rules that I felt were also necessary and made the children aware of their responsibility—in order to be part of the group, they had to agree to follow these rules.

There turned out to be little problem with maintaining confidentiality. When others in the children's classes asked them what they did in their sessions, I heard them state that they played games and talked about feelings.

■■ Evolution of the Group

Working with the Children in a Group

My goal was not to do intensive psychotherapy, for my time was limited and this would have been unrealistic. I did hope to pinpoint some of the children's maladaptive behaviors, teach the children more effective ways of interacting with others, and provide a climate in which the children would feel free to express a range of feelings. It seemed important to teach them ways of expressing emotions without hurting themselves or others. I wanted to convey to the youngsters that negative feelings do not get them into trouble; it's acting on these feelings that can lead to problems. In an effort to teach them ways of safely expressing negative feelings, I got them involved in a variety of activities, including role playing, play therapy, acting out social situations, painting, finishing stories that I began, putting on puppet shows, playing music, and dancing.

I found that the easiest to work with and most productive groups were those composed of three to five children of the same age and same sex. If there were more than this in a group, I found myself (1) unable to relate intensely to individuals, (2) slipping into the role of disciplinarian to counteract the increased distractions, (3) feeling frustrated at the number of children competing for my attention, and (4) not having enough time left over from keeping order to pay attention to underlying dynamics. In addition, children between the ages of 6 and 11 tend to become impatient if they have to wait very long for their turn to speak.

I took care to combine withdrawn children with more aggressive children, but I also felt that it was important for the children to be with others who were experiencing similar conflicts. For example, I put in the same group two boys who felt much anger, hurt, grief, and frustration over their parents' divorces and subsequent remarriages. They slowly learned how to express their feelings about not having much contact with the parent they didn't live with. At first, the boys could only express their feelings symbolically, through play; later, they learned to put words to their emotions and to talk about their feelings with their parents.

As I had planned, I provided some time for each child during which he or she could have my attention alone. I noticed that in the group all the children became less jealous of one another about me and trusted me more once I had begun to provide this individual time. Alone, the children were more cooperative, less competitive, and more affectionate than in the group. They felt less need to show off. Having an adult spend time with them individually gave the children a sense of importance. With the teacher's consent I also visited each child frequently in his or her classroom and on the playground, sometimes just observing and sometimes making a brief contact through touch or words.

Our scheduled group and individual sessions took place twice a week and lasted for half an hour to an hour. It would have been a mistake for me to insist that sessions always last a certain length of time, because the children's patience varied from session to session. When a child wanted to leave a group session, I would say in a friendly manner that that was allowed, but I wished he or she would stay until the session was over. Usually the child stayed. Most of the time the children enjoyed the sessions. I learned by trial and error that it was a good practice to let them know in advance that a session was coming to an end and then to be firm about having them leave and not give in to their demands that the group continue.

My groups were open groups; new members could join. The children already in the group handled this very well. They knew the newcomer from school and didn't meet the child with any negative reactions or resistance, contrary to what I have experienced with adults.

At first, I was eager to get to work on a child's specific problem as it was perceived by teachers, parents, and others. However, I found I needed to go beyond the specific problem area, because the children did not perceive themselves as having a problem. For me to talk to a girl about what was going on when she had violent angry outbursts and suddenly struck out was futile. Therefore, I began to relax with the children, let them lead the way, and listened to what they had to say, directly or through the various symbolic means I've described. Quite by accident, playing with puppets turned out to be an excellent means of revealing a variety of emotions and dramatizing situations that produce conflict. I made puppets available to the first- and second-grade children but found that even the fourth- and fifth-grade children were able to use them to vent their pent-up emotions.

The groups offered the children the opportunity to act out situations that aroused conflicting feelings. Sometimes I would suggest a problem situation, and at other times the children would select a problem to act out. The children would take the role of teacher, friend, principal, parent, brother, sister, or whoever else was involved. In this way they were able to release their emotions without hurting others.

Many times I had to remind myself to be patient and to allow the children to take their time in expressing themselves. Several sessions might pass before a child would speak freely. I sat close to the children during the sessions, often maintaining physical contact, which seemed to have a calming effect by itself. I listened to them attentively, often reflecting for them what they were saying but, more important, communicating to them, usually nonverbally, that I was with them, that what they were saying was important, and that I cared about what they had to say. I insisted that other members in the group listen and assured all of them that each would have a time to speak. This is a very difficult concept to get across, especially to a 6- or 7-year-old, who is still very self-centered and learning to share.

Sometimes, after a session that I felt had got nowhere, I was surprised to hear a teacher comment on a child's changed behavior. After one such session a boy who had previously been very destructive and disobedient became cooperative and able to relate to his peers. Pounding a lump of clay, which I had interpreted as nonproductive, turned out to have been very important for him. It had relieved much of his anger and so reduced his need to strike out at others.

In retrospect I can see that I trusted my intuition to a great extent. However, I found that it was important to have a good understanding of different theories of personality, including psychosexual and psychosocial developmental theories, and to be familiar with various counseling theories. I also discovered that, in order to understand the underlying causes of the child's problem behavior, I would have to include the parents in the treatment process as much as possible.

I often agonized over whether my work with the children was doing any good. Changes in the children's behavior were slow in coming and sometimes temporary. A child would seem to have improved one week, but the next week his or her behavior would again be very negative. My firm belief that a child can change if afforded the opportunity to change was challenged again and again.

However, most children made definite changes, as observed by the teacher, the principal, the parents, and me. Truants began to come to school more regularly. A boy who was in the habit of stealing and giving his loot to other children so they would like him learned that this behavior was one of the reasons that others disliked him in the first place and began to get their attention through more positive actions. A girl who had been conditioned not to trust learned to make friends and to reach out first—to do what at one time she had most feared.

These changes, though encouraging, needed to be reinforced at home. I cannot stress enough the importance of involving parents in the therapeutic process. Although most parents welcomed many of their child's new behaviors, some found the new behavior threatening. For instance, one girl caused her mother some anxiety by beginning to ask probing questions about her absent father. I encouraged this mother—and other parents facing similar problems—to try to listen to the child nondefensively.

Why the Group Format Was Effective

My clients, aged 6 to 11, were at a stage of growth in which they were leaving parents and home part of the day, expanding their relationships to include other adults, exploring and testing out-of-home environments, and developing peer relationships. Since most of my referrals were children who had deficiencies in relating to others, the group was an excellent means for them to learn and practice relational skills.

In addition, using the group format allowed me to spend more time with each child than would have been possible had I used only individual sessions. However, since individual sessions are valuable for their own reasons, I preferred having both types of contact with each child.

Another advantage of the group was that it allowed me to experience the child as the teacher did, thus giving me the opportunity that individual conferences didn't to spot faulty interactions with peers. I could witness interactions firsthand, and I could instantly give feedback; this maximized the chances that learning would take place.

Finally, the group by its very nature encouraged the children to discuss, or otherwise deal with, problems they had in common. After directly expressing emotions that had been bottled up, the children had less need to express these feelings indirectly by withdrawing, fighting, or getting sick.

Termination of the Group

When I began to work with the children, I told them that the sessions would go on only for a limited time during the school year. Several sessions before termination, I reminded the children that the group and individual sessions would be ending soon, and we discussed the imminent termination of our meetings. I had seen some of the children over a period of 8 months, and they had formed a strong attachment to me and I to them. It was as difficult for me to leave them as it was for them to see me leave, and we shared this sadness openly.

Although I had been affectionate with the children during our time together, I hadn't deceived them by becoming a substitute mother or by establishing myself as a permanent fixture who would totally satisfy all their needs. By being realistic about the limits of my job from the beginning, I was able to prevent termination from being a catastrophic experience for the children.

Teacher Evaluation of the Counseling Program

Like the parents, the teachers provided me with ongoing information regarding the children's programs. I was able to use this information in deciding how long to see a particular child or what problem area to focus on. In addition, the teachers prepared written evaluations for my program director, and they shared these evaluations with me. The following are some of their comments:

· "These children have emotional and educational problems, and the individual care given each of them has helped them understand better their limitations and assets."

· "Both children were very explosive and lashed out at other children without provocation. The counselor's attitude and positive outlook helped to calm them, and they now are getting along well in the classroom and with their peers."

· "A student with a high absentee record, who seldom communicated with others, began to change after her involvement in the counseling program. She began to initiate conversation, and she no longer preferred sitting alone; rather, she began to want to be with others. She even began to smile."

· "They are fighting less and are better able to talk things out. The special attention these boys received helped make their second year of school a more successful experience than it would otherwise have been."

· "I believe they have developed a stronger sense of identity—a foundation for self-love—and have developed some positive ways of resolving problems."

· "The counseling program has helped me understand the children and has created a valuable link between the school and the home."

■■ Special Problems Requiring Out-of-Group Attention

Children have a multitude of developmental problems, and there are many avenues of help for these problems. In working effectively with children, counselors must be willing to involve as many resources and people who can assist them as possible. It is a wise policy to let the parents know about these contacts and resources, so they, too, are involved in the helping process.

Academic Problems

The children who were referred to me, almost without exception, were identified by the teachers as children with learning problems. Often these learning disabilities were a reflection of their emotional conflicts. Since I was unable to provide the necessary tutorial assistance, I contacted a nearby university and recruited five graduate students to tutor the children for credit in their child-psychology course. In addition to providing tutorial services, they gave the children additional positive individual attention. This tutoring proved very successful for both the children and the university students, and the program was continued after I left.

Nutrition, Hygiene, and Health Care

Several of my children repeatedly came to school hungry, tired, sloppily dressed, and emanating strong body odors. These children had poor self-images and were victims of teasing by their peers. To deal with these problems, I taught personal hygiene, secured some nicer clothes, and made arrangements for certain children to receive free lunches at school. (The school had a free-lunch program, but many parents had neglected to enroll their children in it.) Besides teaching the children personal grooming, I was able to convince some parents of the importance of their child's hygiene in terms of the child's self-image. Often a change in a child's outward appearance had a significant positive effect on his or her behavior at school. When I detected health problems, I referred the child to the school nurse.

Lack of Supervision, Attention, and Affection in the Home

Because both parents of every child I worked with were employed full time, they had little time for involvement with their children. (This was true not only of the children in my case load; it also applied to the vast majority of the children at that school, which suggests that, in itself, the full-time employment of the parents was not responsible for the children's psychological problems.) Some of these children, as young as 6 years old, spent several hours a day at home alone. In working with the parents of my clients, I became aware that positive contact with the children was almost nonexistent. When the parents did come home, they were tired and burdened with household chores. Many of the parents deceived themselves by saying that the quality, not the quantity, of the time they spent with their children was important. In most cases, I found that the quality was as poor as the quantity was small. Occasionally I discovered that, if I discussed this matter with the parents in a nonaccusatory way, they would accept the fact that they were contributing to their child's school difficulties and realize that their responsibility for their child's healthy development called for them to change. One parent who had many children began to spend a few minutes a day alone with each child. Another parent started regular family sessions during which each family member could discuss his or her concerns about home and school.

Problems Associated with Single-Parent Homes

The divorce rate at this school was extremely high, and all but two of the children I worked with came from single-parent homes. In the group sessions I became aware that much of the children's hurt and anger related to the breakup of their home. I allowed the children to vent these feelings of sadness and anger. I discovered that many parents were unaware of their child's conflict, and I encouraged these parents to listen to their children and allow them to openly express their emotions without fear of the parent's becoming defensive. The children were much more likely to resolve their conflicts if the parent permitted them to talk about the divorce. (Later in this chapter we will describe in some detail a group designed for this special population.)

■■ Working Outside the Group

Working with Families

I've already discussed the fact that I contacted the parents as often as I could in order to involve them in the process of their child's counseling. On several occasions I also had lengthy family sessions, discussing not only the particular child's problems but also the dynamics of the entire family. The purpose was to explore the conflicts that affected all of the family members and to find ways of improving the quality of interaction. Although I felt enthusiastic about working with entire families, it was hard to arrange such sessions, for reasons of time and scheduling. I found stopping by a child's home just to visit or to show movies and pictures of the child that I had taken during a trip to the mountains or at a swimming party just as valuable as "work" sessions. It seemed especially meaningful to show the movies of the children to the families, because this made the children feel special and proud. These visits increased the parents' trust in what I was doing and their willingness to cooperate with me.

Working with Teachers

I've noted my involvement with my clients' teachers. A point I want to emphasize is that I was working with an exceptionally enthusiastic and caring staff. We combined our efforts to come up with ways of improving the children's overall school experience. Our enthusiasm was infectious, and we were able to learn much from one another. The teachers implemented classroom procedures that were extensions and continuations of the work I was doing. For instance, a teacher might give a few moments of individual positive attention when he or she saw that the child was about to ask for attention in a negative way. In addition to meeting with the teachers I also made frequent contacts with the principal, the school nurse, the school secretaries, the school psychologist, and the school librarian, for additional information about the children and feedback about what I was doing.

My work as a counselor would have been a lot harder if I had had to work with a competitive rather than a cooperative staff. Whenever teachers and other staff can be involved and their input received, they are more likely to assist the counselor.

Tapping Outside Resources

Because a counselor works with the total child, he or she needs to know what services, agencies, associations, companies, and individuals can be contacted for help when counseling is not enough. Many children are undernourished, underclothed, and in need of medical assistance, recreational opportunities, or supervision after school. Counseling is more likely to have an effect if the child's basic needs are being met. I found that I had to become actively involved as a kind of social worker to provide for many of the children's physical needs. I learned to rely on myself to do much of the legwork required to obtain food, clothing, money, or special services for the children and their families. Some families resisted turning to outside agencies because of pride or fear that strings would be attached, or simply because of ignorance about where to go for help. When a family did want help with emotional, economic, or medical problems, I referred them to one of the appropriate agencies. I did this rather than dealing with problems I wasn't qualified to deal with or taking on additional counseling loads that I might not have had time to follow through on. However, I often made the contacts with the agencies and did the paperwork they required.

Probably the most important (and most often overlooked) method of obtaining services for children and their families is asking. Private companies, concerned citizens, and the school staff are all potential resources that can be tapped, both for material goods and for suggestions about where else to go for help. I can't stress enough that the total needs of the child must be considered if the child's emotional needs are to be met.

Children's Groups in Community Agencies

One of our colleagues, Randy Alle-Corliss, who is a clinical social worker in a community mental-health agency, has designed groups for children much along the lines of the basic structure and format just described. What follows are some of the highlights of his way of organizing and leading these groups in an agency setting.

Randy originally got the idea to organize groups for children as a result of working with parents who came to the agency complaining about the behavioral problems of their children. When he began his first group, he sought out other therapists on his staff as referral resources, giving them information that would help them determine what kind of children might benefit from his group. He also typically obtains additional information by consulting with teachers, parents, and therapists who have any involvement with the children to be placed in the group.

In much the same manner as described earlier, Randy screens and orients the children, as well as educating parents about the nature of the group. He meets with each child alone to build rapport, he sees the parents without the child, and then he sees the parents and the child together to get a sense of the family situation.

Randy prefers to work with a female co-leader. This structure provides adult modeling and allows for parental-transference issues to be explored in the sessions. His groups are limited to 9 months, with some changing membership. They meet once a week for an hour. During the first 20 minutes the co-leaders talk with the children. The next 20 minutes is devoted to various play activities. The children draw pictures, use sand trays, and engage in both structured and spontaneous play. The leaders are involved in the play, either by observing or by actually participating in the activities. The final 20 minutes is set aside to discuss what happened during the play session, which often serves as a catalyst for brief role playing. Common topics and themes that are explored in these sessions are family conflicts; school problems; peer relationships; abandonment, loss, and death; dealing with frustration, aggression, and anger; and dealing with reactions to one another in the group.

A few of the main goals of this group are learning that feelings are acceptable; learning how to express feelings constructively; identifying with others and feeling less alone with one's problems; learning to change those attitudes, beliefs, feelings, and behaviors that they have the power to change; and accepting the things they can't change, such as the reality of their parents' divorce.

Randy reports outcomes similar to those mentioned earlier, including improved peer relations and social skills, a cohesion within the group, increased ability to express feelings appropriately, and a decrease of target behaviors such as aggression or withdrawal.

Randy and his co-leader deal with the eventual termination of the group by alerting the children to it 4 weeks in advance. Children thus prepared are given opportunities to express their feelings about separation. The co-leaders use many of the techniques described in Chapter 7, including reviewing the highlights of the group's history and doing a lot of reminiscing. The leaders help the children remember what they have talked about and help reinforce the gains they have made during the group. Many times there is food and a party at the final session as a way of celebrating the end of a meaningful experience.

A Group for Children of Divorce

This section describes a counseling group designed for children from divorced families. Marilyn Chandler, an elementary school counselor in North Carolina, compiled many of these ideas from reading and attending workshops pertaining to counseling children.

■■ Overview of the Group

Marilyn reports that she limits her divorce groups to fifth- and sixth-grade children. She finds that divorce groups with younger children are less successful, because these children lack the maturity to generalize from the group experience to daily life. Most of her counseling with children below the fifth-grade level on divorce or stepfamily issues is done on an individual basis.

With her divorce group Marilyn begins by establishing the ground rules of confidentiality. She also stresses to the children that they have been chosen to participate in this group on the basis of their progress with her in their individual counseling sessions.

She reports that, as the sessions progress, the children share more of their feelings and are surprisingly supportive of one another. She makes sure that the children are aware that they can pursue some highly personal issues with her privately. If a child makes what she feels is an inappropriate self-disclosure, she may take the initiative by saying "Maybe this is something you and I might want to talk more about together." She recognizes that, because this group is done in a school setting, issues may come up that are inappropriate for group work.

Before the group starts, parental-permission slips are sent home. Below is a sample copy of this letter to parents.

Parental-Permission Form

Dear Parent,

We are planning to offer a series of small group-counseling sessions for fifth- and sixth-grade students who are interested in working with other students on the topic of divorce. The time will give the students an opportunity to share feelings, concerns, and coping skills with others whose families are also separated. With the help of a supportive group, we hope, the children will learn to accept their own family's situation in a positive way and will be better prepared to handle other life crises.

The six weekly sessions will last approximately 30 to 40 minutes. The group leader, Marilyn Chandler, is the school counselor.

Parent permission is requested for a student to participate in the group. The classroom teachers have been consulted on scheduling, and students will not be penalized for missing class time.

If you have any questions, please call the school. Your support is greatly appreciated.

Sincerely,

Guidance Counselor

I give my child _____ permission to participate in the group counseling series.

_____   _____
Parent's signature   Date

■■ A Format for Divorce-Group Counseling

Following is Marilyn Chandler's six-session program for helping elementary students from divorced families.*

---

* Adapted from *Group Counseling for Children of Divorce*, by Janice Hammond, 1981. Ann Arbor, MI: Cranbrook. (Order from Cranbrook Publishing Company, 2815 Cranbrook, Ann Arbor, MI 48104.)

Goals

1. To help students talk about and come to understand their feelings about their parents' divorce
2. To help students understand that they are not alone in their feelings and experiences
3. To give students an opportunity to learn new coping skills and to share successful coping strategies with others in the group
4. To help students gain a more realistic view of the divorce situation and move toward acceptance of themselves and their family

Session Content

· Session 1: "Getting to Know You"
  A. *Group Introductions.* Have students form pairs, interviewing each other to learn five new things about the other. Have students introduce their partner to the group.
  B. *Discussion of Group Goals and Plans.* Explain goals and activities, answer questions, and ask students to share what they hope to get from participating in the group.
  C. *Set Group Guidelines.* List the guidelines on newsprint and keep for future reference.

· Session 2: Filmstrip and Discussion
  A. *Present Film or Filmstrip.* Suggested titles: *Breakup* (Inside/Out)— 16mm or video casette; *Coping with Your Parents' Divorce* (Learning Tree)—sound filmstrip; *Understanding Changes in the Family* (Guidance Associates)—sound filmstrip.
  B. *Discussion.* Ask for students' reactions. Discuss characters' feelings, using questions in the manual if available. Summarize.

· Session 3: "Things I Wish My Parents Knew"
  A. *Values Voting* [from Simon, Howe, & Kirschenbaum, 1972]. Have students vote on statements and myths regarding divorce and stepfamilies.
  B. *Brainstorm.* List on newsprint the "things I wish my parents knew" about the effects of divorce on children. Discuss.
  C. *Role Playing.* Have students act out and discuss common problem situations, such as where the child goes for holidays, parents' criticism of each other, or meeting a parent's new "friend." This role playing may be structured by writing situations on cards for the students to draw or asking the students to suggest situations. Discuss the feelings shown, and ask students to tell about times when they have felt that way.

· Session 4: Bibliotherapy
  A. *Distribute Booklist.* Compile a list of divorce-related books appropriate for the students' ages. Show them whatever books you have access to, let them peruse them, and allow them to check them out from you if possible.

B. *Reading Aloud.* For younger students, read "Zachary's Divorce," from *Free to Be You and Me* [Sitea, 1984]. Have older students read orally from *My Dad Lives in a Downtown Hotel* [Mann, 1973] or *It's Not the End of the World* [Blume, 1972]. (If the books are available, it would be ideal to give them out the week before and assign the reading in advance.)

C. *Discussion.* Discuss characters' feelings and behaviors. Some common themes are children's feelings of responsibility for their parents' divorce, anger and aggressive behaviors, wishing the parents would get back together, and embarrassment about the new family situation. Encourage personal discussion, and elicit suggestions for dealing with these problems.

· Session 5: Empathic Assertion

A. *"You're Not Bad If You Get Angry."* Read pages 48–58 from *The Boys and Girls Book About Divorce* [Gardner, 1970] on anger.

B. *Teach Assertive Response.* Practice expressing feelings and needs while showing some understanding of others' feelings. (See page 32 of Hammond [1981] for good handout and discussion questions.)

· Session 6: "The Uh-Oh Game"

A. *The Uh-Oh Game.* Available from the Friends Next Door, Inc., 10907 Oakwood Street, Silver Spring, MD 20901. Encourages children to discuss common problem situations, gives them a chance to share their feelings. A fun concluding activity.

B. *Summary.* List on newsprint the lessons that have been learned. Evaluate by asking students what they liked most, what was most helpful, and so on.

C. *Strength Bombardment.* Close on a positive note. Ask students to write one positive statement about each group member on separate stick-on labels. Have them use the labels to make a poster for each member.

■■ Outcomes of the Group

According to Marilyn, her divorce groups help her develop bonds with her counselees. When she works with children on an individual basis, she often makes a remark such as "Remember when this came up in the group?" She finds that children are able to take issues they worked on in group sessions and apply them to one-on-one counseling situations. For her, group counseling is a useful adjunct to individual counseling.

The children involved in these groups develop bonds that they can take beyond the group experience. Many strong friendships develop from the group and last the rest of the year. The children express mutual concern and an interest in helping one another.

Parental response has been positive. An increasing number of parents see the school counselor as an important helper in stepfamily or divorce situations.

Guidelines for Group Work with Children and Adolescents

This section consists of some practical guidelines for counselors who are considering setting up groups for minors. These guidelines apply to groups for adolescents, which we consider in the next chapter, as well as to children's groups.

■■ Developing a Sound Proposal

In designing your proposal, make sure that your goals and purposes are clearly described. Avoid arousing suspicion with global language or loaded words such as *sensitivity group* or *group therapy*. Rather than being mysterious about your work with the children, be open and willing to describe those who are concerned.

Develop a clearly stated rationale for your proposed group. This should include the goals, the procedures to be used, the evaluation devices that will be used to assess the degree to which the goals were met, and the reasons a group approach has particular merit. Too many potential groups fail to materialize because the group leader has impulsively decided to lead a group but has put little serious thought into the planning of an effective design. Refer to Chapter 3 for more information on developing a group proposal.

The support of administrators is essential, and if your rationale for designing a group is well organized, the chances are that you will receive support and constructive suggestions from the people you contact. It may be necessary to make certain compromises in your proposal, so keep an open mind. Remember that the school principal or the agency head—not you—will probably be the target of criticism if your counseling group is ineffectively run or compromises the integrity of the institution. He or she will be the one who, if you've overlooked the need to get parental permission, receives the calls from parents who want to know what right the school has to probe into the personal lives of their children. An intern of one of the reviewers of this book reported that she had encountered resistance from her school principal when she suggested a divorce group for children. She formally proposed a "loss group," which satisfied the principal but confused the children. They reported to the office saying "We're the *lost* group; we're here to get found."

▪▪ Legal Considerations

Be aware of your state's laws regarding children. Know the rules and regulations as they specifically apply to your agency or the setting in which you work. Be familiar with the ethical guidelines related to group work, especially the specific guidelines on confidentiality as it pertains to children. For example, don't tell the children that you can keep everything they discuss confidential and then be put in the position of having to disclose information about the children to your agency or school administrator. Be clear as to what you can and cannot promise by way of retaining the privacy of their disclosures. Be aware of your legal responsibility to report abuse or suspected abuse of minors. In this situation confidentiality *must* be broken, since the law requires you to take action by notifying the appropriate authorities. For other legal and ethical considerations in setting up groups for minors, review the discussion of such standards in Chapter 2.

Become knowledgeable about the legal factors involved in therapeutic work with minors. For some types of group, written parental permission may be a legal requirement. We feel that no harm—and much protection—can come from routinely requiring the written consent of the parents or guardians of any person under 18 who wishes to participate in a counseling or personal-growth group.

▪▪ Practical Considerations

Be aware of the age of the children, taking into account the fact that the attention span of a child age 4 to 6 is quite different from that of a child who is 10 to 12. Know something about these children's present difficulties in deciding what type of group would best meet their needs. The size and duration of the group depends on the age level. As a rule of thumb, the younger the children, the smaller the group and the shorter the duration of the sessions. Another consideration in forming a group is the severity of problems. For example, a group of hyperactive 12-year-olds could be as small as a group of preschoolers. You must also consider your own attention span and tolerance for dealing with children who will test your limits. Avoid becoming impatient at each session, thus becoming more of a disciplinarian than a counselor.

The Setting.   Consider the setting in terms of its effectiveness for the kind of work you want to do with young people. Will they be able to roam around freely and not have to be continually asked to talk softly so as not to disturb others in an adjacent room? Will the place for meetings provide for privacy and freedom from interruptions? Are there objects around that could easily be destroyed accidentally or objects that are obviously unsafe for children?

Communication of Your Expectations.   Be able to tell the children or adolescents in a simple manner about the purpose of your group, what you expect of them, and what they can expect from you. Make sure that they understand the basic nonnegotiable ground rules and, as much as is realistic, attempt to involve them in the establishment and reinforcement of the rules that will govern their group. In stating certain rules, it is essential to follow through with firmness (without an autocratic tone and style). For example, you may have the policy of not allowing members to return to a session if they leave before that session ends. Be careful not to give in to the demands for a "second chance." Young people will quickly learn that you mean what you say. They may not always like what you do at the time, but your chances for earning their respect are increased.

Preparation.   Prepare adequately for each session. Working with children or adolescents does not justify lack of preparation and absence of an agenda. In fact, you may need to prepare and structure sessions even more carefully than in some adult groups. However, be flexible to adjust your format and whatever you have planned for a given session in order to attend more sensitively to spontaneous situations. Avoid insisting on "covering your agenda" no matter what; be creative but not careless.

Involvement of Parents.   By preparing and involving parents you increase your chances of earning their cooperation. As with the young people, you need to explain to the parents your expectations and purposes in such a way that they can understand and not become suspicious. You reduce the chances of encountering resistant and defensive parents by making it a practice to approach them with an attitude of "How can you assist me in my work with your child, and how can we work as a team for a common purpose?" Rather than communicating to them in subtle ways that they are incompetent and you are the expert who can remedy the situation, be sincerely interested in their reactions to your program. You might spend an evening presenting your program in a group meeting of parents, or you might send them a letter briefly describing your program. This letter can be sent with the parental-consent letter.

▪▪ Tactics in the Group

Use Judgment.   Consider the purposes and goals of your group in deciding how much to encourage self-disclosure, especially in matters relating to family life. It is difficult to say what is the right degree of disclosure. The counselor needs to be careful, as children may not keep confidentiality and may talk to other children about disclosures made in the group. It is more difficult to maintain confidentiality in a school setting than in private practice, where the children may have no contact outside of the group. Should you encourage an open discussion of personal matters? For example, in a group in an elementary school, you may not want to let a child go into detail about a parental fight. An important intervention is directing this child to express how he or she was affected by the incident. In any case, the focus of disclosure should be the child, not the parent.

Don't Take Sides.   Avoid siding with children or adolescents against their parents or a particular institution. They may like and admire you for your patience and understanding and complain about missing this with parents or teachers. Deal with this complaint realistically, keeping in mind that you are spending an hour each week with them as opposed to living with them every day. Try to get the young people to understand the other side, through role playing, for example.

Use Appropriate Exercises and Techniques.   If you use certain interaction exercises, explaining their purpose in a general way will not diminish their effects or impact. Realize that young people should be granted the right of not participating in some activities. Although their unwillingness to take part in structured exercises is often due to lack of understanding, there are times when children or adolescents will be resistant because they see such exercises as inappropriate. For example, counselors should keep in mind the children's ages in suggesting exercises. It may be appropriate to ask 6-year-olds to hold hands with the other sex, but you are likely to meet with resistance if you ask 12-year-olds to do the same.

Listen and Be Open.   Learn to listen to young people; let them say what they need to say in their own words. Let them lead the way and follow their clues. Listen to their words and also pay attention to the possible meanings of their behavior. For example, if a child is acting out, is she telling you "Please stop me because I can't stop myself"? If a child is continually screaming, he might be saying "Notice me! Nobody else does." Remaining open to what children are trying to tell you about themselves is difficult if you cling to preconceived labels and diagnoses. The children you work with are often categorized and labeled. Be careful not to limit their ability to change by responding to them in terms of rigid categories.

Prepare for Termination.   Children are quick to form attachments with adults who display a concerned and caring attitude toward them. Long before your group ends—for example, 3 sessions before the end in a 16-session group—you must let the children know that the termination point is not far off. This allows the children to express their sadness, and it allows you to share your sadness with them. Avoid promising them that you will keep in contact with them, if that is not possible. If you don't deal with these issues, they may see you as running out on them and consider you as one more adult they cannot trust. (At this point it is a good idea to review the guidelines for the final stage of a group, described in Chapter 7.)

Know Your Limitations.   Be realistic and realize that you cannot work effectively with every child or provide all the needed services. It is essential that you know the boundaries of your competence. You should also make it a practice to know referral resources and be willing to make use of these resources when it is to the child's best interest.

▪▪ Personal and Professional Qualifications

Some of the *personal* characteristics that we see as important in working with children include patience, caring, playfulness, a good sense of humor, the ability to tune into and remember one's own childhood and adolescent experiences, firmness without punitiveness, flexibility, the ability to express anger without sarcasm, great concern and interest in children, and the other characteristics of group leaders that were described in Chapter 1.

Four of the *professional* qualifications that we believe are especially important for those leading groups with children are:

1. a thorough understanding of the developmental tasks and stages of the particular age group
2. a good understanding of counseling skills, especially as they pertain to group work
3. supervised training in working with minors in groups before leading a group alone
4. knowledge of the literature and significant research pertaining to counseling children and adolescents

In addition to the above qualifications there are other specific knowledge competencies and skills that are essential to effectively lead groups of children or adolescents. For a listing of these competencies, refer to Chapter 2 and review the *Professional Standards for Training of Group Counselors* of the Association for Specialists in Group Work.

▪▪ A Concluding Thought

It is easy to overextend yourself in working with children and adolescents whose problems are pressing and severe. You might find yourself working with youngsters who are abused and neglected and find it difficult to separate yourself from their life situations. If you are consistently preoccupied with their problems, you may discover that this is affecting your life and your relationships negatively. It is a personal matter for counselors to discover how much they are capable of giving, as well as how much and what they need to do to replenish themselves in order to stay excited and creative in their work.

Where to Go from Here

If you were to have time to read only a few additional books on counseling groups of children, our top recommendations would be *Windows to Our Children: A Gestalt Approach to Children and Adolescents* (Oaklander, 1978) and *Developmental Groups for Children* (Duncan & Gumaer, 1980). *Windows* is a how-to book that describes Oaklander's work with children in a very sensitive and straightforward manner and points out cautions and pitfalls to the counselor. Duncan and Gumaer's collection has several excellent articles that group leaders will find useful in working with children, including pieces on peer-facilitated groups, assertive training in groups, parent groups, rational-emotive groups for children, growth-centered group procedures, group techniques for staff development, and an overview of developmental groups for children.

An excellent resource is *Counseling Children* (Thompson & Rudolph, 1983), especially Chapter 15, which deals with group counseling, and Chapter 18, dealing with special needs and problems of children. The latter chapter contains an extensive and useful compilation of suggested readings for children in the following areas: abandonment, adoption and foster homes, child abuse, death, divorce, family, friendship, relationships with the older generation, and single parents.

Group Work in the Helping Professions: A Bibliography (Zimpfer, 1984) is another comprehensive source of articles and books dealing with group procedures for children (see section 6.12, pages 225–230) and with minority groups and multicultural groups (see section 6.15, pages 262–270).

Counseling and Therapy for Children (Gumaer, 1984) contains several chapters on counseling children in groups, including a detailed description of child-centered, growth-centered, and problem-centered group counseling. Gumaer also has a fine chapter on family therapy and consultation procedures. Other chapters deal with play therapy, art therapy, music therapy, bibliotherapy, behavioral counseling, and relaxation and guided fantasy. If you are interested in group techniques specifically designed for children, this book will be a most important reference.

Other books that contain chapters of specific interest to those conducting groups with children include:

- *Group Counseling: Theory and Practice* (Dinkmeyer & Muro, 1979). Chapter 9 covers group counseling with children and adolescents; Chapters 10, 11, and 12 deal with group counseling in the school.
- *Group Counseling: A Developmental Approach* (Gazda, 1984). It discusses group procedures for children in preschool and the lower grades.
- *Group Counseling* (Ohlsen, 1977). It has a section on counseling children in groups.
- *Assertiveness: Innovations, Applications, Issues.* There is a chapter entitled "Developing Assertiveness in Children" (Thoft, 1977).
- *Therapeutic Use of Child's Play* (Schaefer, 1979). You can find ideas and techniques for integrating play therapy into groups.

Suggested Readings*

Alberti, R. E., & Emmons, M. L. (1982). *Your perfect right* (4th ed.). San Luis Obispo, CA: Impact.

Axline, V. M. (1974). *Play therapy* (rev. ed.). New York: Ballantine.

* Axline, V. M. (1976). *Dibs: In search of self.* New York: Ballantine.

* Baruch, D. (1964). *One little boy.* New York: Delta.

Blume, J. (1972). *It's not the end of the world.* New York: Bantam Books.

Brown, M. C. (1984, June 5). A special kind of help for children of divorce. *Family Weekly*, p. 10.

Cochrane, C. T., & Myers, D. V. (1984). *Children in crisis.* Beverly Hills, CA: Sage Publications.

* DiGiuseppe, R. A. (1981). Cognitive therapy with children. In G. Emery, S. D. Hollon, & R. C. Bedrosian (Eds.), *New directions in cognitive therapy* (pp. 50–67). New York: Guilford Press.

* Dinkmeyer, D., & McKay, G. D. (1982). *The parent's handbook: STEP—Systematic training for effective parenting.* Circle Pines, MN: American Guidance Service.

Dinkmeyer, D. C., & Muro, J. J. (1979). *Group counseling: Theory and practice* (2nd ed.). Itasca, IL: F. E. Peacock.

Dougherty, A. M., & Fore, P. (1983). Surveying: An adjunct to group counseling for middle grade students lacking social skills. *Guidance Clinic, 15*(10), 8–9.

* Duncan, J. A., & Gumaer, J. (Eds.). (1980). *Developmental groups for children.* Springfield, IL: Charles C Thomas.

Ely, D. F., & Associates (1981). *California laws relating to minors.* Gardena, CA: Harcourt Brace Jovanovich.

Gardner, R. A. (1970). *The boys and girls book about divorce.* New York: Bantam Books.

*Books and articles marked with an asterisk are recommended for further study.

* Gazda, G. M. (1984). *Group counseling: A developmental approach* (3rd ed.). Boston: Allyn & Bacon.

Ginott, H. (1973). *Between parent and child.* New York: Avon.

Glasser, W. (1969). *Schools without failure.* New York: Harper & Row.

Gordon, T. (1970). *P.E.T., Parent Effectiveness Training: The tested new way to raise responsible children.* New York: New American Library.

Gumaer, J. (1984). *Counseling and therapy for children.* New York: Free Press.

* Hammond, J. (1981). *Group counseling for children of divorce.* Ann Arbor, MI: Cranbrook.

Hetherington, E. M. (1979). Divorce: A child's perspective. *American Psychologist, 34,* 851–858.

Kraft, I. A. (1983). Child and adolescent group psychotherapy. In H. I. Kaplan & B. J. Sadock (Eds.), *Comprehensive group psychotherapy* (2nd ed.) (pp. 223–234). Baltimore: Williams & Wilkins.

Krumboltz, J. D., & Krumboltz, H. B. (1972). *Changing children's behavior.* Englewood Cliffs, NJ: Prentice-Hall.

Lederman, J. (1973). *Anger and the rocking chair: Gestalt awareness with children.* New York: Viking Press.

* LeShan, E. (1976). *Learning to say goodbye when a parent dies.* New York: Macmillan.

Lewis, D. K. (1984). *Working with children: Effective communication through self-awareness.* Beverly Hills, CA: Sage Publications.

Lifton, W. M. (1966). *Working with groups: Group process and individual growth.* New York: Wiley.

Manela, R., & Lauffer, A. (1984). *Health needs of children.* Beverly Hills, CA: Sage Publications.

Mann, P. (1973). *My dad lives in a downtown hotel.* New York: Doubleday.

Milner, D. (1983). *Children and race.* Beverly Hills, CA: Sage Publications.

Moustakas, C. (1973). *Psychotherapy with children.* New York; Ballantine.

Moustakas, C. (1974). *Children in play therapy.* New York: Ballantine.

Moustakas, C. (1975). *Who will listen? Children and parents in therapy.* New York: Ballantine.

* Oaklander, V. (1978). *Windows to our children: A Gestalt approach to children and adolescents.* Moab, UT: Real People Press.

Ohlsen, M. M. (Ed.). (1973). *Counseling children in groups: A forum.* New York: Holt, Rinehart & Winston.

Ohlsen, M. M. (1977). *Group counseling* (2nd ed.). New York: Holt, Rinehart & Winston.

Reppucci, N. D., et al. (Eds.). (1984). *Children, mental health and the law.* Beverly Hills, CA: Sage Publications.

* Rogers, C. (1983). *Freedom to learn in the 1980's.* Columbus, OH: Charles E. Merrill.

* Rose, S. D. (1972). *Treating children in groups.* San Francisco: Jossey-Bass.

* Schaefer, C. (Ed.). (1979). *Therapeutic use of child's play.* New York: Aronson.

* Scheidlinger, S. (1984). Short-term group psychotherapy for children: An overview. *International Journal of Group Psychotherapy, 34*(4), 573–585.

* Simon, S., Howe, L., & Kirschenbaum, H. (1972). *Values clarification: A handbook of practical strategies for teachers and students.* New York: Hart.

Sitea, L. (1984). Zachary's divorce. In Thomas, M. (Ed.), *Free to be you and me.* New York: McGraw Hill.

* Thoft, J. S. (1977). Developing assertiveness in children. In R. E. Alberti (Ed.), *Assertiveness: Innovations, applications, issues* (pp. 195–203). San Luis Obispo, CA: Impact.

* Thompson, C. L., & Rudolph, L. B. (1983). *Counseling children.* Monterey, CA: Brooks/Cole.

Wilkinson, G. S., & Bleck, R. T. (1977). Children's divorce groups. *Elementary School Guidance and Counseling, 11,* 204–213.

* Zimbardo, P. G. (1978). *Shyness.* New York: Jove Press.

* Zimpfer, D. G. (1984). *Group work in the helping professions: A bibliography* (2nd ed.). Muncie, IN: Accelerated Development Inc.

10

Groups for Adolescents

Introduction: Special Needs and Problems of Adolescents

A detailed description of the unique needs and problems of adolescents is beyond the scope of this book. For group leaders who work with adolescents, good courses in the psychology of adolescence are essential. Reading and reflecting on one's own adolescent experiences and perhaps reliving some of these experiences are also valuable means of preparing oneself to counsel adolescents. Those who wish to review the field of the psychology of adolescence can refer to suggested readings at the end of this chapter.

The adolescent period is a time of searching for an identity and developing a system of values that will influence the course of one's life. One of the most important needs of this period is to experience successes that will lead to a sense of self-confidence and self-respect. Adolescents need to recognize and accept the wide range of their feelings, and they need to learn how to communicate with significant others in such a way that they can make their wants, feelings, thoughts, and beliefs known.

The adolescent years can be extremely lonely ones; it is not unusual for adolescents to feel that they are alone in their conflicts and self-doubt. It is a period of life in which people feel a desperate need for universal approval yet in which they must learn to distinguish between living for others' approval and earning their own. During these years the dependence/independence struggle becomes central. While part of the teenager yearns for independence from parents, another part longs for security. Adolescents must cope with decisions, such as vocational and educational choices, that will influence their future. In order to make these choices wisely, they must have information both about their abilities and interests and about such realities as job opportunities and college entrance requirements.

Sexual conflicts are also a part of this period; adolescents not only need to establish a meaningful guide for their sexual behavior but also must wrestle with the problem of their sex-role identification. Teenagers may have real difficulty clarifying what it means to be a man or a woman and what kind of man or woman they want to become.

Adolescents are pressured to succeed; they are expected to perform, frequently up to others' standards. They need to be trusted and given the freedom to make some significant decisions, and they need the faith and support of caring adults. But they also need guidelines and limits.

Adolescence is a time for continually testing limits, for this period is characterized by an urge to break away from control or dependent ties that restrict freedom. Although adolescents are often frightened of the freedom they do experience, they tend to mask their fears with rebellion and cover up their dependency needs by exaggerating their newly felt autonomy. Their moods are quick to change, and often they are negativistic and rebellious. The rebellion of adolescents can be understood as an attempt to determine the course of their own life and to assert that they are who and what they want to be, rather than what others expect of them.

A central part of the adolescent experience is peer-group pressure, a potent force that pulls at the adolescent to conform to the standards of friends. Because of adolescents' exaggerated need for approval, there is a danger that they will sell themselves out and increasingly look to others to tell them who and what they should be. The need for acceptance by one's peer group is often stronger than the need for self-respect. This can lead to a range of behaviors that cause problems for adolescents, such as dependence on drugs or alcohol in order to feel anything or to escape from painful feelings.

Adolescents tend to be more aware of what the world does to them than of what they do to the world. Thus, they can be highly critical and fault finding. At times, they may want to drop out of society, yet at other times they may idealistically strive to reform society. Adolescents confront dilemmas similar to those faced by the elderly in our society: finding meaning in life and wrestling with feelings of uselessness. Older people are often forced to retire before they feel ready to do so, and the young have not yet completed their education or acquired the skills essential for many lines of work. Thus, adolescents are continually preparing for the future, which is often marked by uncertainty.

In sum, for most people adolescence is a difficult period, characterized by paradoxes: they strive for closeness, yet they also fear intimacy and often avoid it; they rebel against control, yet they want direction and structure; although they push and test limits imposed on them, they see some limits as a sign of caring; they are not given complete autonomy, yet they are often expected to act as though they were mature adults; they are typically highly self-centered and preoccupied with their own world, yet they are expected to cope with societal demands and go outside of themselves by expanding their horizons; they are asked to face and accept reality, and at the same time they are tempted by many avenues of escape; and they are exhorted to think of the future, yet they have strong urges to live for the moment and to enjoy life. With all these polarities it is easy to understand that adolescence is typically a turbulent and fast-moving time, one that can accentuate loneliness and isolation. Group experiences can be very useful in dealing with these feelings of isolation and making constructive choices for a satisfying life.

This brief sketch of some of the main currents of adolescent life should make obvious the need for developmental counseling. And group counseling is especially suitable for adolescents, because it provides a place in which they can express and experience their conflicting feelings, discover that they're not unique in their struggles, openly question their values and modify those they find wanting, learn to communicate with peers and adults, learn from the modeling provided by the leader, and learn how to accept what others offer and give of themselves in return. Groups provide a place in which adolescents can safely experiment with reality and test their limits. A unique value of group counseling is that it lets adolescents be instrumental in one another's growth; group members help one another in the struggle for self-understanding. Most important, a group setting gives adolescents a chance to express themselves and to be heard and to interact with their peers.

Sample Proposal for an Adolescent Group

The following example of a proposal for a group could be modified to fit many types of special-interest adolescent group and some children's groups as well. It could be adapted to various settings such as mental-health clinics, community centers, public schools, family-services agencies, and so on.

■■ 1. Rationale

Adolescence is a time of paradox; conflicts often lead to considerable anxiety and feelings of separateness. At this time of life people need to learn how to cope with increasing freedom and the responsibilities that accompany it. A group can provide the opportunity to share common struggles and to find ways of making responsible choices.

■■ 2. Type of Group

This will be a self-exploration group composed of young people between the ages of 15 and 19. The group will be limited to eight participants, and entry into the group is voluntary. This is basically a therapeutic group, with the focus on providing an open atmosphere to explore typical developmental concerns and conflicts facing the adolescent; it is not group therapy aimed at treating emotional disturbances. The group will meet for 15 weeks, each Wednesday from 7:00 to 9:00 P.M. If all the members have an interest, one all-day Saturday extended session can be arranged at some time during the 15-week period.

The initial session will be devoted to teaching the participants how to get the maximum benefit from a group experience and will orient the members to basic ground rules and to working toward the establishment of trust.

■■ 3. Goals and Objectives

The group will be a place for self-exploration and for sharing of ideas and feelings. Participants will be invited to examine their values, behaviors, and relationships with others and to look at the direction of their life to determine what changes they might want to make. It is the members' responsibility to decide for themselves the nature and extent of the changes they want to make. The members will decide when to share personal issues and how much to share. Participants are expected to be active in the sessions, at least to the degree of sharing their reactions to the here-and-now events within the group.

Although each member will be assisted in developing specific, concrete, and personal goals early in the group, the following are some general goals that will provide direction for this group:

- to grow in self-acceptance and self-respect
- to clarify values and examine one's philosophy of life
- to become sensitive to the needs of others
- to explore conflicts and look for one's own answers
- to develop sufficient trust within the group to allow for an honest sharing of attitudes and feelings
- to learn ways of applying what is learned in the group to everyday situations

■■ 4. Basic Information

- names of the group leaders (group will be co-led)
- qualifications and experience of the leaders
- pertinent information concerning fees (if any), dates, and how to sign up for screening interview

■■ 5. Basic Ground Rules

- Members are expected to attend all the sessions and participate by sharing themselves and giving feedback to others.
- Members must maintain the confidential nature of others' disclosures.
- It is the participants' responsibility to decide on specific personal goals that will guide their participation. This will be done within the

first few sessions by developing a contract that clearly states what members want to change and to discuss in the group and how they might go about this.

· Members will not come to group meetings under the influence of drugs or alcohol.
· Smoking is not allowed during the sessions.
· Members must have the written consent of their parents to participate in the group.

▪▪ 6. Topics for Possible Group Exploration

During the history of this group the members and the leaders will collectively decide on certain common themes and personal issues to provide some structuring to this group. Some examples of theme-oriented sessions are the following:

· dealing with alcohol and drug abuse
· learning how to cope with feelings (of depression, guilt, anxiety, anger, rejection, hostility, loneliness)
· exploring conflicts related to school
· discussing careers and post–high school plans
· discussing love, sex, and intimacy
· defining sex roles
· exploring identity issues
· considering the struggle toward autonomy
· discussing conflicts with parents; learning how to live with and appreciate parents

Other topics of concern to group participants will be developed as the sessions progress.

▪▪ 7. Special Considerations in Getting Adolescent Groups Started

There are a number of practical, ethical, and legal issues that need to be carefully considered in designing groups for adolescents. For a detailed discussion of these issues, refer to the section at the end of Chapter 9 dealing with guidelines for group work with children and adolescents.

The Evolution of an Adolescent Group

In this section we discuss ways of involving and motivating the adolescent to become an active group participant and guidelines for conducting the sessions and keeping the meetings moving in a meaningful direction. We address dealing with resistance, facilitating action, making role playing meaningful to the adolescent, sustaining the interest of the group, involving as many members as possible in the interactions, and other topics relevant to the unfolding of the adolescent group.

We show how these guidelines can be put into practice, using as an example our experiences as co-leaders of a weekly counseling group for adolescents. Our group consisted of students from a local high school. This was an experimental program, offered free to the school district and to the participating members. The members were expected to attend all the sessions, which met on Wednesday evenings from 7:00 to 9:00 for one semester. In addition to these 15 meetings we held one 10-hour marathon. The group consisted of ten members, all of whom were there by choice. Most of the participants were functioning relatively well, so the focus of the group was developmental and preventive rather than remedial. In many respects the group became a personal-growth group; members were encouraged to initiate discussion of matters important to them at this time in their life.

During the initial sessions we talked to the members about the need to specify group, as well as individual, goals. We devoted the beginning sessions to encouraging the participants to formulate their personal goals as concretely as possible. Contracts were useful in this respect. Some of the personal goals that members set were (1) "to feel less self-conscious around members of the other sex," (2) "to decide whether to go to college," (3) "to increase my feelings of self-esteem and self-confidence," (4) "to learn how to get along with my parents," (5) "to develop a closer relationship with my parents," (6) "to feel less isolated and different," (7) "to learn how to communicate what I really feel," (8) "to learn how to be more assertive without alienating others," and (9) "to learn to distinguish my parents' values from my own." Granted, a few of these goals are not very precise, but this vagueness was one of the reasons these adolescents had joined the group. Part of our task was to teach the members to translate their broad goals into behaviors that could be practiced both within and outside the group.

▪▪ Establishing Trust and Dealing with Resistance

At a point early in an adolescent group's history we might say something like: "This is a place in which, we hope, you will come to feel free enough to say what you think and feel, without censoring or rehearsing. It is a place where you can reveal personal struggles and find, with the help of others, a way of recognizing, understanding, and perhaps resolving certain problems. We hope a climate develops in which, because you feel that what you say is important and that you're respected for who you are, you will be able to discover the many selves within you. To a great degree, the value of the sessions depends on your level of commitment. If you merely show up and listen politely, you may leave disap pointed. We hope that, as the sessions progress, you will think about what you want from this group and ask the group to help you get it. Our agenda will include anything about you that you want to explore; there are no forbidden topics. We hope you will take risks here, saying and doing things that you don't feel safe saying or doing in other social settings. In order to make many of the changes you wish to make, you'll have to take such risks."

Although this speech suggests that we give group members a great deal of freedom, it's not meant to imply the absence of realistic limits and rules. For example, in our weekly group we wouldn't permit marijuana smoking, which would have threatened the very existence of the group. Also, we pointed out to members that their freedom to act had to be balanced by a respect for the rights of others.

It must be remembered that many of the freedoms a group offers typically do not exist for adolescents. Their teachers may not be interested in their personal views or concerns; the atmosphere of their school may be one of oppression and control; and their parents may miss hearing what they say or appreciating them as young adults, instead attempting to fashion them according to a certain set of standards. Thus, we've found that adolescents will test us to determine whether we mean what we say about what can go on in the group. How we respond to their testing tells the members how much they can trust us as group leaders. If we accept their testing in a nonjudgmental and nondefensive way and resist giving lectures about how they should be, we come a long way toward gaining their acceptance. We've found that adolescents are quick to detect phoniness (and sincerity) and that practicing what we preach is the surest way to earn their respect and to generate an atmosphere of trust in the group.

■■ Working with Involuntary and Resistant Adolescents

Although the group we have described consisted of voluntary members, many groups are composed of court-referred or school-referred clients. In working with adolescents who are reluctant to participate, some of the following interventions have proved helpful to us, and we suggest that you consider how these ideas could be applied to some groups you may lead or co-lead.

First of all, much of the resistance of adolescents to participating in a group can be effectively explored by meeting with them initially on an individual basis. At this meeting you can find out about their reservations about being in a group; give them specific information about the group; and in a nondefensive way explore their negative attitudes with them and provide them an opportunity to express their reactions to being "forced" into the group. You can also point out to them that they *did* make a choice to come to the group. They could have refused and then taken the consequences of not complying with the directive. During the individual pregroup meeting it is helpful to explore any of the adolescent's past experiences with therapy. You can do a lot to demystify the process of therapy by providing accurate information about the goals of a group, your role as a group leader, and other considerations that we discussed in Chapters 2 and 3.

Another way to work with uncooperative adolescents is to go *with* resistance, rather than fighting *against* it, and to attempt to work out alternatives to a group. One example of such an option is to continue seeing these adolescents individually for a number of sessions to establish a relationship with them before putting them in a group. You might also invite them to join the group for three sessions, in which they make a sincere effort to participate. Then if they are still reluctant, allow them to leave. The rationale for this strategy is that these adolescents will have some basis for a decision after they have been to a few group sessions. Even though they were directed to "get counseling," this is one way to provide some increased element of choice. Since forced therapy would only entrench negative attitudes, the leader may genuinely be able to help them find another solution.

Another alternative is to invite a skeptical adolescent to attend the group for a session or so without any pressure to participate. It is important to let other members know that this person is an observer, there to determine if he or she wants to continue. They are less likely to resent the nonparticipant, and they can let him or her know whether they themselves have overcome resistance to being in this group.

Adolescents who show up for a session involuntarily often show their resistance through sarcasm and silence. It is important to respond not with defensiveness but with honesty, firmness, and caring confrontations. Assume that an adolescent says "I don't want to be here!" A nonhelpful response is "Look, I don't want to be here either." A productive response could be "Tell me where you would rather be." Then follow the adolescent's lead and go with the resistance, instead of fighting it or taking it personally. Although you might feel personally rejected, it is essential not to get bogged down in feeling useless and unappreciated. A group counselor cannot afford the luxury of feeling vulnerable to rejection. Taking as a personal affront all the abrasiveness and defensiveness some adolescents display is a quick route to burn-out.

We are not suggesting that you give resistant adolescents permission to verbally beat up on you. It is possible to stand up for yourself in a direct and nondefensive way. If an involuntary client taunts you with "You're a phony, and you're only in it for the money," it is not helpful to lash out and then proceed to defend your altruistic bent and your dedication to helping others. Doing this can easily lead to becoming entangled in countertransference. An alternative response could be: "I don't like being called a phony by you. We've just met, and you don't have enough information about me to make that judgment. I'd like to have a chance with you before you dismiss me!'' This is an example of speaking for oneself and keeping the lines of communication open.

■■ The Influence of the Leader's Personality

Our experience with adolescents continues to teach us how great an influence the personality of the group leader has on the evolution of the group. We find that adolescents respond well to leader characteristics such as a willingness to share one's self with the group, a caring attitude, enthusiasm and vitality, openness, and directness. They do learn from watching the leader model, but the behavior of the leader doesn't have to be perfect in order for them to benefit. In fact, adolescents can relate well to adults who reveal their personal struggles. Adults who genuinely respect and enjoy adolescents will typically be rewarded with a reciprocal respect.

Adolescents are also sensitive to the adult who, never having fully experienced his or her adolescence, attempts to experience it now by ''becoming one of the gang.'' Some group leaders do this by imitating the slang and manner of speaking of the adolescents. Young people are quick to detect the insincerity of a group leader who uses expressions to impress them and to give the appearance of being ''with it.'' Because of this insincerity, the leader may have difficulty gaining the adolescents' trust and respect. Group leaders would do well to remember that they hold a different position and role from that of the members and that clients usually expect their leader to act differently. Leaders who are powerful but who don't use their power to control and stifle members are viewed with respect by adolescents.

Finally, adolescents have taught us that we have the most influence on them when we are seriously attempting to be in our life what we are encouraging them to become. This does not mean that, in order to be effective, we must be ideal people whom the members can imitate. Rather, it means that we are most effective when the members feel that we practice what we preach.

We want to mention why it is sometimes extremely difficult for people to lead adolescent groups. We think that those who work intensively with adolescents experience a reliving of many of their own unresolved adolescent conflicts. For example, an adult who never faced or resolved certain adolescent fears related to sexuality or lovability may find these fears resurfacing as he or she leads an adolescent group. For this reason, it is crucial that those who lead adolescent groups be willing and courageous enough to explore, and perhaps relive, much of their own adolescent experience so that it will not interfere with their work with adolescents or so that they won't become enmeshed in countertransference.

In addition, adolescents may be psychologically threatening to adults, for they are full of energy, are often free from major responsibilities, have the capacity to have fun and experience joy, and are able to feel intensely. Leaders may feel that they have lost some of these lively qualities. They may be faced for the first time with the facts of their aging and their loss of the capacity to savor life. Such leaders can prevent the growth of resentment by first accepting the fact of their aging and then looking for new meaning and excitement in their life.

■■ Keeping the Sessions Moving

In our weekly adolescent group a valuable skill was keeping the sessions moving, which was accomplished mainly by assisting the members to speak for themselves in concrete terms. This was not an easy task; it was hard to get the participants to focus on themselves in the here and now. Especially in a beginning adolescent group, members have a tendency to tell stories endlessly, going into every detail. We found that the best way to teach members not to ask questions or storytell was to make the group aware of this dynamic as it occurred, by saying something like "I'd like to stop for a moment to check out your reactions to Betty and to find out where you are at this moment." Very often we found that the members felt lost, unsure what the point was, and bored; they had tuned Betty out. This feedback served to teach the members that storytelling and excessive questioning had a tendency to be nonproductive, both in the group and in their outside life.

Action-Oriented Techniques.   It is sometimes useful to say to a member after a long-winded story "If I allowed you only one sentence to express what you have just said, what would be the bottom line?" In this way a very detailed story that has the effect of boring others could be simply and directly stated by "I sometimes resent my girlfriend for the way she treats me!"

If members are well prepared for action-oriented techniques, Gestalt and psychodrama techniques can bring vitality to the sessions. For instance, if Scott is complaining about how his girlfriend, Dawn, treats him, he can be asked to imagine that Dawn is sitting in an empty chair and to tell her how he feels around her at times. If appropriate, another member can "sit in" for Dawn and carry on a dialogue with Scott. Scott might "become Dawn" and tell everyone in the group what she thinks of Scott; this could be useful in helping Scott stand in Dawn's shoes. Through these kinds of action-oriented techniques, more feelings are elicited, and boring stories are minimized. Members also get a chance to say out loud things that they have kept inside. Through role reversal, members can gain empathy for others in their life.

Using Personal Statements. We have asked members to try to state how they were affected by a situation rather than how other people acted toward them. For instance, Carol began by talking about how she felt misunderstood by her mother. Soon she slipped away from her own feelings and focused on her mother. She told stories about her mother, blamed her mother for her unhappiness, focused on her mother's feelings, and so on. After a while one of us remarked "You seem to be talking more about your mother right now than about yourself. Why not tell us how you're affected when your mother does so-and-so?"

Another problem frequently encountered during a session with adolescents is the apathy of some members. At times there can be a general lethargy in the group. Participants may wait for the group leaders to do something to get them going. Even though we may suggest certain themes or use interaction exercises, there are times when the members go through the motions and then wait passively for another exercise. At times like this one of us might say: "It seems that the energy level is very low in this group tonight. I suggest we go around and have each of you state where you've drifted off to and why, as well as what you're willing to do about it."

Another dynamic that commonly keeps a group from reaching an intensive working level is one member's bombarding of another with questions. When such questioning occurs, it is appropriate for the group leader to make a comment such as "Marco, instead of questioning Charlene, tell her what it was that provoked you to ask the question." Unless the questioning is stopped in this way, the intensity of Charlene's emotional experience may soon be dissipated. The leader can try to prevent this from happening again by stressing that it is far better for members to state how they are affected by someone's emotional experience and in what ways they're identifying with the person than to distract the member with questions.

Teaching members how to share themselves through statements rather than questioning is more effective when done in a timely, appropriate, and sensitive manner—when certain behaviors or interactions are occurring in the session. If members experience the intimidation of being bombarded by questions, they are receptive to learning alternative behaviors.

Structuring Sessions. We favor active intervention and structuring for adolescent groups, particularly during the initial stages. In our judgment adolescents do not cope with uncertainty as well as adults do, and some structuring can provide the direction needed to keep the sessions moving. Structuring might involve specifying a theme or topic for the group to deal with. Such topics should be related to the interests and needs of the adolescents and not merely issues the leader feels are important, such as: How can we improve our study habits? What can be done to reduce the absentee rate in classrooms? How can we learn to respect our teachers? The group may well have little interest in these topics, and the sessions are bound to get bogged down.

In our adolescent group we developed themes with the participants in the sessions. We didn't say "Since this is your group, what do you want to talk about?" Instead, we structured by limiting the choices somewhat, saying: "In working with groups like this, we have found that certain themes are of concern to most young people. A few of these are: What do I want from my life, and what is stopping me from getting it? Can I be who I am and be sincerely accepted by my parents? How can I better understand my feelings of loneliness? In what ways am I like others in my struggles? These are only a few of the topics that we might consider. Every group moves in its own direction. What, in particular, would each of you like to see us focus on in this group?"

A general agenda for the next session can be decided on at the end of each session. Flexibility should be built into the structuring, though, for often members will spontaneously bring up pressing problems that are not related to the scheduled theme, and this deviation from the plan can be very fruitful. A theme, like an interaction exercise, is only a means to the end of involving the members in meaningful group work; it is important that topics or techniques not become ends in themselves. Our adolescent group once planned, at the end of a session, to deal with a certain theme the next week; however, a classmate of the group members committed suicide the night before the next session, and the group was preoccupied with this. The session was devoted to exploring the effect that this tragedy was having on each group member, and the topic of death was explored in a very personal way.

■■ Role Playing

In our adolescent groups we usually rely heavily on role playing and other action-oriented methods. We find that this is an excellent way to keep the interest level high, to involve a lot of the members, and to give a here-and-now flavor to the work being done. Role playing fosters creative problem solving, encourages spontaneity, usually intensifies feelings, and gets people to identify with others. By role playing, participants can learn how to express themselves more effectively. They can test reality and practice new behavior.

We've found that it helps members become comfortable with role playing more quickly if we participate at first. For instance, if a girl has been describing how she views her parents and how frustrated she feels when she tries to talk with them, we might take the part of her mother and father. That will allow her to deal directly, albeit symbolically, with her parents and feel her frustration intensely. We can then stop the action and ask her: "What are you experiencing now? What would you most like to do now? If you could reach us, make us really hear you, what would you most want to say?" The role playing may be brief. When it's over, the person should discuss the experience and plan how to handle this situation when it arises in the future.

Adolescents are often self-conscious about getting involved in role playing. Both the timing and manner of introducing techniques are directly related to the degree to which adolescents are likely to cooperate. It is useful to provide a general orientation to the techniques you employ, which could be done at an orientation session. At times, you might respond with humor when an adolescent says he or she feels silly in role playing. "I know it seems silly and a bit awkward," you could say, "but how about trying it anyway and seeing what you might learn about yourself?" Or you could say "I know it seems silly, but who says we always have to be serious?" Generally, if we approach role playing in this light and gentle way, the resistance dissipates, and before the participant knows it, he or she is playing a role with gusto. Frequently we check to see whether a person wants to explore a particular problem and is willing to use role playing to do so. One of us might say: "You seem to be unclear about how your mother really affects you and how you should deal with her. Are you willing to try something?"

There are many variations of role-playing techniques. To illustrate, we'll use the example of Sally, who discloses that she feels she can never please her father and that this hurts her. She says that she and her father are not close and she would like to change that. She is afraid of her father, for she sees him as critical of her, and she feels that, unless she is perfect, she cannot win his approval. Several role-playing situations are possible:

· Sally can play her father. To get a picture of how she perceives her father, we can ask her to give Sally a long lecture and tell her all the things that she must become before she is worthwhile in his eyes. Speaking as her father, Sally might say something like: "I know you have a lot more ability than you show. Why didn't you get all A's? Yes, I'm proud of you for getting five A's, but I must confess I'm let down by that one B. If you really put your mind to it, I know you could do better." We would encourage her to stay in her father's role for a time and say things that she imagines he is thinking but not expressing.

· A group member who identifies with Sally can play Sally while Sally continues playing her father. From the dialogue that ensues, Sally can get an idea of how her father feels with her. A group member with a similar conflict can benefit from involvement in the situation.

· A member who feels that he or she can identify with the father can play that role. If nobody in the group jumps at this opportunity, the leader can take the parent role. This situation allows Sally to intensify her feelings and to demonstrate how she deals with her father. As the role playing continues, Sally may achieve insight into herself that will help her grow.

· Sally can also play both herself and her father. She can be directed to say (as her father) what she wishes he would say to her. This is a future projection, and it taps the person's hopes.

· Sally can present a soliloquy, talking aloud as her father, saying what she imagines her father might say about her. Sally can also use the soliloquy approach when she is in her own role, after she finishes an exchange with her father. She can express many of the thoughts and feelings she generally keeps locked within herself when she talks with her father.

· Several other group members can sit in for Sally and show how they would deal with her father. This may suggest to Sally options she hadn't thought of.

· Other members who role-played Sally's father can provide helpful feedback to her by telling her what they felt as they listened to her. Sally may be less defensive in hearing from her peers about how they were put off by her abrasive style than if an adult provided this feedback.

As it is important for members to process these dramas, the leader should ask them to think about the implications of what they observed in themselves in the role-playing situations. At this time feedback from other members and interpretations from the leader can enable the members to see with more clarity their own part in their conflicts with others.

▪▪ Getting Group Members to Participate and Initiate

During the sessions we look for many ways of bringing uninvolved group members into ongoing interactions. After Sally's role playing, for example, we might encourage other members to tell what they were experiencing as Sally was working with her father. We might request: "Can any of you give Sally feedback? What did you see her doing? Did Sally spark any feelings in you?" Adolescents are usually most eager to become personally involved when other members touch vulnerable spots in them. As we've mentioned, one real advantage of group counseling is that the members can be of service to their peers by giving their perceptions, by revealing similar problems, by suggesting alternatives, by supporting them in times of despair, by reflecting what they hear them saying, by confronting them on inconsistencies, and so on.

Therefore, we try to involve as many members as possible in the group process. In addition, we try to shape the group so that we will be required less and less to give direction. As we have pointed out, in an effective group, the members gradually assume a larger and larger share of the leadership functions. For instance, if a group that usually functions effectively begins to stray aimlessly, a member will probably point this out. If a group member gets bogged down in storytelling and intellectualizing, we expect a member to call the person on this. In short, one of our aims is to teach adolescents to monitor their own group and become less dependent on us for direction.

▪▪ The Use of Peer Counselors

Peer counselors can be used both in the classroom in human-relations classes and as a part of the outreach program of the counseling and guidance program of the school. Given proper training and supervision, peers can often be as effective in reaching fellow students as counselors or teachers.

An important consideration in using peer counselors is teaching them the boundaries of their competence. For instance, a counselor we know commented that an issue explored in her groups is adolescent suicide. Many of her counselees experience depression and alienation, and some are suicide prone. A number of her counselees use drugs and alcohol heavily, to the point that it has interfered with their life. Such situations highlight the importance of peer counselors' and counselors' being aware of their own limitations. It is essential to know the agencies to which to refer students who need further professional assistance, and a valuable skill is being able to present information to a young person in such a manner that he or she is likely to accept a referral in those situations that call for it.

There is a strong possibility that peer counselors might become deeply involved in others' lives when professional expertise is called for. Peer counselors can play a supportive role, they can challenge fellow students to evaluate their behavior honestly, and they can share their own life experiences and learning with others. They are not qualified to attempt to render psychotherapy. Thus, it is critical that peer counselors learn how to function as liaisons so that students who need professional assistance can get it.

Finally, in working with adolescents in personal areas, it is important for both counselors and their peer counselors to learn how to set personal limits so that they do not become burned out. For example, adolescents can easily become dependent on an adult or a peer counselor whom they respect and have affection for. Counselors who make it a practice to say "Here is my phone number, and don't hesitate to call whenever you'd like" are likely to find themselves swamped by demands and not able to live up to what was promised. To remain effective in working with young people in groups, the counselor must recognize personal limitations and take care to ensure that resentment does not build up over constantly being asked to help others in crisis situations.

Involving Parents

■■ Parent-Consultation Groups

Leaders of adolescent groups are potentially valuable as consultants both to parents and to teachers. Most parents care about their children. Yet most parents go through a period when they would like to "divorce" their adolescent, for the possibility of any real communication seems remote. Like their adolescent children, parents need some assistance. They need more than general information about parent/adolescent relationships or methods of control. They need to talk about their feelings of inadequacy, guilt, resentment, and rejection. Many feel deeply unappreciated and feel that, no matter how sincerely they try to improve relations at home, things won't get better. A consultation group can give parents a chance to express some of their frustration and ambivalence about being parents. A good group leader can sensitize parents to the dynamics of adolescence. The leader can present short, informal talks that widen the perspectives of parents, and parents can raise questions and bring up problems that they would like to discuss with other parents and with the group leader.

Certain programs can also be designed for the parent willing to invest a lot of time and energy in becoming a better parent. Many group leaders offer parent-effectiveness training groups. Such groups can be held at the local high school or at one of the parents' homes one evening a week. Parents in such groups are encouraged to read books such as Gordon's (1970) *Parent Effectiveness Training*, Ginott's (1973) *Between Parent and Teenager*, Dinkmeyer et al.'s (1983) *Systematic Training for Effective Parenting of Teens* (STEP/Teen), and to discuss them in the group. Role playing gives parents a chance to examine their relationships with their children and experiment with new, more effective behaviors.

■■ Groups with Parents and Adolescents

Many community mental-health agencies and schools provide groups composed of adolescents and their parents. It takes considerable skill and sensitivity to keep group meetings from degenerating into gripe sessions. The focus needs to be on both parents and teenagers learning how to listen with understanding. The group can be kept small, especially if the group leader has not led such a group before. Groups with parents and adolescents have the potential for improving relationships at home, especially if contracts are formed that include both parents' and adolescents' taking specific steps toward agreed-on changes.

A Group for Unwed Teenage Fathers

Wayne Huey, a counselor at Gordon High School in Decatur, Georgia, designed a group called MALE (Maximizing a Life Experience). It included eight students, age 14–18, who were already fathers or expectant fathers. He created this group after one of his school-board members commented on his school's counseling program for pregnant girls and wondered what help was available for the teenage fathers. After reviewing the literature, Huey concluded that counseling programs for unwed teenage fathers were practically nonexistent, especially in the schools. Although he realized that the "other half" of the teenage pregnancy problem was being overlooked, he was not sure whether the young men might need or even want help. And he had few ideas about how to set up a program for them if one was warranted. The remainder of this section describes the steps taken in setting up and evaluating this creative program.

■■ Initial Steps

The pregnant girls in the school were contacted, but it was found that none of them was pregnant by a student at the high school. Huey then contacted counselors, teachers, administrators, and coaches, and eight names were eventually secured. The program was outlined to each of them, and they were asked if they wanted to make a commitment to participate in the group. Parental consent was required to join. All eight identified males got parental consent, all made the commitment, and all completed the nine-session group.

■■ Goals and Objectives

The MALE group had the general goal of offering assistance in a nonjudgmental way. The initial plan focused on three R's: rights, responsibilities, and resources. The specific objectives were for the participants (1) to learn more about themselves and their feelings in relation to their situation, (2) to understand their legal and emotional rights and responsibilities, (3) to identify and explore present and future options, (4) to learn to make sound decisions, (5) to realize what resources were available to them, (6) to accept that pregnancy is not an accident, and (7) to obtain information about contraception.

▪▪ Structure of the Group Sessions

The nine sessions were held for an hour each week. They were held during the school day on a rotating schedule, so that no class was missed more than once or twice. The members were to make up all missed assignments. The nine sessions were structured as follows:

Session 1. An overview of the program was explained, as were general group goals and ground rules. Members got to know one another and developed their own personal goals.

Session 2. The group viewed and discussed the film *Teenage Father*.

Session 3. The group viewed and discussed the filmstrip *His Baby, Too: Problems of Teenage Pregnancy* (available from Sunburst Communications, 39 Washington Avenue, Room KT7, Pleasantville, NY 10570). The members also prepared questions on legal issues.

Session 4. The group explored legal issues, with a focus on the rights and responsibilities of unwed teenage fathers in Georgia. A guest speaker from the Legal Aid Society was heard.

Session 5. The reproductive system and contraception were discussed. A guest speaker from Planned Parenthood appeared.

Session 6. There was a field trip to Planned Parenthood and a presentation on sexually transmitted diseases.

Session 7. A session on problem solving and decision making was held, including models and practice activities.

Session 8. Problem-solving and decision-making models were used with actual personal situations.

Session 9. At the final session members summarized what they had learned about their rights and responsibilities, and there was discussion of school resources. The members completed a written evaluation and discussed the effectiveness of the program.

▪▪ Outcomes of the Program

Results.   According to Huey, the program was a tremendous success. The overall group rating was 9.5, on a 10.0 scale, when the members were asked if the group had been helpful to them. The young men wanted the group to last longer, and they considered it very helpful. They had shared their feelings of anger, guilt, frustration, confusion, and fear. They explored concerns about their situation and the impact it might have on their future and the future of their baby.

Follow-Up.   At 1- and 2-year follow-ups, none of this first group had fathered a second child, and all were progressing toward their career goals as they had imagined that they might be without a child. Three were in college or technical school, two were in the military, two were working full time, and one was still in high school. None of them had married the mother of his child; in fact, only two were still dating her a year later. All of them were contributing something toward the support of their child, and those who were close enough to visit were seeing the baby on a regular basis.

■■ Summary

This group is another example of a specific program designed to meet the needs of a particular population. Such a group can be replicated in a community agency. The steps taken to set up this program and the general structure of the sessions can also suggest a model for other specialized short-term groups for adolescents. This group illustrates the possibilities involved in combining an *educational* program (one designed to impart certain information) with a *therapeutic* program (one geared to helping members explore their feelings, attitudes, and values and make decisions). If you are interested in more detailed information on this type of group, write Wayne Huey at Gordon High School, 2190 Wallingford Drive, Decatur, GA 30032, or telephone him at (404) 241-5662.

A Systemwide Program for Counseling Young People in Groups

This chapter has thus far described the formation of specific counseling groups for adolescents in schools and agencies. Now we consider organizing a group-counseling project on a larger scale for adolescents in senior and junior high school, as well as for children in the elementary grades. The project about to be described demonstrates that it is possible to set up a program, including training and supervision of professional group counselors, on a systemwide scale.

■■ Background of the Program

Public schools are responsible under federal law for guaranteeing the right of free and appropriate education for all children. Iowa developed a comprehensive system of special education for students who otherwise could not successfully compete in "regular" education. Essential to the teaching of special-education students is an emphasis on their integration into as many regular classes as possible.

Project Group Work is funded by a grant from the Iowa Department of Education. This project involves a regional education agency that provides support services to 29 local school districts in a six-county area. Project Group Work is designed to provide training in group-counseling skills to school social workers, psychologists, and special-education teachers who work with the behaviorally disordered. (Iowa defines the behaviorally disordered as those students who have observable problematic behaviors in the school setting. Of the 60,000 students in the area, 2128 are identified as learning disabled, 1142 as mentally disabled, and 454 as behaviorally disabled.)

The Focus of Project Group Work.   This project is noteworthy in that it

- emphasizes group work with special-education students
- provides supervised group work training in the school setting
- emphasizes the importance of therapeutic relationships between the group leader(s) and students
- uses the discussion approach to identify problematic issues
- utilizes the special-education class as a peer-support system
- promotes the concept of special-education teachers as co-leaders in the therapeutic discussion groups
- blends concepts from a variety of theories of group counseling

The groups are viewed as therapeutic discussion groups for elementary- and secondary-age behaviorally disordered students. The purpose of the groups is to provide a safe environment in which the students feel comfortable discussing issues that are interfering with their educational functioning. The group, with a range of 6 to 12 students, meets for one class period each week.

Topics or issues discussed in the groups include academic difficulties, feelings associated with having a disability, peer-relationship problems, value conflicts, family problems, and child abuse. Often these students are poorly motivated or exhibit behavioral difficulties in school because of their personal stress. The group is viewed as a support group for these students, as it becomes a place for expressing feelings, gaining insights into alternative ways of behaving, and receiving positive reinforcement.

▪▪ Basic Elements of the Group Experience

Phil Piechowski, the director of Project Group Work, reports that the following elements have been found to be essential in conducting counseling groups in the school setting:

1. **Positive focus.** The students must be hopeful that change will result from their participation in the group and in their special-education program.

2. **Focus on the here and now.** Although an understanding and discussion of the student's past history is helpful, the student is encouraged to identify goals for the present and the future.

3. **Emphasis on overt behaviors.** Since groups are typically limited to one class period a week, the focus tends to be on those behaviors that

are identified by the teacher, psychologist, and social worker as most interfering with the student's academic success.

4. **Reinforcement system.** A system for reinforcing appropriate behavior is often necessary in the initial stages of a group.

5. **Enhancing self-concept and coping skills.** Feelings about self and social skills are general deficit areas for the students participating in these groups. Therefore, the goals of group work are largely related to these two areas.

6. **Changing an image.** Many of the students perceive special-education placement as a "punishment," because they have less contact with the regular educational program. Students are encouraged to explore their perceptions and feelings regarding their placement, and it is hoped that they will learn to accept such a placement.

7. **Teacher participation.** The involvement of the teacher as a co-leader with the social worker or psychologist is essential. The teacher adds significantly to the group because he or she is involved on a daily basis with the students and can lend support to them throughout the week. The teacher's capacity for understanding and accepting these students is increased because he or she becomes aware of some of the students' personal struggles through the group sessions.

■■ Training Group Leaders

Since the project's inception in the fall of 1983, twenty master's- and doctoral-level school social workers, psychologists, and special-education teachers have received intensive training in group skills. The training has included theories of child development, elements of group process, and group-leadership skills. No single theoretical model is promoted; these practitioners have been exposed to a variety of counseling theories. The group leaders are supervised by the supervisor of school social-work services and the head psychologist. Each group is observed, and several practitioners are video-taping their group sessions.

The practitioners meet once or more a month to discuss the progress of their groups. On attaining the desired degree of proficiency, each group leader assists in the training of additional professionals.

■■ Conclusions

Project Group Work has been well received by special-education teachers. It is often the first opportunity the teacher has had to work with the social worker or psychologist. The co-leaders meet both before and after the group meetings. This process has helped improve the communication between the teacher and the mental-health professionals serving the special-education program.

Students who are offered the opportunity to discuss personal concerns begin to view the school as a more caring institution and the teacher as a helping person. This project has demonstrated students' behavior and school work improve when they perceive the school as supportive.

For additional information about Project Group Work write Phil Piechowski, Supervisor, School Social Work Services, Mississippi Bend Area Education Agency, 729 21st Street, Bettendorf, IA 52722, or telephone him at (319) 359-1371.

Where to Go from Here

One book that has impressed us is *Psychotherapy with Adolescent Girls* (Lamb, 1978). Many of her ideas and the issues she addresses can also be applied to boys. Group workers with adolescents will find her ways of working therapeutically with this age group both stimulating and challenging. Although she mostly describes individual therapy, many of the concepts can be used in group work.

A few other resources you might want to consult in setting up groups for adolescents include *Assertiveness: Innovations, Applications, Issues* (Alberti, 1977) for three good chapters on assertiveness-training groups for adolescents; *I Never Knew I Had a Choice* (Corey with Corey, 1986) for a theme-oriented approach in groups; and *Group Techniques* (Corey, Corey, Callanan, & Russell, 1982) for examples of ways to develop action-oriented techniques.

The following group-counseling textbooks contain a chapter on groups for adolescents: *Group Counseling: Theory and Practice* (Dinkmeyer & Muro, 1979); *Group Counseling: A Developmental Approach* (Gazda, 1984); and *Group Counseling* (Ohlsen, 1977).

A series of four books, all by Jeanne Warren Lindsay, can be used in conjunction with group work: (1) *Teens Look at Marriage: Rainbows, Roles and Reality* (1983); (2) *Teenage Marriage: Coping with Reality* (1984); (3) *Teens Parenting: The Challenge of Babies and Toddlers* (1981); and (4) *Pregnant Too Soon: Adoption Is an Option* (1980). This series is published by Morning Glory Press, 6595 San Haroldo Way, Buena Park, CA 90620.

For an extensive bibliography of group procedures for adolescents, refer to *Group Work in the Helping Professions: A Bibliography* (Zimpfer, 1984), section 6.16, pp. 270–274. This source also contains a wide range of references on group procedures directed at behavior problems, substance abuse, unwed pregnancy, battering, child abuse, acting out, antisocial behavior, social withdrawal, dating inhibition, and groups in correctional settings (section 16.4, pp. 240–262).

Special chapters on peer-facilitated groups, assertion-training groups, parent groups, and growth-centered groups can be found in *Developmental Groups for Children* (Duncan & Gumaer, 1980).

For those interested in the application of Gestalt techniques to adolescent groups, *Windows to Our Children* (Oaklander, 1978) is an outstanding resource. The author describes a variety of techniques, including drawing and fantasy, storytelling, poetry, sensory experiences, creative drama, play therapy, and making things. Most of these Gestalt techniques can be applied to working with adolescents in groups.

Readers who are interested in using concepts and techniques drawn from a variety of therapeutic group models can find concise summary overviews in *Theory and Practice of Group Counseling* (Corey, 1985). The following theoretical approaches to group counseling are described: psychoanalytic, Adlerian, psychodrama and role playing, existential, person-centered, Gestalt, transactional analysis, behavioral, rational-emotive, and reality therapy.

---

*Suggested Readings**

* Alberti, R. E. (Ed.). (1977). *Assertiveness: Innovations, applications, issues.* San Luis Obispo, CA: Impact.

* Bedrosian, R. C. (1981). The application of cognitive therapy techniques with adolescents. In G. Emery, S. D. Hollon, & R. C. Bedrosian (Eds.), *New directions in cognitive therapy* (pp. 68–83). New York: Guilford Press.

Bingham, M., Edmondson, J., & Stryker, S. (1983a). *Challenges: A young man's journal for self-awareness and personal planning.* El Toro, CA: Mission Publications.

Bingham, M., Edmondson, J., & Stryker, S. (1983b). *Choices: A teen woman's journal for self-awareness and personal planning.* El Toro, CA: Mission Publications.

* Bloomfield, H. H., with Felder, L. (1983). *Making peace with your parents.* New York: Ballantine.

Bolles, R. N. (1984). *What color is your parachute?* Berkeley, CA: Ten Speed Press.

Bolton, F. G., Jr. (1980). *The pregnant adolescent: Problems of premature parenthood.* Beverly Hills, CA: Sage Publications.

Burgess-Kohn, J. (1979). *Straight talk about love and sex for teenagers.* Boston: Beacon.

* Corder, B. F., & Cornwall, T. (1984). Techniques for increasing effectiveness of co-therapy functioning in adolescent psychotherapy groups. *International Journal of Group Psychotherapy, 34*(4), 643–654.

* Corey, G. (1985). *Theory and practice of group counseling* (2nd ed.). Monterey, CA: Brooks/Cole.

---

* Books and articles marked with an asterisk are recommended for further study.

* Corey, G., with Corey, M. (1986). *I never knew I had a choice* (3rd ed.). Monterey, CA: Brooks/Cole.
* Corey, G., Corey, M., Callanan, P., & Russell, J. M. (1982). *Group techniques.* Monterey, CA: Brooks/Cole.
* Dinkmeyer, D., et al. (1983). *Systematic training for effective parenting of teens (STEP/Teen).* Circle Pines, MN: American Guidance Service.
* Dinkmeyer, D. C., & Muro, J. J. (1979). *Group counseling: Theory and practice* (2nd ed.). Itasca, IL: F. E. Peacock.
* Duncan, J. A., & Gumaer, J. (Eds.). (1980). *Developmental groups for children.* Springfield, IL: Charles C Thomas.
  Elkind, D. (1984). *All grown up and no place to go: Teenagers in crisis.* Reading, MA: Addison-Wesley.
  Ely, D. F., & Associates. (1981). *California laws relating to minors.* Gardena, CA: Harcourt Brace Jovanovich.
* Erikson, E. (1968). *Identity: Youth and crisis.* New York: Norton.
  Frankl, V. E. (1963). *Man's search for meaning* (rev. ed.). Boston: Beacon.
  Gazda, G. M. (1984). *Group counseling: A developmental approach* (3rd ed.). Boston: Allyn & Bacon.
  Ginott, H. (1973). *Between parent and teenager.* New York: Avon.
  Gordon, T. (1970). *P.E.T., Parent Effectiveness Training: The tested new way to raise responsible children.* New York: New American Library.
  Green, H. (1964). *I never promised you a rose garden.* New York: Holt, Rinehart & Winston.
  Harris, T. (1976). *I'm OK—You're OK.* New York: Avon.
  Hart, G. M. (1978). *Values clarification for counselors.* Springfield, IL: Charles C Thomas.
  Hesse, H. (1951). *Siddhartha.* New York: New Directions.
  Hesse, H. (1965). *Demian.* New York: Harper & Row.
  James, M., & Jongeward, D. (1971). *Born to win: Transactional analysis with Gestalt experiments.* Reading, MA: Addison-Wesley.
  Kelly, G. F. (1977). *Learning about sex: The contemporary guide for young adults.* Woodbury, NY: Barron's Educational Series.
  Kraft, I. A. (1983). *Child and adolescent group psychotherapy.* In H. I. Kaplan & B. J. Sadock (Eds.), *Comprehensive group psychotherapy* (2nd ed.) (pp. 223–234). Baltimore: Williams & Wilkins.
* Lamb, D. (1978). *Psychotherapy with adolescent girls.* San Francisco: Jossey-Bass.
  Leaman, D. R. (1983). Group counseling to improve communication skills of adolescents. *Journal for Specialists in Group Work, 8*(3), 144–150.
* Mencke, R., & Hummel, R. L. (1984). *Career planning for the 80's.* Monterey, CA: Brooks/Cole.
  Moustakas, C. E. (1972). *Loneliness and love.* Englewood Cliffs, NJ: Prentice-Hall.
* Oaklander, V. (1978). *Windows to our children: A Gestalt approach to children and adolescents.* Moab, UT: Real People Press.
  Ohlsen, M. M. (1977). *Group counseling* (2nd ed.). New York: Holt, Rinehart & Winston.
  Rice, F. P. (1981). *The adolescent: Development, relationships and culture* (3rd ed.). Boston: Allyn & Bacon.

Rogers, C. (1983). *Freedom to learn in the 1980's.* Columbus, OH: Charles E. Merrill.

Russell, E. E. H. (1984). *Sexual exploitation: Rape, child sexual abuse, and workplace harassment.* Beverly Hills, CA: Sage Publications.

Zelnik, M., Kantner, J. R., & Ford, K. (1981). *Sex and pregnancy in adolescence.* Beverly Hills, CA: Sage Publications.

* Zimbardo, P. G. (1978). *Shyness.* New York: Jove Press.

* Zimpfer, D. G. (1984). *Group work in the helping professions: A bibliography* (2nd ed.). Muncie, IN: Accelerated Development Inc.

11
Groups for Adults

Introduction

This chapter describes a variety of special-interest groups for adults, with emphasis on these areas: themes and topics as useful catalysts for group interaction, the structuring of adult groups, special considerations in designing and conducting groups for adults, leader characteristics needed to work with various special-interest groups, and the rationale for group approaches. The discussion will be based on our style of leading groups, in that we will describe strategies we've found useful in working with a variety of adult populations. Our attempt is to be as practical as possible, so that as leader of your own adult groups you will be able to incorporate some of our suggestions in your practice.

We begin this chapter with some observations on a theme-oriented approach to adult groups. We then describe several special-interest groups for college students, including structured groups, which can be done in public and private agencies as well as in college counseling centers. Also described are groups for substance abusers, a transition group in a community agency, a women's support group for victims of incest, a residential workshop for couples, and a weeklong residential personal-growth group.

Theme-Oriented Groups

We believe that theme-oriented groups have many advantages for adults. Topics can generate considerable interest within a group and, if they reflect the life issues of the participants, can be powerful catalysts. You should consider several factors if you decide to structure your groups around topics.

It helps to think about the population you are working with, especially the common struggles that members face. For example, if the group you are leading is made up largely of adults in their early 20s, some major areas they are concerned about are choosing a career, choosing a life-style, revising their life plan, finding meaning in life, and wrestling with unresolved dependence/independence issues. If your group is composed of many people who are making the transition from the late 20s to the early 30s, you could expect concerns such as dealing with changes in their values and beliefs, parent/child issues, concerns related to success in the world of work, and depression over not meeting goals they've set for themselves.

For groups made up of middle-aged participants, leaders can structure the group around such themes as coping with the pressure of time, adjusting to children's growing up and leaving home, marital crises, changing roles of men and women, coping with aging, the death of one's parents, divorce and separation, stagnation in work, changing one's occupation or career, finding meaning in life apart from rearing a family, learning how to deal effectively with stress, and facing loneliness.

Who decides on the themes for a group? This depends on many factors, including your leadership style and the level of sophistication of your group. Topics do not have to be imposed on members in an insensitive way; members and leaders can cooperatively develop themes that will provide direction for the sessions. We do think it is important that leaders consider the readiness of members to fully explore these themes. Death, loneliness and isolation, anger, depression, and other potentially intense topics can trigger the opening of feelings that have been repressed for many years, and both the leader and the members need to be able to handle the emotional intensity that is likely to be generated. If members select the themes, rather than being pushed into exploring a given topic, there is a greater chance that they will be able to face them.

Groups for College Students

A common complaint we hear from students is that it is easy to feel isolated on a university campus. Students feel that, whereas much attention is paid to their intellectual development, relatively little attention is paid to their personal development. From our work in the counseling centers of universities, we have come to realize that many students seek counseling services not only because of serious problems but also because they want to develop aspects of their personality in addition to their thinking abilities. These students are hungry for personal nourishment, and they actively seek group experiences in which they can be nourished and can grow by nourishing others. In a weekly group with fellow students (and a group leader) they can formulate goals, explore areas of themselves they've kept hidden from themselves—areas that are presently causing them difficulties in interpersonal relating—and identify the internal blocks that have been impeding the full utilization of their capacities. By dealing with their personal problems, students are able to free themselves of certain emotional blocks to learning. Many who have clarified their values and made decisions about what they want from life have become far better students, approaching their studies with a sense of enthusiasm and commitment.

When we speak about college students, we are not restricting ourselves to a population of those in their late teens or early 20s. The groups that we've led and co-led on university campuses draw a cross-section of students composed of people in their 20s and 30s as well as many middle-aged people. There are, for instance, women who are returning to college after their sons and daughters leave home and many middle-aged men and women preparing for major changes in their career and life. We have found a diversity of special needs on the college campus that can be partly met through a group experience.

▪▪ Common Topics in College Groups

Some themes seem to arise often in our college student counseling groups. These common themes, which provide the content of the group encounters, include the following: the desire to be genuine, problems of college life, interpersonal difficulties, psychosomatic illnesses, denial of problems, the search for pat answers, sexual conflicts, dealing with hostility, feelings of rejection, the desire for acceptance and approval, wanting to love and be loved, relationships with parents, uneasiness about one's body, trusting self and others, feelings of loneliness, emptiness and alienation, how to feel alive, value confusion, search for meaning in life, dependency problems, identity confusion, problems associated with drugs and alcohol, religious conflicts, vocational indecision, anxiety, intimate relationships, insecurity, and lack of self-confidence.

It is possible to structure a personal-growth group, either in a community agency or in a college counseling center, around topics appropriate for the clientele. As an example of structuring a group along thematic lines we offer the following topics, which we have used both in personal-growth groups and in self-exploration courses in college.

1. **Identity.** Who are you? What is important in your world now? What are the main factors that have influenced your life? What kind of person do you wish to become? How do you perceive the world?
2. **Independence.** To what degree have you gained psychological independence from your parents?
3. **Sex roles.** What are the implications for you of the changing concepts of masculinity and femininity? How can you resolve your conflicts about your role?
4. **Love.** How capable are you of loving? What are the barriers in your life that prevent love? What is it like for you to experience love?
5. **Sex.** What are your views regarding sexuality? What are your main concerns regarding your own sexuality?

6. **Marriage.** What are the dynamics within and between two individuals that determine the success or failure of the relationship? What are your feelings about marriage?
7. **Loneliness.** What are the creative aspects of loneliness? Do you cope with your own loneliness, or do you escape from it?
8. **Death.** How do you feel about death? Does this affect the way you live?
9. **Search for meaning and values.** What are the values that give your life meaning, and where did you get them?
10. **Evaluation of the group experience.** What has this group meant to you? What have you learned about your own attitudes, values, beliefs, and behavior? To what extent have you carried this learning into your outside life? What areas do you need to continue working on in your life?

As an example of the variety of structured groups, consider the following group program at one university: (1) dealing with an alcoholic parent, (2) self-hypnosis, (3) staying well, (4) the aftermath of suicide, (5) stress management for law students, (6) developing assertive behavior, (7) eating disorders (binge/purge syndrome), (8) overcoming perfectionism, (9) gaining control of your life-style, (10) managing and ending relationships, (11) mid-life transition, (12) women in transition, (13) depression management, (14) managing the stress of graduate school, and (15) jealousy—taming the green-eyed monster. All of the preceding groups were short term, lasting from 4 weeks to the entire semester, and all were offered in an academic year by the Counseling-Psychological Services Center at the University of Texas at Austin. The counseling staff found that group programs could meet a variety of special needs and that it was possible to combine a therapeutic and an educational focus.

▪▪ Our College Groups

In Jerry Corey's work as a psychologist at university counseling centers, some of the types of group he himself led and co-led were groups with students on academic probation, weekly two-hour personal-growth groups, assertion-training workshops, and marathon weekends. Colleagues who worked in these university centers offered other special-interest workshops and weekly groups, including career development and life planning, skills in living, stress management, consciousness-raising for men and for women, returning-students groups, veterans' groups, groups for women who were abused or raped, groups with gay people, meditation workshops, and groups designed for specific ages.

In Marianne Corey's work with graduate students in counseling and marriage- and family-therapy programs, she has led weekly self-exploration groups as well as weekend and weeklong residential workshops and personal-growth groups. She has found that students in a master's program often discover their own personal issues being brought to light through their contact with clients in their field placements and internships. Weekly groups give these students an opportunity to identify and work through some of their personal problems, which often get in the way of establishing a therapeutic relationship with their clients. In weekend training workshops it becomes apparent that they are able to challenge clients to the degree that they have been willing to examine their own struggles. These graduate students typically discover that they can take a client only as far as they have gone in their own life personally.

■■ Leading Your Own College Group

We wish to emphasize the possibilities that a university counseling center holds for those who want training and supervision in group leading. A counselor on the staff might be willing to assume responsibility for training students to lead groups of their peers. This kind of program would be of real benefit to the volunteer, to the many students who would relate well to a peer leader, and to the counseling center, which would be able to serve more students at no additional expense.

If you should ever work as a group leader on a college campus, consider developing a group that will allow you to share your talents and experiences with others. For example, a woman who begins a counseling career during middle age might decide to form a group composed of women who want to discuss their struggles in adjusting to university life in middle age and finding their way into the world of professional work. Similar groups can be developed to work with substance abuse, weight control, certain behavioral changes, and other life-choice areas.

One caution is in order. It is possible for leaders to develop a special-interest group as a way of working on their own unresolved issues. For example, a male leader who is stuck with resentment toward women may form a men's group and use it as a forum for his own catharsis. We are not implying that leaders should be completely free of their own problems before they lead a group; however, we do see it as a misuse of groups if leaders use session time to grind an axe over some personal issue. Leaders who are unaware of their motivations are not facilitating participants' growth. This problem can be avoided with careful supervision during the leader's training period, as well as continual self-examination and in-service training experiences for those who lead groups.

Groups for Substance Abusers

A large number of people drink, use drugs, or have eating patterns that cause them severe problems in daily living. One therapeutic approach to dealing with the impact of substance abuse on individuals and society is group counseling. We recently gave a professional development workshop on group counseling for the European Branch of the American Association for Counseling and Development. Many of the participants in the workshop, which was held in Germany, specialized in drug and alcohol counseling for military personnel. Most of them were using group approaches with this population. These counselors were eager to learn more about strategies to work with their population, especially techniques in dealing with the resistance they experienced in working with involuntary groups.

Groups such as these, and other groups designed for people with problems controlling the use of alcohol, drugs, and food, appear to be gaining popularity in public and private mental-health agencies. A special issue on substance abuse in the *Journal for Specialists in Group Work* (March 1984) describes group approaches that represent merely a few of the hundreds, and maybe thousands, of programs in the United States. If you are interested in more detailed information on designing a group for substance abusers, we suggest that you consult this reference as an excellent place to begin. Since you may eventually lead this type of special group, we briefly present the rationale for group treatment, requirements for member participation, group techniques, and a summary of commonalities of most group programs for substance abusers.

■■ Rationale

As a rule, substance abusers feel socially isolated and lack interpersonal skills. Further, they are dependent and manipulative and use defenses such as denying, blaming, and rationalizing as ways to avoid accepting personal responsibility for their problems. Some of the specific values of group treatment for substance abusers have been identified by Fuhrmann and Washington (1984a, 1984b) and Altman and Plunkett (1984):

- Groups provide a safe setting for members to break through their sense of isolation.
- Groups can teach such clients that they are not alone with their concerns and that they have the capacity to learn new and more appropriate social skills.
- The protected setting offers members both the support and the confrontation they need for resocialization and for problem-solving.
- The group can encourage clients to let go of some of their defenses.

· Especially through feedback from peers, members can begin to see themselves as others do and can learn how they affect others.
· The group can help the abuser confront difficult issues and learn to cope more effectively with the stresses of daily life.
· A group provides relationships with others with similar struggles and also offers a support system that is typically lacking in their life.
· Clients can explore a range of mutual issues besides those related directly to substance abuse, such as problems in their personal relationships at home and at work.

■■ Requirements for Member Participation

Although specific groups designed for substance abusers will have particular criteria for inclusion, the following are some general requirements for being included in these groups as an outpatient: for a drug and alcohol population, abstinence is necessary if they are to function effectively in a group; clients should show some degree of motivation to change; they need some capacity to look at themselves and to interact with others; and it is helpful if they have some social-support system outside of the group. Clients with psychoses are excluded. Another criteria for admission is the client's being involved full time in structured activities such as work, school, or home-care responsibilities. Although most programs prefer voluntary clients, some will accept involuntary members as long as they meet the other criteria for inclusion.

■■ Group Techniques

In their review of the programs on group work for substance abusers, Fuhrmann and Washington (1984b) conclude that a factor common to most of these groups is an eclectic orientation of the leader. Such groups draw on affective, cognitive, and behavioral techniques, and all of these approaches appear to be appropriate at some time for particular clients. The needs of the clientele determine the appropriateness of particular intervention strategies. Most of these group practitioners employ a high degree of structuring during the early phase of a group's development, with a decrease in leader direction and more emphasis on an interactive style during the later phases of a group. For those clients who are experiencing a crisis, more directive cognitive-behavioral techniques are generally utilized. Many of these groups use a co-leader of each sex. There is an emphasis on here-and-now interaction and action-oriented techniques, which focus not only on the problem of substance abuse but also on all the needs and concerns of the participants. These groups frequently employ present-oriented techniques such as role playing, problem solving, coaching, modeling, interpretation, self-disclosure, feedback, confrontation, and imparting of information; creating a social-support network outside of the group; and the use of referrals and community resources (Fuhrmann & Washington, 1984b).

■■ Implications

A group approach is especially useful in the treatment of substance abusers, because they can observe and participate in the treatment of other group members. Doing so is therapeutic and reinforces newly acquired insights and behavioral skills. Being able to help others is a key therapeutic factor, for many of these individuals have long felt devalued and worthless and thus would not offer their views to others. The group process involves elements of psychotherapy, resocialization, and reeducation. These factors help individuals in dealing with barriers to their personal growth and in completing unresolved developmental tasks (Altman & Plunkett, 1984). An increasing number of mental-health professionals and paraprofessionals are being trained in the treatment of substance abuse. Now the challenges facing these practitioners are to learn as much about the prevention of substance abuse as they know about treatment and to design group approaches aimed at prevention.

A Transition Group in a Community Agency

Our friend and colleague, Randy Alle-Corliss, the clinical social worker in a community mental-health center whose children's group we described in Chapter 9, also created and co-leads adult groups in the agency to help clients make the transition from a hospital or partial hospital program to independent living in the community. The primary goal of the transition group is to teach the members basic coping skills needed to reengage in the world.

■■ Structure and Policies

The transition group, consisting of eight members, meets once a week for 90 minutes. Even though these groups are open, in that membership can change, they typically develop cohesion, and significant learning occurs. Being an open group does not mean that the group is loosely structured, without any ground rules. There is a core of regular members who make cohesion possible. Clients are expected to make at least a 6-week commitment. They also agree to be on time for all sessions, to give 24 hours' notice if they need to cancel a group session, and not to miss two sessions in a row. The members sign a contract, which is also signed by the co-leaders, providing that failure to meet any of the above conditions means they will be terminated from the group. Any extenuating circumstances need to be discussed with the co-leaders. If members are dropped from the group and want to return, they must set up a private conference with both co-leaders. These policies tend to promote commitment and consistency.

■■ Topics

Although each group develops a unique "personality," most of the transition groups deal with themes such as the following: socialization issues; communication skills; problem-solving skills; fears and struggles in independent living; individuation issues, such as learning to take care of oneself; family conflicts; topics related to work, such as getting a job or dealing with supervisors; relationships issues, including meeting people and making and maintaining friendships; fears of going out into the community; fears of being alone and learning to express and deal with loneliness and isolation; coping with loss and death; expressing and working through suicidal thoughts and feelings; and learning constructive ways of expressing and dealing with anger.

Topics such as these are generally dealt with through verbal techniques, although the co-leaders do employ role playing to make the sessions come to life. For instance, if a member is working on her fear of interviewing for a job, one of the co-leaders is likely to take on the role of an interviewer. In addition to identifying her specific fears about the interview situation, she also benefits from the feedback of others in the group, and she learns specific behavioral skills that she can practice to help her overcome her fears and increase her chances of succeeding in a real interview situation. The co-leaders make attempts to involve the other group members by inviting them to bring up their own related fears that they would like to explore.

Participants are also strongly encouraged to carry out behavioral homework assignments in between the sessions. They are expected to return with a report of what they thought, felt, and did in situations in which they applied newly acquired skills. By using the group as a laboratory for learning and practicing these social skills, the members do more than simply ventilate emotions and talk about problems. The emphasis is on dealing with interpersonal problems in the here and now in an action-oriented way.

■■ Stages of Group Development

The transition group has all the characteristics of a closed group, but the stages are focused more on individual members than on the group as a whole. Some members are functioning at the initial stage, others may be transitional, and some have advanced into the working phase. New members are introduced into the group as old members terminate.

The core members are usually at the same stage, and their work provides modeling for others and gives the group direction. As a member terminates, separation and loss issues emerge into the forefront and are explored.

■■ Implications

Many agencies expect that groups will be open to new members, since there is a constant turnover of clientele in typical community clinics. Practitioners must learn how to adapt group process to an open and changing structure. It is a mistake to cling to the defeating notion that such an arrangement is "secondary" in preference to a closed group, because there are some unique values of the open structure. In families, new babies are born, grow up, and eventually leave, all of which have an impact on the entire family system. In a like manner, the open group incorporates new members as others in the "family" leave, and everyone has opportunities to work through issues of separation and change within the group structure. If participants are prepared, such changes do not necessarily result in fragmentation or superficial group interaction. The group just described demonstrates that open groups can have identified goals and a clear structure and can result in many of the same member outcomes as a closed group.

If you are interested in obtaining a more detailed description of this transition group, the children's group described in Chapter 9, or the following women's support group, write Randy Alle-Corliss (or Lupe Alle-Corliss) at the Tri-City Mental Health Center, Pomona, CA 91767, or telephone him at (714) 623-6131.

A Women's Support Group for Victims of Incest

Another colleague and friend, Lupe Alle-Corliss, a clinical social worker in a community agency, co-leads groups for women who have incest in their family background. She designed these support groups along the lines of a time-limited therapy group for women with a history of incest (Herman & Schatzow, 1984). The following description includes key features of both the group described by Herman and Schatzow and the one designed by Lupe and her co-leader, Myrna Samuels.

Sexual abuse of children by family members is increasingly coming to the attention of mental-health professionals. Approximately 10 percent of White, middle-class women in the United States indicate that they had a childhood sexual experience with an older male relative (Herman & Schatzow, 1984). A sexual encounter with a trusted family member not only typically results in a major psychological trauma itself but also frequently leads to emotional problems for the victim later in life. Some of the common problems include impaired self-esteem, negative identity formation, difficulty in intimate relationships, sexual dysfunction, and repeated victimization (Herman, 1981; Meiselman, 1978).

■■ Purpose and Rationale

A group approach, or a combination of group and individual therapy, is generally considered to be the treatment of choice. The aim of the group is to provide a safe and therapeutic environment for women who were sexually abused during their childhood. Other objectives are to help women share their secret and recognize that they are not alone, understand the current impact of this experience, and begin to work through and resolve feelings associated with their trauma and to make changes. In a group situation women find a commonality and a basis for identification. The supportive environment within the group tends to encourage women to make contacts with others outside of the group. A new type of family can emerge, one that is different from the clients' original family, which may have been dysfunctional.

■■ Setting Up the Group

Both Randy (whose group we described earlier) and Lupe have learned the value of recruiting potential members by publicizing their groups within their own agency. They do this through memos, announcements, and personal contact with colleagues. In considering members for the women's support group, they seek clients who display a readiness to deal openly with the trauma of incest. Typically, most of these women are already in individual therapy. If the women have a therapist other than the group leaders, a release form is asked for so that the co-leaders can consult and coordinate with the individual therapist.

As far as screening is concerned, both co-leaders meet individually with each potential member. Clients are asked about why they want such a group, and an attempt is made to determine how ready each individual is to talk in a group setting about the incest and its impact. Other questions sometimes asked during the screening include: "If there is any previous group experience, what was this like for you?" "Were you, or are you now, involved in individual therapy, and what was (is) this experience like?" "What are your personal goals for the group?" "What are your expectations, hopes, and fears about participating in the group?" Applicants are also encouraged to interview the co-leaders, asking questions about the group. The co-leaders let each applicant know that they will get back to them with a decision after they have had a chance to talk over all the candidates.

It is critical that members possess the ego strength to deal with the material that will be explored during the sessions. Members need to have enough interpersonal skills to deal with others in a group situation. People with suicidal and extremely self-destructive tendencies and people who do not have adequate contact with reality are screened out. Care is taken not to include family members or friends in the same group. Also excluded are those who are not ready or willing to talk openly about their experiences.

Herman and Schatzow (1984) use three criteria for inclusion in a group: (1) the clients must express generally positive feelings about participating in a group with others who have experienced incest; (2) the potential participants must not be in a crisis state—that is, must be functioning reasonably well in daily life; and (3) they must have an appropriate ongoing relationship with an individual therapist.

■■ Structure of the Group

The group is closed and meets for 75 minutes for a 12-week period. This time limitation is designed to facilitate bonding and to produce a reasonable degree of pressure necessary to work through the members' resistances. Although each group has its own process, these groups generally go through the phases to be described.

Initial Phase. The initial stage involves getting to know one another and establishing ground rules. Aspects that are emphasized are the importance of regular attendance; being prompt; confidentiality; the limitations of time; and bringing any unresolved issues back to the group, rather than dealing with them outside of the group. A date for a postgroup meeting, which is typically about 3 months after termination, is established at the first session. In the early phase of the group, members express empathy with one another over the difficulty of sharing the incest issue. The following guideline questions are provided to help them deal directly with the impact of incest on them: "How did the molestation happen? Who molested you? How old were you? How long did it go on? How did you deal with it? How did you feel toward the people who were in a position to protect you from the molestation, but failed to do so?"

Much of the initial phase is focused on identifying personal and specific goals in writing and then discussing them. This procedure allows all in the group to know of each person's goals and provides a direction for the sessions. Members generally feel much anxiety and apprehension at first. A member often feels that she is the only one with such a terrible burden, and she may feel that she would be an outcast if others knew about her secret. As the women realize that they have a common experience, they begin to open up and find the support that is available in the group. By sharing the incest experience, the women free themselves to look at how it continues to affect them. The focus of the sessions is not merely on reporting the details of the specific acts but also on exploring their feelings, beliefs, and perceptions about what happened.

As well as gaining insight into her own dynamics, a woman learns that she can be of help to others through her disclosures. Initially, a woman may show resistance by becoming the "helper" or "caretaker" of others in her group. Herman and Schatzow (1984) observed that the increased risk taking involved in discussing feelings and beliefs about the incest story led to an increase in the group's cohesiveness. They found that the discharging and sharing of intense emotions resulted in a bonding, mutual supportiveness, and a safe climate that allowed for exploring common themes of secrecy, isolation, shame, helplessness, fear, hurt, and anger.

Middle Phase.   During the middle stage there is a focus on accomplishing the individual members' goals. Connections are made between a woman's past behavior and her present behavior. In this way she begins to see patterns in her behavior and to understand her own dynamics. For instance, a woman may have chosen men who dominated her, abused her, or in some way took advantage of her. She sees with greater clarity her own part in allowing this type of treatment to continue. A group is a good way to help such a woman become aware of and challenge her faulty belief system. For example, women may hold themselves responsible for initiating the molestation. Through the group process, these women can rid themselves of destructive self-blame and can learn to create functional self-statements. There are a number of therapeutic strategies that promote a change of feelings, attitudes, and behaviors. Examples include learning that they behaved normally in an abnormal situation; reading books in a personal way; keeping a diary or journal that includes thoughts, feelings, and behaviors in certain situations; writing letters that are not sent; talking to other family members; and recording and sharing dreams.

Final Phase.   Toward the end of the group the women are reminded of the upcoming termination. The co-leaders assist them in reviewing what has happened in the group as a whole as well as what they have learned individually and how they can continue to apply their insights and newly acquired behaviors to situations outside of the group. Role playing helps in this consolidation process. The co-leaders give a structured questionnaire to help the members pull together and assess their learning. The members evaluate their progress and determine future plans, including what work they still need to do. They write down and give feedback to one another, and they identify certain people in the group whom they are willing to contact should they feel a need for help and support. Although the women cognitively know that the group will soon be over, it is a common reaction for them to say that they do not want it to end. Members are asked how they want to celebrate the ending of the group, within limits. The follow-up meeting 3 months later reinforces what was learned and provides renewed support.

■■ Implications

You might want to organize a group such as the one described above or another specific type of group for adults. We encourage you to follow your interests. Do additional reading in this area. Seek out a colleague with some experience with the population you will work with. And then design a group that will allow you to try out some therapeutically creative ideas. As we mentioned in Chapter 7, building follow-up procedures into your design gives you a basis for understanding the longer-term value of the group experience as well as improving your design for future groups. In the short-term groups reported on by Herman and Schatzow (1984), the results of a 6-month follow-up survey of 28 women supported their assumption that this therapeutic approach had been particularly effective in resolving the issues of shame, secrecy, and stigmatizing associated with incest. The single most helpful factor was the contact with other women who had been incest victims. Should you be interested in learning more about designing groups with women with a history of incest, we strongly recommend reading the article by Herman and Schatzow (1984) as a beginning. Then follow this up by reading books and articles on incest, some of which are among the Suggested Readings at the end of this chapter. Some especially useful resources include Butler (1978), Courtois (1979), Courtois and Leehan (1982), Finklehor (1984), Forward and Buck (1978), Goodwin (1982), Herman (1981), Justice and Justice (1979), Meiselman (1978), Rush (1980), and Sprei and Goodwin (1983).

A Weekend Workshop for Couples

■■ Purpose and Themes

Our couples workshop is designed primarily to provide an opportunity for people in an intimate relationship to examine the quality of their relationship, to determine what barriers are preventing genuine intimacy, to make decisions concerning how they want to change their life with each other, and to explore their conflicts. The workshop is for any woman and man who define themselves as a couple. Whereas most of the couples who participate are married in the conventional sense, some couples are living together. We've had newlyweds, and we've had grandparents; generally, there's an interesting variety of people in each group. To avoid cumbersome phrasing, we will use the terms *spouse*, *marriage*, *wife*, and *husband* to apply to all the couple relationships.

During the workshop we sometimes ask questions to provide some focus. For the most part, however, the couples determine what topics will be explored; they are asked to think before they arrive for the weekend about what they want to deal with in the group. The content of the workshop thus varies from group to group. Still, certain themes regularly emerge:

· how to remain separate individuals while benefiting from an intimate relationship
· the myths about marriage and how they lead to unrealistic expectations
· sex roles as they affect a marriage
· alternatives to traditional marriages
· open versus closed marriage
· the importance of commitment in a relationship
· how to reinvent a relationship
· sex and loving in intimate relationships
· the sources of conflict in a marriage
· how to detect communication pitfalls and learn to express one's thoughts and feelings directly
· how to deal with stress

■■ Structure

Generally, the five or six couples who attend the workshop have been in one of our groups for individuals. If we don't know a couple who have applied for the workshop, we like to arrange a meeting with them before deciding whether to accept them. At the meeting we ask what they're seeking from the group and explain its purpose. We deal with any questions or concerns they have. Thus, by the time the workshop begins, none of the participants is a stranger to us.

The workshop is held at our home in the mountains; hence, it has the special feature of being away from the usual city distractions. We believe that this setting improves the quality of the work done; maybe for the first time in years, a couple can be alone together in nature, and all the couples can reflect without disruption on what they're learning in the group.

The members arrive at 9:00 A.M. on Friday, not to leave until 5:00 P.M. on Sunday. In the interim we all live together, and everyone helps with the preparation of the meals. This communal living is another special feature that enhances the experience.

We work as a group for approximately 24 hours, or eight sessions of at least 3 hours. During the afternoon session of the second day we frequently work near a running creek, among boulders, trees, flies, and mosquitoes. We divide into pairs and talk informally, and by the end of the afternoon most participants have had a chance to spend some time on a one-to-one basis with most of the other participants. This allows for discussion of commonalities or of anything that may have emerged in the preceding workshop sessions.

■■ The Initial Stage

To begin the workshop we generally call together the entire group for a short time and ask a few questions:

· What was it like to come here today?
· How have you felt since you decided to join the group? What were you hoping to get from the weekend when you signed up?
· Did you leave anyone behind whose welfare preoccupies you now, so that you're not fully present?

After the members have discussed these questions and any related concerns, we have them devote the remainder of the morning session to working in pairs with someone other than their mate. The reason for beginning this way is that it breaks up the exclusive focus on the couple; we've discovered that more honesty is generated this way. This pairing also helps the members get acquainted and builds up trust. We ask the members to work for approximately 15 minutes with one person of the opposite sex and then change partners, and so on. Before each new set of dyads is formed, we suggest a question to the members, the answer to which they can discuss with their partners. These questions lay the groundwork for later group work by getting the members to begin thinking about themselves and their mate. During later workshop sessions we will usually delve in depth into the issues raised by these questions, which include:

· Why did you come to this particular couples group? What are you hoping to leave with?
· What are you afraid you might find out about yourself, your spouse, or your relationship? Explore your fears about this workshop.
· How would you describe your marriage?
· How do you imagine your spouse just described your marriage?
· Become your spouse, and describe what it is like to be married to you.

· What changes would you most like to make in your relationship with your partner?
· If no change took place in your marriage, what do you imagine your future would hold? How do you think your partner answered that question?
· How would your life be different if you were not married?

While the group members are working in dyads, we sometimes rove about and listen in on their conversations; at times we join a dyad, pairing off with one member to form a twosome. At other times we talk with each other about our initial reactions to group members.

After the pairings the group usually reconvenes before lunch to share reactions to the work in dyads. We find out a little about what came out in these exchanges, and we begin to see what the goals of the workshop should be. Members may express fears or reservations, and we deal with these concerns at this time so that they won't interfere with the main work of the group.

▪▪ The Working Stage

After the initial session the direction of the group is somewhat unpredictable, for we do not tightly control the process with techniques or themes. Our philosophy is that these groups function best if there is some structure to provide a focus but enough flexibility that the members can draw up their own agenda. Our main functions are to see that the discussion stays on a meaningful, not a superficial, level and to encourage members to participate.

We do make use of techniques, though, when we feel they'll deepen the level of interaction. For most of the remainder of this section we describe approaches that we use in the workshops. Remember that what we do varies with each workshop, in accordance with the unique development of the group. As you read about the exercises and techniques that we describe, you may get the impression that the entire weekend consists of doing exercise after exercise. This is not the case, for as we said earlier, our techniques are typically invented and adapted to assist a couple in working therapeutically on a meaningful level. We present these techniques as examples of ways you might work with couples in groups.

Inner and Outer Circles.   The men form a circle, and the women form a circle outside it. Pretending that their wife is not present, the men talk about how it is for them to be married. The women listen silently. After the men have said all they want to say, they discuss what they imagine their partners would say about their marriage if *they* were sitting in the inner circle. When the men are finished, the women and men change places. The women begin by sharing their reactions to what they heard their partner say. Then, as though the men weren't present, they tell how they perceive their marriage and to what degree they feel understood by their husband.

This exercise usually brings meaningful issues out into the open. After the exercise we focus on the mates who apparently don't understand each other. The exercise is useful in that it allows us to detect distortions, projections, and conflicts.

Variations on the Circles Exercise.   Throughout the workshop we suggest variations on the preceding exercise when they seem timely and when they will bring about interaction on a more profound level. For instance, we may reintroduce any of the questions we asked the dyads to answer at the opening of the workshop. Or we may have the inner circles answer one of these questions:

· What are some of the best (or worst) features of your marriage?
· In what concrete ways would you like to change your relationship? What are you doing about making these changes? What more could you do?
· How much do you depend on your partner for confirmation of your worth, and what effect does this have on you? on your relationship?
· What was it in your partner that influenced your decision to form the relationship?
· What was it like for you when you first met? What were your expectations?

Exercise in Separate Identity and Mutuality.   A very important part of our philosophy is our belief that, in order for two people to have a productive relationship, they must be separate individuals who can exist without each other. If two people depend on each other completely, it will be extremely difficult for them to examine their relationship, and they will be reluctant to challenge each other. If one partner is excessively dependent on the other, his or her freedom to grow as a unique person will be stifled.

A fantasy exercise can get the members to think about how separate they are from their partner and what would become of them if their partner were not in their life. The participants are asked to imagine that they come home and find a note from their spouse that says that he or she has left and may not return. The participants are to fantasize about their immediate reactions and tell what they would do if the partner didn't return. They might tell what they think they would be doing, thinking, and feeling a week, a month, a year, or even longer after their mate's departure.

Brainstorming.   At different points in the workshop, we use brainstorming to provide alternatives for consideration. One theme that comes up in most couples groups is how to enhance a dull relationship. Couples tend to settle into comfortable but boring patterns; many workshop participants are seeking ways of revitalizing a stale marriage. In the brainstorming exercise members think of as many ways of reinventing a relationship as possible. The entire group throws out suggestions, and the guideline is the more suggestions, the better. Nobody is to question or comment on any of the ideas during the 10 or 15 minutes of freewheeling brainstorming. Then the participants can focus on the suggestions that seem exciting to them, and a discussion of ways of using these suggestions can follow.

Women's Group and Men's Group.   An approach that we have used at some workshops is separating the participants into a women's group and a men's group, with each of us leading the appropriate group. The agenda is determined sometimes by the group and sometimes by us. These subgroups can last an hour and a half to 2 hours, depending on how much time the participants are willing to invest and what topics are introduced. One common focus of the subgroups is sexuality. Some questions we might ask are: "How do you feel about your own sexuality? Do you enjoy your body? Are you able to enjoy sensuality as well as sexuality? In what ways do you feel that your sex life could be improved? What do you most enjoy receiving from your partner? What do you most like to give to the other? What are some attitudes or guilts that interfere with your sexual fulfillment? What is it like for you to be a woman (man)?"

We separate the sexes in this way because we believe this allows members to openly discuss topics that they might feel shy about discussing with the entire group, at least at first. However, it is our hope that much of what goes on in the subgroups will eventually be discussed in the general group. After the whole group has reassembled, we ask members to share any aspects of their subgroup experience that they're willing to disclose. Considerable time can then be devoted to discussion of these issues or to role playing. Unless a general discussion of what went on in the subgroups takes place, there is danger that the group will be divided.

Opposite-Sides Exercise.   The women sit on one side of the room, and the men sit on the other side. Each side has 5 minutes to issue any and all of its complaints about the opposite sex. The people on the other side are not to respond. After each side has had its 5 minutes, the floor is open to any couple who wish to explore a comment that was made. The purpose of this exercise is not to set up debates but rather to facilitate open expression of certain resentments that are usually concealed. We try to get partners to express pent-up hostilities without attacking each other.

A variation of this exercise involves using the same structure but having the men and women tell what they appreciate, respect, and like about the opposite sex. This variation is designed to teach the importance of expressing feelings of love, tenderness, gratitude, and respect. Married people often fail to express these positive feelings to each other.

Incomplete-Sentence Exercise.   Each person in the group in turn finishes an incomplete sentence. (Of course, a person may say "I pass" in response to any sentence.) We usually ask the members to finish a number of the following sentences:

· My greatest joy in marriage is . . .
· I feel disappointed in my relationship when . . .
· What I'd most like to change in myself is . . .
· What I'd most like to change in my spouse is . . .
· I feel the closest to her (him) when . . .
· If I were not married, . . .
· If our relationship continues to be as it has been, in 5 years . . .
· When I get angry with my spouse, I . . .
· It is difficult for me to show . . .
· My greatest fear concerning our relationship is . . .

Sometimes we ask the participants to suggest incomplete sentences.

This exercise can bring out valuable material, which needs to be pursued openly in the group if full advantage is to be taken of it. After everyone has completed the sentences, the members are invited to tell what the exercise was like for them or how they felt when their spouse completed a particular sentence.

Marital-Interactions Exercise.   One function of the workshop is to increase the participants' awareness of the interactions that prevent intimacy. A task of the participants is to examine the benefits they derive from these interactions and decide whether they're willing to forgo these benefits and deal directly with their partners. These interactions should be pointed out by either the members or the leaders as they become evident in a couple's relationship. Some common marital issues can be described as follows.

· The husband does not state directly what he needs or wants from his wife; instead, he questions her about her wants.
· The wife punishes her husband by savoring her hostility.
· The husband tries to meet what he imagines are his wife's expectations and, in the process, loses most of his identity.
· The wife does not do certain things that she wants to do and then blames her husband for her situation.

· The husband initiates an argument in order to prevent closeness.
· The wife plays helpless and weak and then explodes when her husband tells her what to do.
· The husband is usually too tired to have sex when the wife initiates it.

Examining One's Parents' Marriage. A variation of the marital-interactions exercise involves examining one's parents' marriage and then comparing it with one's own. To help the participants carry out this examination, we ask such questions as: "In what ways is your marriage like your parents'? How do your parents deal with disagreement? How do they treat their children? What do they most want from life? What do they do for fun? What have you learned from them about marriage?"

To do this exercise, each member joins another—preferably someone other than the spouse—and answers one question. Then everyone changes partners. After several pairings have taken place, the members all get together again and examine in depth the influence that their parents' marriage has had on their own marriage. The rationale for this approach is that it helps couples see what attitudes of their parents they've incorporated and gives them a chance to decide whether they want to continue holding these attitudes. In this exercise the members engage in a critical examination of the degree of influence that their parents still exert on them and, if they want to, look for ways of lessening this influence.

Examining Partners' Values. Couples can be encouraged to examine openly the compatibility of their values. We see this as a most important function of the workshop. Couples can explore the extent to which they agree on:

· the value of a sexually exclusive relationship
· how children should be reared
· how money should be spent
· the importance of doing things together as a couple or as a family
· the importance of self-awareness and personal growth
· what constitutes success
· religion and a philosophy of life
· what constitutes a good sex life
· the need to devote time and energy to renewing the relationship
· divisions of tasks and responsibilities

The purpose of the workshop is not to teach couples what to value, but rather to have them clarify their values as separate individuals and as a couple and to help them communicate in an honest way about what they value. We feel that we've done an important service if couples begin to talk openly about their values and to respect one another's differences.

Critical Turning Points.   The participants generally spend at least one session focusing on the times and occurrences they judge to have been critical turning points in their married life. The members are asked to examine the significance of these incidents with respect to some of their current marital struggles. This exercise is designed to facilitate a review by each participant of his or her married life. This review brings submerged issues to the surface, where they can be dealt with.

For instance, a woman may identify her critical turning points as the births of her children, her decision to complete college, and her decision to commit herself to a career as well as to marriage. Her husband may harbor bitter feelings regarding her decision to go to college and her quest for independence; he may have encouraged her dependence on him and have been threatened by her success in college and in her career. The more successful she became, the more he withdrew from her. The identification by the wife of her critical turning points may bring this dynamic to the surface and thus offer a chance for both partners to develop new perspectives. The husband can work on his insecurity while learning to accept his wife's strengths and can, it is hoped, begin to feel that he is worthwhile even if his wife is not dependent on him—that it is possible for both to be strong at the same time.

How Have You Changed?   Many individuals change over the course of their relationship with their partner. At some point in the workshop we usually focus on the nature of these changes and on how each person perceives and reacts to the changes his or her partner has made or is making.

For example, a man may have married a woman he viewed as strong because at the time he felt a need for someone who would make decisions for him and even take care of him. As time went by, he painfully came to recognize that he related to his wife as to a mother. He then decided to treat his wife as a wife, not as a mother, and to take the responsibility of deciding things for himself, instead of playing helpless in order to make her take over. Crucial questions are: How has she responded to his changes? Does she encourage his redefinition of himself, or does she attempt to thwart these changes? This exercise can give this couple the chance to reflect on and discuss the changes that have taken place in their relationship.

We encourage the participants to recognize that the need that made them choose a certain partner may change or the partner may change and no longer fill the need. We encourage a dialogue between spouses about the changes they perceive and about the impact these shifts in needs and motivations are having on the relationship at present.

Role-Playing Exercises.   As much as possible we use action-oriented approaches, in which people act out their conflicts rather than merely talking about them. When participants say that they would like to understand a specific conflict more fully, we design a situation in which the difficulty can be acted out.

For example, Sam becomes extremely jealous when Carole expresses any interest in other men. He immediately interprets her regard for another man as a sign of his deficiency as a man, and he tends to feel that, if he were man enough, she would not be interested in others. The role playing can be set up by having Carole talk to Sam about her feelings of attraction for another man in the group. It is presumed that a dialogue like the ones they have at home will ensue. Then the other members can give Sam and Carole feedback. They may find that Carole's manner of communicating her feelings ignites Sam's jealousy with hints, which she maintains are unintentional, of a sexual interest in the other man. In other words, she sends conflicting messages: she says directly that he has no grounds for his fears and indirectly that she's interested in other men. As a variation on this exercise Carole and Sam can exchange roles; Carole can play Sam as she sees him while Sam becomes Carole as he perceives her.

In another case Betty may complain that all Bert ever talks about to her is his work as an engineer. Betty might play her husband, showing how he talks to her when she would like to discuss something other than engineering. This can give Bert some idea of how Betty feels, and he can discuss how accurate he considers Betty's portrait of him.

In still another case Elsie may struggle with Jack's insistence on being "logical" and his inability to deal with the realm of feelings. The two can be asked to reenact a typical situation so that the group gets a sample of their interaction. Or Elsie can be asked to exaggerate Jack's logical behavior while Jack exaggerates Elsie's emotional behavior that causes him so much difficulty. By reversing roles and exaggerating each other's styles, Elsie and Jack may come to appreciate each other's position. Again, feedback from group members on how they experience Jack and Elsie can help the couple see themselves more clearly.

Other group members can join the role-playing activities at times by sitting in for someone. For example, in the dialogue between Elsie and Jack, Joan might sit in for Elsie and demonstrate another way that Elsie might respond to Jack when he becomes cold-bloodedly logical. There are also some exciting possibilities in involving several people in a piece of work by having alter egos (that is, by having two members stand behind two partners and say what they imagine the partners are thinking or feeling) or by having several couples work simultaneously on a similar problem.

We find that the manner in which we suggest role playing determines the willingness of the members to participate. We strive for an informal manner and, in many instances, model the role playing. This action-oriented approach reduces the boredom and detachment that come from intellectualizing about problems.

▪▪ The Final Stage

During the final sessions we emphasize review of what was learned during the workshop, practice of newly adopted styles of behaving, and formulation of contracts to be fulfilled and homework assignments to be carried out before the follow-up session in 2 months. But we especially emphasize participants' giving feedback to one another individually and as couples.

There are several methods of making feedback interesting and meaningful. One approach involves the members' forming dyads, much as they did in the initial session. This time, the participants tell their partners how they imagine it would be to live with them. At this point there are plenty of observations to draw on, and the participants are usually willing to be very honest. The advantage of this one-to-one format in giving and receiving feedback is that it tends to lessen the defensiveness of the receiver and to increase the independence of the giver's observations.

In another exercise the focus is on each couple for 10 or 15 minutes. During this time the rest of the group gives the partners feedback based on what they experienced of them in the workshop. This feedback helps the couples see their interactions with increased clarity. As part of the feedback, members can tell each couple the strengths they see in each person and in the relationship, the ways the partners undermine these strengths, the hopes they have for them, and their fears and concerns about them. Again, if this feedback is given with care, directly and honestly, it can be a tremendous resource for partners who are trying to improve the quality of their life together.

During the final session we like to get the participants to think about ways they can sustain the growing process they've begun. We ask the members to tell what significant things they've come to understand about themselves and their manner of relating to their spouse, and we encourage them to state briefly some of their decisions for change. To increase the chances that the couples will indeed change, we ask them to give themselves certain homework assignments to do before the follow-up session. A realistic contract that involves specific actions can be very fruitful in enabling couples to make progress. For example, a couple might say that they learned in the workshop that they have drifted away from each other and buried themselves in outside responsibilities. Their contract might commit them to a variety of new activities. They will go away for a weekend together to a place they've both been wanting to visit. They will keep journals for the next 2 months concerning their reactions to the workshop and what they learned about themselves as a couple, and they will devote at least 15 minutes a week to talking with each other about the quality of their relationship. They will take square-dancing lessons together—something they've wanted to do but have put off for years because of their busy schedules. She will do something for herself that she has long dreamed of but continued to tell herself that she couldn't do: enroll in an evening class in the community college. And he will do something just for himself: go with his buddies on a long-overdue fishing trip.

It is important that contracts be realistic—that they require activities that the people are willing to carry out—and that the activities they call for be chosen by the couples themselves rather than by other members or by workshop leaders. However, at times it may be appropriate for others to suggest assignments that the couple might not have considered. Suggestion of options is also an important part of the feedback process during the closing session.

Before the workshop ends, we usually make a few suggestions concerning how the members can sustain in their daily life the focus they learned in the workshop. We give them the names of books that offer ideas they can talk about, and we encourage them to record in a journal their reflections on the themes that emerged during the workshop. We also suggest resources for individuals or couples who want to join another couples group, get individual or family counseling, or join a therapeutic group for individuals. Participants are encouraged to think about other therapeutic experiences that will assist them in making their desired changes.

Finally, we are always interested in some kind of evaluation at the end of a workshop with couples, so we typically ask the members to assess the sessions and to suggest ways of improving the workshop. Not only is this important for us as leaders, but we think it is also valuable for the members, for it allows them to review their own process as a group.

■■ Implications

Many variations on the workshop for couples can be designed. For instance, the group can involve a series of six or more 3-hour weekly sessions, then a weekend workshop, and then about six more weekly sessions. Another alternative we've considered involves several presessions, with the usual presession work spaced out, allowing members to practice what they are learning, followed by two weekend retreats and a series of follow-up meetings. This pattern can be spread out over a period of 3 to 9 months. We feel that there are some advantages to a combination of ongoing weekly sessions and occasional intensive weekend workshops. Under this plan, members can learn from a variety of experiences; can practice outside the group and report on the results; and can benefit from ongoing feedback, challenge, and support. A concern we have about the one-weekend approach is that couples may receive only a "booster shot" and temporary excitement; we wonder about the permanence of changes that are not intensively and continuously reinforced, as they are in an ongoing group.

In concluding this section we want to describe what our experience in working with couples has taught us. One important lesson is that, if two people are to keep their relationship alive, they must be committed to working hard at it. Both individuals have to consider their relationship to be among their highest priorities. They must be willing to stay with each other during times of crisis and upheaval as well as when everything seems to be going smoothly. We've found that some people file for divorce just when they might have made a breakthrough and begun a new kind of marriage. And we've seen people leave their spouse because they feel that the spouse is stagnating while they are growing. Lately we've begun to encourage the "growing" person to give the other person a chance. Perhaps the spouse will relate vastly differently to the changed partner or even be inspired to seek the same kind of therapeutic experiences that led to the partner's changes. We are not saying that couples should stay together at any cost; rather, we are observing that a couple working together can make some dramatic, constructive changes, provided the commitment to improving the relationship exists. This is one reason it is so exciting to work with couples: they can be challenged together and can participate in each other's growth.

A Residential Group for Adults

■■ Description and Purpose

Along with some of our colleagues we have designed what we consider a unique type of course and experiential workshop in personal growth—one with combined educational and therapeutic aims. We have done these workshops through California State University at Fullerton's Continuing Education Program on a regular basis since the summer of 1972. These week-long residential workshops include 16 participants, ranging in age from 18 to 65, and four co-leaders. The groups are composed of people from various socioeconomic classes representing a wide range of occupations. With the experience of over 40 of these weeklong groups, we have found themes that appear to have universality for the participants.

The purposes of the workshop are to provide the tools for self-confrontation and self-help methods to make change possible. Basically, we hope that participants will leave the group with a greater awareness of how they typically initiate and respond in their world, how they avoid coming to grips with their full potential, and how they can take specific steps to challenge areas in their lives where they feel stuck.

■■ Structure and Format

We follow most of the guidelines that we described in Chapter 3 relating to preliminary procedures, screening and selection, conducting individual interviews and a pregroup session, preparing the participants, asking them to do some reading and write personal papers, and teaching them ways of getting the most from this workshop. We place considerable emphasis on ways of translating what they experience in the workshop into practical changes in their everyday behavior.

Of course, many of the procedures we use in organizing and getting this group going can be applied to other types of group. For example, even though you might not employ a residential format, you could still use some of the preliminary procedures in setting up a group for parents without partners, a women's group, or some type of support group.

We find that one of the exciting features of any type of adult group is the fact that a group of strangers can drop their social masks and become more intimate with one another, building a caring community that leads to taking action in their daily life. Once they decide to risk opening up to their inner experiencing, a wide range of feelings and thoughts emerges, and the basis is formed for pursuing some universal themes that unite the members.

A residential group is particularly valuable in this regard. The structure of the group provides for about 10 hours daily of leader-directed groups, in addition to many opportunities for informal interactions with other individuals and in small groups. The residential setting makes this a unique experience in living and learning with a community, something that is difficult to achieve in meetings that last for only a few hours once a week. Moreover, the structure allows participants to block out other distractions of daily living and focus for a week on what they want to change in their life.

The themes that are explored in a residential workshop are the same as those we have discussed earlier. It should be emphasized that we don't expect the issues explored intensively to be resolved in a week; our intention is to give the members an opportunity to view themselves in a new light and to figure out what they will need to do after the group. For this reason, we describe for the members the resources for individual and group counseling that are available to them both on the university campus and in the community.

■■ Exploring Inner Conflicts

A great deal of what members do in the residential workshop has to do with resolving inner conflicts (such as between self-awareness and blissful ignorance) and learning that certain apparently conflicting parts of themselves (such as the experiences of joy and sorrow) are in fact complementary. The members find that much of their energy has been invested in the struggle between their conflicting inner selves. The follow-ing are a few of the conflicts that come to light during a workshop.

· **The struggle between the desire to know oneself and the fear of discovering only emptiness inside.** Members often fear that, if they search themselves, they will find that they are merely reflections of what everyone expects them to be, having introjected their parents' and others' standards. They fear finding out that, if the other people in their life are subtracted from them, there will be nothing left.

· **The struggle between the desire to know oneself and the fear of finding that one is like one's parents.** Some people are very upset by their awareness that they have turned out to be just like their parents. They may want to reject all of the qualities they have in common with their parents, including the positive ones.

· **The struggle between the desire for security and the desire to break new ground.** A young woman in one of our workshops found herself bored with her life—with herself, her husband, and her children. She described how one part of her was saying: "Accept what you have. Settle for security. Don't rock the boat. After all, things could be a lot worse. Don't make waves, or you might lose what you have now—and then what?" But the part of her that wanted more than security was saying: "Is this all I'm worth? Don't I deserve more? I'm bored and growing stale. If I accept that now, what will my life be like 5 years from now? I will challenge myself. I will take the risk of revealing to my husband what I'm thinking and feeling. I will demand more, although I realize that I may wind up without security."

· **The struggle between the desire to be self-sufficient and the desire to lean on others.** A woman in one of our workshops had been on her own for a long time. She had not suffered from this; her life was ar-ranged in such a way that she experienced success in her personal en-deavors. Yet she had never fully allowed others into her world. During the workshop she realized that she feared being hurt by others. She began to see how she distanced herself from others and suppressed her need for them. In short, she began to let herself experience the conflict between her need for others and her desire to go it alone.

· **The struggle between the desire to drop one's hard exterior shell and the desire to protect oneself.** Some people who come to a workshop have developed a hard exterior shell, behind which they hide. These people may have acquired their tough exterior in response to a great number of disappointments and hurts. In the workshop they may let themselves feel their gentleness and compassion and may consider anew whether their suit of armor is necessary.

· **The struggle between the desire to respect oneself and the desire to feel sorry for oneself.** This struggle is exemplified by the group member who was very much overweight and who seemed to make running him-self into the ground a way of life. His obesity prevented him from liking himself, and it also made him unattractive to others. It was as though he was wearing a sign telling people that he was worth little. And he was treated accordingly. His dependency, self-pity, and helplessness were a drain on others. During the workshop he realized that, before he could begin to appreciate himself, he would have to allow himself to experience the depths of his self-hatred. When he hit bottom, he decided to climb out of the pit of self-pity.

· **The struggle between the desire to get revenge and the desire to forgive.** In every group we hear the angry cries of those who feel that they were abandoned by their parents. Our cushions are torn, and our battacas are ripped at the seams. The desire to hurt the father or mother who was not there when needed is expressed in most groups. Yet when people have purged themselves of the hatred and rage, they often find that there is room in themselves for acceptance and that they have freed themselves from an obsession. They may realize that they might do better to express to their parents their need for them than to wait indefinitely for the parents to make the first move.

■■ The Final Stage

During the closing days of the workshop our primary goal is to help the members integrate and consolidate what they've learned. At this point the emphasis is on conceptualization and on integrating the experiences of the workshop. We pay particular attention to the points we developed in Chapter 7.

In Chapter 7 we described procedures designed to assist members in consolidating their learning in a group, termination issues, follow-up procedures, and evaluation measures. We apply these procedures to the residential workshop in a systematic way; however, such procedures also work for us in groups for adults that we've led in other settings and in using conventional time structures of weekly meetings. For example, if you were leading a group composed of divorced women, a group in private practice, a gay-people's group, or an assertion-training work-shop—to mention only a few—you could ask the same types of question that were used during the initial, the working, and the final stages of the workshop for personal growth we've just described. The process, as well as the content (themes and topics explored), are similar across many groups for adults, regardless of the format used and of the special inter-ests of the participants.

The closing phase of the group is designed to bridge for the partici-pants the gap between the world they've experienced for a week and the world they will soon reenter. The workshop is not meant to be an end in itself but rather a means by which people can come to a better under-standing of their internal world in order to be able to reshape their external world. The aim of the workshop is to help the participants see the richness of their capacities, the ways they prevent themselves from realizing their potentials, the mechanical ways they relate to others, and the advantages of recognizing and utilizing the power they have as individuals.

As we mentioned in Chapter 7, follow-up procedures are of great value; therefore, we schedule a group session 3 months after the weeklong residential group has come to an end. In this way the members have an added incentive to keep their commitments, and a note of accountability is added to the workshop. As leaders, we find these follow-up sessions useful in evaluating the outcomes of the workshop experience.

Concluding Comments

Our preferred format for working with adults is a residential one that provides for intensity and the time to work in a sustained way. However, the outcomes and directional changes that appear to result from successful group participation seem strikingly similar among all types of adult groups. We've found that the participants take an honest look at the quality of their life, they make certain decisions after their experience in the group, and they take active steps to carry out their plans. We have observed in working with various special-interest groups (including, but not limited to, residential workshops) that participants often achieve such outcomes as:

- an increased desire to get more from their relationships with significant people
- a tendency to be more direct and honest in relating with selected others
- a greater willingness to take risks and to live with uncertainty
- a willingness to challenge others and to be challenged by others
- an awareness of how and why they keep themselves from getting what they say they want from life
- an understanding of ways they often sabotage their own growth
- a recognition that they are to a large degree the product of their choices and that, if they don't like the direction of their life, they have the power to do something to change this direction.

Where to Go from Here

Since groups for adults represent such a wide variety of special interests, it is difficult to list one or two books as a place to begin. The suggested readings below do not all pertain to group work, but ideas for leading various adult groups can be found in these resources. Depending on your interests, you might find the following books particularly helpful in getting ideas for your groups.

The theme-oriented approach to group work was described in this chapter. If you want to do further reading in topics that can be applied to groups, see *I Never Knew I Had a Choice* (Corey with Corey, 1986), which deals with existential concerns that people bring to groups. The book contains many exercises and activities that leaders can use for their groups. Each chapter is followed by numerous annotated readings appropriate for developing themes and topics for adult groups.

If you are interested in organizing an assertion-training group, two of the best resources are *Assertiveness: Innovations, Applications, Issues* (Alberti, 1977), and *Your Perfect Right: A Guide to Assertive Behavior* (Alberti & Emmons, 1982).

For those interested in reviewing the developmental tasks and critical turning points of the adult years, the following books are our recommendations for interesting and informative reading: *Transformations: Growth and Change in Adult Life* (Gould, 1978); *Passages: Predictable Crises of Adult Life* (Sheehy, 1976); and *The Seasons of a Man's Life* (Levinson, 1978).

Some books with a cognitive-behavioral slant, all of which are aimed at the popular market, can easily be used as the basis for structuring themes in adult groups. These books include *Feeling Good: The New Mood Therapy* (Burns, 1981); *A New Beginning: How You Can Change Your Life through Cognitive Therapy* (Emery, 1981); *Take Effective Control of Your Life* (Glasser, 1984); and *A New Guide to Rational Living* (Ellis & Harper, 1975).

Group leaders who work with adults can find an excellent discussion of both the theory and practice of therapy groups in the works of Irvin Yalom. His classic work is *The Theory and Practice of Group Psychotherapy* (1985). In his *Existential Psychotherapy* (1980) is an outstanding discussion of ways in which the themes of death, freedom, isolation, and meaninglessness can be integrated into clinical practice and group work. His latest book, *Inpatient Group Psychotherapy* (1983), is highly readable for group practitioners who work with both higher- and lower-level inpatient groups. He integrates techniques with relevant research findings.

A key resource for an extensive bibliography of interest to practitioners with adult groups is *Group Work in the Helping Professions* (Zimpfer, 1984). Of special use are the references dealing with group procedures for parents, relatives, families, couples, and spouses; separation and divorce groups; parent education; enrichment; marriage encounter; and premarital counseling in groups (section 6.10, pages 200–224). This work also is an excellent source of articles pertaining to women's groups (section 6.20, pages 303–315) and men's groups (section 6.21, pages 315–320).

Readings that are particularly appropriate to groups with couples include *The Intimate Enemy* (Bach & Wyden, 1969); *I Never Knew I Had a Choice* (Corey with Corey, 1986); *Becoming Partners: Marriage and Its Alternatives* (Rogers, 1973); *The New Male* (Goldberg, 1979); *Passive Men, Wild Women* (Mornell, 1979); *A Casebook in Group Therapy: A Behavioral-Cognitive Approach* (Rose, 1980), which has a chapter on couples groups; and *Marriage Counseling in Groups* (Ohlsen, 1979).

An outstanding book that contains informative articles on the process of Gestalt groups (with techniques applicable for various populations) is *Beyond the Hot Seat: Gestalt Approaches to Group* (Feder & Ronall, 1980). This book includes descriptions of the use of art therapy, movement therapy, and marathon groups.

If you want to read further about the ways of creating your own techniques in working with various adult groups, we recommend *Group Techniques* (Corey, Corey, Callanan, & Russell, 1982), which describes our approach to techniques for all the stages of group development.

Suggested Readings*

* Alberti, R. E. (Ed.). (1977). *Assertiveness: Innovations, applications, issues.* San Luis Obispo, CA: Impact.

* Alberti, R. E., & Emmons, M. L. (1982). *Your perfect right: A guide to assertive behavior* (4th ed.). San Luis Obispo, CA: Impact.

Altman, L. S., & Plunkett, J. J. (1984). Group treatment of adult substance abusers. *Journal for Specialists in Group Work, 9*(1), 26–31.

Anderson, W. P., & Otto, R. L. (1984). Designing groups for use with special populations: A case history. *Journal for Specialists in Group Work, 9*(4), 179–185.

Azima, F. J. C. (1983). Group psychotherapy with personality disorders. In H. I. Kaplan & B. J. Sadock (Eds.), *Comprehensive group psychotherapy* (2nd ed.) (pp. 262–268). Baltimore: Williams & Wilkins.

* Bach, G. R., & Wyden, P. (1969). *The intimate enemy: How to fight fair in love and marriage.* New York: Morrow.

Bankoff, E. A. (1982). Widow groups as an alternative to informal social support. In M. A. Lieberman, L. D. Borman, & Associates, *Self-help groups for coping with crisis* (pp. 181–193). San Francisco: Jossey-Bass.

Bridges, W. (1980). *Transitions: Making sense of life's changes.* Reading, MA: Addison-Wesley.

Bumagin, S., & Smith, J. M. (1985). Beyond support: Group psychotherapy with low-income mothers. *International Journal of Group Psychotherapy, 35*(2), 279–294.

* Burns, D. D. (1981). *Feeling good: The new mood therapy.* New York: New American Library (Signet).

* Books and articles marked with an asterisk are recommended for further study.

Buscaglia, L. (1972). *Love*. Thorofare, NJ: Charles B. Slack.

Butler, S. (1978). *Conspiracy of silence: The trauma of incest*. New York: Bantam Books.

Cargan, L., & Melko, M. (1982). *Singles: Myths and realities* (Vol. 1). Beverly Hills, CA: Sage Publications.

* Cole, S. A. (1983). Self-help groups. In H. I. Kaplan & B. J. Sadock (Eds.), *Comprehensive group psychotherapy* (2nd ed.) (pp. 144–150). Baltimore: Williams & Wilkins.

Corey, G. (1985). *Theory and practice of group counseling* (2nd ed.). Monterey, CA: Brooks/Cole.

* Corey, G., with Corey, M. (1986). *I never knew I had a choice* (3rd ed.). Monterey, CA: Brooks/Cole.

Corey, G., Corey, M., Callanan, P., & Russell, J. M. (1980). A residential workshop for personal growth. *Journal for Specialists in Group Work, 5*(4), 205–215.

* Corey, G., Corey, M., Callanan, P., & Russell, J. M. (1982). *Group techniques*, Monterey, CA: Brooks/Cole.

* Courtois, C., & Leehan, J. (1982). Group treatment for grown-up abused children. *Personnel and Guidance Journal, 60*(9), 564–566.

Cox, A. A. (1984). A description of behavioral group treatment for depression. *Journal for Specialists in Group Work, 9*(2), 85–92.

* Cunningham, N. J., & Brown, J. H. (1984). A parent group training program for single parents. *Journal for Specialists in Group Work, 9*(3), 145–150.

Dell Orto, A. E., & Lasky, R. G. (1979). *Group counseling and physical disability*. North Scituate, MA: Duxbury Press.

* Dowling, C. (1981). *The Cinderella complex*. New York: Pocket Books.

* Ellis, A., & Harper, R. A. (1975). *A new guide to rational living*. Englewood Cliffs, NJ: Prentice-Hall.

* Emery, G. (1981). *A new beginning: How you can change your life through cognitive therapy*. New York: Simon & Schuster.

Emery, G., Hollon, S. D., & Bedrosian, R. C. (Eds.). (1981). *New directions in cognitive therapy: A casebook*. New York: Guilford Press.

* Feder, B., & Ronall, R. (Eds.). (1980). *Beyond the hot seat: Gestalt approaches to group*. New York: Brunner/Mazel.

Filene, P. (1981). *Men in the middle: Coping with the problems of work and family in the lives of middle-aged men*. Englewood Cliffs, NJ: Prentice-Hall.

* Finklehor, D. (1984). *Child sexual abuse: New theory and research*. New York: Free Press.

Forward, S., & Buck, C. S. (1978). *Betrayal of innocence: Incest and its devastation*. Los Angeles: J. P. Tarcher.

Fromm, E. (1974). *The art of loving*. New York: Harper & Row.

Fuhrmann, B. S., & Washington, C. S. (1984a). Substance abuse: An overview. *Journal for Specialists in Group Work, 9*(1), 2–6.

Fuhrmann, B. S., & Washington, C. S. (1984b). Substance abuse and group work: Tentative conclusions. *Journal for Specialists in Group Work, 9*(1), 62–63.

* Glasser, W. (1984). *Take effective control of your life.* New York: Harper & Row.

* Goldberg, H. (1979). *The new male.* New York: New American Library (Signet).

* Goldenberg, I., & Goldenberg, H. (1985). *Family therapy: An overview* (2nd ed.). Monterey, CA: Brooks/Cole.

Goodwin, J. (1982). *Sexual abuse: Incest victims and their families.* Boston: John Wright.

* Gould, R. L. (1978). *Transformations: Growth and change in adult life.* New York: Simon & Schuster (Touchstone).

* Goulding, M., & Goulding, R. (1979). *Changing lives through redecision therapy.* New York: Brunner/Mazel.

Hanson, S. M. H., & Bozett, F. W. (Eds.). (1985). *Dimensions of fatherhood.* Beverly Hills, CA: Sage Publications.

Hawes, E. C. (1985). Personal growth groups for women: An Adlerian approach. *Journal for Specialists in Group Work, 10*(1), 19–27.

* Herman, J. (1981). *Father–daughter incest.* Cambridge, MA: Harvard University Press.

* Herman, J., & Schatzow, E. (1984). Time-limited group therapy for women with a history of incest. *International Journal of Group Psychotherapy, 34*(4), 605–616.

Jourard, S. M. (1971). *Transparent self: Self-disclosure and well-being* (2nd ed.). New York: Van Nostrand Reinhold.

Justice, B., & Justice, R. (1979). *The broken taboo: Sex in the family.* New York: Human Sciences Press.

Kibel, H. D. (1983). Group psychotherapy with neurotic disorders. In H. I. Kaplan & B. J. Sadock (Eds.), *Comprehensive group psychotherapy* (2nd ed.) (pp. 234–242). Baltimore: Williams & Wilkins.

Koestenbaum, P. (1974). *Existential sexuality: Choosing to love.* Englewood Cliffs, NJ: Prentice-Hall.

* Levinson, D. J. (1978). *The seasons of a man's life.* New York: Knopf.

Lewis, R. A. (Ed.). (1981). *Men in difficult times: Masculinity today and tomorrow.* Englewood Cliffs, NJ: Prentice-Hall.

Lieberman, M. A., & Bond, G. R. (1982). Women's consciousness raising as an alternative to psychotherapy. In M. A. Lieberman, L. D. Borman, & Associates (Eds.), *Self-help groups for coping with crisis* (pp. 150–163). San Francisco: Jossey-Bass.

Lieberman, M. A., Bond, G. R., Solow, N., & Reibstein, J. (1982). Effectiveness of women's consciousness raising. In M. A. Lieberman, L. D. Borman, & Associates (Eds.), *Self-help groups for coping with crisis* (pp. 341–361). San Francisco: Jossey-Bass.

Lieberman, M. A., Borman, L. D., & Associates (Eds.). (1982). *Self-help groups for coping with crisis.* San Francisco: Jossey-Bass.

* Lindbergh, A. (1975). *Gift from the sea.* New York: Pantheon.

Lowinson, J. H. (1983). Group psychotherapy with substance abusers and alcoholics. In H. I. Kaplan & B. J. Sadock (Eds.), *Comprehensive group psychotherapy* (2nd ed.) (pp. 256–262). Baltimore: Williams & Wilkins.

Martin, P. A. (1983). Group psychotherapy with couples. In H. I. Kaplan & B. J. Sadock (Eds.), *Comprehensive group psychotherapy* (2nd ed.) (pp. 278–282). Baltimore: Williams and Wilkins.

May, R. (1981). *Freedom and destiny.* New York: Norton.

* Meiselman, K. (1978). *Incest: A psychological study of cause and effects with treatment recommendations.* San Francisco: Jossey-Bass.

* Mornell, P. (1979). *Passive men, wild women.* New York: Ballantine.

Moses, A. E., & Hawkins, R. O. (1982). *Counseling lesbian women and gay men: A life-issues approach.* St. Louis: C. V. Mosby.

O'Brien, C. P. (1983). Group psychotherapy with schizophrenia and affective disorders. In H. I. Kaplan & B. J. Sadock (Eds.), *Comprehensive group psychotherapy* (2nd ed.) (pp. 242–249). Baltimore: Williams & Wilkins.

* Ohlsen, M. M. (1979). *Marriage counseling in groups.* Champaign, IL: Research Press.

* Rainwater, J. (1979). *You're in charge: A guide to becoming your own therapist.* Los Angeles, CA: Guild of Tutors Press.

Rogers, C. (1961). *On becoming a person.* Boston: Houghton Mifflin.

* Rogers, C. R. (1973). *Becoming partners: Marriage and its alternatives.* New York: Dell.

Rogers, C. R. (1980). *A way of being.* Boston: Houghton Mifflin.

* Rose, S. D. (Ed.). (1980). *A casebook in group therapy: A behavioral-cognitive approach.* Englewood Cliffs, NJ: Prentice-Hall.

Rush, F. (1980). *The best kept secret: Sexual abuse of children.* Englewood Cliffs, NJ: Prentice-Hall.

Sadock, V. A. (1983). Group psychotherapy with rape victims and battered women. In H. I. Kaplan & B. J. Sadock (Eds.), *Comprehensive group psychotherapy* (2nd ed.) (pp. 282–285). Baltimore: Williams & Wilkins.

Schlossberg, N. K., Troll, L. E., & Leibowitz, Z. (1978). *Perspective on counseling adults: Issues and skills.* Monterey, CA: Brooks/Cole.

Schwartz, J. (1982). *Letting go of stress.* New York: Pinnacle Books.

Schwartz, R., & Schwartz, L. J. (1980). *Becoming a couple: Making the most of every stage of your relationship.* Englewood Cliffs, NJ: Prentice-Hall.

* Sheehy, G. (1976). *Passages: Predictable crises of adult life.* New York: Dutton.

* Sheehy, G. (1981). *Pathfinders.* New York: Bantam.

* Sprei, J., & Goodwin, R. (1983). Group treatment of sexual assault survivors. *Journal for Specialists in Group Work, 8*(1), 39–46.

Stein, A. (1983). Group psychotherapy with psychosomatically ill patients. In H. K. Kaplan & B. J. Sadock (Eds.), *Comprehensive group psychotherapy* (2nd ed.) (pp. 250–256). Baltimore: Williams & Wilkins.

Vannicelli, M., Canning, D., & Griefen, M. (1984). Group therapy with alcoholics: A group case study. *International Journal of Group Psychotherapy, 34*(1), 127–148.

Watson, D. L., & Tharp, R. G. (1985). *Self-directed behavior: Self-modification for personal adjustment* (4th ed.). Monterey, CA: Brooks/Cole.

Woodman, N. J., & Lenna, H. R. (1980). *Counseling with gay men and women.* San Francisco: Jossey-Bass.

* Yalom, I. (1980). *Existential psychotherapy.* New York: Basic Books.
* Yalom, I. (1983). *Inpatient group psychotherapy.* New York: Basic Books.
* Yalom, I. (1985). *The theory and practice of group psychotherapy* (3rd ed.). New York: Basic Books.
* Zimbardo, P. G. (1978). *Shyness.* New York: Jove Press.
* Zimpfer, D. G. (1984). *Group work in the helping professions: A bibliography* (2nd ed.). Muncie, IN: Accelerated Development.

12

Groups for the Elderly

Introduction: Some Personal Observations *

My interest in working as a counselor with the elderly is associated with my German background. When I was growing up, old people were always present. In Germany, old and young live together. More often than not, children grow up in households that include their grandparents. Today, there appears to be an increase in the construction of homes exclusively for the elderly, but the practice of living with one's children still prevails among old people, because Germans continue to believe that the elderly should be taken care of by family members rather than by strangers.

Our children, Heidi and Cindy, frequently spend their summers with their grandparents in Germany. They experience old and young people living together harmoniously—and sometimes not so harmoniously. These regular interactions of all ages, I believe, prevent the development of certain stereotypes and negative attitudes toward the elderly. During a recent trip to China my family and I visited a home for the aged. I noted with interest that the home was referred to as "the respected home for the elderly." Only older people who have no relatives to take care of them live in these homes. Throughout my stay in China I observed that older people are highly respected and generally live with younger generations.

My long contact with elderly people has left me with fewer fears about aging than most Americans seem to have. I have noticed that many Americans are threatened by the aging process, perhaps because they fear their own deterioration. This is truly sad, for I take pleasure in looking at an old person's face, in which I see a treasure of character, beauty, and wisdom. I remember rumors circulating to the effect that in the United States old people were considered useless and were locked up. Since I have been in the United States, I've learned that the facts are

* This chapter is written from the perspective of Marianne Corey.

not so horrible as I had imagined; however, I do detect many differences between the United States and Germany in the treatment of and attitudes toward the aged.

Until recently it was considered unusual for a young person to be seriously interested in a career working with the aged. People, even old people, asked me "Why does a young person like you want to work with old people?" I hear such comments less frequently now, and the number of young people working in the field of geriatrics is increasing with the passing years. Americans are beginning to perceive old people as vital members of society and to treat them with more respect.

A liking for old people does not alone make a good counselor. This unique population requires special skills and knowledge. To further my understanding of this age group, I attended the summer institution that is part of the geriatrics program at the University of Southern California. I have attended many workshops, listened to many lectures, read extensively, and visited numerous homes for the elderly in several countries. Although I have not recently been involved in leading groups for the elderly, I have continued my involvement with them through individual counseling, by giving lectures on the elderly (both to the elderly and to other age groups), by personal contacts with older people, and as a consultant for group leaders in training who work with the elderly.

Much of this chapter is based on a description of my group work with the elderly in institutions, which was a part of my graduate internship in counseling. After encountering some difficulties in having a program for the elderly accepted as a legitimate part of my training for a master's degree in marriage, family, and child counseling, I developed the position that the elderly are a vital part of the family and that a family counselor should have exposure to their unique needs and problems. Once the university had accepted this rationale, and thus my proposal to work with the elderly, I met other difficulties. I had a hard time locating an agency that could give me an opportunity to work in a meaningful way with the aged. The human-service agencies I contacted were not very involved in providing counseling services for the elderly. Today it is not so difficult to find an agency that offers groups for the elderly. There has been a definite increase in groups offered for this population. Nevertheless, counselors may encounter many obstacles in organizing such groups. Some of the barriers are due to the unique characteristics of this population, but other obstacles are found within the system or the institutions themselves—for example, lack of interest in therapeutic work for the elderly, lack of administrative support for group work, and lack of cooperation from staff workers. Beginning leaders are likely to find it difficult to obtain adequate supervision in working with this specialized population. Because of these restraining factors, group leaders might find themselves losing their enthusiasm and motivation for setting up such groups. I want to encourage you to persist in this very important area of group work.

Unique Characteristics of the Elderly

Leaders who are forming their first group for the elderly will find some definite differences from other age groups. They need to be aware of the particular life issues faced by older people. Although not exhaustive, the following is a list of observations I have made over the years as a result of my personal and professional contact with the elderly.

1. Themes that are more prevalent with the elderly than with other age groups include loneliness and social isolation; loss; poverty; feelings of rejection; the struggle to find meaning in life; dependency; feelings of uselessness, hopelessness, and despair; fears of death and dying; grief over others' deaths; sadness over physical and mental deterioration; and regrets over past events.

2. Some older people are more difficult to reach, for they may not be so likely to come to a counselor's office. They may be more resistant and skeptical about the effectiveness of counseling than are other populations, and it may take more time to establish trust. It is very important to carefully consider the titles you use in describing your services for the elderly, because older people are more sensitive to feeling stigmatized when they seek out a mental-health professional.

3. Their attention span is often short because of physical or psychological difficulties. Consequently, the pace of the group needs to be slower.

4. Old people are often taking medications that interfere with their ability to be fully present.

5. With some who are in advanced stages of senility, reality orientation becomes a problem. Sometimes they simply forget to come to sessions.

6. Regular attendance at group sessions often becomes problematic for a variety of other reasons, such as physical ailments, transportation problems, interruptions in the schedules of institutions, and conflicting appointments with doctors and social workers.

7. Older people often need support and encouragement more than they need confrontation. Therefore, group work is oriented less toward radical personality reconstruction and more toward making life in the present more meaningful and enjoyable. However, never to challenge or confront older people could be seen as patronizing and may be based on the distorted belief that they cannot change.

8. The elderly have a great need to be listened to and understood. Respect is shown by accepting them through hearing their underlying

messages and not treating them in a condescending way. The elderly often suffer from "conversation deprivation." To be encouraged to share and relate with others has therapeutic value in itself (Burnside, 1984b).

Special Types of Group for the Elderly

Not all old people can be placed in the same type of group. Leaders must take into account the special needs of potential group members. Some groups that are commonly offered include those with a special emphasis on reminiscing, physical fitness, body awareness, grief work, occupational therapy, reality orientation, music and art therapy, combined dance and movement, preretirement and postretirement issues, remotivation, preplacement (preparing people to move from an institutional to a community setting), organic brain syndrome, education, poetry, health-related issues, family therapy, and assertion training. This is certainly not a complete list; leaders can invent ways to bring their particular talents into a group setting to promote interaction among elderly members. For example, later in this chapter I describe a master's degree project that involved designing a group composed of adolescents and the elderly. Leaders who have artistic hobbies can have members do something with their hands; in the process of creating products, the members often feel the freedom to talk about themselves in spontaneous ways. Groups that entail the members' doing something specific can promote more interaction than groups that are limited to discussion.

I want to share an example of a group that naturally evolved from an exercise class at a senior citizens' center in our community. Jerry and I were invited by a 70-year-old man to attend the class, which was very physically challenging. The leader of this class, who was also an elderly person, had several talents that she combined fruitfully and shared with her group. She not only directed activities designed for physical fitness but also provided a climate that fostered meaningful personal and social interactions. For example, she was very patient with members who interrupted the exercises by talking about problems that were preoccupying them that day. Sometimes they described the details of an enjoyable weekend, at times they listed numerous complaints ranging from home problems to world problems, and often they engaged in nonmalicious community gossip. If the leader had had a rigid notion of what an exercise class should be, many of these spontaneous and therapeutic interchanges would not have evolved. Her talent and enthusiasm inspired both humor and seriousness of purpose; she had a special gift of gently pushing and confronting the members to exceed what they thought were their physical limits. Thus, people typically left feeling both physically rejuvenated and psychologically uplifted.

A Program for Institutionalized Elderly People

As I mentioned, I faced some obstacles in securing a group for the elderly as a part of my internship. I was finally able to arrange to work with geriatric patients in a state mental institution—the only institution I could find that provided counseling for a large number of old people. During a 2-hour interview conducted by the program director and a staff member, I was questioned (at first with suspicion) concerning my motives for seeking this kind of experience. The staff member expressed her surprise about my request to work with the elderly, since, as she put it, "Nobody wants this assignment." However, the general tone of the interview was very positive; how my needs and the needs of the program could be integrated was given serious consideration.

New group leaders should be aware that they may not be accepted by the staff of an institution until they prove themselves, especially in facilities where group work has not been part of the treatment plan (Burnside, 1984b). Program directors or others with influence may do anything they can to undermine the newcomer's well-intentioned design for a group. Therefore, it is good to provide the personnel in charge of an agency with a detailed description of the goals and procedures of the group and to do anything you can to solicit trust for and cooperation with your plans.

My initial impression of the ward I was assigned to was that it was very unattractive. The atmosphere seemed depressingly lifeless. Many of the 44 male and female patients were either standing by themselves or sitting in front of a television set; most were staring blankly into space. I noticed very little contact among the ward members. They seemed quite isolated from one another, even though they shared a relatively small area. Eight to ten beds occupied a single room, so there was a complete lack of privacy. The old people were dressed in unattractive state-issued clothing that could have added nothing to their self-esteem. I was convinced that the surroundings were having a strong negative effect on the patients' ability to change. I felt that their environment contributed to their sense of hopelessness and isolation.

One staff member was setting a patient's hair; another was working with patients on art projects. However, most of the staff were in a centrally located glass-walled office from which they could view the activities of the patients on the ward.

I was soon accepted by the ward members; they seemed willing to talk to me if I approached them first. I was to work with a social worker assigned to the ward 2 days a week, and he and I decided to form two groups. One was to be a preplacement group for people who were ready to leave the institution and were waiting either to be placed in some type of home for the elderly or to return to their own home. The other group would be for patients suffering from organic brain syndrome

(OBS), a condition associated with impaired cognitive abilities. People with OBS evidence severe impairments of memory, intellectual functioning, and judgment; they are disoriented and show little emotional response.

■■ The Preplacement Group

As with other group populations, it is necessary to give careful consideration to the selection of members. A group is not likely to function well if severely disturbed and hallucinating members are mixed with clients who are psychologically intact. It is a good practice, however, to combine talkative and quiet people, depressed and ebullient types, excitable with calmer clients, suspicious with more trusting individuals, and people with different backgrounds. The size of the group is determined by the level of psychological and social functioning of the participants. A group of ten relatively well-functioning people is much easier to manage than even a smaller number of regressed clients.

The preplacement group that my co-leader and I formed consisted of three men and four women—a good balance of the sexes and a workable number for two leaders. Before the first meeting I contacted the members individually and gave them a basic orientation to the group. I told them the purpose of the group, what the activities might be, and where, when, and for how long the group would meet. I let each person know that membership was voluntary. When people seemed hesitant to attend, I suggested that they come to the initial session and then decide whether they wanted to continue.

Before the first session my co-leader and I decided on a few general goals for the group. Our primary goal would be to provide an atmosphere in which common concerns could be freely discussed and in which members could interact with one another. We wanted to provide an opportunity for members to voice complaints and to be included in a decision-making process. We strongly felt that these people could change their life and that the group process could stimulate them to do so.

The group met once a week for an hour in the visitors' room. Before each group session I contacted all the members, reminded them that the group would meet shortly, invited them to attend, and accompanied them to the group room. I learned that it was difficult for them to remember the time of the meetings, so individual assistance would be important in ensuring regular attendance. Those who were absent were either ill or involved in an activity that couldn't be rescheduled, such as physical therapy. The group was an open one; members would occasionally be discharged, and we encouraged newly admitted patients to join. This didn't seem to bother the members, and it didn't affect the cohesion of the group. As leaders, we also attempted to make entrance into the group as easy as possible. We always allowed some time for the new members to be introduced and to say anything they wanted to about being new to the group, and we asked current group members to welcome them.

The Initial Stage.   During the initial sessions the members showed a tendency to direct all of their statements to the two leaders. In the hope that we could break the shell that isolated each person in a private and detached world, my co-leader and I immediately began to encourage the members to talk to one another, not to us. When members talked about a member, we asked them to speak directly to that member. When members discussed a particular problem or concern, we encouraged others to share similar difficulties.

In the beginning the members resisted talking about themselves, voicing complaints, or discussing what they expected after their release from the institution. Their usual comment reflected their hopelessness: "What good will it do? No one will listen to us anyway." Our task was to teach them to listen to one another.

The Importance of Listening and Acting.   My co-leader and I felt that one way of teaching the old people to listen would be by modeling—by demonstrating that we were really listening to them. Thus, when our clients spoke of problems related to life on the ward, my co-leader and I became actively involved with them in solving some of these conflicts. For example, one member complained that one of the patients in his room shouted for much of the night. We were able to get the unhappy member placed in another room. When some members shared their fears about the board-and-care homes they were to be released to, we arranged to take them to several such homes so that they could make an informed choice of placement. One woman complained that her husband did not visit her enough and that, when he did take her home, he was uncaring and uninterested in her sexually. On several occasions my co-leader and I held private sessions with the couple.

Some men complained that there was nothing to do, so we arranged for them to get involved in planting a garden. Another group member shared the fact that she was an artist, so we asked her to lead some people in the group and on the ward in art projects. She reacted enthusiastically and succeeded in involving several other members. One member complained during several sessions that he felt trapped and that he did not belong in the hospital; the staff agreed with this assessment of the situation. He was waiting for something to happen, and with the passing of time he became increasingly depressed. After discussing his case with the director and the social worker, I encouraged this man to take steps to get himself released instead of depending on others to do it. He then obtained a pass that permitted him to leave the ward, and on several occasions he visited his conservator (the legal guardian appointed for him by the state) in an effort to make himself visible to the authorities. Too often patients like him, who are ready to be released, are lost in the paperwork required for hundreds of other cases. Despite our help, it took this man almost a year to get out of the institution.

All these stories illustrate the importance of a counselor's working with the immediate problems that old people face. Our philosophy was to encourage them to again become active, even in a small way, in making decisions about their life. There were two things that we learned *not* to do: (1) encourage a patient to participate in an activity that would be frustrating and thereby further erode an already poor self-image, and (2) make promises we couldn't keep.

Listening to Reminiscences. In addition to dealing with the day-to-day problems of the members, we spent much time listening as they reminisced about sadness and guilt they had experienced, their many losses, the places they had lived and visited, the mistakes they had made, and so on. By remembering and actively reconstructing their past, old people can hope to resolve the conflicts that are still affecting them and decide how to use the time left to them. In addition, they enjoy remembering happy times, when they were more productive and powerful than they are now. I believe that this life review is an important and healthy process and that old people need to experience it.

Most agencies that work with the elderly offer reminiscence and life-review groups. According to Lewis and Butler (1984), the life review is seen as a universal psychological process that is associated with increased awareness of one's finiteness. The myth of immortality gives way to an acceptance of one's death. The life review involves a progressive return to consciousness of earlier experiences, a resurgence of unresolved past conflicts, and the bringing up of memories that have been deeply buried in the unconscious. Although some older people are aware of a need to put their entire life into a meaningful perspective, others avoid this type of review as a protection against painful memories.

The Use of Exercises. My role as a leader of this group differed from the roles I had played in other types of group. I found that I was more directive, that I was much less confrontive and much more supportive, and that I spent a lot of time teaching the members how to express themselves and listen to others. My co-leader and I designed a variety of exercises to catalyze member interaction. The exercises often succeeded in getting meaningful discussions started, and sometimes they were just plain fun. We always began by showing how an exercise could be done. Some of the exercises we assigned the group were as follows:

· Go on an imaginary trip, and pick a couple of the other group members to accompany you. (Although you may have to deal with feelings of rejection expressed by those not chosen, this exercise is very helpful for people who are reluctant to reach out to one another and make friends.)
· If you could do anything you wanted, what would it be?
· Pick a new name for yourself and talk about what that name means to you.
· Bring a favorite photograph and share it with others in the group.
· Draw a picture of you and your family and talk about your place in the family.
· Describe some of the memories that are important to you.
· Tell what your favorite holiday is and what you enjoy doing on that day.

Another exercise that helps the elderly focus and contributes to member interaction is the sentence-completion method as described by Yalom (1983) for inpatient group psychotherapy with low-level clients. Incomplete sentences can be structured around a variety of themes such as:

· self-disclosure (One thing about me that people would be surprised to know is _____ .)
· separation (The hardest separation that I have ever had is _____ _____ .)
· anger (One thing that really irritates me is _____ _____ .)
· isolation (The time in my life when I felt most alone was _____ _____ .)
· ward events (The fight on the ward last night made me feel _____ _____ .)
· empathy (I feel touched by others when _____ _____ .)
· here-and-now interactions (The person that I am most like in this room is _____ .)
· personal change (Something I want to change about myself is _____ _____ .)
· stress (I experience tension when _____ .)

Working with incomplete sentences can trigger intense emotions. Thus, the group leader needs to be skilled in dealing with these feelings.

We used exercises as simple means of getting group interaction going. One of our group sessions fell on the day before Thanksgiving. We asked the participants to remember a special Thanksgiving day from the past—to recall all of the people who were with them and everything that happened. The members received these instructions enthusiastically, and everyone participated. My co-leader and I pointed out to them that the fun and excitement they had experienced during past holidays was due partly to their interaction with people and could certainly be experienced again if they made a special effort this Thanksgiving to reach out to and make contact with one another. The Thanksgiving celebration did, in fact, go well for the group members. Several of them made a point of sitting together, and they reported at the next session the fun they had had.

These exercises, by encouraging the members to express themselves, led to their getting to know one another, which led in turn to a lessening of the "what's the use" feeling that was universal in the beginning.

Debunking Myths. With the old people's group, my co-leader and I explored some myths and attitudes that prevail regarding the aged. Our intention was to challenge the members' acceptance of these myths. The following are some of the beliefs we considered.

· Old people can't change, so it's a waste of time and effort to try to help them with counseling or therapy.
· All people who retire become depressed.
· It is disgraceful for an old person to remarry.
· Young people are never forgetful; old people always are.
· Forgetfulness is a sign of senility.
· Old people cannot contribute to society.
· There are many child molesters among the aged.
· Most young people want to neglect the elderly members of their family.
· Old people are always emotional and financial burdens, whether their children take them into their home or not.
· People should retire at 65.
· Old people are not creative.
· An elderly person will die soon after his or her mate dies.
· Becoming old always means having a host of serious physical problems.
· Old people do not understand the problems of younger people.
· Old people are no longer beautiful.
· Old people are dependent and need to be taken care of.
· Most old people are lonely.

· There is a high degree of alcoholism among the aged—higher than among younger people.
· Old people are no longer interested in sex.
· Old men are impotent.
· Old people are not afraid to die.

Outcomes.   To work successfully with the elderly, one must take into account the basic limitations in their resources for change yet not adopt a fatalistic attitude that will only reinforce their sense of hopelessness. Had my co-leader and I expected to bring about dramatic personality changes, we would soon have been frustrated, because the changes that occurred were small and came slowly. Instead, we expected to have only a modest impact, and so the subtle changes that took place were enough to give us the incentive and energy to continue. The following are some of the outcomes we observed.

· Members realized that they were not alone in experiencing problems.
· The participants learned from one another's feedback.
· People in the group felt an acceptance of their feelings and realized that they had a right to express them.
· Members said that they liked coming to the meetings, and they told this to patients who weren't members.
· The group atmosphere became one of trust, caring, and friendliness.
· The members continued the socializing that began in the group outside group sessions.
· The members learned one another's names, which contributed to increased interaction on the ward.
· Participants engaged in activities that stimulated them rather than merely waiting for their release.
· The members began to talk more personally about their sorrows, losses, hopes, joys, memories, fears, regrets, and so on, saying that it felt good to be listened to and to talk.
· The enthusiasm of the members and the staff led to the formation of another group for ward members.
· The nurses reported seeing a change in the patients and expressed a desire to learn the skills needed to facilitate such groups.
· Staff members noticed positive changes, such as elevated spirits, in some of the members.
· Staff members became involved in thinking of appropriate activities for different members and helped the members carry them out.

My co-leader and I encountered some frustrating circumstances during the course of the group. For instance, the members occasionally seemed very lethargic. We later discovered that this occurred when the participants had received medication just before the group session. Still, it was difficult to discern whether a member's condition was due to the medication or to psychological factors. It was not uncommon to find a member functioning well one week and feeling good about herself and then to discover, the next week, that she had had a psychotic episode and was unable to respond to anyone. Another heartbreaking reality was the slowness with which patients who were ready for placement in outside agencies had their papers processed for release. People who had to remain in this institution after they no longer needed it could be seen to suffer, both physically and psychologically.

Some small changes that occurred in the group sessions were undone by the routine of ward life. On the one hand, some of the members resisted making their life on the ward more pleasant for fear of giving the impression that their stay would be a long one. It was as though they were saying "If I communicate that I like it here, you might not let me go." On the other hand, some members resigned themselves to institutional life and saw the ward as their home, expressing very directly that they did not want to leave. These people had developed such a fear of the outside world that they were willing to give up the chance that it offered of a richer life.

Termination.   I was to be co-leader of this group for only 3 months, and I prepared the members for my departure several weeks in advance. After I left, my co-leader continued the group by himself. On occasion I visited the group, and I was remembered and felt very welcome. One year later this group was still in existence, although the membership had changed.

■■ The Group for Patients with Organic Brain Syndrome

Some of the patients on the ward were severely handicapped by organic brain syndrome, and my co-leader and I decided to form a group with these people that would provide them with some sensory stimulation. The group would have the same format as the preplacement group, but the activities would be somewhat different.

The group consisted of three men and three women, and the sessions lasted from half an hour to an hour. We felt successful after a session if members had not wandered off or fallen asleep. I sat in front of the group and touched the members to make sure they could see and hear me. Each week I told them who I was, where they were, why they were there, and who was present. I moved around a lot, making physical contact with each member; I called them by name. The other leader and I developed a routine of opening the session by providing chocolate candy or, in some cases, a cigar, and the members very much enjoyed this ritual. Once I brought in a bottle of perfume, let everyone smell it, and helped the women put it on, which brought many giggles. This allowed for touching, which these people very much needed. The members sat holding hands and sang favorite old tunes while one of them plucked away at a guitar. It was a touching experience to see these people enjoying singing an old and much-loved song; they still remembered the words but had to struggle with their physical handicap to sing them. I can still hear the group singing "You Are My Sunshine."

We generated another activity in the OBS group by bringing in a beach ball and encouraging the members to throw it to one another and to go through the struggle of retrieving it. This stimulated the members into activity. We brought in large, colorful pictures and had the members describe what they saw. The members had a tendency to talk very little, so we encouraged them to notice one another's presence and address one another. We brought a tape recorder to some sessions, recorded the songs, and then listened to everyone's voice. We brought in clay one day, but this proved to be a disaster because several members started eating it. This problem could have been prevented, though, had we paid closer attention to what was going on. Bringing my two daughters and introducing them to each member of both my groups delighted my children as well as the group members. This was a natural catalyst; afterward there was much talk among the members about the fun they had had with my children. Weather permitting, we took the members on walks, having them touch and smell flowers, trees, and shrubs. In all of these ways we encouraged members to employ all of their senses, so that they could be more alive.

Obviously, the goals of this group were much more limited in scope than those of the preplacement group. Few changes were observed outside of group; members continued not to react to or recognize one another much of the time. However, I felt that it did them good to be aroused from their lethargy, if only for short periods of time. The following are notes I made after the second session.

> The OBS group was slow. In the beginning, two people insisted on going to sleep. One member kept wandering off. Later, some talked about a birthday party and shared the fun they had. Everyone sang some songs and held hands. I contacted everyone in group, touching and talking with each one. It is difficult not to get discouraged, and I have to continually keep my goal—to get any of them to converse or react about anything—in mind. As I did last time, I made a point of saying good-bye to each of them individually.

With this particular group, it was rewarding to see even the most minute changes. It was exciting for me to hear one 87-year-old man, who usually showed no responsiveness, giggle when I put some perfume behind my male co-leader's ear. During the initial sessions he had never uttered a word; now, slowly, he began to talk and sing with the rest. One lady who had not allowed anyone to touch her reached out one day and held another member's hand.

I visited this group 3 months after I had left it, not expecting to be remembered. I was touched when some members approached me in recognition and reminded me that I had not been to the group meetings! This group was continued after my departure for about a year.

■■ Groups for the Families of the Elderly

I see a pressing need for therapy groups for people who have aged relatives in an institution. Very often a family's feelings of guilt, anger, failure, and hopelessness will keep them away from their hospitalized member, depriving him or her of the joy of visits. Or the family members may visit but transmit their negative feelings to the old person. In either case, everyone suffers from the loss of true contact. By allowing families to share their concerns with other families, groups can relieve much of the tension that normally results from the responsibility of caring for a loved one who is old.

My co-leader and I experimented with this idea by holding several sessions with one member and his entire family. The family members talked about the shame they felt over having one of their relatives committed to a mental institution, and the patient expressed the anger he felt over being ignored by his family. After expressing their feelings, the family members made the decision to visit the institutionalized member more often.

■■ Involvement with Other Ward Residents

Due to a lack of staff members qualified to lead groups, many patients were not assigned to a group. One way for me to make contact with these unassigned residents was by seeking them out, so each time I came to the hospital I spent some time walking around the ward. During my first day on the ward I noticed a woman who was crocheting and told her about my liking for this activity. On my next visit I brought wool and several crochet hooks. I put a table and several chairs in an area in which I could be seen by a lot of patients. I invited the woman who had been crocheting to sit with me. Very soon other women approached us and sat down. They took yarn and hooks and began to crochet, much to the amazement of the ward staff. One patient who seldom sat down and who instead usually ran around the ward cursing and uttering obscenities sat with me and crocheted. I crocheted in that spot again and again, and each time she stayed a little longer. It surprised everyone to hear her talk about her life. An informal group of five women and myself was thus spontaneously formed. It proved to be a great catalyst of interaction among ward members. Several men would often stand around and watch the women, who would show off what they had crocheted. I encouraged the women to get together and crochet during my absence, but they didn't do so. As with many other activities, this one only held them as long as a staff member was there to encourage them. I taught two staff members how to crochet, and it became a good means for them to make contact with patients.

I moved around on the ward, meeting as many members as possible. I talked with them, sat by their bedside, put my arms around one or held one's hand, laughed with them, and teased them. It was a good feeling to walk into the ward in the morning and hear many familiar hellos. I danced with many of them, and I encouraged them to dance with one another when the dance band came each week.

■■ General Reactions and Observations

At times I felt depressed, hopeless, and angry, but these feelings were seldom directly connected with my activities with the patients; the smallest changes I observed in them were rewarding and gave me the incentive to go on. Rather, I experienced these feelings whenever I saw the system contributing to the physical and psychological deterioration of a person, such as when the staff appeared uncaring and lacking in enthusiasm. I've already mentioned that some members were forced to stay in the institution because everyone claimed to be too busy to do the paperwork necessary to get them out. I felt angry when I saw student psychiatric technicians or other staff members show disrespect for the patients and when I heard these same individuals call an elderly person by his or her first name yet insist that they themselves be addressed by their surname. I felt discouraged and helpless when, as happened occasionally, an agitated patient would be restrained physically or with medication without ever being asked what had made him or her so upset in the first place. Another misuse of medication occurred, I felt, when patients were given strong doses to put them to sleep at night. In many cases a glass of wine would have had the same effect and might have stimulated satisfying socializing among the patients. Another upsetting sight was a patient in a wheelchair being pushed around and not being told where he or she was going.

At times the behavior of a patient was treated as crazy when in reality there was a good reason for it that could have been discovered if anybody had tried. One day a student brought a blind member of my OBS group to the meeting. The blind man proceeded to take off his shoes, and the student shouted at him to put his shoes back on. I approached Mr. W. and kneeled in front of him. I simply said "Mr. W., you are taking your shoes off in our group session. How come?" He apologized, saying that he had thought that he was being taken to the physical-therapy room.

In another case, a 75-year-old patient kept taking his shoes off all day long, always gathering up newspaper to put around his feet. Everyone considered this behavior very bizarre. I remembered that during my childhood in Germany I was often told in the winter to put newspaper into my shoes to keep my feet warm. After spending some time with this man, I found that this "strange" behavior was based on the same experience. I learned to be careful not to judge a patient as bizarre or delusional too quickly but rather to take the time to find out whether there was a logical reason for a peculiar behavior.

I felt very helpless when I had to struggle with the heavy diagnostic language used by the staff to record the patients' behavior in their official records. I often found it difficult to understand the notes in the records, and I was concerned that the simple language I was using to describe the members' behavior in group might be considered inappropriate. A number of staff members apparently had reservations about the use of technical language, too, for one day, during an important hospital meeting, it was decided that from then on there would be a minimum of labeling of patients and that, instead, their behavior would be described in a way that anyone could understand. Instead of labeling a patient withdrawn, a staff member would describe the behavior of the patient. This would, of course, be more time consuming, and several staff members resisted it.

It was sad to see that patients were sometimes discouraged or made to feel shameful when they physically expressed affection for another ward member. Sensuality was perceived by the staff as bad because of "what it could lead to." There is one positive note, however. I had several very good discussions with staff members about our attitudes toward the sexuality of the aged. I felt very encouraged by their willingness to explore their attitudes and their openness to change. By dealing with our own attitudes, misperceptions, and fears, the staff members and I were able to be more understanding and helpful to the patients. Several of us attended seminars on the sexuality of the aging.

It was also sad to see an elderly person describe himself or herself as ugly, having accepted the standard according to which only the young are beautiful. In our groups my co-leader and I talked about attitudes toward old people's physical appearance. We were able to work with the members on accepting and liking themselves.

A Combined Group for the Elderly and Adolescents

At a recent convention of the American Association for Counseling and Development I met Michael Nakkula, who had designed an innovative group combining older people with adolescents. Nakkula's (1984) research design, under the direction of Joseph Morris of the University of Minnesota at Duluth, was aimed at assessing members' changes in attitude as a result of their experiences in eight group sessions.

▪▪ Basic Assumptions

Nakkula's study was based largely on a review of the literature and his personal observations on the developmental tasks of the young and the old. Some of his key assumptions were:

· Part of maintaining mental health in the elderly is staying in contact with all age groups.
· The old need to have an opportunity to pass on their wisdom to the younger generation.
· The young need exposure to the elderly to gain wisdom.
· The elderly can become a "living history book" to young people.
· There is a need to bring these two age groups together to exchange elderly wisdom and youthful vitality.
· Older people benefit from the knowledge that their investment in society can live on beyond their own life.
· Adolescents need role models for their developing value systems.
· The benefit of interaction between the young and the old is based not only on what they can learn from their differences but also on what they can learn from their similarities.
· Contact between the two age groups can lead to less fear and more realistic attitudes about the aging process among adolescents.
· The two age groups display a striking resemblance in their struggle to understand the purpose of their life.
· Both groups suffer from apparent alienation within our social structure.
· The elderly are stifled in their attempts to realize their full potential; adolescents are stifled by their limited power and control and lack experience in using the power they do have.

Based on the above assumptions, Nakkula hypothesized that combining the two age groups would result in positive changes in attitude toward members of the opposite age group due to increased knowledge and understanding. He also hypothesized that the group experience would lead to an increase of self-esteem in the elderly.

▪▪ Structure of the Group

The group consisted of five junior-high-school students, aged 12 and 13, and five elderly people, all of whom lived in a nursing home. They met for eight sessions, with each session being structured as follows:

Session 1. The purpose of the group was explained. The members were asked to interview one another and later introduce one another to the rest of the group.

Session 2. The objective was to help members look at their similarities and differences. Classical music was played, and they were asked to think about the most critical task in their life. The differences and similarities of these tasks were then discussed in the group.

Session 3. The goal was to discuss the significant aspects leading to personal strength, which will lead to personal happiness. The members were asked to think about their assets and how they thought their strengths contributed to their happiness. They were asked to choose a strength from the other age group they would like to possess.

Session 4. The purpose was to assist the elderly in putting their life experiences into perspective and to teach adolescents that life is an ongoing process that demands work. Members brought to the session photographs of themselves at different points in their life cycle. They talked about their favorite picture, explaining why it was associated with special meaning.

Session 5. The aim was to look and examine how the young and the old were represented in the media. Members shared and discussed news articles. They also identified adjectives used by the media in describing the young and the old.

Session 6. The purpose was to examine the messages found in music and to compare yesterday's with today's music, as well as to look for common themes. After listening to selected pieces of music, members discussed the feelings that were aroused and the people and situations they associated with each piece. They also talked about what was happening in the world at the time these songs were written. All the members sang a song known to everyone.

Session 7. The elderly were given an opportunity to share the significance of their heritage with the young, and the young had an opportunity to realize the importance of the elderly in connecting them with their roots. The members discussed their ethnic backgrounds. Adolescents discussed what they knew about their heritage. The elderly talked about how their families had come to the United States and what it had been like for them, their parents, and their grandparents from the beginning.

Session 8. The purpose was to say good-bye and to leave one another having earned mutual respect. The members divided into pairs and talked about what they had learned from and enjoyed about each other. They also identified at least one misconception they had had about the other age group and how it had been clarified. They exchanged names and addresses so that they might stay in touch.

■■ Outcomes

This study included a pretest and posttest design to assess adolescent attitudes toward the elderly and to assess the degree to which the elderly felt useful in society. It was found that young people who participated in the group were much less biased toward older people at the time of the posttesting. The elderly showed an increased sense of self-esteem. In addition, they appreciated the break from routine and the chance to socialize with curious and enthusiastic youngsters, who seemed to enjoy listening to their reminiscences.

■■ Implications and Commentary

I am excited about a project like Nakkula's. Many people today grow up in single-parent families and can benefit from contact with other significant adults such as grandparents. In my talks to the elderly I encourage them to spend more time with young people, especially those who are significant to them. My message to them is not to underestimate the tremendous power and influence they could have in the lives of young people if they foster a relationship with them early on. In my adult therapy groups I often hear about a grandparent who had a significant impact on a person's life when a parent was too busy.

There are many ways to combine the elderly and the young. It is up to the creativity of the group practitioner to come up with variations of a group such as the one just described. Should you like more detailed information regarding the structure and format of this group, write Michael Nakkula, 509 West 121st Street (512), New York, NY 10027.

Suggestions for Working with Healthy Aging People

It is crucial to realize that there is a large population of the elderly who are not institutionalized but who do have problems coping with the aging process. These people have to deal not only with the many losses associated with old age but also with the pressures and conflicts that the younger generation experiences, and they can profit from personal-growth groups that serve people of all ages.

The following are a few suggestions for helping healthy, well-functioning elderly people.

1. I find it very exciting to combine a group of people over 65 with a group of adolescents and have them explore their common struggles—their feelings of uselessness, difference, and isolation from the rest of society.
2. Aging people can be employed or asked to volunteer as teacher aides in elementary and secondary schools.
3. High school or college students who are learning to speak a foreign language can be given the assignment of visiting homes for the aged that include people who speak the language as their native tongue. This plan, in addition to helping the student, provides some badly needed stimulation for the elderly person.

4. Groups of old people can be formed to explore such themes as love, sex, marriage, meaning in life, death, failing health, and body images. Many of the myths about the meaning of these issues for old people can be examined in depth.
5. Teachers can invite elderly people to be guest speakers in their classes and ask them to discuss special historical events they experienced that are being studied by the students.
6. People in senior citizen centers could be asked to teach young people arts and crafts and many other skills that are often not taught at home or at school.

Summary of Practical and Professional Considerations

■■ Issues in Group Process

All of the issues addressed in Part Two of this book pertaining to stages in the development of a group have some applicability to designing and conducting groups for the elderly. This section provides brief examples of practical issues group leaders need to think about in forming specialized groups for older people.

The Group Proposal.   It is especially important for leaders to develop a sound proposal, since they will often encounter resistance from agencies dealing with the elderly. I have already mentioned ways of enlisting the support of the agency. Refer to Chapter 3 for the elements that might be included in a proposal for groups for the elderly.

Screening and Selection Issues.   As I have discussed, the needs of the elderly are diverse, so leaders need to consider the purposes of the group in determining who will or will not benefit from the experience. The decision to include or exclude members must be made appropriately and sensitively. For example, to mix regressed patients with relatively well-functioning older people is to invite fragmentation. Leaders may have a rationale for excluding people who are highly agitated, are delusional, have severe physical problems that could inhibit their benefiting from the group, or display other behaviors that are likely to be counterproductive to the group as a whole.

Purpose of the Group.   Elderly people generally need a clear, organized explanation of the specific purposes of a group and why they can benefit from it. Some of them are more closed to the potential values of group participation than are other populations. In short, leaders must be able to present a positive approach to the members. The anxiety level may be high among an elderly group, which calls for clear structure and a repetition about the goals and procedures of the group.

Practical Issues.   Practical considerations regarding the size, duration, setting, and techniques to be used depend on the level of functioning of a particular group. For example, more members could be included in a well-functioning group than in an OBS group. The attention span of a group of outpatients would be longer than that of patients who are out of contact with reality. The leader must have a good understanding of the members' mental and physical capabilities.

Confidentiality.   Institutional life is often not conducive to privacy. Elderly group members may be suspicious when they are asked to talk about themselves, for they may fear some sort of retaliation by staff and fellow members. Leaders must take great care to define the boundaries of confidentiality, to ensure that confidences will not be broken, and to provide a safe and nonthreatening environment.

Labeling and Prejudging Group Members.   Institutions are quick to diagnose and categorize people, and they are slow to remove such labels when they no longer fit. Those working with the elderly must be careful not to be rigidly influenced by what they hear or read about a given member, be open in forming their own impressions, and be willing to challenge any limiting labels.

Visitors to Groups.   As is often the case in institutions, visitors and other staff members may wish to attend a particular group session. A good practice with even severely regressed patients (who may or may not be aware of another's presence) is to announce visitors in advance of their attending a session and again at the beginning of the session. In addition, the purpose of their visit should be mentioned in order to lessen suspicion.

Value Differences.   Leaders must have a good understanding of the social and cultural backgrounds of their members in order to work with their concerns in a sensitive way. Many times the group leader is younger than the members, and this age span may represent significant value differences. For example, a group leader in her early 20s might consider unmarried couples living together an acceptable norm, whereas a member in her mid-70s might suffer great guilt and shame for doing so. It is essential for the leader to take this member's anxiety seriously and not simply reassure her that she has no need to feel guilty. Another issue to consider is that group leaders typically assume that there is therapeutic value in discussing personal problems and conflicts openly; however, not doing so may be a deeply engrained habit in the elderly members. It is a special challenge to the leader to teach these members about the benefits of expressing and exploring personal experiences.

The Issue of Touching.   Aging people have a special need for being touched. They may be alone, and the leader and others in their group may be their only source of touching. Therefore, a group leader needs to be comfortable in being touched and in touching others and must be careful not to misinterpret an older person's touching.

The need for touching among the elderly was vividly expressed during my recent visit to the respected home for the elderly in China. I observed an elderly woman lying on her bed, mumbling to herself and looking extremely withdrawn. As I stood near her bed I struggled with myself over the appropriateness of touching her, not knowing if it would be accepted in a different cultural setting. I gave in to my urge to hold the woman's hand, and she reciprocated immediately by pressing my hand and turning toward me. She slowly began to talk and I asked our tour guide to translate. He introduced my daughters and me to her, and she showed great interest in where we were from and what we were doing. She kept repeating how lucky I was to have such daughters. She touched my daughters and me again and again. Within a short time this woman sat up on her bed and began laughing and talking. She had been an artist, and my daughters and I shared our interest in art with her. The young tour guide, who had never been in a home such as this, told me how surprised he was by the lady's intellectual sharpness. When he initially saw her lying on her bed, he thought that she might be dying.

The attending nurse mentioned that this woman had indeed been very withdrawn and depressed, and the nurse was surprised over her excitement and interest in us. Within a span of 20 minutes she had become completely animated. This episode reminded me again how much we can communicate with a touch or a smile.

Difficult Group Members.   The leader may encounter many types of difficult member in this age group. Some may refuse to speak or make any contact, some may never stop talking or interrupting, some may be highly agitated and hostile, and so forth. Leaders must be able to set firm limits and deal with these members nondefensively.

Some Cautions.   The following are a few cautions in the practice of group work with the elderly:

1. Be careful not to treat people as frail when they are not.
2. Don't keep your members busy with meaningless activities.
3. Don't insult their dignity, intelligence, and pride.
4. Make use of humor appropriately. Avoid laughing at your members for failing to accomplish tasks, but laugh with them when, for instance, they have created a funny poem.
5. Be careful not to change your way of speaking with them; avoid talking to them as if they were small children.

6. Allow your members to nag and complain, even if there is nothing you can do about their complaints. You don't need to burden yourself with the feeling that you should do something about all of their grievances. Sometimes it is enough to simply let them get the problems off their chest.
7. Avoid probing for the release of strong emotions that neither you nor they can handle effectively in the group sessions.
8. Each leader must determine how much he or she can do without feeling depleted and must find avenues for staying vital and enthusiastic.
9. Working with the elderly can be very rewarding and challenging. Nevertheless, there will be days when the work is more draining than nourishing. Not every leader is capable of working with the demands often made by the elderly.

■■ Attitudes and Skills of Leaders

It is especially critical that group workers be aware of how their own feelings and attitudes will affect their work with the elderly. Such leaders must find ways to successfully deal with the feelings that are generated within them as a result of their work. They must also acquire special skills and knowledge to work effectively with the concerns of the elderly. Their range of life experiences, as well as their basic personality characteristics, can either help or hinder them in their work. I consider the following as important assets for group work with the elderly:

· genuine respect for old people
· a history of positive experiences with old people
· a deep sense of caring for the elderly
· an ability and desire to learn from old people
· an understanding of the biological aspects of aging
· the conviction that the last years of life can be challenging
· patience, especially with repetition of stories
· knowledge of the special biological, psychological, and social needs of the aged
· sensitivity to the burdens and anxieties of old people
· the ability to get old people to challenge many of the myths about old age
· a healthy attitude regarding one's own eventual old age
· an understanding of the developmental tasks of each period of life, from infancy to old age
· an appreciation for the effects that one period of life has on other stages of development
· a particular understanding of how one's ability to handle present life difficulties hinges on how well one dealt with problems in earlier stages

- background in the pathology of aging
- ability to deal with extreme feelings of depression, hopelessness, grief, hostility, and despair
- personal characteristics such as humor, enthusiasm, patience, courage, endurance, hopefulness, tolerance, nondefensiveness, freedom from limiting prejudices, and a willingness to learn
- an ability to be both gentle and challenging
- the sensitivity to know when it is therapeutic to provide support and when to challenge
- a working knowledge of group process along with the special skills needed for group work with the elderly

■■ Concluding Comments

The elderly make up a significant part of the population of the United States. By the year 2000, it is estimated, there will be 29 to 33 million older Americans. Currently, one-fourth of the elderly population is 75 and over; by the year 2000, this proportion will rise to one-third (Burnside, 1984b). It should be evident from this chapter that this population has special needs and problems that should not be ignored by any helping profession. The helping professions must continue to develop special programs for the elderly; they must also find the means to reach this clientele.

I feel angry when old people are perceived as near dead, cute, or strange; I certainly will not care to be regarded as such when I'm older. As I once told a friend, if I am to get old in this country, I want to change a few things before I get there. I decided to include a chapter on groups for the elderly in this book because I strongly believe that group approaches can be developed that would help bring about such changes by helping to meet the needs of this growing segment of our population.

Where to Go from Here

If you are interested in working with the elderly, it would be a valuable experience to participate in group counseling both with older people and with families of the elderly. This experience could be a catalyst for exploring your feelings about responsibilities toward older family members, which would help you understand the struggles of the members of the groups you lead. There are a number of other steps that you can take to better prepare yourself to work with the elderly:

- Take courses and special workshops dealing with the problems of the older adult.
- Get involved in practicum and internship experiences in working with the elderly.

- Visit agencies for the care of the elderly, both in your own country and on any trips you take abroad.
- Attend conventions on gerontology, a mushrooming field.
- Investigate institutes that provide training in leading groups for the elderly.
- Explore your own feelings toward aging as well as feelings you might have toward older people in your life (Hammond & Bonney, 1983).

Hawkins (1983) maintains that counselors who lead groups for the elderly not only provide a valuable service for their clients but also grow themselves. Her recommendations for entry-level workers include doing extensive reading about the elderly, getting to know older people, demonstrating a genuine sense of caring, and imagining what their own life might be like as they age.

Irene Mortenson Burnside has had a valued impact on my views about working with the elderly. In my opinion her latest book, *Working with the Elderly: Group Processes and Techniques* (1984b), is a must for any person considering group work with the aged. Many people with experience in working with the elderly are contributors to the book. It contains a wealth of practical information on subjects such as training and supervision of group workers, suggestions for contracts in working with older people, group membership issues and procedures, responsibilities of group leaders, special groups, guidelines for group workers, and the future of group work with the aged.

Another good reference for group workers is the special issue "Counseling Psychology and Aging" in *The Counseling Psychologist* (1984). A resource listing articles and books of interest is *Group Work in the Helping Professions: A Bibliography* (Zimpfer, 1984). This reference guide has sections on types of group experience, groups for specific clienteles and in specific settings, and outcome studies. For references on group work pertaining to old age, suicide, death, survivor grief, and adaptation see section 9.4, pages 508–515).

For practical suggestions on strategies in working with the elderly in groups, see *Inpatient Group Psychotherapy* (Yalom, 1983). It has especially good points on ways of assisting group members to work in the here and now and to translate in-group learning to everyday life.

Suggested Readings*

* Altholz, J. A. S. (1984). Group psychotherapy with the elderly. In I. Burnside (Ed.), *Working with the elderly: Group process and techniques* (2nd ed.) (pp. 248–258). Monterey, CA: Wadsworth.

Beck, A. T. (1976). *Cognitive therapy and emotional disorders.* New York: New American Library (Mentor).

---

* Books and articles marked with an asterisk are recommended for further study.

Beck, A. T., Rush, A. J., Shaw, B. F., & Emery, G. (1979). *Cognitive therapy of depression.* New York: Guilford Press.

Biegel, D. E., Shore, B. K., & Gordon, E. (1984). *Building support networks for the elderly: Theory and applications.* Beverly Hills, CA: Sage Publications.

Birren, J. E., & Schaie, K. W. (Eds.). (1977). *Handbook of psychology of aging.* New York: Van Nostrand Reinhold.

Birren, J. E., & Sloan, R. B. (Eds.). (1980). *Handbook of mental health and aging.* Englewood Cliffs, NJ: Prentice-Hall.

* Blake, D. R. (1980). Group work with the institutionalized elderly. In I. Burnside (Ed.), *Psychosocial nursing care of the aged* (2nd ed.). New York: McGraw-Hill.

* Booth, H. (1984). Dance/movement therapy. In I. Burnside (Ed.), *Working with the elderly: Group process and techniques* (2nd ed.) (pp. 211–224). Monterey, CA: Wadsworth.

Brammer, L. M. (1984). Counseling theory and the older adult. *The Counseling Psychologist, 12*(2), 29–37.

Burnside, I. (1970). Loss: A constant theme in group work with the aged. *Hospital and Community Psychiatry, 21*(6), 173–177.

Burnside, I. (Ed.). (1973). *Psychosocial nursing care of the aged.* New York: McGraw-Hill.

* Burnside, I. (1984a). Self-help groups. In I. Burnside (Ed.), *Working with the elderly: Group process and techniques* (2nd ed.) (pp. 234–247). Monterey, CA: Wadsworth.

Burnside, I. (Ed.). (1984b). *Working with the elderly: Group process and techniques* (2nd ed.). Monterey, CA: Wadsworth.

Butler, R. N., & Lewis, M. I. (1982). *Aging and mental health* (3rd ed.). Saint Louis: C. V. Mosby.

Capuzzi, D., & Fillion, N. G. (1979). Group counseling for the elderly. *Journal for Specialists in Group Work, 4*(3), 148–154.

Davidson, H. (1979). Development of a bereaved parents group. In M. A. Lieberman, L. D. Borman, & Associates (Eds.), *Self-help groups for coping with crisis.* San Francisco: Jossey-Bass.

* Dennis, H. (1984). Remotivation therapy. In I. Burnside (Ed.), *Working with the elderly: Group process and techniques* (2nd ed.) (pp. 187–197). Monterey, CA: Wadsworth.

* Donahue, E. M. (1984). Reality orientation: A review of the literature. In I. Burnside (Ed.), *Working with the elderly: Group process and techniques* (2nd ed.) (pp. 165–176). Monterey, CA: Wadsworth.

* Emery, G. (1981). Cognitive therapy with the elderly. In G. Emery, S. D. Hollon, & R. C. Bedrosian (Eds.), *New directions in cognitive therapy* (pp. 84–98). New York: Guilford Press.

* Erikson, E. H. (1982). *The life cycle completed.* New York: Norton.

Foster, J. R., & Foster, R. P. (1983). Group psychotherapy with the old and aged. In H. I. Kaplan & B. J. Sadock (Eds.), *Comprehensive group psychotherapy* (2nd ed.) (pp. 269–278). Baltimore: Williams & Wilkins.

* Hammond, D. B., & Bonney, W. C. (1983). Counseling families of the elderly: A group experience. *Journal for Specialists in Group Work, 8*(4), 198–204.

Harrington, C., Newcomer, R. J., Estes, C. L., & Associates. (1984). *Long-term care of the elderly.* Beverly Hills, CA: Sage Publications.

* Hawkins, B. L. (1983). Group counseling as a treatment modality for the

elderly: A group snapshot. *Journal for Specialists in Group Work, 8*(4), 186–193.

* Hennessey, M. J. (1984). Music therapy. In I. Burnside (Ed.), *Working with the elderly: Group process and techniques* (2nd ed.) (pp. 198–210). Monterey, CA: Wadsworth.

Herr, L., & Weakland, J. (1979). *Counseling elders and their families: Practical techniques of applied gerontology.* New York: Springer.

Hickey, T. (1980). *Health and aging.* Monterey, CA: Brooks/Cole.

Ingersoll, B., & Silverman, A. (1978). Comparative group psychotherapy for the aged. *Gerontologists, 18,* 201–206.

* Johnson, D. R. (1985). Expressive group psychotherapy with the elderly: A drama therapy approach. *International Journal of Group Psychotherapy, 25*(1), 109–127.

Kalish, R. A. (1975). *Late adulthood.* Monterey, CA: Brooks/Cole.

* Kalish, R. A. (1985). *Death, grief, and caring relationships* (2nd ed.). Monterey, CA: Brooks/Cole.

* Keller, J. F., & Hughston, G. A. (1981). *Counseling the elderly.* New York: Harper & Row.

Koestenbaum, P. (1976). *Is there an answer to death?* Englewood Cliffs, NJ: Prentice-Hall.

* Kübler-Ross, E. (1969). *On death and dying.* New York: Macmillan.

Kübler-Ross, E. (1971). *What is it like to be dying?* American Journal of Nursing, *71*(1), 54–62.

* Kübler-Ross, E. (1975). *Death: The final stages of growth.* Englewood Cliffs, NJ: Prentice-Hall.

Landreth, G. L., & Berg, R. C. (Eds.). (1980). *Counseling the elderly.* Springfield, IL: Charles C Thomas.

Leszcz, M., Feigenbaum, E., Sadavoy, J., & Robinson, A. (1985). A men's group: Psychotherapy of elderly men. *International Journal of Group Psychotherapy, 35*(2), 177–196.

Levin, J., & Levin, W. C. (1980). *Ageism: Prejudice and discrimination against the elderly.* Belmont, CA: Wadsworth.

Lewis, M. I., & Butler, R. N. (1974). Life-review therapy: Putting memories to work in individual and group therapy. *Geriatrics, 29,* 165–173.

* Lewis, M. I., & Butler, R. N. (1984). Life-review therapy: Putting memories to work. In I. Burnside (Ed.), *Working with the elderly: Group process and techniques* (pp. 50–59). Monterey, CA: Wadsworth.

Lieberman, M. A., & Bliwise, N. G. (1985). Comparisons among peer and professionally directed groups for the elderly: Implications for the development of self-help groups. *International Journal of Group Psychotherapy, 35*(2), 155–175.

Lieberman, M. A., & Gourash, N. (1979). Effects of change groups on the elderly. In M. A. Lieberman, L. D. Borman, & Associates (Eds.), *Self-help groups for coping with crisis* (pp. 387–405). San Francisco: Jossey-Bass.

Lopez, M. A. (1980). Social skills training with institutionalized elderly: Effects of precounseling structuring and overlearning on skill acquisition and transfer. *Journal of Counseling Psychology, 27,* 286–293.

Marshall, V. W. (1980). *Last chapters: A sociology of aging and dying.* Monterey, CA: Brooks/Cole.

* Martin, A. (1984). Family sculpting: A combination of modalities. In I. Burn-

side (Ed.), *Working with the elderly: Group process and techniques* (2nd ed.) (pp. 225–233). Monterey, CA: Wadsworth.

Matthews, S. H. (1979). *The social world of old women: Management of self-identity.* Beverly Hills, CA: Sage Publications.

McNeely, R. L., & Colen, J. N. (1983). *Aging in minority groups.* Beverly Hills, CA: Sage Publications.

Medler, B. W. (1980). A selected review of the research on helping the elderly. In G. L. Landreth & R. C. Berg (Eds.), *Counseling the elderly.* Springfield, IL: Charles C Thomas.

Meyer, G. R. (1980). The new directions workshop for senior citizens. In S. S. Sargent (Ed.), *Nontraditional therapy and counseling with the aging.* New York: Springer.

Mintz, J., Steuer, J., & Jarvik, L. (1981). Psychotherapy with depressed elderly patients: Research considerations. *Journal of Consulting and Clinical Psychology, 49,* 542–548.

* Nakkula, M. J. (1984). *Elderly and adolescence: A group approach to integrating the isolated.* Unpublished master's project, University of Minnesota, Duluth.

Nissenson, M. (1984). Therapy after sixty. *Psychology Today, 18*(1), 22–26.

Nouwen, H. J., & Gaffney, W. J. (1976). *Aging: The fulfillment of life.* New York: Doubleday.

Palmore, E. (1980). Facts on aging: A short quiz. In G. L. Landreth & R. C. Berg (Eds.), *Counseling the elderly* (pp. 51–61). Springfield, IL: Charles C Thomas.

Poon, L. W. (Ed.). (1980). *Aging in the 1980's.* Washington, DC: American Psychological Association.

Rubin, I. (1976). *Sexual life after sixty.* New York: Basic Books.

* Sargent, S. S. (Ed.). (1980). *Nontraditional therapy and counseling with the aging.* New York: Springer.

Shanas, E. (1980). Older people and their families: The new pioneers. *Journal of Marriage and the Family, 42,* 9–15.

Sherman, B. (1979). Emergence of ideology in a bereaved parents group. In M. A. Lieberman, L. D. Borman, & Associates (Eds.), *Self-help groups for coping with crisis* (pp. 305–322). San Francisco: Jossey-Bass.

Smyer, M. A. (1984). Life transitions and aging: Implications for counseling older adults. *The Counseling Psychologist, 12*(2), 17–28.

Spiegel, D., & Glafkides, M. C. (1983). Effects of group confrontation with death and dying. *International Journal of Group Psychotherapy, 33*(4), 433–448.

* Spiegel, D., & Yalom, I. D. (1978). A support group for dying patients. *International Journal of Group Psychotherapy, 28*(2), 233–246.

Springer, D., & Brubaker, T. H. (1984). *Family caregivers and dependent elderly: Minimizing stress and maximizing independence.* Beverly Hills, CA: Sage Publications.

Storandt, M. (1983). *Counseling and therapy with older adults.* Boston: Little, Brown.

* Szafranski, L. M. (1984). Using patients as co-leaders. In I. Burnside (Ed.), *Working with the elderly: Group process and techniques* (2nd ed.) (pp. 132–140). Monterey, CA: Wadsworth.

* Taulbee, L. R. (1984). Reality orientation and clinical practice. In I. Burnside

(Ed.), *Working with the elderly: Group process and techniques* (2nd ed.) (pp. 177–186). Monterey, CA: Wadsworth.

* Waters, E. B. (1984). Building on what you know: Techniques for individual and group counseling with older people. *The Counseling Psychologist, 12*(2), 63–74.

Wellman, F. E., & McCormack, J. (1984). Counseling with older persons: A review of outcome research. *The Counseling Psychologist, 12*(2), 81–96.

Wheeler, E. (1980). Assertive training groups for the aging. In S. S. Sargent (Ed.), *Nontraditional therapy and counseling with the aging.* New York: Springer.

Wikler, R., & Grey, P. S. (1968). *Sex and the senior citizen.* New York: Fell.

* Yalom, I. (1983). *Inpatient group psychotherapy.* New York: Basic Books.

Yalom, I., & Terrazas, R. (1968). Group therapy for psychotic elderly patients. *American Journal of Nursing, 68,* 1690–1694.

* Zimpfer, D. G. (1984). *Group work in the helping professions: A bibliography* (2nd ed.). Muncie, IN: Accelerated Development.

To the owner of this book:

We hope that you have enjoyed this book and found it useful. We would like to know as much as possible about your experiences with *Groups: Process and Practice* (Third Edition), so that we can take your reactions into consideration in future editions. You can write your comments on this convenient form and send it to us care of Brooks/Cole Publishing Company. Many thanks for your help.

School: _____

Your Instructor's Name: _____

1. In what class did you use this book? _____

2. What did you like *most* about *Groups: Process and Practice?* _____

_____

_____

3. What did you like *least* about the book?_____

_____

_____

4. How useful were the exercises at the end of the chapters in Parts One and Two? Did you use any of them in class? _____

_____

_____

5. How useful and informative were the chapters on specific groups in Part Three? Were there any chapters in this section that you did not read?

_____

_____

6. In the space below or in a separate letter, please make any other comments about the book you'd like. For example, what were your general reactions to the book? Were any chapters *or* concepts particularly difficult? Do you have any suggestions for future revisions? We'd be delighted to hear from you!

Optional:

Your name: _____   Date: _____

May Brooks/Cole quote you, either in promotion for *Groups: Process and Practice* (Third Edition) or in future publishing ventures?

Yes _____   No _____

Sincerely,

Marianne Schneider Corey and Jerry Corey

CUT PAGE OUT AND

FOLD HERE

NO POSTAGE
NECESSARY
IF MAILED
IN THE
UNITED STATES

BUSINESS REPLY MAIL
FIRST CLASS   PERMIT NO. 84   MONTEREY, CALIF.

POSTAGE WILL BE PAID BY ADDRESSEE

Marianne Schneider Corey and Gerald Corey
Brooks/Cole Publishing Company
Monterey, CA 93940